THE PSYCHOLOGY
OF TRADING

Founded in 1807, John Wiley & Sons in the oldest independent publishing company in the United States. With offices in North America, Europe, Australia, and Asia, Wiley is globally committed to developing and marketing print and electronic products and services for our customers' professional and personal knowledge and understanding.

The Wiley Trading series features books by traders who have survived the market's ever changing temperament and have prospered—some by reinventing systems, others by getting back to basics. Whether a novice trader, professional, or somewhere in-between, these books will provide the advice and strategies needed to prosper today and well into the future.

For a list of available titles, visit our Web site at www.WileyFinance.com.

THE PSYCHOLOGY OF TRADING

Tools and Techniques for Minding the Markets

Brett N. Steenbarger

John Wiley & Sons, Inc.

For general information on our other products and services, or technical support, please contact our
Customer Care Department within the United States at 800-762-2974, outside the United States at
317-572-3993 or fax 317-572-4002.

Wiley also publishes its books in a variety of electronic formats. Some content that appears in print
may not be available in electronic books.

For more information about Wiley products, visit our Web site at www.wiley.com.

Library of Congress Cataloging-in-Publication Data:

Steenbarger, Brett N.
    The psychology of trading : tools and techniques for minding the markets / Brett N. Steenbarger.
        p. cm.—(Wiley trading series)
    Includes index.
    ISBN 0-471-26761-9
        1. Stocks—Psychological aspects.   2. Speculation—Psychological aspects.   3. Investments—
Psychological aspects.   I. Title.   II. Series.

    HG6041.S76 2003
    332.64'01'9—dc21

                                                                                        2002190744

Printed in the United States of America.

10   9   8   7

For Margie,
who has made it all possible

Preface

Preface

In our debts to others, we find the true measure of our wealth.

If there is a single theme to this book, it is this: *Trading is a microcosm of life.** In trading, as in life, we pursue values. In both trading and life, we manage the risks of those pursuits: lost opportunities and realized losses. How we seek values and manage the associated risks will determine our personal and professional success.

Many times, our responses to the uncertainty of outcomes interfere with the achievement of our goals. In careers, romantic relationships, and trading, we find ourselves enacting self-defeating patterns: cutting promising situations short and lingering in unprofitable ones. It doesn't matter that we are virtuous people, hardworking and otherwise successful. It doesn't matter that we have attended all the latest seminars, read the hottest books, and purchased all the best trading tools. If our coping with risk distorts our efforts at

---

*The term *trading* is used in this book to cover all active forms of managing one's financial investments. Anyone who attempts to time investments, whether over hours, days, weeks, or months, is a trader.

pursuing values, we will fail to attain the stature that can be ours—as traders and as human beings.

For the past 20 years, I have provided counseling and therapy services to approximately 130 people a year. Almost all of these people have been high-functioning individuals tackling demanding career fields. I learned during these years of practice that the problem patterns of physicians, executives, students, and traders are surprisingly similar. These patterns arise when strategies for emotional risk management—efforts to minimize pain and maximize pleasure—fail to make it possible to successfully navigate life's matrix of risks and rewards. Every problem pattern we experience is a once-successful coping effort that has outlived its value. Conversely, newly created patterns that meet life's present challenges lead to success. We are best positioned to achieve our goals when we can extract ourselves from the mindless repetition of the past and fashion fresh life solutions.

The purpose of this book is to help you identify your patterns of success and failure and exercise greater control over these. My deepest hope is that the case studies, the research, and the ideas contained in these pages will provide you with the intellectual and emotional ammunition to face yourself and to transform your approach to life's risks and rewards.

The following pages can help you cultivate new ways of thinking, feeling, and acting; but they cannot perform magic. For the trader, no amount of psychological assistance can substitute for concrete trading plans that have been tested across a variety of markets. As Robert Krausz neatly stated in his *New Market Wizards* interview with Jack Schwager, self-help methods by themselves can no more make you a great trader than they can make you a great chess player or baseball star. You can only learn to master the markets by immersing yourself in the markets.

Indeed, there is a sense in which the process of developing and testing your market strategies is the best of all methods for cultivating a positive trading psychology. Many traders fail with mechanical systems simply because they cannot tolerate the inevitable periods of drawdowns or flat performance. When you create and test your own approaches to the market, you develop an inner knowledge of how those methods work. During periods when the market throws a curve ball, your confusion is more readily replaced by the sense of "been there, done that." *Nothing* substitutes for the confidence born of experience.

Still, it is difficult to underestimate the degree to which traders can utilize identical trading methods and arrive at wildly different results. Possessing the right tools is necessary, but not sufficient, for success. As Krausz observed, traders have an uncanny knack for acting out their repetitive and destructive emotional patterns in their trading. Such enactments will derail even the most carefully constructed and tested systems.

An important goal of this book is to help you approach trading the way a psychologist approaches his or her clients. I call this "trading from the couch," which means learning to utilize your thoughts, feelings, impulses, and behavioral patterns as *market data.* Trading from the couch entails an important shift from traditional thinking. Instead of trying to overcome or eliminate your emotions, this self-aware trading calls on you to *learn* from your reactions. Your goal is to turn yourself into a finely calibrated instrument for detecting and acting on the patterns of both the trader and the trading.

Note that cultivating such sensitivity does *not* mean simply going with your feelings in placing orders! As you will see in the coming pages, it often means the opposite: learning to use excess confidence and risk aversion as valuable *contrary* indicators. Surprisingly often—for the trader, as for the therapist— acting counter to one's initial impulses is the winning move.

In trading from the couch, you become your own psychologist. That is not an easy task in the markets or in everyday life. The rewards, however, are considerable. Trading, like competitive sports, is a powerful crucible for cultivating the emotional skills crucial to life success. In few arenas are the pursuit of values and the management of risk so tangible and immediate. Nothing so drives home lessons in self-understanding as brutal hits to one's bottom line.

Self-aware trading also presumes a vital symmetry: In mastering the markets, you can further yourself as a human being; and in developing yourself as a person, you can enhance your trading success. *Once you are able to extract the information contained within your emotional, cognitive, and behavioral patterns, you will be better equipped to identify and to exploit the patterns that appear in the financial markets—and vice versa.*

BRETT N. STEENBARGER

Fayetteville, New York
November 2002

Acknowledgments

My appreciation for the emotional intricacies of trading expanded exponentially when I began writing trading psychology columns for a web site that was known as WorldlyInvestor and for MSN's Money site (www.moneycentral.com). In response to those columns, I heard from traders around the world who were experiencing difficulties strikingly similar to the ones I had encountered in my years of trading. Some of my correspondents were neophytes, trading by the seats of their pants, engaging in little more than gambling. But most were dedicated practitioners, who had dutifully read books, learned trading methods, and undertaken their own research. With remarkable frequency, I heard the plaintive refrain: Inconsistency was robbing them of profits and exposing them to occasional, debilitating losses. It is difficult to express how frustrating trading can be when success seems so tantalizingly close and yet remains ever so elusive.

How is it that we can *know* the right things to do—regular exercising, healthful eating, good parenting—and yet so often fail to follow through? What distorts our trading, preventing us from acting on the information clearly in front of our eyes? These are the questions that have haunted me for nearly two decades as a professional psychologist and market participant. My attempts to answer them have taken me from the literature on trading and psychology to philosophy and leading edge research in cognitive neuroscience. If I have accomplished anything in this book, it is in synthesizing contributions from these fields, contributions that are far worthier than my own.

Authors face a curious paradox indeed: With each intellectual debt accumulated, they are enriched manyfold. In that regard, I feel wealthy indeed, having benefited from the insight and the assistance of many inspiring influences.

My first forays into writing about the markets came through the Speculator's List, an online group of traders, money managers, academics, and accomplished individuals in the arts and sciences. I am forever indebted to Laurel Kenner, Victor Niederhoffer, and James Goldcamp for their role in establishing the List and for their kind encouragement of my many posts to the group.

When I needed to understand the dynamics that distinguished successful from unsuccessful traders, Linda Raschke was incredibly supportive, allowing me to study the many individuals who participated in her seminars. I quickly found that Linda was a worthy model of exemplary trading and an accomplished mentor. I am deeply grateful for her friendship and for her insights into the business and human sides of trading.

Some of my most important influences have been those who have pushed me to write with ever greater clarity and precision. Jon Markman, editor at MSN Money, has been a valued friend and colleague, as well as a role model for his trailblazing research. The book has greatly benefited from my editor at Wiley, Pamela van Giessen, whose humor, practical bent, and commitment to quality have carried me through the long writing process.

To be sure, none of this would have been possible without the salutary influence of my academic colleagues in the Department of Psychiatry and Behavioral Sciences at SUNY Upstate Medical University, most notably Roger Greenberg, Mantosh Dewan, and John Manring. My good friends and trading correspondents Henry Carstens, Saurabh Singal, and Steve Wisdom have enriched this book with their inspirations and ideas. I am also indebted to Mark Mahorney for his excellent work on the Great Speculations site (www.greatspeculations.com) and to Frank and Kris Linet, Susan Niederhoffer, and Arnold and Rose Rustin for their warmth, humor, and insight. To Yale Hirsch, Andrew Lo, Sam Eisenstadt, and Jeff Carmen, my hat is off in salute and appreciation for their exemplary research and personal support.

Finally, I gratefully acknowledge my family for their ongoing love and encouragement. My parents, Jack and Connie, have been role models and inspirations for longer than they realize. The support of Marc, Lisa, Debi, Peter, Steve, Laura, Ed, Devon, and Macrae has meant more than I can express. But no single person deserves credit for this book more than my wife, Margie, who has taught me most of what I know about life, love, and the navigation of risks and rewards. It is my greatest joy to dedicate this book to her.

A VIEW FROM TALL SHOULDERS

I count July 4, 2001, as a special day. That marked the completion of the first draft of this text. Until that day, I hadn't explicitly identified why I had written the book. Yes, I had wanted to share insights and ideas, but that wasn't the major purpose. After all, I had written the book with no publishing contract in hand. And although I wanted to see it published, it was clear to me that the writing held a personal significance beyond its status in the marketplace.

On July 4, sitting in a Seattle hotel lobby with laptop at my side, I suddenly recognized the source of that personal significance. Feeling the need to capture my insight in words, I took out the laptop and composed the following letter to my friend and mentor Victor Niederhoffer:

Dear Victor,

Nothing is quite so conducive to reflection as travel. The combination of distinctive scenery and breaks from normal, daily schedules helps us think in new ways, see things in a new light. What we vacate during vacation are our routine ways. It is during those breaks from the routine that creative impulses are most likely to find expression.

This was particularly evident to me during this past holiday, as I brought my book manuscript on a trip to the West Coast. I expected that the writing would find inspiration on the road, and I anticipated that the writing would be most enjoyable without the distractions of the workaday world. I was not disappointed in these respects. More surprising, however, was my emotional reaction to the writing. As I crafted page after page, I found myself experiencing a profound humility. I recognized, with a deep emotional certainty, the extent to which so few of my ideas were truly original. With each line I could recognize an inspiration from another source: a teacher or mentor, a book I had read, a piece of research I had studied, a personal hero. There was little on these pages that was truly my own. Instead, the writing was a synthesis of what I had absorbed from those greater than myself. At a profound level, I could appreciate Newton's statement that if he had seen farther than others, it was because he had stood on the shoulders of giants.

Perhaps this is why the immortals do not write for self-aggrandizement and why charlatans are so quick to credit themselves and deny credit to others. The greats recognize the fountainhead of their inspirations. Their dominant emotion is the humility of gratitude, of having been the recipient of gifts that can never be fully repaid.

In this state of humility, I also gained a unique perspective on your own book. My first reading of *The Education of a Speculator* [John Wiley, 1997] focused on its personal story: the formative experiences that contributed to success in the markets. Upon rereading, I saw the book in a different light: as a tribute to those moral and character influences—particularly those of your father—that made for success as a human being. After this vacation, however, a wholly new reading became possible. I could appreciate your book as a broader tribute to the exemplars in your life. It is a testimonial and a statement of thanks to Arthur Niederhoffer, Jack Barnaby, Tom Wiswell, Francis Galton, and those many others who gave more than can ever be wholly repaid.

And yet, in writing a book of tribute, perhaps we do repay at least some measure of indebtedness. Even the great ones die. Their voices are stilled, and subsequent generations never gain the privilege of sitting by their sides and hearing their words. My children will never directly encounter Artie or Galton and absorb their personal examples. Through a book of tribute, however, exemplary individuals gain a degree of personal immortality. As long as the book graces the shelves of libraries and bookstores, there is hope that the lessons taught by the greats will not be lost, that their examples can live well beyond their years.

This is the beauty of writing a book: In telling the stories of heroes, we contribute to their immortality and immeasurably enrich generations to come. Before I went on this vacation, I vowed to write a book that informed, entertained, and enriched. Now, however, I have set the bar far higher. I will only be satisfied with a work that does justice to those who have inspired the best within me.

As I sit here now, writing early in the morning, it strikes me with sincerity and gratitude that the only way to stand on the shoulders of giants is to hoist them on our own.

Sincerely,

Brett

Trading, indeed, is a microcosm of life. If you long to develop yourself, as a person and as a trader, search high and low for the immortals. Find the heroes and the heroines who have lived their lives with passion, nourishing all who have come in contact with them. Discover those who have lived, breathed, and studied the markets, enriching the world with their ideas. Then hoist them on your shoulders, remaining ever mindful of your debt. You will be surprised how high you stand, how far you can see.

B. N. S.

Contents

Chapter One

The Woman Who Could Not Love

Solutions are the patterns we enact between problems.

I suppose it's only natural that you would expect a book on the psychology of trading to begin with a description of the various emotional afflictions experienced by traders. In this chapter, however, we are going to approach the topic from a different angle. We are going to adopt what is known as a "solution focus" to trading and explore how many of the answers to our problems are *already occurring*. If you have a template for identifying and understanding what you are already doing right, in life and in the markets, you are well on the way to creating a model for your future success.

MANUFACTURING CARS AND SUCCESS

Many years ago, I read something in a management text that made a lasting impression. At that time, Japanese car manufacturers were making distinct headway in their competition with their U.S. counterparts. On both price and quality, the Japanese seemed to be winning the race.

The account I read described the difference in the management approaches of the U.S. and Japanese manufacturers. The U.S. automobile manufacturers, it appeared, were very concerned about the possibility of breakdowns on the assembly line. To avoid the disruptive effects of a breakdown, they kept the line moving sufficiently slowly to prevent any glitch from bringing operations to a halt.

The Japanese manufacturers adopted a radically different approach. When manufacturing was proceeding efficiently, they would speed up the line *until a breakdown occurred*. Then they would intensively study the source of the breakdown and institute preventive measures. Over time, they identified many weak links in the production process and improved both their efficiency and their quality.

The U.S. manufacturers looked on breakdowns as failures and on failures as outcomes to be avoided. The Japanese looked at production problems as opportunities for learning and improvement. These were two philosophies of management and two approaches to life, with very different sets of results.

The lesson applies to trading as well as to manufacturing: *Successful market participants seek out their weaknesses and learn when they fail. Unsuccessful ones avoid their shortcomings and, thus, fail to learn.*

SUE, THE SURVIVOR

When Sue[*] came to my office, I knew immediately that she was not the typical Upstate New York medical student. She looked and sounded like a person from the inner city. As we became acquainted, I learned that, indeed, she was exactly as she appeared. From the clothes she wore to her street English, Sue was a student from the 'hood. Little did I know that she was to become one of the most inspiring individuals I have had the honor of assisting. She also taught me a great deal about the power of the solution focus.

At the time of our first meeting, Sue was distraught. Her school perfor-

---

[*]The names and identifying details of all clients and characters in this book have been altered to protect anonymity and confidentiality. To further protect my clients' privacy, all of the cases and incidents described are composites of actual counseling cases. I have endeavored to preserve the essence of those cases, even as the creation of composites introduced elements of fictionalization into the accounts.

mance was solid, befitting a young lady who had graduated with honors from a highly competitive undergraduate institution. Nevertheless, she told me in no uncertain terms that she was thinking of withdrawing from school. Her grandmother had died a few months earlier, she informed me through tears, and she could not handle that.

Sue, it turned out, had grown up essentially without parents. Her father left the family when she was several months old, and she never knew him. Her mother suffered from a chronic crack cocaine addiction and was unable to maintain a consistent parenting role. When it became clear to child welfare authorities that Sue's mother was selling her body as well as drugs to finance her habit, Sue was formally removed from the home and placed in the custody of her grandmother. Though she was only five at the time, Sue had witnessed a parade of men in and out of her mother's life, several shootings and stabbings, and multiple run-ins with the police.

Sue's grandmother, Nana, was a religious woman with strong ties to her church. The church congregation formed a strong social network, in which people supported one another through poverty, illness, and the suffocating absence of opportunity. Perhaps most important, it was a community that emphasized education, and Nana worked fiendishly to ensure that Sue kept up with her studies.

Naturally shy and slight of stature, Sue could not excel in athletics, so she found early success and approval in her studies. Over the years, she stayed involved in her mother's life and, in a way, became a parent to her parent. Her greatest concerns were for the abusive relationships that punctuated her mother's skirts with the law. One particular man, Davis, put Sue's mother in the hospital several times with broken bones and multiple bruises. Sue could never comprehend why her mother would not press charges, why she would never leave the relationship.

Perhaps because of men like Davis, Sue showed no interest in dating. Her grandmother had warned her many times of the dangers of unmarried pregnancies and the ways in which young men would be out to take advantage of her. The only way to better herself, Nana stressed, was through God and her studies.

"I had good friends in school," Sue explained. "We used to help each other out when things were rough. Tasha's daddy used to drink away the family money, so Nana would have her over for dinner just to make sure she got fed. Nana was like that. If she saw you needed something and she liked you, she'd give you everything she had."

"Are you still in touch with your friends, like Tasha?" I asked.

Sue shook her head. "Tasha got pregnant and dropped out of school. She hooked up with a guy just like her daddy. Daryl got caught dealing drugs; he's in jail. Rhonda—you don't want to know about her. She's worse than my mom. The only one there for me was Nana."

The other medical students found Sue to be aloof, with an "attitude." One professor suggested that she meet with me, indicating that the "chip on her shoulder" would make it difficult to succeed in school. In fact, Sue was warm and engaging—once you got to know her. Few people, however, were allowed inside. She had learned to trust no one, especially men. When they approached her, her instinctive reaction was to turn them aside. "I can't love anyone," she stated plainly, "because I can't trust anyone." Staying aloof was a protective mechanism, and it worked for many years.

"So why are you telling me all this?" I asked Sue in our second meeting. "I'm a man, I'm a white guy, and I've never lived in a neighborhood like yours. Why are you trusting me?"

"'Cuz you didn't ask me my MCAT scores right when we first met," she laughed.

This was an inside joke among the school's black students. A number of faculty questioned the academic fitness of some of the minority students, though they were too discreet to raise the issue directly. So whenever such a student came in with a problem, the faculty would find a way to inquire about their undergraduate campus of origin and their scores on the Medical College Admissions Test (MCAT). Such questions were rarely, if ever, directed to the white students. The implication was clear: You're having problems because you shouldn't have been allowed into the school to begin with.

"I need to be able to talk to someone," Sue said, "and I can't talk with the people in my class. We had to pair up for work in the anatomy lab, and you should have seen everyone scurry so they wouldn't have to work with me. One boy told me I would slow him down in the dissection. I told him to stand still, and I'd cut him good to show him how fast I could open a body."

Sue, I gathered, was not to be messed with. She was a survivor. But, now, sitting in my office, contemplating a withdrawal, she was ready to pack it all in. She could handle shootings in her neighborhood, the slights of racist students, and the ongoing spectacle of her mother's torture at the hands of a man.

But she could not handle the loss of her Nana.

How People Deal with Losses

"I was doing this for Nana," Sue sobbed. "I wanted her to see me graduate. She was so proud of me for making it into medical school. She'd always talk at church about how her little girl was gonna become a doctor. And now she's not going to be there. It just isn't fair. Since she died, I haven't even been going to class. What's the point?"

For the most part, people can tolerate losses well, whether in the markets or in life. Losing trades, lost business opportunities, lost friends—these are painful but generally not overwhelming. Far more debilitating is the loss of hope. When a trader loses a good portion of capital on a butched trade, it is not so much the dollars-and-cents impact that becomes depressing, as it is the loss of hope that one can ever recoup. I recall one trader pointing out to me that his portfolio was down 50 percent in just three months. "I could double my money now and still not be profitable," he explained in a flat monotone. Lost was his horizon for success. Like Sue, he could not find a rationale for going on.

Although Sue valued her medical school career, she had much more invested in her education than time and effort. Success in school had come to symbolize her way of repaying her grandmother, of making all Nana's sacrifices worthwhile. Sue confided to me her fantasies of becoming financially secure someday. "After I paid off my loans," she said, "I was going to buy my grandmother a new house. I didn't want her living the rest of her life in a little apartment." These dreams kept Sue's hope and motivation alive, even as she endured troubles at home and humiliations among classmates.

What is the significance of one's life undertakings: one's education, career, brokerage account, or 401(k) statement? It cannot be reduced to a dollars-and-cents figure. Invested in people's efforts are their hopes for a successful trading career, their dreams for a secure retirement, and their self-image as individuals competent to navigate the future. What happens when these ideals are threatened, when people's hopes and visions for the future are shattered? One of my graduate school professors, Jack Brehm, described depression as *motivational suppression*. Once valued outcomes are deemed unattainable, it no longer makes sense to muster the energy and the enthusiasm for their pursuit. Depression is nature's way of conserving energy, damping the diversion of resources toward ends deemed unreachable.

Most depressed traders identify losses as the source of their blues. They forget that many system traders lose money on half or more of their trades and endure occasional strings of multiple, consecutive losses. The difference is that the depressed trader has lost hope as well as money. The mechanical trader pushes forward precisely because losses are built into the system. With no mechanisms for anticipating or handling losses, the depressed trader sees no future and loses all motivation.

Motivational suppression would be an accurate description for Sue's state of mind. School, her longstanding passion, no longer felt like the priority that it had been. The hopelessness that had no doubt engulfed her childhood friends was now descending on her. Why make efforts if they can go nowhere?

"But why withdraw from school?" I asked Sue. "Do you really think this isn't the field for you? What are you going to do for a career?"

Sue looked down, her voice barely audible. "Dr. Steenbarger," she said, addressing me as she might address a parent, "I *have* to go. I'm pregnant."

The Enduring Pain of Self-Betrayal

I valiantly tried to hide my shock.

"I can't believe I let it happen," she said. "I was weak. Nana was gone, and this guy Kenny was really good to me. I felt I could trust him. And don't get me wrong. He's great. He says he'll go along with anything I want to do, and he says he loves me. But one night we didn't use protection, and that's it. I'm not getting rid of my child, and I can't be a mother in school. No way. I'm not going to do what my mother did. I'm going to be there for my child."

I knew Sue's religion would dictate her response to the situation. She felt that she had committed one sin in her premarital pregnancy; she would not commit another by ending the pregnancy. But I had the feeling this was not the source of her greatest anguish.

"You know," she sobbed, "when I found out, I felt so guilty. I thought to myself that it was good that Nana had died first. I don't know how I would have told her. I couldn't have stood to see the look on her face. She'd have been so disappointed in me. I can't believe how I've ruined everything."

Loss is painful; guilt can be devastating. Worse than losing one's dreams is the knowledge that the loss was self-inflicted. Like many traders that have sought me out, Sue could overcome the dreams that had died, but not the ones she had killed.

FINDING SOLUTIONS AMIDST PROBLEMS

In the midst of experiencing problems, it can be difficult to focus on solutions. Guilt and shame were Sue's dominant emotions. Yet if ever she needed to draw on her skills as a survivor, it was now. Much of the change process in therapy consists of finding the solutions that lie between the problems. And Sue, I believed, possessed just such a solution in her love for her child. Was she contemplating dropping her education because she no longer wanted to be a doctor? Was she making the decision out of self-punishment?

Of course not.

Sue was going to leave school because she felt that it was the right thing to do for her child. She was pushing Kenny away because years of duress had taught her that men were not to be trusted. She wanted to be a parent like Nana, not a parent like her mother. And she would give up anything to avoid replaying her past—*anything*—which both creates her problem and opens the door to change.

You see, the key to understanding Sue's dilemma lies in recognizing that her problem—her sudden desire to terminate her education and her rejection of the boyfriend who cared for her—is actually a solution. Sue survived a traumatic childhood by emulating her grandmother; Sue's way out of her misery was to adopt Nana's values and to please. Now, with a birth looming and her world shaken by the loss of her one supportive figure, Sue is doing the only thing she knows how to do: She is trying to be like Nana. Nana would not end a pregnancy; children were the priority in her life. Nana would not let a man ruin her life. This could only mean one thing to Sue: Her child must become the most important thing in her life. She must give up school for her baby. She must give up her man.

This theme will be explored repeatedly in this book: *Problems are solutions that have outlived their usefulness.* Problems are patterns that were learned in emotional circumstances during one period of life and that now have taken an existence of their own.

Take a concrete example: the trader who developed his methods during a long bull market. Buying dips consistently made him money. Now he finds himself buying weakness in a very different market. Those gaps and oscillators that seemed so reliable during the strong market now become traps for the unwary. Despite the indications that the trading methods are no longer working, the trader continues to do the only thing he knows. He adds to positions on the way down, only to be caught in a waterfall decline.

Many times, outdated solutions replay themselves in a variety of life situations, leaving people mindlessly repeating their mistakes in work, love, and trading. The philosopher George Ivanovitch Gurdjieff taught that people are shockingly mechanical. Their repetitive patterns rob them of the free will that would otherwise be theirs. In a very important sense, the goal of therapy is the expansion of personal freedom, the capacity for self-determination. There can be no free will for people who are locked into patterns developed for past challenges.

Sue, at the moment she was meeting with me, lacked a measure of self-determination. All she knew was that she had to be like Nana, regardless of the cost to her. Nana put children first; Sue had to put her child first. To do otherwise would be to defile her grandmother's spirit. At some level she realized that forfeiting her education would make it difficult for her to ever rise above the economic circumstances of her childhood. She even could see that continuing on the path of her medical education would make her a better provider for her child. And, deep inside, she knew that Kenny loved her.

But all of that was intellectual. Emotionally, she could not countenance the idea of pursuing her goals. It wasn't what Nana did, and she had to be like Nana to survive. Sue's head told her to persevere in her studies and work things out with Kenny; her heart told her to give them up. Torn between priorities, wracked by learned helplessness—like a trader frozen in front of the screen—Sue could not take a step in any direction.

ACCELERATING CHANGE BY DOING WHAT COMES UNNATURALLY

My particular specialty is brief therapy: Instead of talking about issues and problems, which can take months and even years of weekly sessions, brief therapists seek to accelerate change by creating hard-hitting emotional experiences. The idea is that these experiences are processed more deeply than common conversation. As a result, they are readily internalized and can become the foundation for new patterns in day-to-day life.

Years ago, I met with a young man who sought therapy because of his sense of loneliness and social isolation. He began the session by loudly declaring that he had no business in my office, that all therapists were fakes, and that counseling was a waste of time. I immediately leaped to my feet and expressed my joy that he felt the same way about the field that I did.

There were too many unqualified, untrained therapists, I declared, and he was right to be wary of them. I then invited him to ask me any and all questions so that he could decide if I were qualified to help him. If I failed to answer his questions adequately, I told him, I would gladly refer him to a colleague who might have more to offer.

I was not especially surprised when he only asked me two questions about my training and then dropped all protest. After all, I had passed his test by not responding defensively to his attack. It later came out in our meetings that he had been badly hurt in prior relationships. He had learned to avoid further hurt by pushing people away before they could reject him. But this solution had lost its value. It now left him lonely and isolated.

By embracing the very behavior that was designed to push me away, I convinced him—in ways that words never could—that I would never reject him. To create that experience, however, I had to behave in a counterintuitive fashion. Was I put off by his abrasive attack? Of course! This repulsion, however, was my cue that I had to reach out to him. To be a good therapist, I had to be aware of my natural reaction so that I could act in precisely the *opposite* way. If I had shown him that I was miffed, I would have fallen into the same trap as everyone else, isolating him and destroying all hope for our work.

Know what you're feeling and use that information to go the other way: Successful traders and therapists both learn *to do what comes unnaturally.*

GOING AGAINST THE FLOW WITH SUE

Of course, the natural response with Sue would be to try to convince her that she should continue on with her studies and bring Kenny into our sessions. However, she would hear this as a demand to betray her grandmother and would not only refuse, but possibly leave therapy altogether. No, the natural response would not do. It's like those situations we've all faced when a nice trend leaves the station and we're not on board. The market is moving, the trading pace is quickening, and every fiber of our being wants to pile on. But that's generally when a reversal is at hand. Once a trend is evident, the majority of players have made their move. It takes real discipline to notice your own urge to jump in and then use that information to wait, wait, wait for the retracement.

That is what therapists do: They watch for those countertrend moves, the things that people do when they are *not* immersed in their problems. Few people are continuously dysfunctional; if they are navigating through life, they must have certain strengths and emotional capacities. It is valuable to focus on these: They are the foundation for solutions. A solution-focused approach to brief therapy is grounded in a simple understanding: *The resolution to problems can be found in what people are doing when those problems are not occurring.* If problems are the "trend" in counseling, the therapist waits for the countertrend move before making an entry.

What is the natural thing to do when a person is crying in front of you, submerged in self-blame? Reassure them, of course. That, too, wouldn't work. Sue would toss aside comforting words because she wouldn't feel worthy of comfort. She has done wrong, and she must bear the consequences. But, remember, she would do *anything* for her child. That was Nana's way.

"It's a shame you can't really be a parent like Nana," I said to Sue through her tears. "Nana enjoyed people; she loved being with you. You're not really enjoying this pregnancy are you? I bet if your baby knew how you were feeling, she wouldn't even want to come out of the womb."

Sue's head jerked upward and she glared at me. "That's not true!" she insisted. "You don't know what I've been doing for my baby."

"What have you been doing," I asked, "besides feeling that she was a big mistake?"

Sue was unprepared for my tone of voice. I realized that if I were to reassure her, she would stay helpless, an object of pity. Under the lash of my criticism, however, she now sounded defiant, not depressed.

"We've been making a collage," Sue sputtered.

"A collage?" I asked in surprise. "What kind of collage?"

"I want my child to know all about Nana," Sue stated with feeling. "We've been collecting pictures and letters and everything we can find of Nana's and putting them on a big poster board. When the baby's old enough, it's something we can look at together."

My tone lowered a few notches. "That's beautiful," I said. "You're keeping Nana's spirit alive. And as long as your child learns that spirit and passes it along to her children, something of Nana will live on."

I waited for a moment before asking my question in a near whisper. "Will your med school diploma be part of the collage? Will this be how you pass on to your child Nana's influence on your education?"

Sue didn't respond. But neither did she argue.

I picked my words carefully. "I love the idea of your collage. It will mean so much to your child. But I want to ask something of you. It's going to be very difficult, but you've got to do it for the baby."

"What?" Sue asked quietly.

"You've got to let Kenny contribute to the collage. I know you might not stick with him. That's your choice. But he *is* the baby's father, whether he's in your life or not. Your child deserves to know her story, where she came from. And maybe it will also be a way for Kenny to understand Nana and why you're making your decisions."

Sue stayed silent for a long time. I could tell she was deep in thought. "Maybe," she finally said. "Maybe."

FINDING SOLUTIONS

With Kenny's help, Sue finished the collage. I know because they brought the finished product to me in a joint session. It was a true work of art.

The process got Sue and Kenny talking. Sue wouldn't lower her guard for a man, but she would do it for her child. And once Kenny showed an interest in Nana, the two of them really began talking. Suddenly the relationship wasn't such a betrayal of Sue's upbringing. It could even become an extension of it.

And, yes, Sue left space on the collage for her medical school diploma. Nana valued education; there was no getting around that! So Sue and Kenny would somehow have to make a good home for their child, even with the demands of work and school. Together they were determined to make it work. There was no more learned helplessness.

A simple collage formed the basis for a solution. In the middle of her problems—pushing away love and education—Sue had hit on the idea of leaving her child a memorial to Nana. The key was extending this memorial to Sue's entire life. Sue, after all, would do *anything* for her child—even finish her education, even break down the walls and allow herself to love.

Sue came to me focused on her problem. When she left, it was not with a solution that I had given her. Rather, it was with the realization that *she* had initiated a solution before we ever met.

The problem with many traders is not that they have problems, but that they are *focused* on their problems. It is this problem focus that prevents them from appreciating what they are doing right, that blinds them to solutions already under way.

what's working?

THE FEARLESS TRADING INVENTORY

failure
is
valuable
debt (+)

In the introduction, I mentioned my debts of gratitude for the ideas contained in this book. If the truth is to be told, some of the greatest debts are to my trading failures. When I began as a trader, I believed that what I needed most of all were clean data, a reliable online connection, a good computer, and some well-crafted and well-researched indicators. I obtained all of those and more. I compiled a multiyear database of intraday data for backtesting short-term trading strategies. I obtained decades of market data for examining longer-term market patterns. Not satisfied with normal statistical analysis, I purchased the finest modeling software to ferret out nonlinear patterns in market time series. I read the gurus and compiled an enviable library of books on trading.

And I lost money.

Consistently.

It was a sobering experience. I am a reasonably bright individual, with two advanced degrees to my name. It was humbling, but I had to acknowledge the truth: State-of-the-art tools and IQ points were not going to make me into a trading success. I had the raw materials for success and occasional flashes of promise, but something was getting in the way of making the most of them.

'moral
inventory'

I have the greatest respect for individuals in Alcoholics Anonymous who undertake a "fearless moral inventory." It takes considerable courage to stand in front of a group of people and announce, "My name is Brett, and I am an alcoholic." Even greater courage is required when it comes time to review one's life and the many hurts and wrongs that have been inflicted due to one's addiction. Such a moral inventory is a look in the mirror with eyes wide open. Not many people can tolerate speeding up their personal production process and, like those Japanese automakers, tackle their shortcomings.

I knew, however, that unless I conducted my own fearless trading inventory, I would never take my market game to the next level. So I reviewed my trades, one by one, the winners as well as the losers. I searched for patterns: What did my winning trades have in common? What were the repeated elements in my losing trades?

It was not a pretty sight, but it was educational.

What I found was that my actual trading methods did *not* differ wildly across the winners and losers. I tended to utilize the same market indicators and to piece them together in similar ways. I maintained a core data set and largely relied on this for my trading decisions. These methods had worked well for me in historical backtesting and in paper trading. That suggested an important conclusion: I could succeed or fail with the methods I was using. Developing new and more intricate methods was not necessarily the answer.

The patterns I detected among the winning and losing trades supported this impression. Several conclusions jumped out from my diaries, as I inspected the assembly line of my trading.

position size / consistent ?

• *I was not consistent in my position size.* Too often, I increased my size after a series of successful trades, only to take a large hit when the inevitable losing trade occurred. As well-known trader Mark Cook noticed early in his trading, it is possible to have a respectable overall batting average but still fall short if the size of the losers relative to winners is badly askew. When I placed small trades—so small that the profits and losses almost didn't matter—my percentage of winners was quite respectable. My batting average was painfully lower on large trades.

• *I was not consistent in my preparation.* The single most outstanding feature differentiating my successful trades from my unsuccessful ones was my state of mind during the trade. Winning trades tended to follow from hours of immersion in market data, accompanied by active rehearsals of what-if scenarios. Losing trades were made much more impulsively, without either the focus or the preparation of the winners. Perhaps this sounds mystical, but when I was immersed in the market and my research, winning trades *came to me.* I wasn't looking for the trade; it simply appeared to my conscious mind with a deep, inner feeling of certainty. The losing trades were trades that I attempted to impose on the market. Once I had made my mind up that I was going to trade that day, I found it easy to talk myself into all sorts of patterns and rationales for entering and exiting positions.

• *I was not consistent in my execution.* I am a short-term trader, and I have always been best in that mode. When I reviewed my track record, however, I discovered a disturbing tendency to let losing trades turn into longer-term ones. Invariably this magnified, not rectified, my losses. Ironically, I was most apt to let the short-term trades run when my drawdowns were greatest, almost ensuring that I would wipe out many days of profit in a single, botched trade.

LT term pow(-)

• *I was not consistent in my perspective.* Very often, during trades that ended up as modest losers, I became so immersed in tick-by-tick action that I failed to pay attention to the larger trend. Many trades that would have become large winners were cut short this way. On the successful trades, I tended to work from the top down, aligning my shorter-term positions with the larger trend. At other times, amazingly, I became so caught up in the tick-by-tick action that I placed trades without having even looked at the big picture!

• *I was not consistent in my exits.* On average, I spent far longer analyzing when I should get into the market than how I should get out. The absence of an explicit exit strategy for every likely market scenario left me rudderless at those times of drawdown when I most needed guidance. A significant proportion of my losing trades would have become winners had I followed a planned and tested exit strategy. With the exception of those occasions when I allowed short-term losing trades to become longer-term ones, I tended to be overly risk averse. I cut profits short and tolerated so little drawdown that positions did not have ample opportunity to move in my favor.

The results of my fearless inventory stared me in the face. They could be condensed to a single word: *consistency.* Despite everything I had read about cutting losses, letting profits run, and preparing for each day's trading, I was inconsistent in almost every facet of my game. Worse yet, I hadn't realized I was so inconsistent. Somehow I had talked myself into believing that because I read a great deal about the market, collected megabytes of data, and poured over reams of statistics and charts, this meant that I was working hard and was well prepared. Nothing could have been further from the truth.

But why? I am hardly undisciplined. If I can wake up at 5 A.M. each morning, teach my classes, conduct my counseling practice, amass 50+ professional publications, carry on my trading, and maintain a family, surely I can muster the energy and the focus to create and to adhere to a trading plan! No, something was getting in the way. Something was robbing me of the focus I needed. Like Sue, I had the nagging, guilty sense that when it came to trading, I was my own worst enemy.

AN INVENTORY OF SOLUTIONS

What followed was an intensive period of ruthless, real-time self-observation and evaluation. My goal was to isolate those factors most responsible for maintaining or for losing my trading consistency. I realized, in a humbling moment, that my problems were not unlike those of clients I saw in counseling, people who had difficulty sticking to plans to stop smoking or maintain a diet. Helping them with their problems gave me fresh perspectives on my own. The problem was not one of trading per se. It was more fundamental: *a difficulty in sustaining effortful, purposive activity of any type.*

An important clue to the dilemma was the fact that my trading results were far better when I made small trades than when I made larger ones. When the trades were small, I was much more likely to tolerate normal drawdowns and let profits run. Because the amount at stake—and the amount to be gained or lost—was modest, I felt no need to micromanage the trades. On reflection, I also realized that I tended to place the smallest trades when I was first testing out new trading ideas. Those were the times when I was most immersed in my homework and in the markets. They were also the times when I had best followed the advice of Victor Niederhoffer and kept my trading methods simple, data-based, and direct.

The fearless trading inventory was modesty inducing, to be sure. But it helped to be reminded that when I kept my positions small, my methods direct, and my head in the market, I was capable of placing some very good trades.

That recognition led to a *solution focus* to my market woes. As we saw with Sue, it is often helpful for therapists to *not* focus exclusively on their clients' presenting problems, searching instead for *exceptions* to the problems. If a couple seeks counseling for marital disputes, it is worth delving into occasions when they do not argue. Eating problems? Depression? Solution-focused therapists take the path less traveled: They ask about times when the person *does* eat in a healthy way or about occasions when they *are* happy. Sue's collage was *her* exception: a healthy attempt to face her issues rather than to push them away.

The solution-focused approach works because it utilizes a person's existing strengths as a lever, making weighty problem patterns easier to lift. Couples in counseling are often amazed to find that they go for lengthy periods without arguing. Depressed people have so taken on the identity of being depressed that they fail to appreciate the frequent intervals during a day or a week when they are not down. Once people can turn their mindset from a problem focus to a solution focus, they can identify the adaptive things that they are already doing and do more of them.

This is a very important concept: *You will not become a better trader by emulating a market guru. You will become a better trader by identifying the occasions when you are already trading well and then modeling your future per-*

formance on those. If you are struggling with your trading, thinking of hanging it up (like Sue), you need to identify your own collage—the things you are currently doing that break your problem patterns.

When you learn to trade from the couch as a psychologically sophisticated market participant, you don't become a different trader. *You become more of the trader that you already are in your best moments.* In a very real sense, every trader who has done his or her homework has at least two selves: the one capable of entering the zone and executing his or her strategy; the other so filled with inner urges, fears, and conflicts that the trader winds up trading less in the zone than the ozone. It is interesting that by the time frustrated traders look to psychology for help, they are more in touch with their destructive patterns than with their competencies. The most helpful part of a fearless trading inventory is the firsthand recognition that, even amidst failure, one does indeed harbor the seeds of success.

ENACTING THE SOLUTIONS

You know streak shooters in basketball? Unfortunately, I tend to be a streak trader. I can go through periods of incredible feast and withering famine. At the time I am writing this, I am on a particularly hot trading streak, with about three-quarters of my trades profitable and a net average of several Standard & Poor's (S&P) points per trade. It is at such times that it might seem that keeping a trading journal is least necessary. The solution-focused mindset, however, suggests just the opposite. It is when you are enacting exceptions to problem patterns that you most want to be mindful. If you are meeting with consistent success, the odds are good that you're doing something consistently right. Psychologically minded traders create models of themselves at their best and then consciously strive to embody those models. A great man, Nietzsche once remarked, is only the play-actor of his ideals. That is a wonderful formula for life and market success—to become the play-actor of your own highest strivings.

At first, it does indeed feel like play-acting. The fearless trading audit raised my awareness of many subtle factors associated with successes and failures. For example, the physical comfort of my back and my right hand was highly correlated with the eventual success of trading positions at those times. When I placed high probability trades with proper preparation, I generally felt comfortable with my decision and sat comfortably in my chair, occasionally clicking on different charts and tables to monitor the progress of the trade. When I placed trades for the wrong reasons or with improper preparation, however, I found myself prematurely concerned about their success. I leaned forward in my seat and began furiously clicking charts in a frantic attempt to bolster my confidence in the trade. Eventually, my hand and my back hurt from the hunched-over mouse action. Our bodies often know how our trades are faring more quickly than we do!

Play-acting entered the picture when I consciously adopted a relaxed position when preparing and entering trades. Over the daily course of trading, one can create a powerful association between state of body and state of mind. Entering a facilitative physical state is one of the quickest ways of placing oneself in a winning frame of mind. This principle is well understood by basketball players or major league pitchers who perform little routines before taking a foul shot or delivering a pitch. The ceremonies of religion are similarly filled with such rituals and symbols, as are such formal social occasions as weddings. Once a state of mind has become anchored to a ritual, we need only invoke the ritual to summon the desired state.

Particularly powerful results can be achieved if you can develop rituals out of the patterns you observe during your most successful trading and avoid those patterns associated with trading failures. Once again, think of Sue and the way she was able to expand her collage to include her education and her relationship with Kenny. Even the solution that seems the smallest can serve as an anchor for life-altering change. Here are a few "solution" rituals that emerged from my self-observation: *take break.*

- *Taking breaks from trading.*   Active traders tend to balk at taking vacations. Vacations entail time away from the markets, which means lost opportunities. Nothing is more frustrating than a big move that occurs while you're away from the action, oblivious to the markets. Nonetheless, I have found that trading is especially successful after an extended break. The change of routine allows you to return to trading with a fresh perspective and to perceive patterns that would otherwise not have stood out. Many active traders take breaks around midday (when the markets are least volatile), indulging themselves in activities that are highly noncognitive, such as physical exercise. The renewed energy becomes critical in those later-day situations in which it becomes necessary to sustain concentration for extended periods.
- *Immersing oneself in what-if scenarios.*   My audit found that the amount of time spent in pretrade preparation was positively correlated with the suc-

what-if scenarios ?

cess of trading. It appeared to be the quality as well as the quantity of time spent that mattered for success. As a result, I initiated a daily ritual of looking over the past several years at all days that were similar to the current market. Statisticians refer to such occasions as "nearest neighbors." If today's market declines on high volatility following three days of flat, low-volume market action, I will scour my database for all occasions when this pattern occurred in the past. I will then print out one- and five-minute charts of each of those occasions and review patterns that emerged in subsequent market action. This qualitative exercise primes my mind for things to look for in the coming trading session. As Yale and Jeff Hirsch note in their *Stock Trader's Almanac*, drawing on Pasteur, "Chance favors the informed mind."

- *Playing loose.* I have found that if I am loose during the day, I am most likely to be flexible in my thinking and quick in responding. It is when I am tense and take things far too seriously that I am apt to freeze up and compound a situation that has gone sour. One of my trading colleagues, Henry Carstens, frequently marvels over what a great "game" trading is. It is not surprising to me that he is successful: He plays with trading ideas as spiritedly as he plays with his little son, Everett. Another trading colleague consistently describes trading as a battlefield. It is not surprising that he seems to experience post-traumatic stress with each loss, setting him—and his equity curve—back for considerable periods. Many successful traders learn to keep loose at the trading station in the same way that boxers or ball players stay loose before and during their contests: with uplifting music, banter with friends, and pregame warmup drills. I have recently begun using biofeedback for this purpose.

- *Achieving nonattachment.* There is a Buddhist principle that states that suffering comes from one's attachment to the things of this world. As soon as you *need* something, or need something to occur, it gains control over you. For traders, a most deadly scenario results when they need trading results to bolster their self-esteem. My audit convinced me that I was at my best when I didn't *need* the trades to work out. Indeed, my best trades were ones that were so small that it didn't really matter all that much (in the financial sense) whether any particular one was successful. One of Jack D. Schwager's market wizards, Larry Hite, observed that he had no war stories to tell his colleagues. Every trade represented no more than one percent of total equity, and every trade was like every other one. That is a worthy model of trading psychology: Do a few things well, and perform them often and consistently. Confidence does not result from positive thinking; it results from the ability to face defeat with equanimity and to avoid attachment to market outcomes. Like sex, trading is most enjoyable and fulfilling when participants are immersed in the process rather than concerned about outcomes.

• *Creating symbols.* A symbol is an object that acquires meaning through its association with something significant. The flag is a symbol of one's homeland and crystallizes all that that represents. Depending on one's philosophical proclivities, the dollar sign is either a symbol of the root of all evil or the source of the accomplishments that emerge from personal initiative. Successful traders create their own symbols, immersing themselves in the mindset of success. One practice I have found especially helpful in this regard is to periodically withdraw a portion of profits from the account and use the proceeds to purchase something special for myself or for loved ones. This may be a prestige or a luxury item on which I would not normally splurge, but which is associated with achievement. Some may deride such accumulation as mindless materialism, but this criticism fails to appreciate the psychology of the symbol. Your surroundings are both a mirror of and a contributor to your mind-state; by surrounding yourself with the earned rewards of effort, you transform your very environment into a celebration of self-efficacy.

As you conduct your own fearless trading inventory, you may discover different solutions associated with your trading successes. Trading from the couch challenges you to alter the problem focus and to examine what you're doing when you're *not* trading poorly. Like Sue, you might just discover that you are creating a work of art without even recognizing the fact!

CONCLUSION

Perhaps you picked up this book because you are not content with your market results. If so, that is good. The research literature in psychotherapy suggests that people with moderate levels of distress are most likely to benefit from help. Too much distress leads to shut down; too little pain takes away the incentive for change. Your failures are there for a reason; like those carmakers, you have something to learn when your efforts fall short of expectations. Such a celebration of defeat best positions you to identify your strengths—the solutions you may be enacting without your conscious awareness.

David Bowie once sang of being heroes just for one day. Perhaps Norman

Mailer was closer to the truth when he described every person's "15 minutes of fame." No matter: A single enactment of greatness can set a template for a lifetime. The first step in transforming yourself as a trader is conducting the most honest, fearless inventory possible, assessing each and every defeat and victory. Examine your patterns: What were you doing wrong in the losing trades? What worked in the winning trades? Each of these patterns has a purpose: to teach you something about your trading, something about yourself.

journal of trade

This fearless inventory will require an extensive trading journal that you can review at the end of each week. The journal should include the trades you made, the research-based rationale for the trades, your profit targets, your stop-loss parameters, your frame of mind during the trades, and the outcome of the trades. Each week you will grade yourself on how well you actually followed your trading plans, and each week you will conduct a review of what you did right and what you did wrong. The goal is to create a feedback loop of continuous quality improvement in your trading.

Note that in keeping such a log, the focus is not whether each trade made or lost money. Rather, the emphasis is whether you did your homework and followed your trading plans. Good percentage trades can lose money; occasional impulsive trades can be winners. *You cannot control whether the next trade will win or lose.* All you can do is tilt the odds in your favor through solid research, formulate plans that utilize that research, and place enough trades for the odds to work in your favor over time. In a very real sense, your goal is not to make money. Your goal is to be faithful to your trading plans. If they are solidly grounded, the money will come. If your plans are not solidly grounded, this too will emerge in your trading journal and can prompt you to re-search for your edge.

Find the exceptions to your problem patterns—the times you are doing things that bring you closer to your goals. Then turn those exceptions into solutions by doing more of them. *That* is the solution focus. Sue was able to love by building on her one loving act: the collage. Traders will be able to trade by building on their successes, becoming more of who they already are at their best.

Chapter Two

The Student Who Wouldn't Study

*Overlearned behaviors become automatic: the source of our freedom—
and our slavery.*

Once we find solutions, our challenge is to enact them consistently. Many of
us know what is right to do in life—be good to our spouse, be patient with
the children, exercise regularly, eat in a healthy way—but we fail to sustain
our good intentions. Trading is the epitome of purposive activity; successful
trading is planful trading. In this chapter, we will explore the topic of *purpose*
and some of the factors that will help you become a more-directed, intentional human being. By learning to sustain purpose—expanding your free
will—you also cultivate the ability to formulate and to follow successful trading plans. The best trading system, however, like the best exercise program,
will not help you if you cannot consistently follow it.

KEN, THE FAILURE

I entered the office early on a Monday morning, large coffee already in hand.
I knew it was going to be a full day of counseling. You've probably already

discerned that mine is not an ordinary therapy practice. I primarily deliver counseling services to medical students, resident physicians, nurses, graduate students, and a variety of other health professionals. Most of these are high-achieving, bright individuals whose positions in the market of life could be described as long on stress and short on time. Working on the hospital floors for 12 hours a day and then studying at night doesn't leave time for lengthy psychoanalysis. That is why students come to me as a "brief therapist." People in busy professions appreciate techniques that accelerate psychological change.

Brief therapy, to be sure, isn't for everyone. Some people have chronic emotional problems that require ongoing medical and psychological treatment. The majority of productive people in the working world, however, are not chronically debilitated, even if they do find themselves reliving destructive patterns. Such people have considerable intellectual and emotional resources and, indeed, generally function at a very high level. It is not in jest that I describe my work as "therapy for the mentally well." If you think of people as cars, I am less a repair shop than a performance specialist, helping people tweak those last bits of horsepower and foot-pounds of torque from their factory engines. And in high-risk/high-reward environments that absorb a great deal of time and energy—like medicine or trading—there is a premium placed on every incremental bit of emotional performance.

As I scanned my Monday schedule, I noticed that Ken was my first meeting of the day. I took a long, deep breath. I knew very well that this would not be an easy meeting.

Ken first came to me after he failed the first two pathology examinations. He was petrified at the thought of failing the course, for this would prevent him from moving on to the clinical portion of his medical education. It would also damage his chances of landing a residency in a competitive medical specialty. The remaining two exams, Ken knew, were going to make or break him. He needed every ounce of motivation and concentration he could muster.

But he could muster none.

After studying his heart out—to the point of pulling multiple all-nighters—Ken only had failing grades to show for his efforts. To his complete befuddlement and frustration, he studied the same material as other students and yet scored significantly lower. Even more maddening, he consistently achieved high scores when he took practice exams, only to find the material flying out of his head during the actual test. He was so upset by his lack of success on the first test that he resolved to do whatever it took to pass the course. He spent his evenings, nights, and weekends in nonstop study, losing both sleep and weight in the process.

That came to a crashing halt with the second examination. After his long hours and endless days of studying, Ken's score was no different than the one on the previous exam.

He failed.

With that, for the first time, Ken realized that he might actually fail the largest course of his second curricular year. As he watched his grades fall in his other courses due to the exclusive emphasis he had placed on pathology, he realized with horror that he might even fail out of medical school.

Such a failure would be tragic, given how far Ken had come in his young life. Ken, in fact, was much like Sue, but from a completely different background. After growing up in an alcoholic family, he felt trapped in a small town in New York's Adirondack "North Country." He drove himself mercilessly in high school and gained a scholarship to a reputable college. There he felt painfully out of place amidst peers from wealthier and less-dysfunctional families. He pushed himself to fit in, nonetheless, relying heavily on his academic achievements to carve his niche.

Ken dreaded his returns to the family home. His father constantly reminded him that college was a waste of time, goading Ken to get a job and support himself. During his drunken outbursts, his father would harangue any family member in sight, taking a special delight in belittling Ken's manhood. Ken tolerated this stoically, setting his jaw, and resolving to move forward and win his independence. One pivotal day, after a particularly nasty fight, Ken had enough. He stood toe-to-toe with his father during one of the drunken explosions and announced, quietly but firmly, "I *am* going to make something of myself."

From that time forward, Ken rarely returned to the home of his youth. "My home," he coldly announced in our first session, "is school."

It was hard for me to believe that the Ken now sitting in my waiting room was the same fighter who battled it out with his bitter, drunken father. Ken sat slumped in the chair, and his hangdog look told me that the past few days had not gone well.

"It's really bad," Ken announced as he planted himself in one of the two large reclining chairs in my office.

"What's bad?" I asked. "Your studying?"

Ken gave a brief, self-mocking smile. "I *haven't* been studying," he said, looking down. "I can't get myself to open the books. The test is next week, and I'm behind. I haven't even *started* looking at the new material."

This was bad. Studying hard had not worked for Ken, but hardly studying was not going to be the answer. I could see that his eyes were red-rimmed from sleepless, tear-filled nights. If ever a defeated human being had set foot in my office, Ken was it. From the slumped body to the lifeless voice, Ken was a study in burnout.

"I don't know what to do," Ken lamented. "The more I study, the less I seem to know. But I *do* know it. You wouldn't believe it, but when I was studying with my roommate, I was telling *him* the answers to the practice questions. You know what he got? An 85. Five points away from Honors. What could I say when he asked me my score? He couldn't believe I got a 68. A 68—the same score I got last time!"

He paused, waiting for me to respond. When I did not, he turned his head downward again. "I can't do it any more . . . ," his voice trailed off.

Every ounce of my concentration was focused on Ken at that moment. I *knew* that whatever we accomplished in these next sessions would play a decisive role in shaping his personal and professional future.

These are the moments therapists live for. Therapists are not so unlike major league pitchers or basketball players. The good ones want the ball in their hands when the game is on the line, when each play really counts. Most counseling sessions, like most market sessions, are routine. They offer op- portunities for gains, but most of those gains will be circumscribed. It's those occasional periods of high volatility, when people and markets are reacting most emotionally, that offer the greatest possibilities of large returns.

They are also the periods of highest risk.

I looked at Ken's downcast expression and took yet another deep breath. The ball was in my hands. I had seen Ken for two previous sessions, but the real therapy was now beginning.

DIVERSIFICATION IN LIFE AND MARKETS

What is going on with Ken? Although the particulars may differ, he is not so different from many of the traders who have written to me, lamenting their lack of success in the markets.

Ken wants to succeed in medical school. That much is certain. He so wants to succeed that he will lose sleep and forego food to cover as much material as possible. In fact, he was willing to leave his family to achieve his goals. Although an armchair psychologist might speculate that Ken harbors an inner desire to fail, this would be mistaken. Every fiber of Ken's being wants that medical degree.

Why? What is Ken's motivation to succeed in school?

The obvious answer is that he wants to be a physician. That, too, however, is not quite right. Of course, he wants to be a doctor, but what does that *mean* to him? What is the psychological significance of the ends one seeks? *Why* does anyone want trading profits? Why is it so important for Ken to get that degree?

The answer in Ken's case goes back to his confrontation with his father and, even before that, to his hard work in high school and college. Academic success has always been Ken's niche, the one arena in which he has excelled. His father could berate him and question his suitability for manly work, but he could not erase Ken's inner knowledge that he was an academic success. The philosopher Samuel Johnson, when he encountered the ideas of Bishop Berkeley, was shocked at the notion that the objects people perceive exist only in their minds. Johnson kicked a stone and announced, "Thus do I refute Berkeley!" Well, schoolwork was Ken's way of refuting his father. It was his way of establishing, "I *am* a success."

Success in school possessed an additional significance for Ken: It was his ticket out of the world of his youth. Ken had felt trapped and misunderstood in his small town. He was an anomaly within his family, and he didn't really fit in with his college peers. Medicine promised a personal as well as a professional niche. For once, he could be around people like him who were *doing something* with their lives.

In short, Ken's identity is intertwined with his achievement in medical school. He is not anxious simply about a test. He is petrified, frozen by the possibility of losing *himself*. His self-esteem is dependent on his performance: a sure recipe for anxiety and failure in any arena, whether it's exam taking, public speaking, sports, sexual relations, or trading.

Consider a financial analogy. If medicine is Ken's trading position in life, he is fully leveraged. Ken has invested all of his emotional capital in his medical school career. His poor test performance on the first pathology exam was a normal drawdown, experienced by many other fine students. The other students could weather the drawdown because their emotional eggs were spread across many baskets. Ken, however, was not diversified. He held no cash. Given his 50-to-1 emotional leverage, the normal drawdowns took a fearsome bite out of his psychological bottom line.

"emotional leverage"

Like everyone else, you are a speculator, even if you are not a market participant. If you are to live as a fully functioning human being, you must invest yourself emotionally in the elements of your life. It is only through your emotional investments that you will derive any return, in the form of happiness, contentment, and self-esteem. To be sure, there are chronically depressed and withdrawn individuals who fail to engage the world at all. These individuals realize a paltry return on their lives. In life, as in the markets, the greatest rewards come to those who invest their resources and pursue superior returns.

Most people hold a diversified emotional portfolio, with sizable positions in romantic relationships, children, careers, and other personal activities and social relationships. Such diversification achieves an emotional benefit not unlike its financial counterpart: When things go wrong in one arena of life, the others cushion the blow. The average person holds enough noncorrelated life positions to weather most life stresses.

Such diversification is a potent tool for managing risk. Risk, in part, represents the probability of loss. To achieve superior returns, you must invest emotional capital. But such investment also carries the possibility of significant loss. If you are highly invested in your marriage, you will be severely hurt by the loss of your spouse. If you put dedicated effort into your career, a layoff will hit you hard. When you allow something to mean a great deal to you, you open yourself to significant rewards and losses. The greats in any field of endeavor are those who have dedicated their lives to their pursuits. They are emotional investors, the ones willing to weather the heightened uncertainty that accompanies risk.

Yet even the most dedicated artists or scientists maintain interests beyond their work, just as the most devoted spouses do not limit their interests to their significant others. Few people hold completely nondiversified life portfolios.

But that was Ken. Ken was not dating. Ken was not sleeping. Ken was not eating. Ken had met his personal margin call with the last bit of emotional capital he had available.

And, like many who are living for their trading rather than trading for a living, he came up short.

THE PSYCHOLOGY OF PARALYSIS

Framing Ken's problem as one of emotional investment helps to explain why he would stop studying at a time like this. He is like a shell-shocked trader facing a runaway bear market. Everything is on the line in the market, and he's facing huge paper losses. At some point, the pain becomes so great that he simply can't bear to face the quote machine. Like a turtle retreating to its shell, he is in a protective, shutdown mode.

The difference is that shells really *do* protect turtles. Students and traders only face greater risks when their shutdown modes leave them frozen in the headlights. This lesson was driven home during the dramatic tech bear market of 2000–2001. In a year's time, the Nasdaq Composite Average lost 60 percent of its value; and many former Internet, telecommunications, and networking stalwarts took hits of 80 percent to 90 percent. Funds that had performed admirably since the cyclical bottom of 1998 suddenly found their net asset values considerably shrunken.

During the rout, I wrote several articles for the MSN Money web site, detailing how traders deal with loss. To my surprise, the articles touched a chord among readers, many of whom wrote to me about their devastated financial plans. Several told agonizing stories of watching their retirement savings crumble before their eyes. Having eagerly anticipated their golden years, they now were faced with the prospect of returning to work and/or scaling back their retirement plans. They, like Ken, had placed their emotional and financial eggs in a single basket. Now that the basket was proving unstable, they faced an ominous future.

So how did these readers respond to the difficult combination of risky markets and uncertain minds? To a person, *they did nothing.* Several expressly stated to me that they could no longer bear to look at the stock quotes in the paper. "I can't buy," one reader told me, "and it's too late to sell. All I can do is hold on and wait for it to go back up." At the time the reader wrote that, his largest holding had dropped from 75 to 35. Savings of a lifetime took a 50 percent haircut in a matter of months.

Several months later, the stock—a Wall Street favorite and a core holding of most large, growth-oriented mutual funds—was trading at 16. My reader would need more than a quadruple simply to revisit the old high.

Still later, the market did rebound smartly. The reader's stock made it to the low 20s. At last check, however, it was hovering just above its lows. By not acting, this investor had pursued the riskiest course of all. *There are no nondecisions in the market*. Every decision to hold a long or a short *is* a decision to buy or to sell the market *now*.

If you are holding a position that you would never open as a new order, there's a good chance that you are holding more for psychological reasons than for logical ones. The decision to hold is often framed as a nondecision, when in reality it is an active choice to maintain one's exposure. In a similar way, Ken was not merely making a nonchoice in his academic life; he was actively deciding to not study. The books, like the newspaper quotes for my reader, had become too painful for Ken to open.

Pioneering research by Amos Tversky and Daniel Kahneman helps make sense of this deer-in-the-headlights phenomenon. They found that most individuals are risk-avoiders in handling gains, but risk-takers when faced with losses. In the research example given in Scott Plous's text *The Psychology of Judgment and Decision Making*, an individual is given $1,000 and then offered a choice between two alternatives: She can take a 50 percent chance of gaining $1,000, or she can take a sure gain of $500. Under such conditions, 84 percent of subjects choose the certain gain. If, however, the subjects are presented with a scenario in which they are given $2,000 and then offered a choice between a 50 percent chance of losing $1,000 and a 100 percent loss of $500, nearly 70 percent take the riskier 50 percent bet. In a nutshell, people are far more apt to take chances to reduce losses than they are to extend gains.

Many a winning position has been cut short in the market, and many a loss has been extended, precisely out of this psychology. Ken, like the readers responding to my MSN Money articles, implicitly takes the high-risk bet because of an inability to accept the paper loss. Frozen, he takes the opposite of a solution-focused approach: He continues to do what *isn't* working.

The problem is that people's strategies for managing uncertainty often clash with the strategies needed to manage the objective risks in a situation. To an outside observer, the investor who stops looking at quotes when the market moves against her and the student who discontinues his studies when he is failing are behaving in self-defeating and even masochistic ways. From an emotional vantage point, however, their inactivity makes perfect sense. They are protecting their psyches, not their portfolios or report cards. Like children who hope to escape the bogeyman by drawing the bedcovers over their heads, they hope to make unpleasant realities vanish by banishing them from consciousness.

gains vs losses

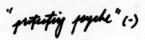
"protecting psyche" (-)

A surprising number of self-defeating patterns can be viewed as misguided attempts to manage the risk and uncertainty of threatening situations. Two years ago, I met with a young man named Bob who was desperate to begin a dating relationship. He had been on a few casual dates, but he hadn't had a meaningful relationship in over a year. Finally, he met someone who interested him. She talked with him after class and seemed similarly interested. He was ecstatic, and he couldn't stop thinking about her.

The following weekend, at a party, they saw each other again. What did Bob do? Nothing!

Why?

"She was talking with other people," Bob explained, "so I didn't think she was interested in talking with me."

"So what did you do?" I asked.

"I left the party," he explained. "I just didn't want to go through rejection again."

Two years later, Bob reentered counseling. He had found a relationship, but it was not fulfilling. For the past year, he had known that his girlfriend was cheating on him, but he could not end the relationship. Like Kahneman and Tversky's subjects and like Ken, Bob tried to protect his self-esteem by taking whatever actions he could to avoid experiencing loss. The young man who was too afraid to talk with a promising woman at a party faced far greater rejection when he was too afraid of losing an unpromising woman.

DECISIONS AND UNCERTAINTY

It turns out that Bob's loss aversion is part of a much larger set of cognitive and emotional biases that affect trading decisions. A growing body of research in behavioral finance has helped traders better understand these distorting influences and their potential impact on the ways traders process market events.

In his book *Beyond Fear and Greed*, Hersh Shefrin summarizes two major biases that influence traders.

1. *Heuristic-driven biases.* Traders create rules of thumb to help them understand and predict events and become overly caught in these imperfect heuristics. Many of the accepted pieces of wisdom among traders, such as the

heuristic-bia

distrust of market declines on light volume and the notion that "the trend is your friend," are convenient heuristics that, unfortunately, do not hold up under the microscope of testing. During periods of uncertainty in the markets, traders are particularly apt to anchor themselves in such heuristics. The opening years of the new millennium witnessed the dangers of such a strategy when traders followed the heuristic that associates high levels of the short-term trading index (TRIN), or Arms Index, with superior upside returns. Thanks to the intensity of selling among large capitalization stocks during 2001 and 2002, very high TRIN readings yielded even more extreme high readings and further significant declines, especially among Nasdaq issues.

2. *Frame dependence.*   The frames, or ways in which situations are presented, affect how people respond to those situations. The risk aversion of Tversky and Kahneman's subjects is an excellent example. As Terence Odean's research has shown, traders who have just made some successful trades are more likely to take subsequent risky trades because they feel that they are now playing with "house money." It is not at all unusual to see traders adopt money management strategies that are a function of their most recent trades. This leads them to become overconfident and impulsive after wins and over-cautious and risk averse after losses.

A good example of how these biases come together in trading can be drawn from breakout trades. The common heuristic among traders is that breakouts from a range will lead to trending movements in the direction of the breakout. Frame dependence, however, helps to determine what traders actually view as a breakout. I have surveyed traders with charts of identical market data plotted on different scales. The points at which traders visually identify a breakout vary as a function of the price scale employed on the *Y* axis and the time frame covered on the *X* axis. I even extended this experiment and plotted chart data on a sonification grid, which assigned a distinct tone to each price level. Subjects were then asked to close their eyes and identify breakouts on the chart from the sounds they heard. The breakout points based on sound were invariably different from those based on visual inspection.

The interesting part of these experiments is that both groups of subjects identified breakout levels well in advance of mathematical algorithms that determined when a breakout was significant. Traders who used charts or sounds to identify breakouts generally made their identification at points at which prices had gone to new highs or new lows, but at which these new highs or lows still fell within the range of random variation. The evidence of the senses, particularly under conditions of uncertainty, is not necessarily an accurate guide for decisions. Traders perceive far more significance in market data than is actually there.

The research of Tversky and Kahneman, moreover, suggests that people continue to hang on to their faulty heuristics and conclusions long after they have obtained contrary evidence. If people can utilize their heuristics to explain most of their experience, they will be reluctant to change those ideas. In trading practice, this creates a dangerous scenario. Only when losses are extreme will traders feel the need for drastic revisions of their scenarios. This imperviousness to new evidence—especially disconfirming evidence—is a major bias interfering with good trading.

Research conducted by Reid Hastie and Bernadette Park helps to explain this perceptual rigidity. Their work suggests that the judgments people make that are based solely on past experience are far different from those that are made "on-line," that is, in the face of fresh incoming data. In the former situation, the quality of long-term memory correlates quite well with the judgments people render. However, in those on-line situations—such as trading—a person's memory is a poor predictor of the decisions that will he made. Subjects, explain Hastie and Park, tend to make new judgments on the basis of earlier judgments and inferences, rather than on the information from long-term memory. Their findings suggest that most spontaneously generated market decisions are apt to be furthest divorced from people's actual experience, a conclusion that reinforces the value of remaining grounded in tested rules and research during the on-line flow of market events.

In sum, it appears that people are far better at generating ideas than at revising them, especially people who are comfortable with the relative balance of risk and reward. Moreover, when uncertainty is high and the volatility of the markets requires on-the-spot decision making, people are most apt to fall prey to their cognitive and emotional biases. In a manner that seems almost cruel, nature has designed human beings in such a way as to be poor traders, ill-equipped to handle the real-time processing of risks and rewards.

ALTERING THE RISK-REWARD EQUATION

I knew that the only way I could help Ken was to alter the balance between perceived risk and reward. He avoided his studies because it was psychologically riskier to try and to fail than to not try at all. The key to helping Ken was the therapist's recognition that failing medical school was *not* his most dreaded fear. His greatest nightmare was that his father was right all along. For years, Ken had felt different from other college and medical students. He had felt a bit like an imposter, coming from a small, rural town and an uneducated, poor family. His desire was to belong. To try and then fail meant facing the devastating reality that maybe he didn't belong. Maybe he would never break free because maybe his family home *was* where he belonged.

Ethologists have observed that animals will fight heatedly until it is clear that one is dominant. At that point, the loser will suddenly stop fighting and bare its throat, as if inviting the deathblow. Interestingly, this inhibits the fighting instincts of the aggressor and allows the weaker animal to go free. If only depression worked so well for people! Ken was losing his battle for independence and now sat in my office, throat bared.

My voice was soft, as I moved closer to Ken. "I need you to do me a favor," I said. "Can you try something for me?"

Ken looked up, a bit puzzled. The last thing he expected was for me to ask help of him. "Sure," he said.

"Whatever you do in the next two weeks," I explained, "I want you to do it honestly. You've always been honest with yourself and your family," I said. "Can you continue that now?"

"Yes, sure," Ken quickly replied.

"Good," I replied, maintaining steady eye contact. "You understand that if you don't study, you'll fail the last exam and the final. That means you'll fail the course. And if you don't study for the other finals, you'll fail those courses as well. That will make you eligible for dismissal, right?"

Ken's eyes grew wider. "Right."

"So if you decide to not study, you're really deciding to leave school," I pointed out. "If we're being honest with ourselves and each other, that's the bottom line."

"But I *want* to study," Ken protested. Some emotion was creeping into his voice. That was good.

Quickly, I shot back, "No, Ken, you want to pass. The last thing you want to do is study . . . especially if you're going to get another 68."

Ken didn't reply.

"How would that feel to you," I asked, my voice rising. "To study your heart out and get another failing grade?"

"I can't do it," Ken moaned, his voice again lowering.

"You don't even want to go there, do you?"

"No," Ken smiled slightly.

"So you don't study. You'll take the default failure rather than put yourself through the agony of trying and then falling short. And, Ken, that's fine," I emphasized. "If that's what you choose to do, I'll support your decision. But it will be important for you to be honest about the decision."

"What do you mean?" Ken asked, puzzled.

"Ken," I said softly, "if you opt out of school, you're going to need a place to stay. You're going to have thousands of dollars of financial aid debt coming due. You're going to need to mend fences with your family."

Ken's face was ashen. But he was looking directly at me, not down at the ground.

"Ken," I intoned slowly, "you'll need to let me call your Dad and explain what happened. You'll need to apologize and swallow your pride—let him know he was right all along. For a while, at least, you're going to need him. You'll need a home base."

"I can't do that," Ken said firmly. "No way. I'm not going to do that. Tell him I'm sorry? Tell him he was right? That I'm not good enough to make it?" Ken's voice rose, his tone indignant, not so defeated.

"But, Ken," I continued softly. "Isn't that what you've been telling yourself? That you're not good enough to make it? All I ask is that you be honest—that what you say to yourself and what you say to your father be one and the same."

Ken stopped short. He seemed to recognize that the emotional bet had changed. Either accept a certain loss—having to move back home, tail between his legs—or take a small chance that he could pass. Ken was still operating in the Tversky-Kahneman mode; but, subtly, we had reconstructed the choice. What had felt like the safest option was now the most threatening.

"I've got to start studying," Ken announced, his determination returning.

"Absolutely!" I said, laughing. "You have to study every minute and drive yourself into the ground. You have to stop eating and stop sleeping. You have to so torture yourself with the fear of failure that you put yourself in a state where you *can't* learn!"

"Or," my voice suddenly turned serious, "you can get back to being Ken and doing the things that have always worked for you. And if you fail, you fail. You won't be the first to fail a course. You'll take it over the summer, get it out of the way, and move on. It won't be fun, but it won't be a killer either. Summer in Burlington, New Orleans, or Chicago sure beats a summer at home, doesn't it?"

Ken laughed. It was one of those transformations that make counseling so rewarding. At that moment, I had no doubt that Ken would find a way to pass. By redefining risk and reward, he had gone from bared throat to emboldened warrior in a matter of minutes.

redefine risk (4)

SHIFTING RISKS AND REWARDS IN TRADING

Ken's therapy illustrates an important idea: It isn't necessary to change your personality to make major life changes. The challenge is to make your personality work for you, rather than against you.

Ken came to counseling desperately wanting to not fail. He left counseling desperately wanting to not fail. Our meetings helped him redefine what failure was by translating his problem from one set of terms to another. And that, as you will see, is a crucial process in all psychological change. Every major change entails a change in perspective, a redefinition of risk and reward.

Many traders express an interest in changing themselves instead of focusing on the specific patterns that they want to alter. They want to talk about their self-esteem, their troubled past, or their poor relationships. Such a problem focus simply reinforces their identities as troubled people. What traders are doing wrong—their impulsive overtrading, their fear of entering positions, their inconsistency in risk management—is looking to solutions that no longer work. Traders caught in such patterns are like Ken: They are managing their emotional distress rather than their current life challenges.

Ken changed by viewing his former solution—avoiding work—as the greatest failure of all. He was achievement oriented to begin with, and we utilized this fact to leverage his emotional change. Once he viewed his old pattern as *failure*, he could make a 180-degree behavior shift without months and years of therapy.

Similarly, traders tend to be achievement minded. They hate to lose. The key to change lies in the recognition that their impulsive or overcautious trading patterns entail the greatest losses of all because those patterns rob them of future as well as current success. *Traders change when they leverage their achievement orientation as a solution, stop beating on themselves*

problem pattern = enemy

and endlessly analyzing their flaws, and make their problem patterns their greatest enemy.

Emotionally troubled traders have defined themselves as the problem, and it is their achievement motivation that then drives them to turn on themselves. They are doing something good—trying to eradicate the problem! By identifying the old solutions that are no longer working and making those the problem, traders can stop the cycle of losing and beating themselves up; and, like Ken, they can use their motivation to fight the *real* enemy.

But how can they sustain the fight against the enemy? How can they get to the point where they *consistently* turn their energy against the patterns that sabotage trading, rather than against themselves?

The answer, oddly enough, can be found in music.

MUSIC, MOODS, AND PIVOT CHORDS

Music is never far away. Almost every movie has a soundtrack: the tubular bells casting a spell over *The Exorcist*, the brass fanfare of *Rocky* impelling the boxer's jog through the streets of Philadelphia, Vangelis's electronic soundscape following the runners through their paces in *Chariots of Fire*, the menacing, brooding sounds of the shark's advance in *Jaws*. It is difficult to think of these movies without their music. The melding of sight and sound generates a powerful set of memories.

sight + sound meld

Advertisers realize this. They create vivid visual and musical images to accompany the presentation of their products. It is not enough to simply explain the virtues of a cola, a bar soap, or an automobile. Advertisers need to show laughing, happy people in a dizzying succession of images, accompanied by up-tempo music and an energetic announcer. In fact, many commercials say very little about their product. Instead, they show the product and link it to memorable images and sounds. The moods anchor the message, helping it stick in the consumer's mind.

In days of old, soldiers marched to music. Now sports teams bring music to the locker room; their fans in the stadium absorb the rhythms of pep bands and sound systems. Boxers and wrestlers enter the ring to the sounds of their favorite, high-energy songs. There is musical accompaniment at funerals, religious services, and graduations. A crying baby is often calmed with a lullaby. Later in life, the sounds internalized, people hum and sing to themselves in the car or the shower. Lives are conducted to a musical score, proceeding to a beat and a rhythm that operate below usual human awareness. Music provides the moods, the emotional texture to many of life's messages.

The therapist Moshe Talmon has referred to *pivot chords* in therapy: points at which a person's meanings can provide a transition to a new way of understanding and experiencing events. In music, a pivot chord is one that contains elements of several different keys, providing a natural transition to a new key. The point at which the pivot chord is struck is one of maximum ambiguity, as the score could proceed in any of several directions.

Composers often sustain a sense of anticipation and drama by prolonging pivot chords, creating a buildup of tension to be released in the subsequent key shift. Philip Glass's musical train in the soundtrack to *Powaqaatsi* is a persistent, intermittent pivot chord (the whistle) accompanied by short, repetitive sequences that capture the sense of motion. When the whistle finally resolves, the involved listener experiences the shift in a visceral manner, as a *change*. Talmon suggests that transition points in therapy—points of rapid change—have precisely this musical structure.

TOM'S PIVOT CHORD

Tom was a trader who came to a counseling session complaining of anxiety. His anxiety typically peaked early in the trading day and inhibited him from entering positions, despite unambiguous signals from his research. Through the day, he would then berate himself for having missed a golden opportunity in the morning. This only added to his agitation, which he then attempted to assuage with a late-day trade. This trade was often impulsively conceived and left him in the hole on a day when he should have been adding to his equity.

All of this became a self-sustaining cycle, as missed opportunities and losses added to his nervousness, which then created further missed opportunities and impulsive trades. By the time he talked with me, he had run through a significant portion of his trading capital.

He was noticeably tense in our conversation, his words running together in a frantic monologue: "I don't know why I am feeling so anxious. When I wake up, I feel this knot in my stomach. I'm all tense and knotted up. I immediately start thinking that it's going to be a bad day, that I'm going to crap out on my trades. Then, all day long, I feel nervous. I don't even want to go outside to take my dog for a walk. I don't want anything to upset me.

I can't stand feeling this way. Yesterday, I was so worked up, I thought for sure I was going to give myself a stroke. My heart was racing and I thought I was making myself sick. But I couldn't stop it."

These kinds of communications are difficult to handle. The person is increasingly experiencing the problem even as they attempt to describe it. The mounting tension can be contagious; it is a challenge for a therapist to maintain a calm, reassuring perspective in the face of such emotional frenzy. As long as that emotional tone persists, however, any reassuring words or helpful strategies will be lost. The person's mood will swamp any message that is offered. The first step, then, is to achieve a mood shift. That is the purpose of the pivot chord.

I responded to Tom with a very even, slow, calm voice. I raised my eyebrow and said, "You have a dog at home? Tell me more about him."

The abrupt shift of topic usually surprises people, but they rarely complain or even comment. Not infrequently, you can help yourself become unstuck in a life situation by changing your pace or by approaching a problem in a different key. At my shift, Tom simply smiled and reported, "She's a girl, a cocker spaniel, only several weeks old. I got her from an ad in the paper. Her name is Nipper."

"How do you feel when you're holding Nipper?" I asked.

Again, Tom smiled and now spoke with a somewhat slower, warmer tone of voice. This was a shift. "Nipper is about the only thing that calms me down. I hold her in my lap and she will let me stroke her belly. When she licks my hand, I feel warm all over."

"Can you close your eyes for a moment and get an image of yourself and Nipper? Can you feel the softness of her fur, her warm tongue? Can you feel her body wriggling underneath your hands as you stroke her?"

Tom nodded and opened his eyes. His look was far mellower now.

It was time for the pivot chord.

"When you wake up with your anxiety, how would you like to *really* experience a stroke?" I asked.

A look of shock flashed across his face. "*What?!*"

"A Nipper stroke," I quickly clarified. "When you are stroking Nipper, you're making that puppy feel loved and wanted, and that feels good to you. Suppose you could stroke yourself the way you stroke Nipper?"

"Funny you should mention that," Tom said. "When I was with my last girlfriend, she used to stroke my face and hair when I would get upset. I calmed down right away."

"Maybe you felt like Nipper," I offered. "What if, next time you get nervous, you think about giving yourself a stroke instead of a *stroke*? Suppose you close your eyes and imagine that you're there with Nipper and imagine what she's feeling like. Try to feel what it's like to be stroked and held. Imagine yourself petting your puppy and getting inside her head, how warm and comforted she must feel. If you're at home, maybe feel Nipper's soft fur and imagine that you're the one being stroked."

Tom liked the idea of "giving himself a stroke." That became a theme for the next several meetings, as he learned to accept his stress and to use it as a cue to evoke nurturance rather than the mounting sense of catastrophe. Emotionally, he made a shift in keys, from the key of anxiety, fear, and negativity to the key of caring and loving. The "stroke" metaphor, delivered at a time of emotional upheaval and following a shift to a warmer feeling, was the pivot chord that made the shift possible.

moods
↓
message

Moods cement messages. We see this cementing in advertising, we make use of it in therapy, and we can harness it in trading. Evoke an enhanced state, and a pivot becomes possible—a new melody, a new rhythm, life in a different key.

BREAKING ROUTINES

Moods and messages—these are the essential building blocks for psychological change. The research literature on the effectiveness of therapy suggests that people are most likely to change when they process information about themselves in new ways. That is why various approaches to therapy make use of role-playing, metaphors and storytelling, personal journals, and dream analysis. Each of these is a way that people can use to capture ideas about themselves in ways that are out of the ordinary. When researchers ask clients to identify the episodes that were most critical to their success in therapy, they invariably mention occasions in which new information and experiences were presented in a novel fashion. Routinely presented information is processed routinely. Novelty breaks routines.

Ken regained his ability to study not because I talked with him about his problems, but because I set up an unexpected situation in which he would have to call his father to admit defeat if he did not study. Faced with that noxious scenario, he could not maintain his pattern of procrastination. The consequence of giving in to his father was much more undesirable than the consequence of failing the test. The novel shift of context allowed him to experience his problem in a different way. Had we simply talked about his fear and the probable consequences of not studying, it is likely that he would never have made it through the course. Changing his behavior required seeing his problem in a different light. Ken redefined "failure"; Tom redefined "stroke." When people change, they effect a translation, a shift in the meaning and the significance of their problem patterns.

A problem patterns

And yet, novelty alone will not generate change. The research on therapeutic outcomes suggests that people are most likely to alter their problem patterns when they are emotionally involved in the change process. A variety of therapeutic techniques are used to enhance the clients' experiencing: confrontations, role-plays, and relaxation techniques, to name a few. Each of these helps to shift an individual from one mode of experience to another. The counseling research suggests that people will process information more deeply and more enduringly when they are in such enhanced states. *The moods anchor the messages.*

Like Sue, Ken, and Tom, many people come to therapy already in a state of high arousal. They are upset about their problems and are already far from a normal, day-to-day state of consciousness. In the heightened state of crisis, they are much more ready to see their problem patterns differently than if they were not suffering. Crisis yields opportunity because it places people in a state where they are open to new life messages.

Skilled therapists help to shift the experiencing of their clients through such simple means as alterations in their tone of voice and the use of shock and surprise. The therapists realize that in routine states of mind, people can only see things in routine ways and behave according to routine. It is when they shift their musical scores that they become able to process even the thorniest emotional patterns in new and constructive ways, opening the door to new behavior.

BREAKING THE ROUTINES OF TRADING

How can these change dynamics be applied to trading, harnessing the elements of change that benefited Ken and Tom? Here is a trading practice that, if it works for you as it has for me, will help eliminate a significant portion of your losing trading ideas before you implement them.

Early in the morning, before the domestic markets open, get yourself in *exercise (4)*

the habit of engaging in a vigorous exercise routine, such as jogging, swimming, martial arts, or aerobics. The only requirement is that it be an exercise regimen that challenges you, raising your heartbeat and respiration for a sustained period of time. My own routine incorporates stretching exercises with rapid series of sit-ups, push-ups, and other calisthenics. Invariably, I feel far more limber and energized after the workout.

review trading-plan

Once you're in your pumped-up state, review your trading plan for the day by *talking it out aloud*. This is important. Do not just look over your charts or computer printouts in the usual way. Talk them out aloud, as if you are delivering a commentary to another person. Your talk will describe the short- and long-term trends, the patterns in the market that you are perceiving, the anticipated points of entry, the proper stops, and so on.

In my morning routine, I deliver my commentary shortly after finishing my workout, on the drive to my office. I cover every contingency I can think of: If the market opens lower, here's what I'll do. If it reverses and makes a new high, here's my plan. And so forth. The key is talking it out aloud in a normal speaking voice, as if you were addressing another person.

exercise = catalyst

The results are quite interesting. When you talk your trading ideas to yourself, you take both roles in a conversation. You are both speaker and listener, presenter and audience. Hearing your own ideas—especially in a fresh, energized state of mind—allows you to evaluate them from a unique perspective. You hear your trading plans differently because you are processing them differently. Exercise is the catalyst that invokes a novel mindset. In a literal sense, you are running your trading ideas by a more objective, neutral party: yourself, in a different state of mind. As the research of James Pennebaker suggests, talking out emotional experiences is a powerful means for reprocessing them. When trading hunches are liberated from the confines of your skull, they are open for more neutral scrutiny.

Incredibly, once they are given voice, many of your ideas won't fly. You'll have that sense of, "What am I thinking?!" That allows you to scratch a trade *before even placing it*. Ferreting out one's own faulty thinking is a powerful technique for building a sense of mastery in trading—and makes it more likely that you will not repeat the error on subsequent occasions. After all, as Yale and Jeff Hirsch point out in their *2002 Stock Trader's Almanac*, "If you don't profit from your investment mistakes, someone else will" (p. 103).

Conversely, you'll find that the best trading ideas *sound* good when you talk them aloud. They just *feel* right. And it is interesting that when you take a break from the screen and return to the charts in a different state of mind, you can actually *see* patterns in the market differently. What had looked like trendless, random action now appears as an important region of consolidation; a vigorous trend that makes you think of doubling down is suddenly reframed as a blow-off top and allows you to take profits. The messages of the market are there to be read, if you can access the proper moods.

One of the problems I continually find with traders is that the frame of mind in which they analyze markets is different from the one in which they are actually making trading decisions. Most traders, like myself, use their late evening and early morning hours to download data, examine indicators, update overseas markets, scan news items, and the like. This is generally a quiet, routine activity. Once the markets open, however, the minute-to-minute price action is anything but routine. There are many indexes and markets to follow; an array of statistics to process; and sudden, unforeseen bursts of volatility to respond to. Under conditions of arousal, people process information very differently than during calm routine. The decisions and the analyses that were prepared in the calm of analysis rapidly fly out the window under the stress of trading, much as Ken's test material abandoned him during his pathology tests.

This is a major reason why traders fail to sustain purpose in the markets. The action of the market elicits unintended pivot shifts, altering how traders process information about themselves and the markets. In a very real sense, the market acts as an antitherapist, shifting traders out of solution mindsets into a greater problem focus!

One of my favorite techniques for handling the novel shifts that the market throws at us traders is to temporarily get away from the screen during periods of uncertainty and stress. During this break, I will quickly update my indicators, rerun my models, and scan the charts of various indexes and markets. This inevitably places me in a calmer frame of mind, similar to the state I am in during those early morning hours of preparation. Often, too, this fresh look at the data will clarify what had seemed uncertain.

Recently, I noticed a nice upside breakout of the Standard and Poor's (S&P) and Nasdaq futures on a one-minute chart. The pattern followed a trade I had just closed, in which I had taken a profit on a short position. Now I was excited about catching a swing in the opposite direction.

Before I could place my order, however, I talked my intentions out aloud and promptly interrupted myself, chastising: "That's not part of the plan!" My research compares current patterns of strength and weakness to similar patterns in past periods. By inspecting how the market moved subsequent to these past periods, I can identify possible future directional bias, which, in this case, had clearly called for a downward trend to the day. Rather than take the exciting, impulsive long trade, I updated the research to assess my earlier trading plan. Sure enough, the edge was to the downside. I let the short-term breakout play itself out (which it did rapidly) and was then better positioned to enter on the short side for the next swing.

Many scalpers and very short term traders convince themselves that they do not have time for such research, that taking time away from the market action will cause them to miss opportunities. "You can't get a hit unless you swing the bat," they insist. They fail to realize that the best hitters protect the plate and, at times, will take a strike in order to wait for their pitch. The key to rapid trading is the *automation* of research, so that statistics and indicators update themselves in real time. I have dozens of Excel sheets dynamically linked to my real-time market feed, updating tables with preprogrammed formulas and displaying these in chart form. A scan through all of them rarely, if ever, causes me to miss a trade but often helps me avoid a bad trade by placing the tick-by-tick action in context.

Such clarification of the market's context is only possible once arousal has been dampened. Activating analytical capacities is one of the most powerful strategies for suppressing excessive emotional processing of events. Well-known traders, such as Victor Niederhoffer, Linda Raschke, and Mark Cook, have written extensively on the value of market research. Less well appreciated, however, is that such research is also a psychological strategy. When people immerse themselves in research, they facilitate shifts in information processing that, as with Tom, open the door to new action patterns. The value of research lies not just in the information it imparts, but also in the frame of mind it cultivates.

Behavior patterns are anchored to one's states of mind and body. As people randomly enter one state after another, they find themselves unwittingly enacting patterns that they would never consciously choose. This is how they fail to sustain purpose—in life and in trading. Once they learn the skill of shifting their emotional and physical states, they are free to create and to enact new patterns. Cultivating a calm, focused state during periods of market research—and then immersing oneself in research during the trading day—is a powerful strategy for interrupting the impulsive and emotional problem patterns that are elicited by volatile periods of price action. Many traders are so afraid of missing a possible market move that they dare not spend time refocusing on their trading plans. They fail to realize the far greater risk of losing sight of their plans and trading haphazardly.

Your trading plan is your anchor; you most want to utilize it when seas are roiling. In developing and following your plans, even in those volatile seas, you extend your ability to act purposefully, and you gain a measure of mastery over yourself and the markets. The psychological antidote to greed and fear is *planfulness*, not calm or confidence.

CONCLUSION

Late in 2001, Linda Raschke invited me to two of her seminars for traders in order to conduct a survey of their personality traits and coping styles. Subsequently, I expanded the survey to include members of her trading chatroom and traders from the Speculators List inspired by Laurel Kenner and Victor Niederhoffer. The 64 traders who responded represented a variety of trading styles, experience, and levels of success.

The personality questionnaire that I utilized was the NEO Five Factor Inventory derived from the research of Robert McCrae and Paul Costa. This assesses personality on five trait dimensions that have been found to be relatively stable across the lifespan:

1. *Neuroticism*—the tendency toward negative emotions.
2. *Extraversion*—an outward orientation toward people and life.
3. *Openness to experience*—a desire for novelty, variety, and risk taking.
4. *Agreeableness*—the tendency to get along well with others.
5. *Conscientiousness*—the capacity to be reliable, steady, and trustworthy.

The findings were eye opening. The traders who reported the greatest success (and who were willing to have me verify their success in case studies) tended to score high in conscientiousness. They were very steady and reliable.

The traders who reported the greatest problems with their trading tended to score high in neuroticism and openness. They were experiencing many negative emotions and tended to use trading for excitement.

The conscientious traders tended to be highly rule-governed in their trad-

rule-governed (+)

ing. There was little excitement in their trading. Instead, they very consistently developed their plans and followed them.

The neurotic and risk-taking traders tended to make their decisions impulsively, without prior planning. They tended to revel in telling stories of their great wins and losses.

stick to plan (+)

The survey drove home one important lesson: *Success in trading is related to the ability to stay consistent and plan-driven.* Traders fail not because of their emotions, but because their emotions deflect them from their purpose. In developing their rules and systems, the successful traders had found a way to immunize themselves from the emotional effects of market volatility. Indeed, in many respects, the successful traders appeared to be every bit as fearful as the unsuccessful ones. It's just that the fears of the successful traders were not those of drawdown or missing a market move. Rather, they feared deviating from their plans. Dedication to purpose was the cornerstone of their success.

'dedication to purpose'

Chapter Three

The Woolworth Man

We rise above what we observe.

'language of market'

Experienced traders learn that the markets speak a language all their own. There are signature patterns for individual stocks, for indexes, and for commodities. A great part of trading success lies in deciphering the language of the markets.

In this chapter, we will look at language—human and market-generated—and see how the tools and tactics utilized by therapists can help us better understand the markets. So far, we have focused attention on the subjective experience of traders. Now, however, we will turn the tables and put the markets on the couch. In so doing, we will learn how to become more adept as observers and how to gain greater control over our trading.

THE INTERVIEW FROM HELL

A most uncanny experience occurred during the first year of my training as a psychologist. My cadre of beginning-level graduate students was scheduled for an observed interview. These were largely enjoyable experiences, in which we took turns interviewing clients from our clinic, finding out about their problems, and formulating ideas for helping them.

The nervous tension within my group betrayed the realization that the interview would be unlike any others. This patient had been recently discharged from the state psychiatric hospital. Indeed, he had spent a significant portion of his life in such hospitals. He displayed the classic signs and symptoms of schizophrenia: disordered thought and language, hallucinations, delusions, and odd emotional expressions. We were warned in advance that much of what he said made no sense whatsoever. We were also told that he rarely stood still and that sometimes, in his agitation, he made physical contact with others. According to the clinic director, he had come to us for help after abruptly discontinuing his medications.

We listened intently to the briefing, our discomfort mounting. Most of my group had never actually talked with a psychotic person. An uneasy silence permeated the observation room as we settled in behind the one-way mirror. Each of us, it seemed, was confronting the inner questions and doubts of the neophyte professional: What will he be like? What will I say? How will I fare as I take my turn interviewing a truly mentally ill person?

We fared poorly.

The man was unshaven and disheveled. He grimaced as he paced back and forth in the interview room, ranting, "I am Woolworth! I am TG&Y Store! I am Woolworth!" His agitated gestures and facial contortions, combined with his fanatical insistence that he was a discount department store, cowed us all. We had no clue as to what to say, what to ask.

Several of us tried in vain to conduct a standard interview. We asked about his problems, tried to elicit details of his personal life, posed our well-honed open-ended questions. He ignored us. It was as if no one was talking to him. He continued pacing, all the while pressing his claims that he was a retail outlet. More than a few of us found ourselves hoping that the class session would run out of time before it became our turn as interviewer.

Finally, a more experienced graduate student tried his hand at the interview. He was unlike the other students, not merely because he had experience but also because there was something *different* about him. It was nothing tangible, just a look in the eyes and a peculiar intensity. He didn't seem altogether *normal*, which, for me, made him especially interesting. Indeed, I had heard rumors that he was quite practiced in dealing with psychotic patients. These rumors were not necessarily spoken in a tone of respect.

He calmly sat beside the raving man. His demeanor conveyed the expectation that he was going to have a normal conversation with a normal person. Meanwhile, his head thrown back and his arms shaking, the client continued the chant, "I am Woolworth! I am TG&Y!"

The student was unfazed. He looked straight at the agitated man before him and quietly asked, "What's for sale?"

From my perch behind the observation mirror, I could feel my heart stop. Instinctively, I knew he had asked the right question.

The man paused. His tone became flat and emotionless. "Nothing," he replied.

"Why not?" the student asked. "Why isn't there anything for sale?"

The man stopped his pacing and gesticulating. For the first time, he looked at his interviewer. "The shelves are bare," he said.

"How about the customers?" he continued. "Where are they?"

His face a contorted, anguished mask, his eyes burning far too brightly, the man whispered, "They're all gone." For hours he had been trying to get people to pay attention. He was not a patient. He was a store—a dark, empty store with barren shelves. He needed to be restocked. I was stunned. The other graduate students seemed indifferent. Some even snickered. I looked from one to another, desperate to see if anyone shared my epiphany, the eye-opening realization that was to forever change my professional perspective: This patient wasn't irrational at all. *He was simply speaking a different language.*

Twenty-three years later, I'm an old hand at the therapy business. I have worked with just about every type of person and problem that exists. In that time, I have witnessed markets that run away to the upside and those that plunge downward. I am still waiting to meet a wholly irrational person.

Or a truly irrational market.

OBSERVING PATTERNS

When people—or markets—seem irrational to you, there's a good chance you are failing to read their language. Dreams, the conversation of young children, artwork—many a profound truth comes packaged in ways that make more psycho-logical than logical sense. Irrational markets suddenly make sense when you recognize that *their volatility is a direct reflection of the emotionality of their participants.* Such markets, like the Woolworth man, are screaming their messages to you—if only you can make the proper translations.

Many traders attempt to predict the market and look for prices to follow. Great traders understand the market's language and follow along. Just as it took a therapist who was a bit off center to appreciate the communications of the Woolworth man, you can best apprehend the market's messages by attending to your own volatility.

There is a myth among beginning therapists and traders that consummate professionals check their emotions at the door and operate under strict logic and reason. Is it possible to shut off your feelings in such a manner? Would this even be desirable?

It is interesting that cognitive neuroscience research has addressed just this issue. A number of studies have investigated individuals with brain lesions who display what would seem to be a trader's dream: Their reasoning mind remains intact, even as their capacity for feeling is blunted. The result is not a superrational, intelligent being, such as Mr. Spock from the old *Star Trek* series. Indeed, the person without the capacity to feel is much like the Woolworth man, issuing tossed salads of words that connote much but denote little. As neuroscientist John Cutting noted, the person who is devoid of feeling is a mere gesturer, issuing words that are divorced from meaning.

Why is this? It appears that feelings are one's guide to the value and the meaning of events. In the language of cognitive psychology, emotions reflect a person's appraisals of the world. Suppose I see a man walking toward me on a dark, empty street. If I interpret the man as the friend whom I am planning to meet, I may feel eager anticipation. But if I interpret the approaching figure as a potential mugger, my emotional response is apt to be quite different. Good/bad; safe/threatening; for me/against me—feelings cast the world in terms of its relevance to the perceiver. It is difficult to imagine a therapist helping people or a trader attending to the significance of market action in the absence of such a guide.

Like the therapist for the Woolworth man, the successful trader feels the market but *does not become lost in those feelings*. Emotions are information, no less than a wide-range bar on a chart. Indeed, a strong emotion can be thought of as a personal volatility breakout. Just as an experienced trader becomes exquisitely sensitive to the patterns emerging from the tape, traders who know themselves well attend to their own patterns. To paraphrase Robert Pirsig in *Zen and the Art of Motorcycle Maintenance*, the real market you're trading is the market called the Self.

One truly accurate market indicator is my own hubris, or pride, in making a successful trade. The setup begins with a series of winning short-term trades. I'm pleased with my success and find myself wanting to get back into the market quickly, to continue the streak. I place my trade—sometimes increasing my size—picking my entry carefully. In this particular scenario, the trade does in fact work to my advantage, and now I have a nice string of successes behind me. Without forethought, I begin to feel my oats. I project my future profits. I start to talk about my positions with others. I entertain wild fantasies of authoring an advisory service or managing a larger portfolio. Before I know it, my emotions have made a high volume move to the upside.

When that happens, the current trade, which is now profitable, very often will reverse. What is more, my subsequent trades are apt to have a poor batting average. It is almost as if I have jinxed myself. What is going on?

In any sport, whether it is basketball, track, or boxing, a successful competitor cannot be a scorekeeper. When I am counting my profits and focusing on my track record, I am no longer attending to the market. I am like the Woolworth man, filled with my inner voices, badly out of sync with the outside world.

How can I escape this trap? Should I make an effort to tune out my feelings? Absolutely not!

The key to self-control is to trade less from the ego and more from the therapist's couch. If I will be a truly successful trader, I will emulate the successful therapist in such a situation. When a strong emotion hits in therapy or trading, the challenge is to activate an Internal Observer. The Internal Observer is a part of myself that stands apart from my moods and calmly observes the situation. If I can identify with the Observer—and not with my grandiosity—I have a chance to profit from the information contained in my emotions.

It takes practice to cultivate the Internal Observer. Practitioners of meditation have long understood that it is easiest to stand apart from the emotional flow if you slow your breathing and your bodily movements and isolate yourself from external stimuli. The mind is apt to be most quiet when the body has slowed down. If I can sit in a darkened room with my eyes closed, breathe deeply and slowly, and focus my mind on a single image—eliminating as many stray thoughts as possible—I will begin to unwind. If I continue the exercise, I will become bored. My mind will hunger for stimulation. That is when real change can occur.

The key to activating the Internal Observer is to *stick with the sensory isolation, deep breathing, and focused concentration beyond the boredom threshold.*

When your body is itching to move and your mind begins to wander, and you think you just can't tolerate a moment's more meditative quiet, *stick with it several minutes longer*. What will happen is quite remarkable. Like a runner who "hits the wall" and becomes exhausted, only to gain a second wind after forging on, your consciousness will find a second wind beyond the boredom threshold. It will take effort, and it will take practice, but the payoff is great. Beyond the boredom threshold lies the Internal Observer.

I always know when I have found the Observer because it feels as though there is quiet inside my head. I feel in the world but strangely separate from it. Things that may have upset or stressed me a few minutes earlier no longer seem so important. When I first tried this exercise, it took quite a few minutes to reach the Observer. Now, more familiar with my mindscape after considerable practice, I can evoke the Observer with just a fixed gaze and a few deep breaths. It's a handy skill in the midst of frenzied trading.

It is at those points of feeling removed from the world, on the heels of indulging in my trading successes, that the Internal Observer pipes up and says, "You know, Brett, you've been feeling awfully good. You've made quite a few good trades, and now your emotional chart is in a parabolic rise. You know what happens to parabolic rises; they end in crashes. This is your signal: The trade you're so happy with is likely to reverse."

If I can heed the Internal Observer, I have an opportunity to keep the focus away from myself. That permits me to become especially attentive to indications that my current position is not working out. Instead of approaching the market as if I'm invincible, I reverse my psychology and *intensify* my concentration and effort, as if I've lost money on the most recent five trades and can't afford to lose more.

Feeling overconfident thus becomes a cue that triggers cautious behavior— *the opposite response from the one that normally would arise*. In trading, as in therapy, the best response is very often *not* the one that comes naturally. If I'm feeling anger toward a client, that's usually a time I need to think about being supportive. If a client seems boring during a session, that often is a sign that *I* need to pursue a more fruitful line of discussion. Therapists think of it this way: The responses that come normally and naturally are what clients have been getting from people all their lives. If those had been therapeutic, you can be sure they wouldn't be wasting their time in your office!

It is exactly the same in the markets. *If the normal, natural emotional response produced profits, the average trader would be making windfalls.* Everyone would be making money, which, of course, is impossible. There would be precious little interest in trading psychology if people could go with the emotional flow and harvest dollars from the market!

INVOKING THE INTERNAL OBSERVER

It turns out that I am not at all unique in my battles against trading overconfidence. Although fear and greed tend to get top billing in the pantheon of trading emotions, researcher Terence Odean has found that retail traders typically suffer from an excess of confidence in their abilities. (It is interesting that he finds that men are more prone to such overconfidence than women are.) For example, in a survey of 10,000 trading accounts, Odean found that traders tend to be successful in their trading prior to opening their online accounts. Once they went online, they dramatically increased their trading frequency and proceeded to significantly underperform the market averages.

I have found a very similar pattern in following the Ameritrade Index (www.ameritradeindex.com), which is a daily tally of the buying and selling activities of Ameritrade's online retail traders. On a significant down day in the market, there is often a swell of buying among the retail traders, who apparently feel confident in picking market bottoms. But there is relatively little *selling* by these same traders on such down days, suggesting that many are initiating overnight long positions in the market. By activating my observing capacity, I can stand apart from the overconfidence of the majority and use the occasion to exercise particular caution. Indeed, many times I have been able to use the information to fade the majority and to benefit from continuation of the downside trend as the stops of the overconfident traders are hit, feeding the decline.

One tool I have found helpful in maintaining my observing stance in the markets is called a sound-and-light machine. There are many companies manufacturing such devices. My unit, the Nova 200 Pro, is made by Photosonix and is offered through many dealers at a discount.

The "sound" part of the sound-and-light machine plays two tones of closely spaced frequencies, one in each ear. The frequencies of these *binaural beats* can be adjusted to correspond to various brain-wave frequencies, from the low-frequency theta and alpha waves associated with relaxation to higher-frequency beta waves associated with alertness. The idea behind such a device is that, over time, one's brain waves will entrain to the frequencies played through the headphones, inducing states of relative calm or vigilance. This phenomenon is known as the "frequency following response."

The "light" machine utilizes a cluster of small lights attached to the inside of a pair of goggles. The lights flash in synchrony with the sounds presented to each ear. Wearers of the goggles keep their eyes closed, but they can perceive the flashes of light through closed eyelids. Each eye receives a frequency of flashing light matching the frequency presented to the corresponding ear. The flashing lights and binaural beats create an immersive stimulus that speeds up or slows down according to programmed routines. (This is not recommended for individuals with a susceptibility to seizures.)

There is limited research evidence to support the notion that brain waves actually do respond distinctively to the stimuli presented to each ear and eye. What I have found in my personal experience is that my biofeedback readings show meaningful shifts in the direction of increased calm and concentration when I am connected to the machine. Particularly useful is the way in which the goggles and sound create a unique stimulus environment that captures the attention of the user. This is helpful because under emotional conditions people tend to become overly focused on internal cues and the self-relevance of events. By shifting attention outward and using the repetitive light and sound patterns as objects of sustained concentration, a trader can very quickly shift out of the fear state induced by a sickening market plunge and into a more neutral mind state.

This last point is especially important. The problem is not that traders experience unpleasant emotions. The problem is that such emotions tend to shift their modes of information processing, diverting the traders from attending to and acting on information in the environment. A large body of literature in social and personality psychology has found that continuously self-focused attention distorts a person's processing of events by activating negative modes of thinking. When traders experience negative emotions, they tend to focus on themselves and their trading—and not on the markets. At such points, they are more likely to abandon their trading plans, to impulsively enter or exit positions, and to otherwise trade in a manner that is contrary to their training and experience.

The value of meditation exercises or sessions with the sound-and-light machine is that the practices interrupt the cycle of self-focused attention that follows emotional events. This is a common psychological technique employed with people who experience traumatic stress. When people are required to perform eye-movement or finger-tapping exercises during periods of "flashbacks," the stress response is interrupted and does not generate a cascade of anxiety, depression, self-blame, and impulsive action. Similarly, interrupting self-focused attention following an adverse market event helps traders learn from the event, and even possibly profit from it.

The beginning therapists could not help the Woolworth man because they were too focused on their own internal states—their discomfort with his irrationality and their fear of looking inept. The experienced therapist also felt uncomfortable with the Woolworth man; but he was able to step back, to observe this feeling, and to use it to initiate a contrary maneuver. If everyone is uncomfortable with the idea that the patient is a retail store, why not take the less traveled path and ask what's for sale? What seemed most crazy was what most people wanted to avoid. It was also what was most worth pursuing.

RULE-GOVERNED TRADING

In Chapter 2, I mentioned the personality survey that Linda Raschke and I conducted with 64 active traders. Some of the findings from that research particularly illuminated the issue of emotions in trading.

One of the survey instruments we administered was the "Ways of Coping" scale developed by Richard Lazarus and Susan Folkman. This scale assesses basic strategies for dealing with stress. Two of the most fundamental strategies involve problem-focused coping and emotion-focused coping.

The person who utilizes problem-focused coping deals with threatening events by developing strategies for action. Investigating the situation, making contingency plans, and consulting others for advice are all problem-focused strategies. The person who employs emotion-focused coping deals with threatening events by expressing their feelings outwardly, by seeking support from others, and by turning their frustration against themselves. Everyone utilizes these different strategies at various points in his or her life. The question is which strategies dominate, especially during periods of high stress.

It is not surprising that traders who scored high on the personality test for neuroticism also scored high in *emotion-focused coping*. They not only experienced a great deal of negative emotion in trading, but also tried to cope with the markets in emotional ways—venting feelings, blaming themselves or others, and so on. These traders tended to report emotional interference in their trading and poor trading results. This group was also poorly research-focused in its trading, relying much more on ad hoc decisions than on carefully constructed trading plans.

Traders who reported greater success in the markets and less emotional interference with trading tended to score high in *problem-focused coping*. They experienced just as many setbacks and frustrations in the market, but generally they channeled these by becoming more immersed in their research and plans, more hands on in their setting and honoring of stops, and so on. These traders were also among the ones scoring highest in conscientiousness, as you might expect from the earlier discussion.

Although traders are sometimes classified in a dichotomous way, as either discretionary (utilizing subjective judgment) or mechanical (automatically following research-tested trading signals), the survey of traders suggested a more complex reality. Traders vary in the degree to which they are *rule-governed*. Some approach the markets with intuition as their only guide, with few rules and explicit guidelines for entering and exiting the markets. Others, like myself, follow basic rules regarding trend and volatility direction, stop-loss levels, and so on, but they permit themselves a degree of discretionary judgment based on the results of historical testing. Other traders mechanize their signals and allocation of capital according to firm rules that are honored to the letter.

My sense, having interviewed many of the participant traders, is that *the net effect of emotion on trading appears to be a disruption of rule-governance.* Most of the surveyed traders did have a set of trading rules to guide themselves, based on their reading of market trends, momentum, and the like. Under emotional conditions, however, their attention became self-focused to the point where they were no longer attentive to their rules. Often, it wasn't so much a case that under emotional conditions they doubted their rules; rather, they simply forgot them!

Psychologists are accustomed to this phenomenon. It is observed most dramatically among people who experience a condition known as *attention deficit hyperactivity disorder* (ADHD). Often diagnosed among children, ADHD represents a chronic inability to focus and pay attention. It also is associated with impulsive behavior and difficulties in delaying gratification. Children with ADHD frequently need reminders from teachers and parents to pay attention to what they are doing and sometimes even need stimulant medications to help them achieve an adequate level of cognitive focus. Russell Barkley's research suggests that ADHD represents an interference with the ability to process and follow rules. With heightened distractibility, children cannot sustain attention to the rules that govern behavior and hence find themselves receiving frequent reprimands in school. It is at those junctures when rules have not yet been internalized—when they require active attention and concentration—that ADHD is most likely to prove disruptive.

It appears that under highly emotional conditions of trading, at least temporarily, traders function in a mode similar to that of the child with ADHD. The high level of bodily arousal serves as a distraction, which diminishes attention and concentration. At the same time, the emotionality triggers negative patterns of thinking and behaving. The ability to plan and to foresee alternate outcomes is impaired as time becomes compressed, generating impulsive actions that fail to take consequences into account. Like the child with ADHD, the emotionally aroused trader becomes less rule-governed. If trading rules have not yet been internalized, this distraction may be sufficient to disrupt the enactment of the rules altogether. In short, *under highly emotional circumstances, traders tend to behave more like the unsuccessful traders in the survey and less like the successful ones.* Little wonder that traders want to eliminate emotions from their trading!

The answer to the dilemma, however, follows the solution-focused model of change. If rule governance and conscientiousness in following rules is associated with market success, then traders want to use emotions to trigger greater attentiveness to plans and rules. This means creating associative cues between emotional arousal and the behaviors responsible for trading success. It is when traders—and markets—are most emotional that they want to become most planful in their approaches to trading.

TAKING YOUR EMOTIONAL TEMPERATURE

An important step in creating links between purposeful behavior and emotional arousal is periodically taking your emotional temperature. During the day, people oscillate between relative states of underarousal (boredom, spacing out) and overarousal (anxiety, enthusiasm). They also move from comparatively positive emotional states (joy, contentment, affection) to more negative ones (stress, depression, anger). As a rule, repetitive behavior patterns lie at the intersection of a person's level of arousal and his or her propensity for action. In overaroused states, some traders will be more likely to be impulsive, whereas others will shut down. In underaroused states, a subset of traders will underreact to situations; others will push to force the action. Taking your emotional temperature periodically and observing your responses to moods will help you identify your own patterns and, when appropriate, target these for change.

Similarly, moods are likely to affect someone's processing of information. Research by Alice Isen at Cornell University suggests that people who tend toward more positive mind frames are less likely to take risks than those who experience negative emotion. Because happy people are generally content with their current state of affairs, they are not as likely to risk a loss as people who are unhappy. In the markets, this could make traders risk-averse following gains (cutting profits prematurely) and risk-seeking following losses (holding losers in hopes of redemption).

Taking your emotional temperature means periodically assessing whether you are overaroused, underaroused, in a positive emotional state, or in a negative one. This assessment in itself entails an activation of the Internal Observer. In taking your temperature, you remove yourself temporarily from the situation at hand, interrupt your normal flow of thoughts and activity, and observe the state of your mind and body at the time. The goal is to *maintain self-awareness*, even as you remain engaged in the flow of market activity.

Once you have noted your cognitive, physical, and emotional state, your first objective, following the physician's creed, is to "above all else, do no harm." *Do not trade* if you are in a bored, underaroused state; a frustrated, aroused state; or a mind-set of excessive optimism or fear. You want to use your mental and physical condition as a formal part of the setup for each trade. Just as you might wait for an upside breakout as a setup for a long trade, you wait to enter the correct mind-set prior to entering a market. Any deviation from your centered, focused state is telling you that something is amiss either in the market or in your processing of the market. *And that is information.*

Very often, you will find that your off-center state reflects both an extreme in the market action *and* your processing of this extreme. Following a low-volatility market can be like watching paint dry. On more than one occasion, I have become bored with such markets and, unthinkingly, attempted to relieve the boredom by searching for short-term trades (i.e., action). These trades rarely prove profitable, as the size of the expected move relative to slippage, commissions, and just plain poor timing does not justify the risk. I don't often lose much money on such trades, but I still find them a distract-

ing source of frustration once a trending movement commences and I need
to have my wits about me.

Similarly, I have found that my level of emotional arousal—especially fear
and overcaution—is well correlated with the volatility of the markets. Because the highest-volatility moves tend to occur toward the opening and latter portions of trending days and especially during market downdrafts, I am
prone to responding to my emotional state by becoming unduly risk-averse
when I have a nice profit in hand. Indeed, I have left a great deal of money
on the table in just such a fashion. "Any profit is better than none" does not
hold if taking your money reinforces poor trading practices.

Attend to yourself before attending to the markets. If you are not in your trading zone, you don't want to be putting your hard-earned capital at risk. Frustration after one or more losses or missed opportunities; eagerness after scoring a win; boredom and a desire for excitement; fear and procrastination at
times of opportunity—these are some of the most common ways in which
emotional shifts alter your perception and response to events and color your
trading.

Once you have taken your emotional temperature and find that you are
running too hot or too cold, that is the time to temporarily remove yourself
from the situation and perform your exercises to reenter a state of focused
concentration. Closing your eyes, keeping your body still, slowing and deepening your breathing, and focusing your mind on a single object (music, an
imagined visual scene, and so on) will help you return to your zone. After
sustained practice, I have found that a quick-burst session with the sound-
and-light machine, combined with the closed eyes and deep breaths, helps
reset my emotional temperature. This is especially valuable for very short term
traders who need to get back in the game rapidly. In the neutral and focused
state, you are then better equipped to extract the information from your
reaction and to formulate and follow your trading plans.

Earlier, I mentioned the value of automating market research so that it is
possible to rapidly shift from an emotional processing of market events to a
more neutral analytic stance. With biofeedback, I have found that I can au-
tomate the readings of my emotional temperature as well, identifying significant deviations from my baseline. Very often the readings will deviate from
their averages before I am consciously aware that I am tense, frustrated, or
anxious. This invites a proactive response, dampening the reaction and shifting gears before the stress response has an opportunity to spill over into decision making.

INOCULATING YOURSELF AGAINST STRESS

The cognitive-behavioral psychologist Donald Meichenbaum introduced a technique that is very helpful in constructively handling emotional trading situations. He referred to the method as *stress inoculation* because it works on the principle of medical immunization. Just as a physician inoculates a patient against disease by introducing small amounts of a virus into the patient's bloodstream and thereby activating the body's natural immune responses, you can activate your desired coping responses for future trading challenges by introducing a small dose of a stressful situation.

This works well in the markets because, although price changes from one time frame to another tend to be uncorrelated, volatility does display significant serial correlation. Volatile periods in the market tend to be followed by other volatile periods, and vice versa; you can roughly estimate the volatility of the next period by observing the previous one.

This information is useful, in that it can help prepare you for the next period's trading landscape. You can observe if volatility is high or low, expanding or contracting, and thereby anticipate how the markets are likely to affect you emotionally. In low-volatility markets, you are likely to encounter underarousal: boredom, distraction, and frustration with lack of trading opportunities. In high-volatility markets, conversely, you are apt to experience the classic fear, greed, and overconfidence responses.

By mentally rehearsing the trading landscape you may face prior to the market open, you can achieve a measure of stress inoculation. Once you have closed your eyes, focused on a stimulus, and slowed and deepened your breathing, the key is *to begin playing a movie in your head.* Your movie will consist of vivid imagined scenarios that you are likely to face in the market, your emotional responses to those scenarios, and the ways in which you plan to deal with those emotional responses. So, for example, on the heels of a downtrending day with expanding volatility, you might imagine yourself, in rich detail, encountering a sharp market drop where the Standard & Poor's (S&P) futures hit a support level on very negative TICK with sharply increased volume. (The New York Stock Exchange [NYSE] Composite TICK is the cumulative total of advancing and declining issues at any moment.) You would vividly imagine yourself feeling your hesitance in entering such a market, fearful of being caught in the downdraft.

At that point, you will imagine yourself performing the activities for focusing your attention (through breathing, and so on) and interrupting your cycle of fear and procrastination. You will then picture yourself in your movie implementing your trading plans and following your trading rules and/or systems. In short, your movie will feature you encountering and coping with the challenges you most anticipate for the coming trading period.

At any point during the movie when you find yourself feeling uncomfortable, simply freeze the image in your mind, continue your deep breathing with eyes closed, and then resume the movie when you are calmer. Your goal is *to play the movie in your head many times without needing to freeze the images before you actually enter the trading arena*. By that time, you have extinguished much of the stress reaction, and you will be primed to enact the right trading maneuvers when your feared scenarios actually unfold.

Stress inoculation works because of counterconditioning. By activating feared scenarios in the context of a controlled state of mind and body, you are training yourself to respond less emotionally and impulsively in those situations. Psychologists utilize this technique to help individuals overcome phobias and performance anxiety problems, such as nervousness in public speaking. The normal human response is to want to *not face* such unpleasant situations. By pushing yourself to face the situations again and again, under controlled conditions, you gain an inner sense of mastery. When the difficult trading situation arises, you can respond with the knowledge that in your rehearsals you've "been there, done that." Such familiarity breeds confidence.

EFFORT AND EMOTIONAL CHANGE

Techniques such as stress inoculation depend not only on the frequency with which they are performed, but also on the intensity. When traders attempt to utilize methods such as meditation, brain wave entrainment, desensitization, and the like, they often give up after a cursory effort, failing to make the essential breakthrough. It is this breakthrough—the concentration of effort—that is largely responsible for the success of these methods.

A good example can be found in the field of bodybuilding. The late trainer and champion Mike Mentzer discovered that building one's physique does not require constant effort in the gym. Instead, he found that relatively short, intense workouts interspersed with days of rest produced the greatest results. Mentzer indicated that the final repetitions in any lifting sequence produced the largest gains because they placed maximal demand on the muscles. This demand forces the body to devote a greater than normal share of resources to the muscles under load, engorging them with blood and nutrients and facilitating their rapid growth. Mentzer discovered that the rest between the intense training episodes was as important as the lifting, as growth occurred during the period in which the body nourished the taxed region.

In an analogous way, the intensity of psychological exercises pushes you to develop extraordinary resources. A single marathon session of deep breathing and imagery accomplishes far more than several briefer sessions performed in succession. Immersing yourself in vivid imagery and real-life situations that evoke fear desensitizes you far more effectively and efficiently than less emotionally immediate exposure. It's back to that principle of the second wind. By exerting yourself beyond the comfort zone, you develop your cognitive and emotional "muscles," much as bodybuilders develop themselves. If the exercise is not taxing you, the chances are great that you are performing the equivalent of bench-pressing 20 pounds. Such exercise could go on for years with no observable development.

This brings up one of the greatest enemies of self-development: time. Most people lead busy lives. Good trading, with its research and planning demands, is a time-consuming enterprise. Add that to home responsibilities, romantic relationships, and family obligations, and the mix can make a trader feel overwhelmed. This stress makes it especially difficult to take extra time out of the day to make supreme efforts. The natural human tendency is to use whatever free time exists for rest and relaxation.

How do some people work long hours each week, undertake multiple projects, and yet seem to have the time and the energy for social and family concerns? To an outsider, such a life seems exhausting. The answer, which is difficult to comprehend until you have experienced it, is that *significant efforts release more energy than they consume.* The breakthroughs at the second and third and fourth winds open you up to new wellsprings of vitality. Without the intensity of practice, however, those wellsprings remain closed.

The bioenergetic psychologist Alexander Lowen has written extensively on the practice of having depressed patients lie on their bed and pound away on their mattress, hitting with their fists and kicking violently with their feet. During this period of at least 25 good hits and kicks, the patients are told to scream as loudly as they can whatever enters their minds. Many—especially those who have been mistreated—end up verbalizing considerable rage. After this exercise (which I invite you to try for yourself), it is not at all unusual for the patients to feel that their anxiety and depression has left them.

Where they were once lethargic and caught in negative thinking, they now feel more alive and energized.

Simply sitting in a chair and raising one's voice a notch cannot duplicate Lowen's exercise in the bed. *It is the radical departure from your daily norms that breaks you out of old modes, opening the door to new ones.*

THE TRADER AS ADDICT: BREAKING STOPS

Perhaps no trading situation so exemplifies the distortion of information processing wrought by emotions as the failure to honor stops. One web site for educating traders, Ken Wolff's Mtrader, has even compiled an Alcoholics Anonymous–inspired 12-step program for those who chronically violate their stops. This is quite insightful. The pattern of overconfidence, getting away from basics, falling off the wagon, and then facing guilt and remorse makes problem trading and recovery from substance abuse very similar.

For active intraday traders and especially scalpers, it is rare indeed for a large gap to force an exit from a position. Most large losses begin as small losses that are allowed to magnify over time. Once those losses occur, they often are processed as failures, with accompanying emotional and physical arousal. Under the aroused conditions, the trader now becomes focused on winning back the lost money and undoing the failure. Instead of honoring his or her stop, a different set of priorities takes over.

A significant proportion of traders with whom I have talked make the lion's share of their money from a relative handful of good market moves. Many of their trades are narrow winners, narrow losers, or total scratches. If, however, they fail to honor stops, those occasional big winners will be balanced by one or two large losers, which will undo many weeks of good trading. Although there may be room for a measure of discretion in entering trades, the use of discretion in honoring stops is a slippery slope that leads to trading ruin.

The stress inoculation exercise mentioned earlier is tailor-made for rehearsing the honoring of stops. Indeed, I have found that a large percentage of my winning trades begin with a rehearsal of negative, what-if scenarios in which I mentally invoke my stop strategy. Conversely, I have found that my worst trades begin with an estimate of my potential profits. By mentally rehearsing stop strategies under conditions of relaxation and cognitive focus— playing movies in your head of experiencing a drawdown and honoring your stops—you can make the minimization of losses an automatic part of your behavioral repertoire. In a very real sense, you want to *normalize the process of losing; making it so familiar that it is no longer threatening.* Uncertainty is built into the market; losses are a cost of doing business. By rehearsing them and your responses to them, you can greatly dampen your emotional reactions over time.

BECOMING MORE RULE-GOVERNED IN TRADING

Recall the situation of the child who is experiencing attention deficits and hyperactivity. School becomes challenging in the face of these difficulties, so teachers typically try to structure the child's setting by emphasizing rules and expectations for behavior. Putting rules into verbal form allows the child to hang onto them and to call them to mind in otherwise distracting circumstances.

Rules in trading serve a very similar purpose. By emphasizing and rehearsing trading rules, traders are more likely to bring them to mind during emotional, volatile times of trading. A survey of the major sites for live training of traders, including those of Linda Raschke and Ken Wolff, suggests that these sites develop explicit rules for traders, which are then reinforced through the presentation of multiple examples.

The formulation of explicit rules for exiting trades is an especially powerful way of moderating the influence of emotional trading events on behavior. Generally, these stop rules fall into one of three categories:

1. *Price-based rules.* These are the most common stop rules, often formulated as a fixed-dollar amount or a percentage that a trader is willing to lose on a given trade. The price-based rules may also be formulated on the basis of perceived support or resistance, in which a particular price target acts as the stop. This latter strategy can be dangerous in the S&P and the Nasdaq futures markets, which feature frequent false breakouts of obvious support and resistance areas. For this reason, I am least fond of price-based stop rules, utilizing them as last-ditch mechanisms for avoiding catastrophic losses.

2. *Indicator-based rules.* These use levels of a market indicator, rather than price alone, to dictate the exit point. A hybrid indicator/price strategy might adjust price-based stops for the current market's level of volatility. If, say, the

market moves against the trader by two standard deviations from its last X period average, this could be construed as a nonrandom (trending) move and trigger a stop.

Other indicator-based rules may dictate exits when a market predictor reaches a predefined level. I have found, for instance, that if the NYSE Composite TICK makes a *significant* (two standard deviations) breakout from its two-hour average, the trend of the breakout tends to continue for the next five hours. Accordingly, I will stop any position after the TICK significantly breaks out of its range in a direction opposite my trade. Many times, the TICK breakout will occur prior to my price-based stop, allowing me to scratch an otherwise losing trade.

Indicator-based rules can also act as profit targets to facilitate market exits. Very often, as I mentioned earlier, I will exit a trade on significant range expansion with high volume. Although I may miss the exact high or low with such an exit, I generally find that closing positions during panic buying or selling is a wise strategy. Similarly, a very high level of ticking action in the Dow Jones Industrial Average (the Dow) stocks (as measured by the TIKI—the cumulative total of upticks and downticks in the Dow industrial stocks) often occurs at short-term market extremes fueled by institutional buying and selling and can serve as a target for exit.

3. *Time-based rules.* These are among my favorite stop rules because they are embedded in the very trades that I research. For example, suppose the market has made a steep two-hour decline on sharply negative TICK early in the morning. This has followed a flat day, breaking to a new low relative to the previous day. I will immediately query my historical database to see how similar markets have performed, say, five hours out into the future. If there is a significant directional bias (perhaps trend continuation, in keeping with the TICK breakout finding), I will then plan my strategy for selling rallies within the coming five hours. If, however, my position does not reach its target profit level in that five-hour period, I close out the trade—regardless of where price is located. To me, this is among the most rational of stops because it suggests that the edge that I had researched is no longer present.

There is a more subtle reason why this exit strategy works, however. Let's say that I am anticipating downside trend continuation for the next five hours but only get a relatively flat move. In such circumstances, I have generally found that my research was right: The flat move was the downside trend continuation that I had anticipated. Because it was so shallow, however, I have a sign that the market may be strengthening. This may alert me to investigate breakout moves to the upside for a possible long trade. In other words, the failure of the market to live up to its historical tendencies can serve as a signal for a counter-trend trade.

By grounding trading in explicit rules that address price, time, and indicator levels, the trader can rehearse concrete strategies even during the most turbulent trading times. If there is one winning strategy I can recommend wholeheartedly for dealing with emotional trading, it is becoming more rule-governed. The kind of historical analysis utilized by Jon Markman in his studies of monthly sector strength and weakness, by Yale and Jeff Hirsch in their research of calendar patterns of market trends, and by Victor Niederhoffer in his statistical analysis of past markets and prospective market moves is a powerful antidote to subjective, impulsive trading. It is in this sense that Niederhoffer's research admonition "Statistics on the table!" is also excellent therapy for the trader.

USING EMOTION TO MAKE THE CONTRARY MOVE

A useful perspective is that if you are feeling cocky or fearful about the market you're following, the chances are good that other traders are having similar feelings. If a downside move is unnerving you and you then notice a wide-range downside movement on the S&P E-Mini chart with a significant expansion of volume, you have real evidence that traders are bailing out of positions. At such times, I use my emotion as a cue to revisit my research, querying my database for all recent times in market history when a similar sell-off occurred and examining what happened subsequently. Very often, I will find a directional bias *contrary to the direction of the market panic*. This allows me to look for an opportunity to enter a long trade and to benefit from the group overreaction.

During such market drops, I compare the expansion in the number of trades to the expansion in the number of contracts or shares traded. Very often the number of trades expands even more quickly than the volume does, suggesting that smaller traders are disproportionately represented among those bailing out. Those small (often undercapitalized) market participants are often wrong during such emotional selling occasions. I also like to look at the expansion of volume in the favorite daytrading vehicles, such as the QQQ and E-Mini indexes, compared to volume changes in the overall markets for evidence of speculative emotional extremes during downturns.

This strategy of using emotional reactions to trigger your observing capacities lies at the heart of trading from the couch. However, it is a strategy that requires considerable practice. At first, the practice occurs outside of market hours, as you simply become adept at reaching the quiet state. In the beginning, it may take quite a few minutes to still your mind and your body. Over time, however, you can become quite skilled at meditation exercises or sessions with the sound-and-light machine, to the point of quieting yourself with a few deep breaths or a few seconds on the machine. This ability to rapidly transition to a calm, focused state is very useful for scalpers and floor traders, who cannot afford an extended exercise period while the markets are in full gear.

I have found that the calm, focused state that facilitates the Internal Observer becomes associated with the stimuli utilized in the practice sessions, much in the manner of Pavlovian conditioning. For example, if you have been performing deep-breathing exercises while focusing your mind on a relaxing piece of music, the state of calm focus becomes associated with that piece of music. Through the associations built by repetition, you can then play that piece during the trading day, taking a few deep breaths and keeping your body absolutely still. This readily summons the Internal Observer, even on the heels of the most emotional trading events.

To make such an approach work, it is first necessary *to treat emotions as useful signals that allow you to begin your Observing.* This flies in the face of the human tendency to want to eliminate unpleasant emotions. I vividly recall one trader, responding to a column I had written for a financial web site, begging me to show him techniques for "eliminating fear" in trading. You don't want to eliminate fear, I responded. Fear is important information, no less than the red light that shows up on your dashboard when you have engine trouble. The red light will make you uncomfortable to be sure; no one looks forward to its appearance. But the answer is not to cover it over with electrical tape. Too many traders want to rid themselves of "negative emotions," taping over their own, personal dashboards. Ignorance is bliss for a while—until the engine seizes and the problems multiply exponentially.

It is understandable to want to rid oneself of fear in trading. Few experienced traders have not had the experience of anxiety during a drawdown, first hoping that their position will recover and then praying that it will do so. To see your position hemorrhaging minute by minute, while you are paralyzed with fear and filled with self-recrimination, has got to be one of the worst experiences known to humankind. At the moment when it seems most clear that your hopes will not be realized and your prayers will not be answered, there is nothing left to do but disgorge the position in a mixture of desperation and relief. Those feelings, however, quickly turn to regret as it becomes painfully evident that your sale has caught the worst possible exit point, almost to the tick.

Painful as it is, this emotional script of hope, fear, and prayer does provide useful information. As you have seen, it often suggests that other traders might be feeling the exact same way and that this might *not* be the best time to liquidate. Among the many intraday indicators I follow and archive, the NYSE Composite TICK is one of my favorites. I am greatly indebted to Mark Cook and Linda Raschke for their insights into the TICK. When you see a TICK of −1000 or lower, signifying that a great plurality of stocks is trading on downticks, it means that people are fleeing the market indiscriminately. The TICK reading is the red light on the trading dashboard, lighting up when emotions are running high.

At those times, the market will seem to make little sense. Even the best stocks, the companies with the brightest prospects, may be plunging, bar after bar after bar. If you can access the Internal Observer at such times, you will be better positioned to read the market's message. Instead of becoming intimidated by the market's craziness, like the graduate students with the Woolworth man, you will have the opportunity to ask, "What's for sale?" You the Internal Observer note the panic of you the Trader and turn that into market data—and a potentially profitable trade.

CONCLUSION

As I have shown, utilizing emotions as information is central to the work of therapists. Therapists experience feelings when they work with people; this is inevitable. The good therapists, however, utilize these as data, not as inconveniences, personal threats, or infallible guides to action. A classic example is a client who is overly dependent. He may express considerable fear about making a decision, emphasize the dire consequences of making a wrong choice, and express considerable anguish over his dilemma. He may even cry and ask the therapist for advice. At that point, it is only natural for the therapist to feel sympathy for the person and offer some guidance. That, however, is almost always the wrong course of action. Whatever advice is given will only reinforce for the individual that he was unable to make his own decision.

Good therapists, therefore, activate their Observer, notice their feelings of sympathy, and think, "Hmmm . . . I wonder why I am feeling this way. I'm tempted to try to rescue this person. Maybe this is how other people feel toward him as well, which would help sustain his diminished confidence. Perhaps I should try the opposite approach and explore situations where he *has* been able to make successful decisions. Then he might be able to use his experience to make his own choice, rather than to rely on others."

I cannot make the point strongly enough: *Successful traders do not eliminate emotions.* Indeed, they experience emotions fully, so fully that they become consciously aware of what they're feeling. At that point, however, they don't become lost in their emotional state. Instead, they adopt the vantage point of the Observer, standing apart from the feelings and making sense of them.

It takes a while to find the exercises that work best for you in cultivating self-observation. I have found biofeedback and the sound-and-light machine to be invaluable in my own work. Others rely on techniques drawn from self-hypnosis or meditation. One interesting variation on the earlier-mentioned movie exercise is to assume a comfortable seated position, slow your breathing, stay completely physically still, and use imagery to create a different movie in your head. In this movie, you vividly image yourself watching yourself as a trader becoming overconfident, panicked, greedy, and so forth.

Notice the important wrinkle in the exercise. You are not watching yourself becoming overly emotional. *You are watching yourself watching yourself overreacting to the market.* Your identification is with the Observer: You can even create images of smiling and shaking your head, comforting and expressing pity for your poor emotional self, and so on. With practice, you, like the therapist, will be able to say to yourself, "Hmmm . . . I wonder why I am feeling this way." Once you cultivate the capacity to observe yourself, you create the freedom to do what doesn't come naturally.

And, very often in the markets, that is the right move.

There is a tendency for financial writers to cloak themselves in gurulike robes, in hopes of attracting the widest audience. I have to be honest with you, however: Dr. Brett is a rather poor trader. He too easily becomes absorbed in market action. Left to his devices, he would usually wind up fully invested at the peaks and troughs of his emotions. He's a lot like the Woolworth man, completely out of sync with the rhythms around him. Thank goodness, however, for the Internal Observer. He is able to make nice money for Dr. Brett's account by fading Dr. Brett.

Chapter Four

Traders Out of Their Minds

One "I" is needed to sustain a vision.

In Chapter 3, we explored how markets elicit emotional responses that color subsequent thought and behavior. This chapter will go a bit deeper and explore the topic from the inside, drawing on research findings from cognitive neuroscience. These findings raise intriguing questions about our identities, challenging the notion that humans have fixed, unitary personalities. Indeed, the presence of multiple personalities—long held to be limited to a relative handful of pathological cases—appears to be the norm. This poses important dilemmas for traders, who may find their well-honed and practiced strategies undermined by qualitative shifts in their patterns of thinking, feeling, and acting.

THE WORLD'S MOST POWERFUL GLASSES

Suppose I were to tell you that the most powerful pair of lenses you could wear are not prescription lenses. They are the simple safety glasses made of clear plastic. You can purchase them at any hardware store to protect your eyes from flying fragments while doing woodwork or gardening.

The catch, as discovered by Harvard Medical School psychiatrist Frederic Schiffer, is that you must purchase two such pairs of glasses. Then you cover three-quarters of the field of vision of the first pair of glasses with electrical tape so that you can see only out of the outer corner of your right eye. You similarly cover three-quarters of the lens area of the second pair of glasses, leaving exposed the outer edge of the left eye.

As it turns out, people not only see differently through the two pairs of glasses; they see themselves and the world differently, as well.

Schiffer's reasoning was elegant and disarmingly simple. Physiological studies have shown that the far right side of a human's visual field maps onto the left brain hemisphere. The far left side of vision is processed by the right hemisphere. In most people, verbal processing of information occurs in the left hemisphere. Much of a person's emotional processing occurs within the right hemisphere. This division of labor between the brain hemispheres is so striking that cognitive neuroscientist John Cutting has argued that humans actually possess two minds. Mind #1, as he calls it, is largely centered in the left hemisphere and helps people understand what things are. Mind #2, right-hemisphere based, enables people to perceive the value, meaning, and relevance of things and events. The crucial quality of these minds, Cutting emphasizes, is that they operate, not serially, but in parallel. At all times, these two minds are continuously scanning the world for the identity of the things a person encounters and the self-relevance of those things. What is experienced seamlessly as thought is actually a delicate coordination of these two minds.

Schiffer's glasses are an elegant way of separating Mind #1 from Mind #2 without undergoing surgery to the corpus collosum, the fibers that connect the brain hemispheres. Years ago, epileptic patients of Dr. Roger Sperry needed such surgery to short-circuit the signals that led to intractable seizures. The researchers were stunned to find that the patients undergoing such surgery could both think and feel but could not readily coordinate the outputs of their "minds."

Subsequent studies conducted by Michael Gazzaniga and colleagues found that when "split-brain" patients were shown an image to their left eye only (connected to the right hemisphere), they could point to a picture of what they saw but could not name the item. They knew what they saw, but their knowing was not of the verbal type. Even more strange, when presented different pictures simultaneously to each eye, patients could point with each hand to what they saw, but they could only verbally describe the picture presented to the right eye. (Only later did Gazzaniga think to ask the split-brain patients *why* they had pointed to the two pictures while describing only one. The answer he received led to one of the most important findings in modern cognitive science, a finding—as you shall see later—that is crucial to understanding the psychology of trading.)

Subsequent studies managed to investigate the two minds without severing the corpus collosum. Patients who experienced severe damage to one brain hemisphere but not the other offered useful insights into the cognitive workings of the brain. A process in which just one brain hemisphere was anesthetized while the other was left alone, called the Wada procedure, was also revealing, in that it allowed patients to be questioned with one of their "minds" turned off.

Schiffer summarized fascinating studies conducted by Geoffrey Ahern and colleagues, in which the Wada procedure was used to investigate the emotional functioning of two patients who had been suffering from epilepsy. Both of these patients were known to experience mood swings so extreme that it seemed they had two completely different personalities. Through the Wada procedure, Dr. Ahern was able to demonstrate that each personality was lateralized to a specific brain hemisphere. When one hemisphere of the brain was anesthetized, the patient was relatively happy and outgoing. When the other half was anesthetized, the same patient would be moody, sullen, and even belligerent!

In a similar vein, Robert Ornstein, in his book *The Right Mind*, described case reports in which a split-brain patient attacked his wife with his left hand while trying to restrain the aggressive hand with his right. Another split-brain patient, when asked to point to words describing his ambition in life, chose "racecar driver" with his left hand (right hemisphere) and "draftsman" with his right hand (left hemisphere). Summarizing a wealth of literature from cognitive neuroscience, psychology, and philosophy, Cutting concluded that people possess a second mind, one that governs emotion, will, and needs-directed action and that is grounded in the right hemisphere and operates separately from the verbal, thinking mind.

The patients described by Ahern and Ornstein were unique in that their subpersonalities seemed completely distinct. It may well be the case, however, that these patients differ from you and me only in the extent of their polarity. In an excellent book entitled *Being of Two Minds*, Arnold Goldberg described how many therapy participants display what he calls a *vertical split* of personality. This is a situation in which an individual experiences a part of himself or herself completely alien to the normal personality. Often, this "part" of the person compels the person to perform actions that are completely at odds with the individual's normal, acceptable behavior, creating considerable guilt, shame, and distress.

I have seen many such examples of vertical splits. Recently, I met with a woman who was generally a self-confident, capable professional who prided herself on her appearance. Every so often, however, she would lapse into periods in which she would feel completely incompetent to make even the most basic decisions. During these episodes, she ate great quantities of chocolates and ice cream and put on significant weight. Afterward, she looked back on her behavior and couldn't believe what she had done. For a while, she would "pull it together"—until the next episode.

An even more dramatic example of vertical split was a successful physician who met with me because of problems in his marriage. He was married to a caring, capable woman who also had a successful career. They had a child and by all accounts loved each other and enjoyed their lives within the family. Every so often, however, the doctor felt a compulsive need to gamble at a local casino. He felt guilty and even "raunchy" engaging in such behavior—many of the gambling participants were unsavory characters—and he did his best to hide his activity from his wife. Eventually, however, she discovered something was amiss when she went into their savings account and discovered a dramatic shortfall. She felt shock and betrayal and was troubled by his inability to explain why he spent his time in this manner. Like other patients who describe impulses to surf pornography sites, expose themselves, or use drugs, the physician could only weakly explain that something "came over him." He loved his wife, he insisted, and didn't want to hurt her or lose her.

Dr. Goldberg's contention is that these clients might well be telling the truth. Something really is coming over them, and they don't have complete control over its emergence. This second personality is "split" from the normal personality that they identify as their own, and it appears to have its own traits, needs, and behaviors. Perhaps when people are caught in dilemmas in which they say, "My heart wants one thing, but my head is telling me something else," they are stating more of a truth than they recognize. At such times, a person really is torn between two selves, two minds.

The implications for trading, I would submit, are monumental. When traders complain of making impulsive trades or of not being able to pull the trigger—when they look back on a trade and wonder, "Why the hell did I take *that* position?!"—perhaps there is a reason for their seeming self-defeat. Maybe *they* didn't place the trades at all. Perhaps, like the gambling physician and Gazzaniga's patients, *they really weren't in their right minds.*

PHIL, THE ADDICTED TRADER

Not being in his right mind appeared to be exactly the case with Phil, a trader with whom I talked over the phone. Every so often Phil would reach a high water mark in his equity curve and then proceed to increase his size, extend his holding periods, and ignore his stops. Needless to say, this led to catastrophic losses, which brought his equity to drastically low levels. At that point, chastised, Phil would reduce his size, trade in a rule-governed fashion, and religiously adhere to his exit plans.

This cycle had occurred several times before Phil e-mailed me. Normally I do not engage in ongoing coaching or therapy for traders, given the demands of work, home, and trading. Nevertheless, Phil seemed to be a genuinely talented trader who was tortured by his seemingly self-destructive behavior. Hopeful that we could address the issue briefly, I agreed to conduct a phone session with him on a courtesy basis.

Phil's Dual Personality

As I collected a history from Phil, it became clear that his irregular trading stemmed from a basic personality inconsistency. Everyone is familiar with the tale of Dr. Jekyll and Mr. Hyde and the story of Superman, who is also Clark Kent. Phil's personality embraced a similar duality.

Most of the time, including his phone conversation with me, Phil was a soft-spoken guy who traded conservatively. He was a real family man, and he took his responsibilities as a father and husband quite seriously. It killed him to think that he was not providing well for the family since going full-time with his trading in the past year. He wanted nothing more than to be a success at his chosen occupation, and he expressed a willingness to work hard to achieve that success.

Once Phil began to reap the benefits of his hard work, however, his per-

spective—and, it seemed, his personality—shifted. His wife noticed this because suddenly he began talking about being a successful trader, making a
lot of money for the family, and so forth. He became unusually expansive
and confident and began making elaborate plans with his wife for expensive
vacations, car purchases, and the like. Even his wife was able to detect this
pattern, begging him to "take it easy" when she saw that he was feeling overconfident in his trading.

This polarity of thought, feeling, and behavior was so dramatic that I would
have thought it to be part of a bipolar disorder, but for the fact that it occurred at no other times in Phil's life. Prior to his trading career, he never
appeared to have such swings; and during periods when he did not trade, he
never demonstrated such overconfidence.

I was perplexed as to the nature of Phil's problem until he revealed to me
that he had abused cocaine as a college student and shortly after his gradu-
ation. He assured me that he hadn't gone near cocaine in many years and
that this was not a factor in his trading.

I asked Phil to describe what it felt like to be high on cocaine. As you
might expect, he experienced feelings of power and euphoria; he described
himself as "on top of the world." At that point Phil stopped himself and
pointed out the obvious: He was getting the same high from trading that he
had experienced with cocaine. Once he had a series of winning trades, he
became intoxicated with his success and was on top of the world.

This made sense to Phil, as he recalled "being a different person" under
the influence of cocaine. He was more gregarious and felt more confident.
He tackled challenges readily and felt that nothing could stand in his way.
With some embarrassment, he described to me how he had recently felt the
same way in the market, boastfully posting his trades to an online bulletin
board and giving advice to others. These trades ended disastrously, as did his
brief online advisory career.

Phil enjoyed cocaine—and trading—because they allowed him to be a
different person. Under the stimulating influence of markets and drugs, he
could catch a glimpse of himself as a heroic being. Unfortunately, it was
counterfeit heroism, artificially induced and incapable of being sustained. But
his basic impulse was a healthy one: to feel powerful and in control of his
life. From a solution-focused perspective, our task was to find constructive
ways in which he was already achieving some of this feeling and to help him
generalize this to his trading.

The most obvious way that Phil was feeling in control of his life was through his success in dealing with his cocaine addiction. Phil stopped using cocaine after he met the woman who was to become his wife. She made it plainly clear that she would leave him if he continued his drug use. Phil realized that this would be a major loss, and he began attendance at a Narcotics Anonymous (NA) group, which operated on the 12-step principles of Alcoholics Anonymous. He subsequently became a mentor and sponsor for many new members, aiding them in their desire to stay clean. Phil experienced himself as a competent individual in NA, and he loved the fact that his wife respected him for his progress against the addiction.

I asked Phil if he would be willing to commit himself to a course of action to change his destructive pattern of trading. I emphasized to him that he had already made great headway against one damaging pattern in this life and that we could make use of this experience in changing his pattern of trading. "I'll try anything!" Phil exclaimed, again asserting that he wanted nothing more than to be a success as a trader.

I asked Phil to put his wife, Rhonda, on the phone. She, too, expressed an urgent desire to help Phil. To my surprise, she stated (within Phil's earshot) that she could not continue in her marriage under the present circumstances. "I need more financial security," Rhonda cried. "We can't pay our bills." Rhonda explained that she had grown up in poverty and could not stand the feeling of financial insecurity. She loved her husband, but she could not go from month to month wondering how the bills would be paid.

I empathized with Rhonda and asked her to put Phil back on the phone. His voice was now shaky; he recognized that the problem was much graver than he realized. And I realized that my simple phone consultation had quickly become a full-blown crisis intervention.

Activating the Observer

At the moment Phil returned to the phone, I was aware of feeling angry toward him. Initially, I thought that I might be blaming him for getting me in deeper than I cared to be. Quickly, however, I dismissed this idea. Generally, I like dealing with crises and high-pressure situations in therapy, and I was genuinely interested in seeing this couple resolve their problems.

No, I acknowledged, I was angry toward Phil because he had upset his wife to such a great degree. It was clear that she was a dedicated spouse and had grown up with her share of life challenges. How could he be so oblivious to her pain? And why, I found myself wondering, didn't he get out of the house after trading hours and take up a job to bring in a little money? Surely he must realize that his wife is struggling with the bills!

It was at that point that my Internal Observer kicked in. I was angry toward Phil for the same reason that Rhonda was contemplating leaving him. In his self-absorption, Phil had neglected her, just as his preoccupation with success allowed him to neglect his trading discipline. Phil, it appeared, not only acted out his pattern with cocaine and trading, but also *went through cycles of diligence and neglect in his marriage.* Only this time, he was threatened with the possibility of losing everything: his trading *and* his wife.

I carefully explained to Phil that I realized that he cared about his trading and his marriage. I told him that his patterns in trading were going to make him lose both of them and that he needed to involve Rhonda in any solution, just as he had done when he joined the NA group. Phil was very open to this idea and readily put Rhonda back on the phone when I asked to speak with her.

I asked Rhonda to help make Phil a good provider for the family. Toward that end, I suggested, she would keep all the books for the trading business. No money would be added to the trading account for at least a year. Once the account gained 10 percent in value—a point that occurred before Phil's overconfidence normally kicked in—the profits would be deposited into the family savings account and not reused for trading. The couple, together, would then chart their savings "equity curve" and use any surplus money to buy nice things for themselves, since this was now a team effort.

I presented the idea to Phil as necessary to help Rhonda. She had been traumatized by the poverty of her childhood, I pointed out, and he needed to be there to support her. The best way he could do that was to concern himself with *her* equity curve—the family's savings account—and not his own.

Phil immediately warmed to the idea. Rhonda was also happy because she felt this would give her better control of the finances and would demonstrate Phil's commitment to her. I was pleased to learn several months later that the couple was out of the hole financially and doing well in their marriage. After all, Phil already had experience helping others in crisis through his work as an NA sponsor. Once we redefined Rhonda as the client, he was more than willing to achieve his sense of mastery by addressing her needs. He didn't have to be a big shot in the market if he could feel needed and effective at home.

Meanwhile, Phil's trading benefited because he was never able to grow his stake by leaps and bounds. Before the account would get to the point of triggering his addictive sense of power, the money had to be withdrawn for the family savings account. In a very real sense, Phil's pattern of making money and then going back to square one continued after our session. Only this time, he and Rhonda were purposely bringing the account back to square one, where he could not afford to take further losses. Because he no longer had the house money of his profits to play with in his trading, he had to strictly adhere to his discipline or risk an end to his trading career altogether.

The solution-focused session recognized that there were two Phils: one who was caring and wanted to do the right thing, and one who craved the high of feeling powerful and who neglected the basic responsibilities of his health, his trading, and his marriage. Rather than label one Phil as bad and the other as good, we set up a situation where the needs met by "bad Phil" could be met by doing the right things. If I had simply asked Phil to give up trading or limit himself to 100-share trades, he would have never complied. However, he was happy to relinquish his profits and to place limits on his account size if it was in the service of a heroic rescue of his wife and marriage. Phil didn't need cocaine if he could achieve a high from helping other addicts. He also didn't need outsized trading profits if he could reach his high by supporting Rhonda.

EXPLORING THE DUAL MIND

Let's return for a moment to the provocative work of Frederic Schiffer and its relevance for the psychology of trading. By covering the lens areas of the clear glasses, Dr. Schiffer in essence duplicated the work of Sperry and Gazzaniga, turning normal people into split-brain patients. Visually, he separated left-brain processing from the workings of the right brain. What he found during this procedure was remarkable.

The subjects for his study were his own therapy patients. Most came to him for problems of depression and anxiety. When Dr. Schiffer had them wear the glasses that covered all but the left side of their vision, they reported feeling anxious and depressed. If anything, they felt worse than usual. To the surprise of the clients, however, when they wore the other set of lenses, covering all but the right side of their visual field, they soon found themselves calming down and feeling better. This did not appear to be a placebo effect. Two control pairs of glasses, which blocked the upper and lower quarters of the visual field (therefore not splitting the brain's processing), produced no such results.

In my own work, I have duplicated Dr. Schiffer's glasses, worn them myself, and used them with clients. The latter have provided the most objective tests because I do not initially tell clients what the glasses are for. My experience is that the glasses do not produce dramatic results for everyone, but they do induce shifts in mind states among individuals who come to counseling with mood and/or self-esteem complaints. Such people typically experience periods when they feel okay about themselves and other periods when they feel nervous, self-blaming, and not confident. These are situations in which vertical splits are most evident.

The glasses in themselves did not cure Dr. Schiffer's patients, and they did not create permanent changes among my clients. But they did dramatically demonstrate to the patients an important reality: *Their problems were not in the world but were a function of how they were viewing the world.* The self who was anxious and depressed coexisted with a self that did not feel that way. This by itself tended to be reassuring to people. They could see in their own experience that their negative views of themselves were a function of their perception, not absolute reality.

Although the glasses are a clever and useful tool, the key to self-development is finding a way to change one's lenses *even when not wearing the glasses.* Traders need techniques for shifting themselves from one mind to another if they are to trade with consistency and an absence of emotional interference.

THE MIND OF THE TRADER

The experience of Dr. Schiffer's clients offers important insights into the plight of the emotional trader who becomes lost in regret, fear, and overconfidence. Experienced traders typically place their trades after they have analyzed the market carefully and weighed their options. They are operating with Cutting's Mind #1 activated, scanning for patterns and relevant data. At that point, they are like the patients wearing the glasses covering all but the far right visual field.

Once the market makes a major move—a move that impacts the trader's position—a shift suddenly occurs. The trader now views the market in terms of self-relevance, evaluating the consequences of the market move for his or her account, esteem, or reputation. This is the equivalent of switching one pair of glasses for another, now covering all but the left corner of vision. Processing the market through the lenses of self-relevance, the trader is no longer "in the zone," fully attentive to market data and patterns. The odds are high that a trading decision will be made for reasons other than those that have been researched and tested.

People lose money in the markets because the person who places the trade very often is *not the same person* who manages and closes the trade. Quite literally, another self has taken over—another mind.

Earlier I questioned why it is so difficult for people to sustain New Year's resolutions, stick to a diet, or maintain an exercise regimen. The split-brain research and the work of doctors Schiffer and Goldberg offer an explanation. At the time people resolve to diet or exercise, they are sincere. They are completely focused on the health benefits of their actions and the many valid reasons for being healthy. Later, however, they become bored, fatigued, or depressed. They enter a different mind state, and their resolutions no longer carry the same force. The person who made the resolution is gone; the other, emotional self is too tired to exercise, too in need of gratification to forego the food. People make exceptions to their rules, and then they forget the rules altogether.

People cannot sustain purpose in their lives—and trading is certainly a purposeful act—because they are fundamentally *divided beings*.

In the early twentieth century, the Russian philosopher George Ivanovitch Gurdjieff anticipated the findings of cognitive neuroscience when he emphasized that people lack a unified self. The average person, Gurdjieff taught, consists of many "I's," each competing for attention and each relatively unaware of the others. As people move from situation to situation, various I's are activated, impelling their behavior. This occurs mechanically, without conscious awareness or participation. In an important sense, Gurdjieff taught, people are asleep; they are not fully conscious. Believing they are free, they are all too vulnerable to situations that trigger their I's and drive their behavior.

This human dilemma, anchored in the reality of multiple information-processing systems within the brain, wreaks havoc among those who hope to profit from the markets. As traders are tossed from state to state by news, hot tips, market movements, and life's distractions, they find it as difficult to sustain a trading plan as it is to stick to a diet. The absence of a unified

I allows the little I's to run amok, executing trading decisions impulsively and creating situations in which even the easiest-to-read market patterns can be missed.

Perhaps you have had the experience of reviewing a losing trade and examining what went wrong. You look at the market data available at the time, ponder your trade, and think, "What in the world was I thinking of?"

Your reaction is more than 20-20 hindsight. You may indeed have had all the information you needed to make the right trade, but you couldn't access the information because you weren't attending to it. Your thinking, driven by the anxiety, boredom, or pride of the moment, was as colored as that of Schiffer's patients wearing the glasses blocked on the right. The "you" that is analyzing the trade is not the "you" that placed the trade.

And that is sobering.

It is also important because it suggests that you can perform endless research, learn every new indicator, and receive the best mentoring and still fall short of your trading goals. If you are asleep—if you are wandering from one mind state to another—you will not be able to consistently implement objectively sound strategies, even if they're handed to you. As P. D. Ouspensky observed in his book *The Fourth Way*, as long as you are asleep, your dreams may change, but you will always be stuck in your bed.

Understanding Schiffer's research also provides a deeper understanding of the Internal Observer. The Observer is the capital "I" in Gurdjieff's scheme— the part of you that stands apart from the various individual moods and states and maintains a constant perspective. The Internal Observer consists of your capacity to ask, "Which lenses am I wearing right now? How am I processing the world at this moment?"

Simply asking these questions introduces a powerful psychological force into one's trading. By taking your "emotional temperature"—recognizing how you are experiencing the world—you create a distinction between yourself as the temperature-taker and yourself as the hot or cold person. *Asking about the lenses you are wearing creates a perspective that transcends the lenses.*

SOLUTION-FOCUSED MONEY MANAGEMENT

Imagine a mutual fund run by several money managers. Some of these managers are relatively astute and quite attentive to market data and patterns. Others tend to take their eye off the market ball and consistently lose money.

The overall performance of the fund, averaging the returns of these managers, is mediocre, as the losses of the poorly performing managers cancel out the gains of the astute ones.

What would you do if you were the chief executive officer (CEO) of this fund?

Easy, you say. You would identify the successful managers and place all of the money in their hands. You would either fire the unsuccessful ones or ensure that they couldn't make final decisions about the investment of funds.

Now imagine that, within yourself, there are actually several different traders, each of whom takes control of your account for a period of time each day. One or two of these traders are relatively astute; others are downright destructive. Your overall performance suffers as a result. As Chief Executive Observer of your own account, what should you do?

If your first inclination is to try to identify the bad traders within you so that you can eliminate them, you haven't learned the lesson from Phil's counseling. The starting point of the solution-focused approach was that Phil's destructive trading—like his cocaine use—was serving a purpose. In fact, it was serving a very positive purpose, albeit in a self-defeating way. The answer to his problem wasn't simply to stop trading or to severely limit the size of his trades. This would never have addressed his reason for trading destructively: his need to feel powerful. Phil and Rhonda found a solution only once that need could be fulfilled in another fashion.

Similarly, if you harbor multiple traders within you—some careful, some impulsive; some successful, some losing—your first task is to avoid labeling these traders and to take an Observing stance. You need to figure out why these lousy traders within you are trading! They evidently are not trading simply for the monetary reward; if that were the case, they would never overrule the successful traders within you. The chances are good that they are trading to achieve something other than a good return on equity: a sense of excitement, a feeling of self-esteem, or an imposed self-image.

You do not fail at trading because you are masochistic or because you love failure or feel you deserve defeat. Rather, you sabotage your trading because you have different facets to your personality, each with its own needs, each clamoring for access to the trading account. Your trading suffers because you are not always trading with the equity stake firmly in mind. In a strange way, a losing trade can be a success to that part of you that is, for example, looking for excitement—not profits—from the markets.

On the whole, I operate on a pretty even emotional keel. I am not prone to bouts of depression, anxiety, or anger—or at least not for any prolonged periods—and I have achieved enough success in various aspects of my life that I don't have to place undue pressure on my trading results. Nonetheless, I find myself prone to lapses in trading that differ from Phil's only in degree.

Because much of my trading is quantitatively driven, based on exploring historical patterns to see where I have an edge, there are many periods of time during which I am out of the markets entirely. Although the markets are not perfectly efficient, they are largely so. Just as nickels don't lie on the sidewalk all day without being picked up, opportunities in the market do not persist for long without someone grabbing them, especially once they are publicized. These opportunities are quickly exploited by well-financed players who can monitor multiple markets with sophisticated data analysis. The real discipline in trading, for me, is not in placing entries and exits but in staying out of the market unless and until I have a demonstrable edge. This means that much of the day, I am watching the markets carefully—and putting on no trades.

Much of the time, I can live with that discipline and use the time to build my research and to attend to the needs of my large database. At times, however, my Type A personality kicks in and begins to feel that the time I spend in front of the screen without placing trades is wasted. I should be accomplishing something! I should be trading! It is at such moments that I am most apt to forego my thorough analysis or to trade a marginal pattern. I trade at those junctures not because the trade is so well crafted as to guarantee a profit, but because it feeds my flagging sense of achievement. I have learned that if I cannot explicitly state—and write down—a sound logical basis for my trade, then I am probably in the trade for psycho-logical reasons and should get out of the market.

But I will only be able to find an enduring solution for my bouts of trading laxity if I can meet my needs for achievement in other ways during those quiet market periods. Just as Phil met his needs for competence by helping others with addictions rather than by continuing his cocaine use, I can gratify my Type A subpersonality by engaging in something challenging and achievement oriented *in addition to my trading*. It is difficult to trade frequently while writing a book (and I have thus curtailed my trading for the past several months), but I do not find it surprising that my trading has gone well during my writing. When the markets are dull, I simply plan my strategy and return to my manuscript, stealing occasional glances at the screen to monitor the action. With my achievement needs nicely gratified by the writing, I can wait patiently for very good setups. My need for results doesn't interfere with my need for profits.

A TRADE FROM THE COUCH

The first psychological step toward trading success, as I emphasized earlier, is keeping a journal of all your trades and the state of mind you were in when placing the trade, the thoughts going through your head at the time, your feelings, and so on. Before long, you'll identify the states of mind that are your good traders and those that are the bad ones. You will know which lenses work for you and which don't. And, most important of all, you will cultivate the habit of being an Observer.

Your journal, however, can be helpful in another respect: It can assist you in identifying the reasons *why* you are trading.

If you can identify your subpersonalities, much as I recognized my own Type A self, you can then use your trading journal to ask yourself, "Which of my internal traders placed this trade? Did I place this trade because the odds were truly tilted my way, or did I place it to compensate for a prior loss or to demonstrate my prowess to my trading buddies?"

Through the journal, you can recognize that you, like Dr. Schiffer's patients and like me, harbor a number of selves within you—each there for a good reason and each more than happy to take the trading reins. This is why trading coaches, such as Alexander Elder, in his book *Trading for a Living*, advise traders to keep a diary of all trades. Such a record allows traders to discern patterns of success and failure so that their past need not be their future.

At the risk of beating a dead horse, I cannot emphasize this strongly enough: The problem is *not* that traders have problems but that traders become *identified* with their problems and thus are unable to gain access to those parts of themselves that can accurately process market information.

You do not want to eradicate your problems. You want to *use them* as signals that help you shift your lenses and activate the best within you.

I recently began feeling so confident about my trading that I briefly entertained the notion of increasing my position size. Quickly, another voice kicked in: Don't go there.

That night, I forced myself to double my preopening homework. I filtered out all but the safest and clearest trading signals and then kept my position size constant. By the early afternoon, I had cleared twelve points on the Standard & Poor's (S&P) futures for a tidy gain. Best of all, "I" felt that I had control over the "I's."

That is trading from the couch.

SHIFTING SELVES IN TRADING

The idea that you can change yourself psychologically by gaining access to alternative minds and selves sounds radical, but it fits very well with the dynamics of change that were demonstrated with Sue and Ken, in Chapters 1 and 2, respectively. When you process a message in a novel state, you are literally accessing another mind. Moreover, when you engage your Internal Observer, you are filtering your problem patterns through a different processing system. The recognition that you are many-in-one opens the door to understanding both how you can sometimes behave so irrationally and how you can accelerate changes in those behaviors.

In his book *Trading in the Zone* (John Wiley, 2001), Ari Kiev summarizes his experience in providing psychological assistance to some of the world's most successful traders. His book describes helpful methods for maximizing trading performance, with a special emphasis on the cultivation of focus and discipline. One of his case studies, that of Kurt, nicely captures the solution-focused mindset of the brief therapist. Kurt was overtrading, trying to make opportunities where none were present. He would experience "seller's remorse"—he castigated himself for a poor trade. This then emotionally colored his subsequent trading decisions. Dr. Kiev observed that Kurt was trading simply to keep his seller's remorse at bay. By holding onto losing positions or by quickly entering new ones, he didn't have to think about what was going wrong. This temporarily made him feel better, but it wreaked havoc with Kurt's bottom line.

Fortunately, through exploration with Dr. Kiev, Kurt observed that he was much more able to handle adversity in his golf game. When he made a bad shot—which happens to all golfers—Kurt would focus on the *next* shot, rather than immerse himself in what had gone wrong with the past shot. By invoking his golf-challenge state of mind during trading, Kurt was able to treat drawdowns and losing trades the way he handled errant shots on the golf course. He became more able to bail out of positions and to reenter them if conditions warranted, adding flexibility to his trading. Dr. Kiev observed that it is helpful to meditate on past success to cultivate a winning mind-set. As his case of Kurt illustrated, such a solution focus can be helpful even when these successes are drawn from spheres of life separate from trading.

Dr. Kiev's astute observations with Kurt imply that anyone may experience a degree of vertical split in his or her trading. It goes back to the Gurdjieffian idea that people consist of many little I's, many traders running around with different needs and impulses. By focusing on past successes and by placing yourself in the mind-set of another domain in which you are successful (such as golf), you can select the I's that will dictate today's trading.

A useful technique when a trading slump hits is to stop trading for a time and immerse yourself in something—anything—that you are very good at. This will invoke the state of mind associated with success, which then can carry over to your subsequent market forays. For me, writing is something that I enjoy and that has been associated with a measure of success. As a result, when markets make little sense to me, I review my charts and data and force myself to *write* a synopsis of my observations. Very often, as I am writing, an insight will come to me that had not been present while I was simply pondering the market action. The process of writing, for me, is like changing the glasses in Dr. Schiffer's office.

Indeed, the dynamics of left- and right-brain hemispheres—and the notion that emotional patterns may be hemisphere-specific—helps to explain the psychological value of market preparation. A theme common to many of the most successful traders is planfulness. Successful traders are highly intentional in their approach to their craft. They treat their trading as a business and follow a careful business plan. They are purposeful with each trade, and they follow well-researched entries and exits. In his work with traders, Dr. Kiev emphasizes the importance of focusing on defined goals and of developing entry and exit strategies consistent with these goals. The very act of focusing appears to be helpful in activating parts of the brain that are responsible for problem solving and in suppressing those parts that process the world in emotional, visceral ways.

I have had the privilege of observing several world-class traders in action and have been struck by the degree to which preparation has been a large part of their success. Victor Niederhoffer uses the term "counting," borrowed from the famous British scientist Francis Galton, to describe his empirical investigations into markets. Each day, Niederhoffer runs a number of studies to examine current market patterns and to see how these have been resolved in the past. Linda Raschke, the well-known Market Wizard interviewed by

Jack Schwager, similarly stresses the importance of planning in market success. Here is an assortment of observations from her *Trading My Way* seminar manual:

• "It is hard work to stay focused and push aside all the distractions that try to come between you and success. Concentration, routine, and ritual are the most powerful tools at your disposal to help ward off distractions and eliminate the emotions and anxieties that hinder good performance" (p. 3).

• "A trader must have a plan, methodology, system, or program! Without a plan, the market already has you beat. The decision-making process can be so overwhelming you will either over-trade or be too conservative (hesitate), and sloppy mistakes will be made. Consistency is the only way to win, and a trading program is the only way to achieve this" (p. 6).

• "Develop your own daily rituals. There is ultimately a freedom to be found in routine and rituals. They help free the mind from 'self-talk' and doubt. They keep one focused in the present and on the process. They add structure in an otherwise abstract environment" (p. 9).

Notice the themes running through Raschke's observations: consistency, planning, rituals. Note Kiev's emphasis on focus and discipline. A problem-solving focus, I hypothesize, activates those verbal, analytic capacities typically associated with the left hemisphere. In suppressing the activity of your more emotional Mind #2, you make a crucial shift without the need for brain surgery, anesthetics, or taped glasses. In this sense, market research, plans, and preparation are more than a computation of probabilities for the next period's price action in the markets. *They are valuable practice in generating and sustaining the quality of mental activity needed for market success.*

STATIONARITY AND THE MOODS OF THE MARKETS

Clifford Sherry has made an important contribution to the trading literature by focusing on the issue of the *stationarity* of price changes in the markets. This concept is foreign to many traders, but it is a vitally important one.

A stationary price series is one that is generated by a single process. If cards are drawn at random from a deck in a game of blackjack, the distribution of cards selected will show evidence of stationarity; that is, they will follow a stable, predictable distribution over time.

If, however, the dealer at the casino shifts from using a single deck of cards to using a shoe of several decks, the distribution of cards selected will change. The distribution will now show evidence of nonstationarity—there will be significant differences in the frequency of cards coming up using many decks versus one.

Stationarity is important to traders because every so often the markets switch the number of decks from which they're dealing. The market will meander in a given direction with low volatility for a while and then suddenly zoom off on high volatility. If you look at the statistical distribution of price changes, you can see evidence of nonstationarity.

Such sudden shifts in market outcomes are not the exception but the rule. Mornings are generally more active and volatile than midday hours in the equities markets. And on average, late afternoons also display more radical price movements than the lunchtime periods do. Preholiday trading is often thin and nonvolatile; trading around periods in which options and futures are expiring is often more hectic, with larger price jumps. Summer months have gained a reputation for doldrums; October has a reputation for violent, downward action.

One of the greatest weaknesses of the methods utilized by many traders I have interviewed is the failure to assess stationarity and factor it into their decisions. Instead of identifying the type of market they are in and trading methods specific to that kind of market, they adopt mechanical signals and uniform chart or oscillator patterns to apply to all markets. As long as the market works from the same number of decks, their methods may produce profits. Once the changing cycles described by Niederhoffer change the decks, however, the formerly useful methodologies will produce substandard results.

Any single set of trading rules or methods is vulnerable to breakdown if repeatedly traded across nonstationary periods. Why is this? Why do markets swing irregularly between trending and nontrending, volatility and quiescence? It may be because of the very same dynamics that have been observed in cognitive neuroscience research. Just as traders shift from one mind state to another, tossed about by their little I's, perhaps markets also shift from state to state. Markets, like people, have their personalities that, like Schiffer's patients, process information in wildly different ways.

If this is so, the ramifications for trading are substantial. Instead of seeking holy grails—methods that can be traded across all markets over all time frames—it may be more fruitful to develop "personality" profiles of markets and to detect when shifts are occurring from one state to another. In my own trading, I integrate several important market variables—price change, acceleration, volatility, and relative strength—into a single composite statistic that I refer to as *Power*. A market with high Power is one that is strongly trending upward; one with low Power is strongly trending downward. Power readings near zero are associated with nontrending markets.

When I conduct my historical analyses, I only investigate those historical market periods that are similar in Power to the present market. Power, as a measure of trend direction and volatility, captures the market's personality at a particular point in time. Shifts in the Power variable signify changes in that personality—and they trigger remodeling on my part to see how the new personality fared in subsequent price action. As the market shifts from upward trending to consolidating to downward trending, the expectations for future price action shift accordingly, making research an ongoing part of the trading process. This embedding of research into the flow of trading is extremely helpful in keeping trades grounded in the logical needs for profit, rather than in competing psychological needs.

Yet even within this quantitative focus, there is a role for intuition and feeling. If you engage in quantitative research, you will start to notice that attentiveness to your own state shifts will provide information regarding those of the market. I encourage you to keep tabs of the direction and volatility of both your moods and the markets you are trading. You may be surprised at the ways in which shifts in your state alert you to shifts in those of the markets. More than once my statistical remodeling of the market has been triggered by a shift in my own state in sympathy with the streaming market data.

It is this intricate interplay between the experiential and the analytic that makes trading so challenging. As you shall see shortly, your emotional, right hemisphere holds the potential both to subvert your analyses and to provide the first, implicit cues for when those analyses are going awry. The image developed by V. S. Ramachandran and Sandra Blakeslee in their book *Phantoms in the Brain* is particularly apt. The left hemisphere of the brain acts like a general during wartime, making executive decisions about the deployment of your capital. The right hemisphere serves the function of scouts and sentinels, feeding fresh information to the general for the updating of strategy. Hysterical scouts and negligent generals are two of the great saboteurs of trading.

CONCLUSION

I have just begun to touch the surface of evidence that the most typical challenges faced by traders are not a function of emotional disorders, but instead are grounded in the very architecture of the brain. The division of labor between the brain's hemispheres, especially in the processing of verbal/conceptual information versus emotional/spatial experiencing, helps create those shifts in information processing that undermine trading discipline.

A major implication of the ideas presented thus far is that traders who are living for their trading will have difficulty trading for a living. Since writing the trading columns, I cannot begin to count the number of desperate traders who have sought me out for advice, beginning their pleas with a statement of how trading is *the* most important thing in their lives. I am obliged to point out to them that this may be their very problem.

If it is true that much bad trading represents a spillover of unmet needs and desires, any failure to meet those needs invites future interference. The trader who lives for his or her trading may be neglecting basic drives for security, stimulation, affection, recognition, and spirituality. These are valid and important needs, but not ones that should be driving entry and exit decisions in the stock and futures markets. Rather than neglecting these needs, it is important to find constructive outlets for them so that they will not color moods and interfere with trading decisions.

I recently spoke with a trader whose lapses in the market were almost entirely attributable to adopting astrological and other mystical patterns as a rationale for trades. Most of the time, he was relatively disciplined in planning and implementing entries and exits. Every so often, however, he would become absorbed in calculating astrological configurations and various numerical patterns in the markets. Hearing him talk about these approaches in reverent tones, it was clear that the very mysticism of the methods—their hints of an underlying meaning and order—was what held his interest. It did not surprise me that he was not inclined to religion or philosophy; his fascination with universal order served to channel these interests. I firmly believe that the best thing he could have done for his trading was to cultivate a creative, spiritual life outside of the markets. With those needs properly addressed, he would have been free to stick to what had been working for him in trading.

Online chatrooms and bulletin boards are filled with lonely, frustrated traders who live for their trading and have precious little to show for their lives if their trading falls short of expectations. Successful traders don't *need* to trade to be successful; their trading success is an extension of—and is permitted by—their other life accomplishments. The markets can be challenging, rewarding arenas; but they are not life and they cannot fulfill the panoply of legitimate human needs. To pursue one's development as a trader at the expense of one's personal development is to court the very emotional interference that generates inconsistent, substandard results.

Chapter Five

Mary, Mary, Quite Contrary

Every change begins with the interruption of a pattern.

We have seen how problem patterns in our personal and trading lives represent well-intended efforts to cope with emotionally stressful situations. These efforts become overlearned and then take on a life of their own when new stressors emerge. People often come to therapy hoping that talking out their problems or immersing themselves in positive self-talk will break these patterns. Change rarely occurs this way, however. More often, people change because they undergo powerful emotional experiences that challenge their old ways and help to cement new patterns. It is not so much that you will trade better once you feel better about yourself, but that you will feel better once potent emotional experiences undermine old ways of trading and contribute to a new set of solutions.

In this chapter, we will explore how therapists help to create these powerful emotional experiences in the context of short-term therapy, utilizing—and even generating—crises to accelerate change processes. We will then map out ways in which traders can accomplish this for themselves, employing emotional arousal as a tool for undermining destructive patterns.

GETTING INSIDE MARY'S JOURNAL

When Mary came to me for her first appointment, I was immediately struck by her attire. Unlike most students, she was wearing a tailored outfit: a silver gray jacket and skirt that would pass muster in any corporate office. Her light brown hair was pulled back away from her face, homely wire-rimmed glasses evoking the look of an elderly English teacher. This struck me as incongruous, because she was actually quite young and attractive.

Mary was holding a large envelope and kept it clutched in her hands as she talked. In a reserved tone, she described how she was unhappy in her relationships with men. She found herself always being the one to give. She felt taken for granted, used. That made her feel very bad about herself. She came to counseling at this time because a relationship with a man had just ended. Despite her best efforts to make it work, he didn't seem to care. He saw her when it suited him, which she suspected meant that he had no other woman to sleep with that night. Nonetheless, she found herself depressed at the loss of this relationship.

"I don't know why I should feel this way," Mary lamented. "I know he doesn't care about me. Why should I care about him? I feel weak. I hate myself this way."

You can learn much about a person from the first few minutes of a therapy session. Counseling is a completely unnatural process. You are asking a vulnerable person to emotionally undress in front of someone they barely know. Only a reasonably secure person—or a completely overwhelmed person—would do that. On the one hand, when people begin their first session in a very guarded mode, it says something about their level of distrust and fear. This in turn probably says a great deal about their experience in previous relationships. On the other hand, when they begin divulging intimate details in the first minutes, you know something is amiss. A gushing firehose is a sure indication of internal pressure.

So when you are a therapist, you look for just the right blend of healthy openness and healthy caution. Mary had that blend. Reserved, straightforward, candid. Not a "sick" person.

I usually test that initial impression, often with humor. My rationale is simple: A person who is completely overwhelmed by a problem cannot stand outside himself or herself enough to laugh. Humor requires an ability to see things from an unusual perspective, or, more correct, an ability to shift perspectives. That kind of shift is central to the change process. If a person can't make a small shift to see humor in a situation, he or she will find the larger shifts required by therapy to be difficult indeed.

I have found that this same principle operates in trading the markets. If I am comfortable with my position, I can stand back and respond to the humor of others, to my e-mails, or to a particular news item. Conversely, if I cannot respond with characteristic easygoing humor, that is a powerful sign that I am absorbed with concern about my position. Very often, there is reason for this concern, and I can use the emotional information as a gut check. Most often, my discomfort stems from having violated one of my trading rules. Although I have talked myself into the "exception," my humorless mind seems to know quite well that I am on dangerous ground!

So I introduced a bit of humor to this first meeting with Mary. When she said, "I work so hard at relationships, but get nothing in return," I smiled and pointed out, "Hmmm . . . that's what I hear from your classmates about the program you're in." Mary was in a very challenging health sciences program, one that is well known for frustrating even the best students. Immediately she cracked a smile and acknowledged, "That's *exactly* how I feel."

Her reaction was another good sign.

(Therapists often come across as humble human beings, insisting that they don't hold all the answers for clients. Don't believe it for a second. My approach to the session is typical therapist arrogance: If you can't find my humor amusing, you *must* be troubled! Anyone who thinks they're going to change a person's life by meeting with them for one out of 168 hours in a week surely has a bit of hubris!)

Mary and I spent much of the remainder of the first session exploring her recent relationships with men and the pattern of giving too much and receiving very little. She made it clear that this was not a pattern in her female friendships. She also indicated that her growing-up experiences were positive, in a home that was supportive and caring. At one level, she recognized that she was bright, attractive, and personable. She should be succeeding at relationships with men. At another level, she felt like a loser because she was unable to sustain those relationships.

"Am I asking for too much?" she implored. "Am I driving everyone away?" Clearly, she was hurting.

One of the greatest mistakes a therapist can make is to become seduced by a person's words. What people say and what they mean can be worlds apart. Often, the nonverbal communications of a person speak far more to their meanings than their words. It is not unusual to encounter clients who are smiling, cheerful, and engaging as they recount the events of the week, their bodies tense with nervous energy, their faces taut with the effort to restrain painful emotions. At times, I make an effort to tune out clients' words and simply absorb the feeling tone of their verbal and physical communications.

This can be of tremendous help in trading, as well. As I have indicated earlier, the state of my body often reflects information that I have processed, but not consciously. A tensing of my muscles and a shift in my posture in the chair at my trade station is often the first clue of a trade that is not living up to expectations.

Respecting the power of nonverbal communication, I waited toward the end of the first meeting to ask about the envelope that Mary had been clutching tightly. A bit sheepish, she mentioned that it contained some of her creative writing. I asked if I could see her work, and she agreed. Several short stories were in the envelope, along with poems and fragments from a journal. I only had to read a few pieces to realize that she had talent. When I pointed this out to her, she brightened noticeably.

"You really like it?" she asked.

"Absolutely."

"I was thinking of entering a creative writing contest," she offered.

"That sounds great," I said. "I think you might have a shot at winning."

We wrapped up our conversation and set our next appointment. It was a nice ending to a first session.

Little did I suspect what was ahead.

Our second session was tumultuous from the outset. No longer was Mary's hair pulled back. It flowed loosely down her shoulders. She was wearing a low-cut blouse and a very short skirt. She was also wearing much more makeup than before, and it was applied with a notable absence of artistry. In place of her straightforward speaking tone, she now talked in a hesitant fashion, looking away from me. Her voice sounded small and distant. I was shocked. *It was as if she was a different person.*

When I pointed out that she seemed uncomfortable, she nervously mentioned that she had a nightmare the previous evening. She didn't see any point in discussing it, however.

"It's only a dream," she said. "It doesn't mean anything."

Gently, I suggested that we explore whether it had meaning. "Dreams sometimes reveal what's on our mind," I explained.

It took a while for Mary to recount the dream. Every few sentences she backpedaled, claiming, "This is crazy. Dreams are made up. They aren't real."

Eventually, she managed to convey her nighttime fantasy. It was quite vivid. She was at home in the dream and suddenly I appeared. I suggested to her that we could hold our sessions in her house. She felt very uncomfortable about that but didn't say anything. I asked her to go upstairs; and in the dream, she noticed my wedding ring and froze with fear. That's when she awakened.

Once she had finished relating the story, we began to explore its significance. "In the house you actually live in," I asked, "what is upstairs?"

Embarassed, she said, "My bedroom." Before I could say anything else, however, she added, "But I know you'd never do anything like that. It's just a dream. I know you don't have a *personal* interest in me."

From her tone, as well as from the dream, I could tell that *personal* interest meant *sexual* interest. A key moment had occurred in the therapy. I could see that she awaited my reply, her eyes practically begging for the reassurance that I was not after her body. Yet, here she was, dressed more provocatively than any client I could recall!

Once again, it was one of those pivotal change moments.

I leaned forward in my seat and looked deeply into her eyes. I was practically touching her. Slowly, kindly—so as to not activate her defenses—I said, "You're wrong. I *am* interested in you in a personal way. And, from the way you're dressed, you seem to be interested in me as well."

At that point, all hell broke loose. Soundlessly, Mary began shaking. For a second, I couldn't tell if she was angry, anxious, crying, or having a seizure.

The real work was about to begin.

AFFLICTING THE COMFORT ZONE

One of the first things I teach my psychiatry residents is that the purpose of therapy is to "comfort the afflicted and afflict the comfortable." The phrase sticks in their minds because it captures an important reality. Some people come to their meetings in need of support. They have been traumatized; they are overwhelmed with anxiety, depression, or anger and need a refuge from their pain. Others enter counseling in a rut. Locked in patterns that bring self-defeat, they are all too comfortable with their old ways. They fear change. They fear the unknown. "I know it's a bad relationship," many people will tell me, "but I don't know if I want to be alone." When a car is stuck in a ditch, it sometimes needs a good nudge to get it going. People aren't so different.

The standard therapeutic maneuver with Mary would have been to reassure her, to establish proper therapeutic boundaries, and to continue to explore the meaning of the dream. By shoring up the safety of the professional relationship, she would feel sufficiently secure to examine the dream's significance.

Taking a look at the dream, however, is very different from *reexperiencing* it. Mary made it perfectly clear that she did not want to go near the nightmare. She had been trying very hard to convince me that it was unworthy of attention. Her discomfort, however, told me otherwise. In temporarily blurring the boundaries by stating my "personal" interest in her, I afflicted the comfort zone—for both of us. I made a bet that my initial impression was right and that she was strong enough to withstand the breach of comfort. When I saw her shaking before me, I wasn't quite so sure.

Mary turned to me, sobbing. She was very upset, but now she looked directly at me. My gentle tone, more than my words, convinced her that I was not a threat, and she spoke freely. Her words poured out. She explained that her father was rarely around when she grew up. He traveled a great deal and divorced her mother while Mary was still young. Her maternal grandfather took care of her while her mother worked long hours to keep the household afloat. Although he was generally nice to her, he had a drinking problem. His moods would change dramatically when he had been drinking. He would become verbally abusive to Mary and her mother, reminding them of all he had done for them and ranting that no one in the family appreciated him. Worse still, when Mary was seven years old, he began fondling her when he was drunk, several times pulling down her panties. This continued until puberty, when she managed to establish residence with her father.

Mary looked at me intently, tears in her eyes. "I feel like it was my fault," she explained. "I let him do that to me. I never told anyone."

Now my voice was quiet. Humbly, I told Mary that I needed to apologize to her. "I'm very sorry," I said.

She looked at me quizzically, and I explained my remorse: When I asked to see the envelope that she was guarding so carefully, I had violated a personal boundary. The envelope and her writing were, strictly speaking, not a part of our meeting. I was displaying a *personal* interest in her. At one level, she was pleased that I appreciated her writing skill. At another level, however, she experienced my interest as yet another boundary violation from a man. Her dream nicely illustrated her fear that I was like her grandfather. And her decision to come to therapy in her dressed-to-kill outfit suggested that she expected to gain my attention the way she had received it in the past.

I explained myself to Mary: "I *do* have a personal interest in you. But I do *not* have a sexual interest. I care much, too much about you to repeat your past." Through her tears, Mary's smile reemerged.

Silently, I breathed a sigh of relief.

REPEATING PATTERNS

Our following sessions filled in the gaps. Each of Mary's relationships with boyfriends repeated her childhood. She became sexually involved very early in these relationships and began to fantasize of a future together. Desperate for acceptance, she did whatever she could to please the man. When he did not reciprocate, her feelings of loneliness and betrayal took over. She felt used, taken advantage of. Symbolically, it was the grandfather all over again.

If all this sounds a bit Freudian, well, it is. One of Freud's greatest insights was what he called the "repetition compulsion." Not too long before Freud, the philosopher Friedrich Nietzsche had called it "eternal recurrence" and made it the center of his worldview. Basically *repetition compulsion* means that evolution is not inevitable. People repeat the same patterns in various ways and on various scales throughout their lives. Freud saw clearly that unresolved conflicts led to a loss of free will. Without resolution, people are condemned to eternally relive the past. The goal of his therapy, called psychoanalysis, was to regain that free will. Freud believed that, if people could become conscious of their unconscious repetitive patterns, they would no longer be controlled by their patterns.

It is difficult to appreciate the degree to which much of people's lives have a scripted quality, as they unwittingly repeat patterns of thought and action. Many of these patterns can be traced back to unresolved conflicts from earlier in their lives. *Talking* about these patterns does not change them. In John Cutting's terms, Mind #1 has a peculiarly difficult time penetrating Mind #2. Only a powerful emotional experience—actually engaging in a relationship with a man who cared about her for more than her body—had the potential to dislodge Mary from her patterns. *Powerful emotional experiences create the pivot shifts that enable people to change their routines.*

Enacting unresolved conflicts in one's financial dealings can be particularly destructive. One physician and part-time trader, Dr. D., sought my counseling after repeatedly facing steep market losses. Dr. D. would take a large position in hopes of making a killing, only to wind up deeply in the hole. At that point, he would follow the market avidly, taking additional positions to balance and bail out his initial faulty trade. Occasionally, he was able to rescue the trade; generally, he fell short and experienced deep feelings of failure. It is interesting that when Dr. D. limited himself to paper trading, he tended to make money, picking stocks with a systematic and well-researched strategy. Only when he entered the emotional arena of actual risks and rewards did his destructive patterns emerge.

Although he was a successful physician, Dr. D. did not feel like a success. He grew up in a neglectful home and felt ignored by his father. Much of his childhood energy was spent in a desperate struggle to gain his father's attention and affection by succeeding in sports and in school. He learned, however, that no achievement was ever great enough: Nothing he did could satisfy his father, who spent long weeks away from home on business.

In later life, even after his father had died, Dr. D. found himself replaying the same emotional scenario in his trading, much as Mary repeated her unsuccessful approaches toward men. Having internalized the sense of not being good enough, Dr. D. now tried to prove himself through his trading accomplishments. Paper trading and small-size trading were not good enough; he had to make huge profits to demonstrate his worth. Ironically, this meant that he was most emotional when he was most financially at risk. When his positions were on paper or limited in size, he could follow his trading plan and take frequent profits. As his size expanded, his focus turned from the market to his emotional script, luring him into decisions he otherwise would never have made.

Dr. D. was an intelligent, educated man. He was a success in his profession. But none of this prevented him from blindly repeating a painful and destructive pattern. It was as if that part of his life were not under his control, activated by feelings of insecurity and playing itself out without his conscious awareness. In a very real sense, he was as out of control as the Woolworth man, living out an irrational life script.

Dr. D.'s therapy proceeded in an unorthodox manner. Simply making him aware of his repetitive pattern would not be sufficient to alter it. As soon as his mood shifted and the not-good-enough feeling overtook him, his perspective would be lost and he would find himself looking for the next market killing. The key to change, as it was with Mary, was to activate the pattern and *then do something different*. Powerful experience—a new ending to the old script—is what changes people.

In Dr. D.'s case, we conducted a funeral: an actual funeral, complete with burial and ceremony. During a marathon session, I asked Dr. D. to write down on paper a complete list of all the things he wanted, but never received, from his father. I also asked him to recount specific incidents in which he felt hurt by his father's lack of recognition. Laboriously, we went through his list, replaying the old, painful memories. Each time we hit on a traumatic memory, I switched gears and asked Dr. D. to recount an unsuccessful market trade. Again and again, we reviewed his trading failures, driving home the destructiveness of his pattern and his inability to win recognition through his trading.

Halfway through our recital, after one particular heart-rending memory in which he recalled his father not showing up to an eagerly anticipated championship Little League game, Dr. D. recalled one of his worst trading experiences. He had taken a fully margined position and, after a decline in the stock, faced a margin call. He added to his trading capital rather than liquidate the position. He lost that money as well. Pale and teary-eyed, Dr. D. looked squarely at me and said in a hoarse whisper, "I can't keep doing this to myself."

The shift from competent doctor to teary-eyed trading failure told me we were ready for the ceremony. We buried the list of hurtful occasions and conducted our funeral, saying goodbye to all his hopes and expectations for his father. After saying our farewells amidst tears and relief, we rehearsed a new pattern. Each time Dr. D. felt unworthy, he was to vividly image the funeral session we had held and picture himself saying, "I can't keep doing this to myself." Whenever that occurred, he was to take a position in the market half—not double—the size of his normal trade. Indeed, drawing on my own experience, I suggested that he initially trade an amount so small that it could not possibly attract the attention and admiration of others.

Freed of the need to be somebody in his father's eyes, Dr. D. was finally ready to succeed in his trading. Quite a few months after our last session, I received a call from him. He was proud of having caught an important bottom in the market. When he mentioned his position, I smiled inwardly. It was a surprisingly modest stake. But it yielded a meaningful profit.

Dr. D. finally got it. He was trading from the couch.

CHANGING REPETITIVE PATTERNS

I wish I could say that Mary's therapy ended successfully with my efforts at providing a powerful new experience in response to her dream. Change is generally not that simple and straightforward. With rare exception, it is not enough to have a single mind shift or emotional experience. Only through repetition do those experiences become internalized as part of one's identity.

That is where *transference* comes in.

Freud referred to transference as the replaying of old conflicts and patterns within the counseling relationship. Mary's second session is a perfect example. I was an older man who showed a personal interest in her. Longing for acceptance, she offered herself to me in the way of her past. All that needed to happen to complete the circle was for me to accept her offering. At that point, I truly would have become her grandfather and she would have repeated the Faustian bargain in which she traded her body for attention.

The goal of therapy has been described as providing new endings to old stories, and that was what I was trying to do with Mary. If my relationship with her was to be truly therapeutic, I could not take her offering. My goal was to provide her with a different kind of relationship: one that offered closeness and caring without exploitation. Perhaps then she could internalize from our interactions the sense of acceptance that had been missing for so long.

Achieving that is more difficult than it might seem. Part of Mary only knows acceptance through offering her body and soul. If I refuse that offering, that part of her is apt to become hurt, angry, and lost—as she has felt in recent relationships. So while a mature part of Mary might appreciate that I am not out to take advantage of her and really do care about her, there is a little girl inside who might not accept that. That little girl will only go down the therapy path kicking and screaming. Freud called this phenomenon *resistance*. The part of the person locked in the past is threatened by change and only knows gratification in the accustomed way. Just as someone might defend himself or herself against external threats, like a mugger or an oncoming car, the mind defends itself against the anxiety of internal threats. New endings to old stories, at some level, are too anxiety provoking for people. As a result, they invoke all sorts of strategies to avoid the new endings, pushing away the very experiences that could help set them free.

This is a very important concept: *The very solutions to people's trading woes are apt to induce anxiety, and they are likely to invoke all sorts of defenses as a result.* This means that one part of the human psyche is likely to fight change—and the uncertainty of the unknown—even as the person ardently desires it and realizes its necessity. Resolving this internal tug of war is an essential step in psychological change.

Ironically, I see this defense against change most vividly among traders who seek me out for emotional assistance. They are often very willing to discuss their problems, including the most intimate details of their histories. To a person, they express the conviction that if they could just overcome their emotional tendencies, they would become successful traders.

As with Mary and the dream, it is often what people are *least* willing to examine that ends up being of the greatest relevance. The traders who avidly seek emotional help are frequently quite reluctant to examine their actual trading methods. It is not that they fear divulging proprietary information. In fact, just the opposite is generally the case: They are uncomfortable with the acknowledgment that they have nothing proprietary to share and are trading very simple price patterns or gut hunches.

It is when I ask how they have tested these trading strategies that the anxiety—and the defenses—rear their heads. "Oh, I'm not a numbers person," one trader informed me. Another one asserted that he was not into any form of "data mining." When I raise the provocative question of how they *knew* their trading strategies could be effective for anyone, regardless of the person's emotional makeup, the responses become even more defensive. "It's worked for X," is a common reply, where X is a well-known trading guru without a well-documented track record. One trader, miffed by my inquiries, justified his tactics by asserting, "It doesn't matter what system you trade, as long as you control your losses!"

It is one of the great ironies of trading psychology that traders desperately seeking the next great system are most in need of emotional guidance, and traders desperately seeking emotional guidance are most in need of a good trading system. People generally seek that which is in their comfort zones (as Mary did), and that generally is what perpetuates old, destructive patterns. The path to successful change is rarely the most comfortable, familiar, or safe one.

In therapy, the uncomfortable changes are often first undertaken within the relationship between counselor and client. What Freud called the *therapeutic alliance* is a sort of bargain between the therapist and the healthy, mature part of the individual. It is as if the therapist says, "Let's make a deal. You and I will team up to understand this other, childlike part of you. Ignoring it won't make it go away. It hasn't gone away so far. But if we can understand the part of you that seeks out unresponsive men and flings yourself headlong into painful relationships with them, perhaps we won't have to repeat that pattern again." Now, of course, all this presupposes that a person like Mary does indeed have a more mature side that can stand apart from her conflicts as an Internal Observer. Fortunately, the fact that she is seeking counseling on her own is a good indicator of such maturity. Part of her desperately wants to be happy, even as she clings to the past.

The idea behind psychoanalytic therapy is that change begins on the couch. The client replays old patterns in the helping relationship, with the opportunity now to experience a different ending. What was missing from earlier relationships can be internalized from the therapist. And once internalized, it can become a template for future life challenges, breaking the cycle of repetition.

Invoke old patterns, activate the Observer, shift the mind state, construct new endings: This is the very essence of emotional change. If you can initiate a new response while feeling the pull of old patterns that haven't worked, you will have made a major step toward change. The first step in transformation is interrupting old patterns as they occur.

DOING WHAT COMES UNNATURALLY

Mary glanced at me, a mixture of fear and defiance on her face. She had just revealed to me that she slept with a man after the first date. This, of course, ran contrary to everything we had been working on in our sessions.

The natural reaction would be to say to Mary, "Why in the hell would you do *that*?" However, the natural reaction in counseling is usually the wrong one. Natural reactions are what Mary has been getting all her life. The last thing she needs from me is another confirmation of how she has fallen short.

That's where something called *countertransference* comes in. Clients aren't the only ones with unresolved conflicts. When therapists fail to work through their past problems, they are apt to repeat them as well. This can have a potentially destructive impact on the therapy. To be honest, there was a part of me that was frustrated with Mary. She knew very well where this would lead, yet here she was inviting yet another rejection and more debasement. That look of defiance in her eyes was all too much like the one I've seen in my young daughter, Devon, when I ask her to clean her room or finish her meal. She'll do it, but in her time, in her way. Rebellion, independence. I'm not going to let you control me. That was the key . . . Mary, Mary, quite contrary.

I turned to face Mary directly. In a firm voice, I announced, "There's something I need to say to you." I paused, creating a moment of anxious silence. Mary looked like a child who has just been told by the teacher, "I want to see you after school." She anticipated the worst.

My tone softened. "I've got to give you credit. It must have been hard for you to come in here and tell me that you did things the old way. What did you expect when you came in today?"

Mary looked sheepish, but a bit relieved. "I thought you'd be angry with me."

"So why did you bring it up? You didn't have to talk about it."

"Because I know it isn't right," Mary explained. "I'm going to get hurt."

"Maybe you will," I acknowledged. "But you are going to change when you're good and ready, aren't you?"

A small smile flashed across her face.

"You've had an older man forcing himself on you for much of your life, Mary. Now we have a great chance for me to be another one. You figure out what I want you to do in therapy and then you'll have another man in your life controlling you."

The smile broadened just a bit.

"If you get hurt, you'll get hurt. We can deal with that. The important thing is that this be *your* therapy. That's why I'm proud of you for bringing this up. It was more important for you to be your own person than to avoid my reaction."

The mood, then the message. Sternness, then praise. When the car slows down, you downshift before accelerating. Stay in the same upper gear, and you stall. Shift and suddenly you have torque. Change cannot occur until you have shifted gears; depressing the accelerator while in the same mental gear halts all movement. Most people come to therapy with a flooded engine: Pressing the accelerator has produced no results, but they don't know what else to do. They haven't yet found their gearshift, that pair of glasses that helps them see the world through another mind. Doing what comes least naturally disrupts their normal patterns of thinking, feeling, and behaving. It is out of this temporary chaos that novel patterns have their best chance of taking root.

RESISTING WHAT IS BEST FOR YOU

Ironically, Mary's greatest crisis came when she finally had the opportunity for a caring relationship. In a perverse way, it was easier to lose men who didn't care for her. The prospect of a true love was a powerful threat, posing the possibility that she would not be able to live up to her dreams.

The opportunity arose, coincidentally, in the pursuit of her creative writing. Mary joined a group of writers in the Syracuse, New York, area and found them interested and supportive. One particular man in the group, Larry, saw Mary's large envelope and asked to read her work. To her credit, she did not complicate his request by reenacting her sexual advance toward me. Openly, with considerable vulnerability, she allowed him to read her work and to relate to her solely at that level. She was shocked and surprised to find that he did, indeed, respond to her as a writer, sharing his own work and expressing further interest in hers. When he asked her to dinner, she responded with a heady mixture of hope, anticipation, and panic.

At times Mary allowed herself to fantasize that this might be *the* relationship. Other times, she worried that he might see the person behind the writing and become disillusioned. Her fears mounted in direct proportion to his continued interest in her.

"How can I tell him about my past?" Mary lamented in therapy. "What is he going to think about me?" Even seemingly simple decisions became torture for her, such as the choice of dress and makeup. "What should I wear?" she asked me several times, mindful that she didn't want to send the wrong sexual signals but still wanted to look her best.

It is not uncommon in therapy that clients will ask for direct advice. Mary's requests, however, went beyond the usual solicitations for feedback. She wanted me to tell her what to do and how to do it. Implicit in her requests was the assumption that she could not handle the situation and make the right choices. She was the helpless female child looking to the power of the older male.

Clearly this was a trap. Any response I could give would implicitly accept a damaging, hierarchical structuring of our relationship. If I told Mary to wear one outfit or another or to share certain things with Larry and not others, I would be conceding that she was incapable of making these decisions on her own. Temporarily gratified, she would be pleased with me, only to become even more dependent in future crises.

This is a major pitfall in trading as well. Many analysts, newsletter writers, columnists, and trading coaches present themselves as gurus, emphasizing that they have the answers to market success. Even if these individuals were successful—and evidence of that is generally woefully lacking—it is far from clear how one could ever gain confidence in one's own trading simply by absorbing the words of the guru. Indeed, by maintaining an aura of special insight or information and appealing to individuals who feel lost, the guru inevitably feeds the very dependence and lack of confidence that undermines successful trading.

To avoid such pitfalls, therapists develop the ability to listen to people with two ears: one for content, the other for process. The content reflects *what* is said, the explicit meanings of people's statements. Process captures *how* that content is conveyed. It is the nonverbal frame in which the person's words are embedded. "What should I do?" could be a helpless request for guidance, a mature request for advice, or an exasperated and angry challenge to a therapist. Process captures the interpersonal context of a communication.

When the process in counseling is problematic, even amidst seemingly positive content, it is usually worthwhile to shift the focus of the session. That means interrupting the conversation and calling attention to what is happening at that moment. This is especially the case when process undercuts content, as in situations where a person might implore: "Tell me how to be more independent!" It is generally not worth discussing a topic if the mode of discussion maintains the very problem under consideration. When correspondents have tried to place me in the guru role, for example, asking me for market predictions, I generally switch to a process focus and ask why they are feeling so uncertain—and why they are feeling the need to take or maintain a position in the market in the midst of such uncertainty.

The shift from content to process can be unsettling and difficult for people, who frequently lack awareness of their interpersonal contexts. Years ago, one of my clients, seen in couples counseling, called his wife a "bitch" in the session, much to her hurt and resentment. When I pointed out the adversarial process and coached him to speak solely in the first person about his own experience, he paused for a long time and reframed his remark: "I *feel* you're a bitch!" As you might imagine, his wife did not find this comforting!

Mary was similarly blind to the process occurring in our session. All she wanted was relief from her anxiety and uncertainty, and this she could get by my providing her with superior wisdom. In typical therapist fashion, however, I responded by pointing out that the situation had become risky. Mary was afraid of losing the relationship; and now, in the heat of her stress, she doubted her own ability to handle matters. I expressed my confidence in her judgment and assured her that, although she may have felt unable to connect with people as a child, she did indeed have that capacity now. I suggested to her that even a wrong choice by her would be superior to a good choice made by me, because she could at least learn from her own actions and maintain her selfhood.

That was not what Mary wanted to hear.

To my surprise, she responded with blind rage. "If you're wanting me out of therapy, just tell me," she yelled. "I'm coming here for help, and you're just telling me to do it on my own. Well, if I could do that, I wouldn't be here!" With that, she stormed out the door, ignoring my requests that she return to talk things out.

Though Mary did return for our next appointment, things went equally poorly with Larry. She focused on his every shortcoming to find reasons for breaking off the relationship. If he failed to call her when she was going through a hard time, she cursed his inattentiveness, ignoring the fact that he could not have known of her hardship. If his eyes strayed to any other female during their dates, she became jealous and insisted that he would not be faithful to her. At first, Larry responded with befuddlement; gradually, he became more defensive and aloof. This only heightened Mary's insistence that he was not right for her, that he didn't care for her, and that things couldn't possibly work out. Oddly, Mary was putting up walls, pushing away the very people she most wanted in her life: her boyfriend and her therapist.

Misery loves lost paradises, writer Jorge Luis Borges once wrote, and Mary understood that she would be miserable without these supportive relationships. It was almost as if Larry was too good to be true, so she had to toss him from the pedestal. The same thing, of course, was happening with me. My expressions of confidence placed too much pressure on her, raising the stakes in the event she failed. It was easier to push me away than to allow for the possibility that she would disappoint me and I would reject her. Once she had destroyed the relationships, her worst fears would have been confirmed, as destiny completed its perfect circle. At least, however, she could find consolation in the knowledge that she, not others, had been the architect of her demise.

I was not so quick to conduct her requiem. I knew that decisive action was necessary. The loss of the promising relationship with Larry, as well as the loss of our alliance, would set her back considerably, convincing her that she had only her body to offer to men. How to convey this to her, however? My intuition said that simply pointing out what was going on, how she was pushing away others to avoid the possibility of rejection, would probably leave her even more defensive and resentful. Indeed, as I consulted my own feelings, I realized that I was *afraid* to point out the pattern to her. I didn't want to risk another blowup and the prospect of her marching out the door for good.

But why was I afraid? Was it because I feared that Mary would never return to therapy and thereby ruin her life? No, that wasn't it. A good part of her knew that she needed help and maintained our work even as she lashed out at me.

As I consulted my Internal Observer, the truth was hard to face: I was afraid of being yelled at. I was hurt by her earlier explosion and wanted no part of another. What an interesting dynamic, I thought: Mary is the abuser; I am the victim. She is angry; I must submit.

With a deep breath of resolve, I pressed forward. "What went through your mind when Larry didn't call you last night?" I asked innocently.

Mary's voice began its escalation. "I couldn't believe it," she said. "For his birthday I spent so much time finding the right present for him. I called him every day when he was going through his exams. When I want something from him, where is he?"

"Just like me," I pointed out. "When you wanted something from me and I wouldn't give you the advice, you marched out of my office."

"I'm so sick of this," Mary yelled. "You have no idea what it feels like to not be appreciated. I give and give and give . . ."

I rose from my seat, interrupting Mary's litany. Her eyes registered surprise, then shock.

"Please excuse me," I said in a soft voice. "I need a break. I'm going out for a minute to get some coffee."

Mary was speechless. I had never interrupted a session in such a fashion.

When I returned, I wasn't sure what to expect. Would she be angry with me for cutting her off? Would she use this as the pretext for leaving for good?

One look and I could tell that she was afraid. She was very afraid. I had walked out on her. Angry Mary was gone. In front of me was a vulnerable child.

I moved my seat closer to Mary, much as I had done in our second session. "I'm really sorry," I explained. "I needed to step out. I didn't feel that I was talking with Mary. I was hearing her grandfather, the angry man screaming that no one appreciated him. It scared me, and it hurt, too. Sometimes grownups need to step away when they feel vulnerable. That's one of the things that makes them different from little kids. Kids don't have the option of stepping away."

Tears flowed down Mary's face. She explained that she didn't want to be like her grandfather. She realized that her anger at Larry hurt him, but she also knew that this was the only way she had found to make her own pain go away.

"Maybe the problem isn't Larry," I offered. "Maybe the problem is that little grandfather that's inside your head. It's like a tape that starts playing whenever you feel hurt, lashing out at everyone."

That idea made sense to Mary and thus, from our experience together, was born the "time-out" rule. Mary was free to do in our sessions what I had done when I felt uncomfortable: She could take a time-out and sort out her feelings. She could use the time-out to ask herself if it was really her or her "grandfather tape" that was responding to the situation. And she could direct her anger toward the tape instead of toward the people she cared about.

Mary took a few time-outs in our subsequent meetings. She also explained the time-outs to Larry and was able to step away from her hurt in situations with him. Ironically, it was by walking away that Mary learned that others would not leave her.

Here it was again: the mood, then the message. Following the gearshift from angry hurt to fear of abandonment when I left the room, Mary was ready to process a different message: Larry is not the problem; Brett is not the problem. The problem is the "tapes" playing in her head. And once the tapes became her enemy—not Larry or her therapist—Mary was ready to engage those people differently.

It was long, grueling work, but it paid off. Eight months later, Mary and Larry sent me a wedding invitation.

CREATING POWERFUL EMOTIONAL EXPERIENCES IN TRADING

Mary's counseling nicely illustrates how therapists act as mirrors to their clients, allowing them to perceive themselves in new ways. If a person is not ready to act as her own Internal Observer, a counselor can assume that role, standing aside from the turmoil of the moment and helping her make sense of what is going on. In no small measure, mirroring this observing capacity so that it can be internalized by others is the heart and soul of therapy. At first, the image mirrored by the counselor may be foreign and uncomfortable. With repetition, however, it becomes increasingly familiar and open for assimilation.

So what does all of this have to do with trading?

When you are trading from the couch, you are acting as your own therapist. You are attending to your own emotional and behavioral patterns, even as you process the patterns of the markets. Your goal, as your own therapist, is to supply repeated new endings to old patterns so that you can internalize new modes of thought and action in the markets.

Much has been written about the power of positive thinking. Many traders attempt to instill positive feelings by imaging favorable scenarios and repeating ennobling messages. There is much to be said for imagery, but perhaps the most powerful rehearsals are not the positive ones. Instead, requiring yourself to image your most destructive patterns—while actively and emotionally reminding yourself of their destructiveness—helps to cultivate the observing capacity to "wake up" and escape the blind repetition of past errors.

As I mentioned earlier, one technique for accomplishing this is "stress inoculation." Like a vaccine that introduces a small dose of a virus to stimulate the body's defenses and ward off the illness caused by the virus, stress inoculation exposes you to measured doses of a challenging situation, allowing you to mobilize your best coping for when the actual challenges hit.

In practice, this means *avoiding* positive thinking when first placing a trade. Almost immediately on placing an order in a superheated market, you want to switch gears, take a time-out (like Mary did), and get yourself in a very focused, relaxed state through deep, rhythmical breathing and a very still body posture. While in this state, you then visualize all of the ways in which your trade can go wrong. It is helpful to think of each trade as a hypothesis: You are a scientist hypothesizing that the market will move in a certain direction, to a particular extent, within a given time span. Framing your trade in this way makes it easier to contemplate all of the ways in which your hypothesis can be disconfirmed.

One of my recent trading experiences nicely illustrates the idea. Following a market decline, the Standard & Poor's (S&P) futures bounced higher and then remained in a fairly narrow range. There was considerable buying during this narrow range market, as evidenced by the consistently positive futures premium and the high TICK figures for the Dow Jones Industrial Average (the Dow) and the New York Stock Exchange (NYSE) stocks. Another of my indicators, which compares the number of trades during advancing one-minute periods to the number of trades during declining periods, similarly indicated buying pressure. Nonetheless, price was unable to break out of its narrow range. My research generally suggests that if high levels of buying pressure cannot take the market meaningfully higher, a correction is likely to ensue.

Soon after I shorted the market, however, the S&P dipped and then broke above the high for the recent trading range. Volume picked up, as traders piggybacked on the seeming volatility breakout. Within a matter of seconds, my trade went into the red, and I could feel a jolt of nervous adrenaline. I turned to my trading screen and punched in the order to cover the short sale for a loss. As soon as my stop was hit, I was ready to hit the button and exit the trade.

I realized that my fear reaction was out of proportion to the situation, however. I never like taking a loss, but I knew that my stop was set closely enough that my account would not be traumatized by getting stopped out. It was at that point that I recalled that a similar market *had* dealt me a difficult loss the prior week. Following a narrow-range period that appeared to be losing steam, I placed an order to go short. Incredibly, I forgot to check the economic calendar for the day and found that my order was executed one minute before the release of an important number. Sure enough, the number beat expectations, and the market broke out of the range with a vengeance. By the time my stop was triggered, the upside gap and slippage ensured that I took a nasty hit.

Realizing that no such economic report was likely to undermine my current trade, I took a few deep breaths and, consciously slowing my pace, examined my Excel screen to see how many stocks in the portfolio I follow were actually breaking out of the recent range. This portfolio consists of 40 stocks (the Dow 30 and 10 additional issues in a variety of industries) that mirror the action of the S&P 500. I have generally found that if the S&P breaks out to relative highs or lows, but the majority of these issues do not, then there is a high likelihood of the move being a false breakout. By dynamically linking the Excel sheets for the stocks to my Townsend Real Tick III platform, I am able to calculate breakouts and breakdowns on a running basis without the need to manually check each of the 40 issues.

To my amazement, only 7 of the 40 issues had broken out of the range to a relative new high. The "breakout" move in the S&P was almost totally accounted for by several stocks making a bounce upward. As soon as I saw this, I said out loud, "There is no way this move can be sustained." I knew from long hours of research that many more issues need to participate if a move is to have legs.

Just as I said that, my price stop was hit. For once, I made a conscious and reasoned decision to override and reconfigure my stop. Instead of basing the stop on a price level, I would stop the trade once 15 or more of the portfolio stocks made a breakout. I waited, and shortly the momentum abated. When the S&P reentered its prior range, I realized that the breakout was false and sat back with a sense of relief. The trade went on to a nice profit when the bottom of the range was violated. The market was thus able to provide me with what I had given Mary: a new ending to an old scenario.

A fun variation on this exercise is to talk aloud or to visualize past mistakes you've made when your hypotheses have been disconfirmed. For instance, if the market moved against me in the opening minutes of a past trade and I magnified my woes by doubling up on my position (trying to achieve a better average entry price), I would visualize doing this again, while laughing at myself or smiling and shaking my head. It is very difficult to become identified with a pattern if you are making it the object of humor. Laughing at oneself is a potent strategy for gaining self-perspective. When contemplating unfavorable market outcomes, think of all the things you could do to really mess up *and then ridicule them before they can ever be enacted*.

Notice how these couch tactics are not so different from the therapy with Mary. In both cases, change occurs when you experience an old, destructive pattern in real time, develop observing awareness of what is happening, shift into a different mode, and try something different. In the therapy with Mary, I helped to shake up her old patterns—afflicting her comfort—by not immediately disavowing my interest in her and by leaving the room when she became enraged. In the trading situation, the shakeup occurred when I checked my Excel sheets and realized the extent to which the breakout was narrowly based. The research, to no small degree, acted as my therapist in the trading situation by challenging my construction of events and helping me see things in another way.

The situation with the false S&P breakout demonstrated how a past trading debacle led me to become overly sensitive to its recurrence the following week. Hours of inoculation practice had taught me to question myself any time an emotional reaction in the market seemed to be excessive. The jolt of adrenaline thus became a cue to take a few deep breaths and question the basis for my reaction. Instead of becoming lost in the fear, I used it to become more deeply immersed in the data. Had the spreadsheet figures confirmed my fears, I most certainly would have exited the trade in haste and ensured that the honoring of my stop would leave my trading capital as dry as possible for the next opportunity. Instead, the figures disconfirmed my fears, allowing me to write a new ending to the script.

A couple of years ago, my 10-year-old daughter, Devon, and I were looking at market charts and preparing a joint e-mail to the Speculators List inspired by Laurel Kenner and Victor Niederhoffer. Laurel and Vic were kind enough to memorialize Devon's e-mail in a subsequent publication of Spec List insights. The market, Devon asserted, was like a school of fish. There are two types of fish that diverge from the pack: (1) the weak and infirm and (2) the leaders. The entire school will shift position in response to the leaders, leaving the weakest behind. To anticipate a prospective move, she suggested, it is necessary to identify the leaders.

I have since placed Devon's insight to good use in many trading situations. Very often, a stock sector, such as semiconductors or financial stocks, will make its breakout ahead of the general market. These sectors sometimes will also telegraph their occasional lead status by refusing to drop during a morning decline and then becoming the first groups to enter positive territory on a rebound. It is easy to become absorbed in market moves, losing sight of what the entire market is up to. For that reason, I keep handy on my screen, in minimized form, the charts of the most common lead fish. Keeping an eye on their action strengthens one's ability to become an Observer to the market and catch nascent moves.

I have found this principle to be helpful even at the finest level of resolution, following the market maker screens for various stocks and exchange-traded funds. The lead fish will be those that demonstrate the greatest stickiness in their bid/ask action in the face of institutional buying or selling. Such stickiness in the midst of premium extremes in the S&P and the Nasdaq futures and Dow TICK levels often points the way to lead fish that will diverge even further from the pack over time. It is when I am most immersed in my preconceived notions of the market that the jolt of seeing the lead fish change direction is most helpful. If you are open to the data, the market will afflict your comfort and create jolts worthy of the best therapists.

CONCLUSION

Because trading is so fast paced and emotional, it is a perfect medium for activating your repetitive emotional patterns. Once those patterns are triggered, only a significant jolt can prevent you from reenacting past solutions that have outlived their usefulness. In therapy, counselors provide this jolt by consciously countering the patterned tendencies of clients. Traders can administer their own shifts by using emotional exercises, such as desensitization, inoculation, and laughing at their old patterns, and by consulting research-based strategies that challenge their perspective on the markets.

The need for such strategies to break patterns of arousal that manifest themselves in trading appears to be especially critical for less experienced traders. In a fascinating study, Andrew Lo and Dmitry Repin of the Massachusetts Institute of Technology connected both experienced and inexperienced traders to biofeedback machines to examine their reactions to the markets. By coordinating the biofeedback with the minute-by-minute market action, the researchers were able to observe the specific market events that triggered emotional reactions from the traders. It is interesting—and perhaps not surprising—that the inexperienced traders displayed the greatest emotional responses to such market events as volatility expansions. This raises the distinct possibility that experienced traders gain their experience and success, in part, by acquiring strategies for reducing their physiological arousal in the face of challenging market events. Their prior experience, coupled with many hours of research and planning, may function as a stress inoculation, desensitizing them to the events that toss novices to and fro.

Lo and Repin's work further suggests that one need not have diagnosable emotional and behavioral disorders to find that his or her patterns sabotage good trading. *Normal and natural ways of processing information are sufficient to interfere with good trading.* A good example of this is the *endowment effect* described by researchers Tversky and Kahnemann. I may be willing to only spend $5.00 to obtain a household item. Once it is mine, however, I may not be willing to part with it for even $10.00. As soon as something becomes mine, I naturally endow it with special value and significance.

This applies to trading opinions and predictions as well. I maintain a weblog on my personal site (www.greatspeculations.com/brett/weblog.htm) in which I share my hypotheses about the markets and my thinking about trading psychology. It has become a useful part of my discipline in writing out my thoughts, obtaining useful feedback, and integrating the feedback into my subsequent trading plans. Recently I posted the results of a nearest-neighbor modeling exercise that suggested a bullish tendency over the coming 40 days. Shortly thereafter, the market made a nice upside move in the overnight session, and I entered a long position at the first morning dip, *without even consulting my other market data*. My grounding in my bullish conviction had become so great that I was no longer scanning for disconfirming data.

Had I looked carefully, I would have seen that the opening breakout was not a breakout for a majority of indexes and, indeed, was part of a larger topping pattern. It took a quick hit of three S&P points, violating my stop, to get me to question my assumptions. By the time I performed the homework I should have finished prior to the market open, my position had not only stopped out but meaningfully continued in a downward direction. Not only had I lost a few points, but I had also missed a shorting opportunity that should have been crystal clear.

It is a rare individual who can form a conviction strong enough to act on and yet remain sufficiently flexible to reverse this conviction in the face of objective evidence. Simple human nature, not any emotional disorder, cuts against this grain, allowing one to interpret the world through his or her beliefs and convictions. Successful traders are trading against their own human nature, making unnatural ways of processing information natural.

It is in this vein that I believe that markets accelerate evolution, selecting for the ability to sustain purpose. The successful trader cultivates his or her ability to stay plan-focused and disciplined even in the face of violent market action. Much as bodybuilders go to the gym to develop their physiques, traders can utilize the markets as workouts for expanding their capacities for intentional action. This makes trading one of the best of all therapy couches.

Chapter Six

The Evil Spiders

In markets as in nature, tornadoes begin in stillness; earthquakes end in aftershocks.

Communication is the therapist's stock in trade. Much of understanding another person consists of being able to read their communications, both verbal and nonverbal. My personal interest in the markets was piqued when I recognized that stocks and futures produced streams of communications not unlike those of clients. As with people, I found that what markets said often conflicted with how they said it, creating complex and rich communications.

In this chapter, we will explore the reading of people and markets and the ways that therapists and traders can become sensitive to the nuances of communication. We will take a particular look at the research of cognitive neuroscience, which suggests that we process far more information than we are aware of. As we will see, the simple but profound fact that we know much more than we know we know holds an important key to our development as traders.

COMMUNICATION AND METACOMMUNICATION

An enduring theme in psychology is the difference between communication and metacommunication. *Communication* refers to what people say—their intended meanings. *Metacommunication* refers to the body language that accompanies communication—*how* people say something. Metacommunication influences what is heard.

Many disagreements arise from discrepancies between a person's communications and his or her metacommunications. A woman, for example, may confront her husband: "Why don't you spend time with me?" If you read the words alone, they appear to be an innocent inquiry. When the words are accompanied by an annoyed tone of voice, arms folded tightly, and an elevated volume, however, a very different message is heard: one of scolding.

The husband, of course, attends to the metacommunications (actions speaking louder than words) and either beats a hasty retreat or responds defensively. Either way, the woman will feel that he has not heard her concern, that he doesn't care about her.

A classic incident once occurred in a couple's counseling session that I held with a successful businessman and his frustrated wife. At one point, she cried out in anguish, "You never say you love me." Eyes rolling upward, he said, "Okay, I love you." The wife, of course, was not satisfied. The metacommunication—the rolled eyes—spoke louder than the content of the communication.

When people are said to have good social skills, it generally means that they are adept at reading the metacommunications of others. These typically take the form of body language, vocal tone, shadings of speech, and the like. A boring person talks continuously, clueless to the shifting body postures and sideways glances of his audience. To a more socially skilled person, those are cues that the listener has tired of the conversation, just as an attentive gaze and a mirroring of tone and posture signify that the listener is tracking a speaker. The socially skilled person makes frequent midcourse corrections in the face of such cues, pursuing topics that elicit favorable nonverbal response and minimizing those that turn off the listener.

The process of attending to cues and making those midcourse corrections should sound familiar to traders. Socially skilled individuals cannot predict the predilections of their companions. But they can be alert for the metacommunications that reveal those predilections—and the shifts in those preferences over time. Nimbleness, not the ability to peer into a crystal ball, is the hallmark of both the skilled communicator and the successful trader.

There are important implications attached to this line of thought. Markets, like people, engage in communications and metacommunications. A market's communications are its movements over time: up 10 percent in three weeks, down five points in the past hour, and so on. The market's metacommunications describe *how* it makes these movements: gradually or suddenly, on high or low volume and volatility, with a majority of stocks participating or not participating, and so on. Much of what we call technical analysis is an effort to read the metacommunications of the market.

Imagine two similar five-minute bar charts: The first depicts a market that has risen from A to B in the span of a day. Its rise was steady and trending. The second chart also shows a market that has risen from A to B during the day session. But this rise was choppy: periods of buying were interspersed with squalls of selling. The market's communications are identical, but the metacommunications are anything but identical.

The market in the first chart is relatively efficient: The distance it traveled over the entire day closely resembles the sum of the distance traveled during each five-minute time span. The second market is inefficient: It traveled a considerable distance from period to period just to arrive at the same end point. Such inefficiency is an important market metacommunication. It means that the primary trend is encountering significant disruption. A decrease in efficiency—the ratio of distance traveled over a time span to the distance traveled within that span—very often precedes a change of trend. Markets, like rivers and humans, begin their lives straight and swift and end in quiet meandering.

The same phenomenon can be observed in therapy. Shifts in efficiency precede important changes in thought, feeling, and behavior. Such shifts are among the most important metacommunications. Before a person ever becomes so depressed that they contemplate suicide, subtle signs of inefficiency emerge: They stop enjoying the things that used to bring pleasure; they cannot tolerate stresses with which they had been coping previously; situations they had tackled with energy now become overwhelming. When people with histories of depression and suicide no longer respond to positive stimuli in their accustomed way, they are exhibiting a useful leading indicator of suicidality. The absence of the positive often is predictive of the future emergence of the negative.

In a similar vein, if you think of the market as a factory—a production system with inputs and outputs—then you can ask meaningful questions about the relationship of inputs to outputs. These are crucial metacommunications for markets, as for people. A market will rise on a given level of advance-decline strength among stocks. Then, suddenly, there will be a shift. A positive advance-decline reading will no longer generate higher prices. The price chart flattens out, even in the face of indicator strength. The market factory is no longer as efficient; it is taking more input to gain the same output. That, for the market as for the depressed client, is a potential leading indicator of trouble.

Conversely, a market may decline for days, bounce, and then hit a new wave of selling, as measured by the New York Stock Exchange (NYSE) TICK. But the selling may not take the majority of stocks to new lows. The market is losing efficiency to the downside. This subtle but meaningful metacommunication precedes a great number of advances, even on an intraday basis.

Skilled tape readers appear to be individuals who have spent sufficient time immersed in the markets that they are able to read the subtle shifts of momentum, acceleration, and volatility that precede trending movements. This seems to especially hold true for floor traders, who scalp small moves over a matter of seconds. With trades lasting such a brief time, there is no opportunity for elaborate statistical analysis. Instead, the traders become exquisitely attuned to the subtle metacommunications of the floor: the activity of trading, the ebb and flow of volume in the pits, the quick shifts in the bids and asks, the pattern of activity among the major and minor players. Little wonder that many floor traders initially struggle with their trading when they move upstairs. Denied their database—those metacommunications that guide their internal sense of rhythm and momentum in the markets—they are temporarily left without a trading rudder.

METACOMMUNICATIONS IN TRADING

I know all too well the experience of trading without a rudder. When I first began analyzing the markets, I treated all rises and declines similarly. If the market rose 5 percent over 20 days, I would scan my database for all occasions in which the market had made a similar move. I would then see what happened subsequently on each of those occasions, in hopes of identifying a nonrandom pattern.

While admirably quantitative, my approach was equivalent to participating in a conversation with my eyes closed. My approach allowed me to pick up the communications of the market, but not the metacommunications. It made me a socially unskilled—and not very successful—trader.

An analogy best captures my predicament. Of the romances I observe among the students I teach, far and away the least successful are those that begin online. Typically, the parties meet in a chat room or through a relationship-oriented web site. They begin a frequent round of communications, often sharing intimate details of their lives. Elated at the prospect of meeting someone who really listens and cares, they arrange a face-to-face meeting.

That is when it all falls apart.

The online medium removes most elements of metacommunication from interactions. When you're chatting online, you can't see that the other person has a depressed tone of voice, a disheveled appearance, or a shifty-eyed charm. The person you fantasize about on the Internet ends up being wildly different from the person you meet. Much of what people experience as personal chemistry emanates from mutual responses to metacommunications.

Trading without an appreciation of metacommunication has about as much chance of success as online dating. As important as *what* the market is doing is *how* it is doing it. Markets are like people: They signal changes in their emotional states with shifts in metacommunication. I refer to these subtle changes as "gearshifts."

If you have ever driven a manual transmission automobile, you are familiar with gear shifting. At a high gear, the car will reach a rapid speed for a given level of engine revolutions per minute (RPM), perhaps 140 miles per hour, before the tachometer hits the redline. At a lower gear, the car will reach the redline well before this maximum speed: Lots of revs produce less speed, but greater acceleration. If you want to pull out into traffic quickly, a low gear will provide maximum torque, propelling you into the flow. If you want to cruise at high speeds along the highway, a high gear will work best.

A capable driver is one who knows when to upshift and when to downshift, depending on road conditions. Driving is an active process, involving continuous adjustment to turns in the road, traffic patterns, road surface conditions, and so forth.

People shift gears, as well, in the course of their conversations. The gearshifts take the form of changes in the volume, the rate, and the inflection of speech. Other gearshifts are manifested as body language, as when a person alters their posture in response to a topic. Often, by watching the metacommunications of two people having a conversation, you can determine whether they are in sync. Rapport between people is evident when each person tracks the metacommunications of the other. The result is an elegant ballet, in which eye movements, vocal tones, and bodily postures are coordinated in a manner that could never be duplicated by conscious effort.

Conversely, you can tell when a conversation is going poorly when the parties are shifting gears at different times and in different ways. The result is akin to a speedway in which some drivers are accelerating, while others are slowing down. A pileup is the likely outcome.

If there is one thing known about therapy, it is that the outcome is highly dependent on the rapport that develops between counselor and client. Therapists are unlikely to have any influence and credibility if their clients do not trust them. Consequently, the first task of a therapist—or anyone in a field where results hinge on the quality of the relationship, whether it is dating, sales, or medicine—is to develop a strong bond. In therapy, like dating or sales, results will occur much more quickly when rapport is present from the start.

As in Mary's case, I invariably begin my work with a new client by engaging in small talk and scanning for the subsequent metacommunications. I especially like to introduce an element of humor or chitchat in the opening minutes of sessions. The responses are instructive, indicating whether people will be able to stand sufficiently apart from their concerns to engage in humor. If the client responds to my "How are you?" by subsequently asking how I am doing, or if they can chat about sports, the weather, or the latest school rumor, it is a sure sign that they are not overloaded by their presenting problems.

I utilize such interpersonal indicators the way a trader employs market indicators. When people do not give the "normal" response to a situation, it is a sign that something abnormal is afoot. Similarly, when markets fail to respond normally to an interest-rate cut or to a piece of good earnings news, it is a metacommunication worthy of attention. It means that the market is not shifting gears when expected. There may be trouble on the expressway dead ahead.

Dashed expectations are one of the most important metacommunications a market can give you. When the market is not doing what it is supposed to be doing, the chances are good that a profitable opportunity is at hand. This is why my early efforts to investigate current periods by investigating all similar past periods missed the boat. The context of that move—whether it occurred after favorable economic news or interest-rate hikes, whether it was achieved on low volatility and breadth, whether it occurred all at once early in the period or was evenly spread throughout—makes all the difference in the world with respect to future expectations. What traders see on the screen is the market's conversation with them. Like psychologists, traders want to be attentive to the tone and the pace of the communications, not just to their literal meaning.

Here is a simple example of such attentiveness. A market moves sharply lower for two or three days in a row, carrying the majority of stocks to multiday lows. The following day, it opens lower still, perhaps aided by the comments of pundits who latch onto the evident weakness. This morning drop, however, is subtly different from that of the past several days. The NYSE Composite TICK—the number of stocks making downticks versus upticks at each moment—stays well above its prior lows. One or more sector indexes may even resist the morning decline, suggesting pockets of strength in the market.

Many traders fail to read the metacommunications. They are wired as human beings to look for patterns—signs of meaning—in the things they perceive. Once something happens two or three times in a row, traders are likely to see it as part of a meaningful pattern. When they experience a market decline for several days, their normal human expectation is to expect continuation.

On such occasions, I generally look to see how traders are responding to the market as a useful piece of body language. One of my favorite ways of doing that is to take an exchange-traded fund (ETF), such as the SPY or QQQ, and watch its action trade by trade. Specifically, I look for the proportion of trades that are being made in small lots—100 or 200 shares—versus very large lots. Very often, it is the smaller, less-sophisticated trader who fails to read the market's language. If the proportion of small trades spikes up during the morning decline, even as pockets of strength are evident, it's generally worth fading the little guys. They are missing the market's metacommunications.

As I indicated earlier, I have also found the intraday volume of the Standard & Poor's (S&P) and Nasdaq E-Mini contracts to be useful in reading the metacommunications of the market. A scrutiny of one-minute volume readings placed in the context of market action suggests that a large proportion of the small, E-Mini traders operate in a breakout mode, piling into the market on new highs and lows. When there is such a rush to enter or exit on a weak breakout—one in which a significant number of sectors and stocks do not participate—these often turn out to be false breakouts and profitable opportunities for fading the crowd. Your position will benefit once the herd has to unwind its positions.

When the market reverses its down open and moves into positive territory, or when it reverses a seeming breakout, the action violates the psychological expectations of traders. They're expecting a fifth-gear cruise downward, and the market suddenly downshifts and heads north. Temporarily they are out of sync with the market, just as I am out of sync with a client who cannot respond to my humor.

Good traders—like good psychologists—know what to do in such circumstances. They have a short throw on their manual transmissions and can shift gears at a moment's notice. Some of the best trades occur when the market violates logical or psychological expectations. A trader's own emotional reactions to such about-face moves can provide some of the best cues for engaging his or her gearshifts.

The majority of very short term traders lack the time to engage in lengthy mathematical analyses of the market and hence rely on more readily available tools, such as chart patterns. These patterns frame the traders' expectations and, as a result, become a useful tool to trade against when those expectations are not met.

While the average trader may be focused on the communication—the chart pattern or oscillator signal—the metacommunications may be pointing in a very different direction. A good example is a region of flat price action following a nice market advance. The flat action interrupts the rise on the charts and thus naturally appears as a forming top. Indeed, the technically minded trader may even monitor volume in the flat region and conclude that a decline is at hand because a waning number of shares are changing hands.

Missing from the trader's analysis is a reading of the market's body language, an appreciation for *how* the market is correcting during this flat period. An instructive exercise is following a basket of stocks and observing new highs and new lows on a short-term basis. In my own trading, the aforementioned basket of 40 stocks (30 Dow issues and 10 tech, financial, transportation, and other issues to mimic the S&P 500) offers a nice reading of metacommunication. Specifically, I monitor the number of new highs and new lows being made on a rolling 30-minute, 2-hour, and 10-hour basis. (Ten hours corresponds to roughly 1.5 days of trading). Longer-term, position traders may utilize a lengthier time frame for counting new highs and new lows, such as a 20-day period. The important thing in trading a consolidating market is that you be able to observe the shifts among new highs and new lows within the period of consolidation.

It is interesting that what appears to be a topping region may end up looking quite different when placed under the metacommunication microscope. With each drop inside the flat zone, fewer stocks make new lows. The negative TICK numbers during selling periods dry up at higher levels. Volatility begins to move a bit upward. Then, bam! The market breaks out of the flat area to the upside. The shorts are forced to cover on the volatility breakout, further fueling the upward move.

Later, the faked-out traders will look at the chart and see an upward trend dwarfing the flat region. They will shake their heads and wonder how they missed such an "obvious" move. They may even search for new chart patterns and advisory services to remedy their errors. All of this is akin to shuffling the deck chairs on the *Titanic*. Reexamining communications will not avail when the issue is one of metacommunication.

THE COMMUNICATIONS OF TRADERS' BODIES

Traders have their own body language, which can be very helpful to monitor. Traders are constantly communicating, even when they are not talking. Their facial expressions, body postures, and gestures all communicate their emotional state to the outside world. Unfortunately, most traders do not attend to their bodies and, hence, are unaware of these most valuable sources of information.

The psychiatrist Wilhelm Reich first introduced the idea that people's emotional defenses are actually bodily phenomena. People tense their muscles and hold their bodies in awkward positions in order to prevent themselves from experiencing uncomfortable emotions or impulses. If, for instance, I am particularly threatened by my own anger toward my children (because it contradicts my image of myself as a loving father), I may become particularly tense during a moment of conflict. I will tighten the muscles in my forehead and try with all my might to banish the evil thoughts that no good dad should have. Later, inexplicably, I will complain to my wife that I have a headache and feel exhausted, completely unaware of the internal, emotional battle I have been waging.

Various approaches to therapy have been developed to utilize shifts in people's physical state as triggers for reprocessing their problem patterns. In bioenergetic work, for example, a person may find herself feeling sad for no apparent reason. After relaxing her muscles and unfolding her arms and legs, she may suddenly gain access to new pieces of information. Only then will she recall that today is the anniversary of an important loss.

The metacommunications of one's body are vitally important because the body often knows things that the mind does not. Or, more properly, you process the world nonverbally before making sense of it through language. If you can read your own body language, you can obtain a deep insight into the goings on of Mind #2.

A parenting example comes to mind. When my son Macrae was in his preschool years, he had periods of frustration where he would tune out adults and even lash out verbally. The imposition of limits seemed to make the problem even worse. He would simply escalate the anger and become increasingly defiant. His day care provider's concern mounted, as she could find no way to communicate with him at those times.

I found these emotional episodes to be draining and unpleasant. After a long day of counseling, I had few emotional reserves for being considerate and sensitive. Indeed, I found myself tensing up when I entered the door, anticipating the worst. I knew, however, that simply discharging my anger would be counterproductive. Like my clients, like everyone, I felt helpless, and I initially tried to bury my frustration.

One evening at home, Macrae was playing on the indoor playground in our basement and broke one of his toys. He immediately launched into a tirade and refused to come upstairs for his dinner. I called to him once . . . then twice . . . then three times. I could hear a slight escalation in my voice. The situation was growing increasingly tense for both of us.

Then I looked down.

Oddly, my right hand was curled in a tight position. It was as if I was trying to make a fist but had stopped myself midway. Indeed, on reflection, I suspect that is exactly what had happened. I was angry toward Crae and wanted to lash out, but I could not allow myself to do such a thing.

Awkwardly, I looked down at my rigid, curled hand and took a deep breath, stepping back from the situation. A strange thought entered my head. My hand looked like a spider.

I tore my eyes away from my hand and looked at Macrae. It was as if I were seeing him in a different light. He didn't seem so angry. He looked sad. I sensed that trying to force the issue would only make his sulking and frustration worse, so I moved next to him. As I approached, I could tell he expected me to reprimand him or threaten consequences if he didn't come upstairs. Maybe he expected to be spanked.

I leaned down, picked him up, and looked directly into his eyes. I set him down on the couch and explained to him that he was going to be attacked by "evil spiders" that tickle boys unmercifully. I showed him my curled hand and explained that these spiders were very fast and difficult to catch. I also explained that the spiders could only be conquered with kisses; forceful blows only added to their strength, whereas kisses made them turn into "nice spiders."

Crae's eyes lit up as the spiders crawled toward him. After a few tickles, he managed to catch one and give it a kiss, whereupon it stopped tickling and, instead, offered gentle strokes to his face. Other spiders were much faster and took a while to chase down and kiss. The downside of the exercise was that our food got pretty cold. The good part was that Crae's attention was entirely absorbed by this new game. By venting his frustrated energies toward a game of affection, a tantrum became a kissing, stroking, and bonding episode, and a broken toy was forgotten.

On my end, by attending to my body, I had learned something about my emotional state. This, in turn, activated my Internal Observer and allowed me to channel my anger differently. Most important, there was valuable information in my curled hand that formed the basis for a creative and constructive response to the situation. Playing "evil spiders" was not a consciously thought-out strategy. *My body had provided the inspiration for the game even before I had given it a name.* From half-formed fist to spider, my body had created a useful pivot chord.

I suspect that most people can identify occasions when their bodies knew something before they were consciously aware of the knowledge. Most of the time they chalk such occasions up to intuition and leave it at that. They fail to realize that their bodies are operating under the guidance of a mind and that it is a different mind from the one with which they consciously identify. This nonverbal, action-oriented, emotion-based mind is a treasure house of useful information if one can only attend to its (meta)communications.

I have repeatedly observed the value of bodily communication in trading situations. A couple of months ago, I placed a routine trade, shorting the market when it appeared that upside momentum had waned. I was trading off one of my favorite patterns, which compares intraday cumulative uptick and downtick readings of the Dow Jones Industrial Average (TIKI) with the readings for price and the NYSE TICK. Because the Dow stocks are heavily traded by institutions, they are quite responsive to program trading. The comparison of the TIKI to both the TICK and the price change of the S&P index gives a rapid reading of the degree to which institutional trading is able to move the market. If there is a great deal of institutional trading in a particular direction and if the general market fails to move commensurately, one can often profit from the market's metacommunication and fade the move.

On this particular occasion, I placed the short trade, as the elevated TIKI was not accompanied by strong upside price or TICK action over a period of two hours. Such a trade is usually good for an intraday countertrend move at the very least. I've researched and traded the pattern long enough to feel comfortable with it.

After placing the trade, however, I was anything but comfortable. I watched each subsequent tick like a hawk, following the fate of my position. Moreover, after a few minutes I suddenly realized I had a headache. I had been hunched forward in my chair, thrusting my eyes closer to the screen. My eyes were fatigued and my muscles felt tense.

It was as if I had awakened. I shook my head and said out loud, "What are you doing?" I *never* follow a trade so obsessively, especially a trade as small as the one I had placed. I realized, however, that my body was not comfortable with the trade, even though I had seemed to be. Despite telling myself I had a high-odds trade, my body was already mobilized for danger.

Now attending to my body's concern, I looked at the charts in a new light, comparing the one-minute time frame to the larger multiday picture. It then hit me that the trade was not progressing as it should. The market had backed off from its highs but was not approaching the support level that I had targeted. Worse still, it appeared that good resistance wasn't to be seen until much higher. I had made a mistake. I had become so wrapped up in the short-term action that I had missed the larger picture. The market was at a relative high, all right, but it was only a way station to higher levels.

Quickly I scratched the trade, turning a potential loser into a useful learning experience.

I swear I had no idea the trade was going sour. But somehow my body knew.

THE MIND BENEATH THE HUMAN MIND

This body-metacommunication stuff seems pretty mystical, and yet it is supported by a wealth of research in cognitive neuroscience. People do indeed know many things of which their minds are not aware.

Tor Norretranders, in his provocative book *The User Illusion*, offers a simple example. Suppose you are at bat in a baseball game and the pitch veers toward your head. In a flash, you hit the ground to avoid being beaned. The pitch, traveling maybe 90 miles per hour, is heading toward you too quickly for you to consciously identify what is happening and formulate an appropriate strategy. In fact, what happens is that you hit the ground and *then* realize that you had almost been hit. The conscious, explicit thought *follows* both awareness and action.

Norretranders points out that this is the case for good reason. Your consciousness operates at a bandwidth far too slow to allow for the efficient processing of information in such dangerous situations. By linking motor channels to a faster mind processor, nature provides you with the highly adaptive capacity to bypass plodding thought and to act to preserve yourself.

The research of Benjamin Libet vividly demonstrates the relative speed of human mind-processors. Libet had his subjects flex their finger or move their hand whenever they chose. All subjects were wired to measure electrical activity in the hand as a way of determining the relationship between the conscious intent of the subjects and their motor activity. Libet discovered, surprisingly, that the electrical readiness potential in the hand starts a bit over half a second before the person consciously executes the finger or hand movement.

For those accustomed to the idea that they *are* their conscious minds, Libet's research is inexplicable. Bodies begin their movement, he found, before the person has consciously formulated the intent to move. The mind does not determine the body's action. It reports what had already begun a fraction of a second earlier. The performance of every conscious, voluntary act, Libet concluded, is preceded by subconscious cerebral processing.

Norretranders refers to the conscious mind as a "user illusion" because it gives the illusion that it is in control of a person's behavior, when generally this is not the case. The term "user illusion" is taken from the computing world. To the uninitiated, it appears that the user interface, such as Microsoft Windows, controls the computer when, in fact, the computer's operations are occurring at a level beneath the interface, in a binary world of machine code.

If your conscious mind is a reporter of your actions and not simply an initiator, it raises an uncomfortable question. How accurate are the reports of your conscious experience? Can you trust your own mind?

Here is where the pioneering research of Michael Gazzaniga and of Joseph LeDoux is particularly relevant. As described earlier, these researchers worked with people with epilepsy who had undergone surgery to the corpus collosum, severing the connection between left- and right-brain hemispheres. They found that individuals with split brains could function reasonably well but also demonstrated certain peculiarities. For instance, people shown different images to their left and right eyes could point to what they had seen with their left and right hands, respectively. When asked what they had seen, however, they could only name the item presented to the right eye. The information to the left eye, wired to the nonverbal right-brain hemisphere, was lost to conscious, verbal awareness—even though the individuals clearly knew what they were seeing and could point to it!

The breakthrough came when Gazzaniga and LeDoux asked the individuals *why* they had pointed to the picture with their left hand. The specific situation, observed with an individual dubbed P.S., was that the left field of vision (right-brain hemisphere) was presented with a picture of snow, while the right field (left-brain hemisphere) was shown a chicken claw. P.S. could then point with his left hand to a snow shovel and with his right hand to a chicken to demonstrate that he had, indeed, seen each item correctly.

When asked what he had seen, P.S. responded that he saw the chicken picture. When asked why, then, he had pointed with his left hand to the snow shovel, P.S. promptly responded that you need a shovel to clean out the chicken shed!

Gazzaniga's conclusion, captured in his book *The Mind's Past*, is that the conscious, verbal mind is actually an interpreter. P.S. had no real idea why he had pointed to the shovel, so his verbal, reasoning mind came up with a plausible—but completely irrelevant—rationale. People's minds, Gazzaniga argues, do not present them with raw data regarding the world. Rather, their verbal, conscious depictions of the world are interpretations taken from more basic data that register at nonverbal levels. *What a person is conscious of is a construction of events, not events themselves.*

In this light, my trading experience with the uncomfortable short sale makes sense. Consciously, I had woven a rationale for the short position. At a nonverbal level, the trade did not feel right because the patterns I perceived did not fit my prior experience. I had looked at so many charts and internalized their patterns that I could detect deviations from the norm before I had consciously identified them.

Some may argue that this line of inquiry destroys the understanding of human reason. If I cannot trust my mind, how can I ever know the world? Such a skeptical conclusion, I believe, is unwarranted. It is not that human beings lack reason, but that *there is far more to human reason than conscious, verbal experience.* When you duck from a thrown pitch prior to consciously identifying what happened, you are behaving most reasonably, albeit nonconsciously. You are at your most rational when you coordinate your minds, gathering information, making sense of it, and testing your understanding with future experience. This, of course, is the task of any trader.

There is much to be said for mechanical trading systems and their potential for reducing the human, emotional element in trading. Like Deep Blue, the chess-playing computer, mechanical systems may ferret out opportunities in the market far more efficiently with brute force than can a good trader. And yet chess masters do not rely simply on brute force. They have so immersed themselves in the patterns of the game that they can see moves far in advance. This allows them to quickly respond to situations that don't neatly follow the scripts of games they've studied. The great chess players, after long years of immersing themselves in the game, have reached the point where they are processing moves on the board nonconsciously, aligning their "intuition" with their "reason."

A similar phenomenon may well be at work in market mastery. While it is comforting to rely on the advice of market gurus, there is no substitute for the deep knowledge that comes from immersing oneself in market patterns. One of my best steps as a trader was to print out every day's market action, along with every reading of every indicator I follow, for a period of years. Reviewing these charts each night cemented into my mind the normal ways the market moves, allowing my body to sense deviations from the norm, those all-important metacommunications of the market.

This, I believe, helps to explain why the development of focus and concentration through daily rituals of market study is a common theme among those who have mentored successful traders. Only daily immersion in the markets can provide the base of information needed for the subconscious mind to discern normal from abnormal events. The psychologist Dean Keith Simonton has summarized research suggesting that greatness in any field of endeavor requires 50,000 chunks of information. Such a storehouse of knowledge can only be acquired through years of intensive study. The average trader, tossed to and fro by various mind states, is poorly equipped to sustain such effort. If immersion is crucial to reading the metacommunications of markets—just as it is critical to learning a foreign language—it is little wonder that emotionally reactive traders fail to master the markets. Their self-focused attention competes with the very processing of subtle information that provides the basis for trading expertise.

KNOWING MORE THAN YOU KNOW: IMPLICIT LEARNING

Step back for a moment and ask how children are able to acquire complex skills, such as speaking their native language and engaging in proper social interaction. When children are very young, they have not yet internalized the rules of grammar and syntax. As a result, they often speak in fragmented sentences, with improper usage. When I was a very young child, I could recognize Chevrolet cars on the road and would call out, "Da-da-da." Although I didn't know the word "Chevrolet," I clearly had an idea of Chevrolet and the fact that it consisted of three syllables. Similarly, before our young son Macrae had the word for "celery," he would ask us for a "lettuce stick."

The rules of social behavior are acquired in much the same way. Young children typically lack an internalized sense of etiquette and manners and will interrupt conversations, take toys from other children, and otherwise fail to contain their impulses. Later, they learn to wait their turn, to ask permission for things they want, and to demonstrate sensitivity to others. Even before they can verbalize these rules, however, they seem to possess rudimentary knowledge of social rights and wrongs. A young child who could never verbally conceptualize rules of proper behavior still will hide a wrongdoing as soon as a parent enters the room. The child knows that he or she is doing something wrong but cannot verbally express the basis for this knowing.

Michael Polanyi has referred to this as *tacit knowledge*. Much of what you know, you cannot verbalize. An excellent example is your recognition of people's faces. You would know the face of a good friend if you saw it, yet it is unlikely that you could provide a verbal description that would allow a stranger to recognize the friend in a crowd. The web of interrelationships that comprise a face is simply too complex and nuanced—too fuzzy—

to neatly fit the categorical terms of language: dark hair, light hair; short, tall; and so on.

As a young child, I knew Chevrolet, but my knowing was not amenable to verbalization. This is common among children in general: Their receptive language competencies precede their skills at spoken language. Long before a child can say, "I want a banana," she can nod "yes" to "Do you want a banana?" or reach out when she sees a banana. The concept of *banana* is there in some form; but it is tacit, rather than explicit.

Cognitive scientist Axel Cleeremans and colleagues in Brussels believe that all knowledge is graded in consciousness, beginning as tacit, implicit knowing and moving through various levels of awareness until it is fully explicit and verbal. Macrae's "lettuce stick" is a nice example of an intermediate level of verbal knowing. He clearly knew that there was a resemblance between celery and lettuce (green vegetable), and he knew the shape of celery (stick-like); but he did not yet possess the word *celery*. Cleeremans's provocative contention is that most learning begins as implicit knowing—people acquire knowledge and skills but are not able to verbalize what they have acquired. This *implicit learning*, he believes, captures how people acquire language, learn faces, and internalize rules of social interaction.

Later in this book, I will explore implicit learning and its profound implications for acquiring expertise in trading. For now, one implication stands out above others: Traders can know things about the markets without necessarily being able to verbalize them. If reading a market's communications and metacommunications is like reading social interactions, it is not surprising that beginning traders would be as unskilled in their readings as children might be in social situations. Moreover, it would not be surprising if their first dawning awareness of patterns in the market manifested itself tacitly and implicitly, rather than explicitly and verbally. Traders are going to feel what they know, point to it, and utilize imprecise language to express their knowledge long before they can accurately describe and convey it to others. Much of the accumulated wisdom of technical analysis is like Macrae's "lettuce sticks": a halting effort to capture, in words and pictures, pieces of internalized knowledge.

Are such efforts necessarily accurate? Perhaps not. The successful trader utilizing a Fibonacci method or a chart-reading technique may be very much like Gazzaniga and LeDoux's patient P.S. Recall that P.S. was the split-brain patient who was shown snow and a chicken claw to his left and right eyes, respectively. When asked to point to a picture that described an aspect of what he had seen, he could point with his left hand to a snow shovel and with his right hand to a chicken. But he could only verbalize what he had seen with his right eye, the chicken. When asked why he had responded with his left hand to the shovel, he invented a rationale: He asserted that one needed a shovel to clean out the chicken coop!

It may well be that theories of trading are similar rationales: The verbal, explicit mind attempts to make sense of what the trader is experiencing tacitly. The Gann, Elliott, oscillator, chart, and candlestick patterns on which many traders rely are constructed explanations for their felt understandings, helping them make sense of their experience. As with P.S., however, the explanations may have little to do with underlying reality. They fill more of a psychological need—traders' need for coherence—than an epistemological one.

This phenomenon is not unique to trading. Studies of psychotherapy processes and outcomes consistently find that what therapists do in sessions and what they *say* they do are widely discrepant. In short, therapists rely on their favorite theories to describe their behavior in sessions—cognitive, psychoanalytic, humanistic approaches—but rarely adhere to these schools of thought in any systematic fashion. Indeed, studies suggest that skilled, experienced therapists across these different schools behave surprisingly similarly. Moreover, these similar elements appear to be more crucial to the success of therapy than the specific, unique techniques advocated by each of the schools of thought.

In trading terms, the various theories of charting, indicator analysis, cycle behavior, and waves may have more to do with how traders describe their actions than with their actual behaviors and understandings. I have noticed this during my own participation in Linda Raschke's trading chatroom, an educational service that allows traders to watch Linda trade the markets in real time. Many times, Linda has pointed out a buy or a sell signal at the same time that I have noticed it. However, whereas Linda might explain the pattern as a function of a chart configuration and a volatility-based oscillator reading, I might describe the pattern in terms of a waning level of buying or selling on the intraday advance/decline and new high/low data. We saw the same thing—and traded very similarly on those occasions—but captured our understandings quite differently. One can only wonder if both of us didn't first detect the waning velocity tacitly, only later scanning for the evidence to support our felt understandings. This would fit with Libet's research, in which our bodies respond to situations before our conscious minds.

If this line of research and reasoning has validity, it points to a central dilemma of trading psychology: *At the same time that traders need to dampen emotional reactions that skew information processing, they need to be sensitive to the felt tendencies that capture their implicit knowing.* On the one hand, if the general in the field (the left hemisphere) is overly sensitive to the data accumulated by the sentries and scouts (the right hemisphere), adhering to a plan of attack will be difficult. On the other hand, if the general does not heed the scouts, there is a risk of failing to update those attack plans in the face of changed realities. Learning to distinguish between the distortions of emotional arousal and the tacit knowledge of one's body—to remain open to experience while not lost within it—is perhaps the greatest challenge a trader faces in cultivating trading expertise.

MINDING THE COMPLEXITY OF THE MARKETS

This brings up a second, and perhaps even more problematic, dilemma. The patterns of the markets may be fuzzier—more nuanced and complex—than the language traders use to describe them. This would make describing trading much like describing a person's face. Although a description could capture the gross contours of shape of eyes, skin color, and so on, it is unlikely that it could fully capture that person's look. Similarly, attempts to describe markets in terms of "head and shoulders" patterns, "double tops and bottoms," and "rising wedges" capture the gross contours of price action—what I have called the market's communications—but hardly the contexts in which the action has occurred (metacommunications).

The coarse grain of language relative to market action suggests that the answer to this dilemma is not the discovery of a better indicator, chart pattern, or technical analytic approach. All of these are like the blind men's description of the elephant in the famous tale—approximations that cannot possibly capture the whole. "If you see the Buddha on the road, shoot him!" captures the understanding that Buddhahood—enlightenment—is to be found within experience, rather than in any self-proclaimed expert. Similarly, if you find a trading guru on the road, the best course of action is to dismiss him. The real trading guru may also exist within, at that tacit level of knowing.

Expertise in other fields of endeavor is similarly difficult to capture in words.

Chess players, football running backs, and racecar drivers often know the right move to make without first engaging in an explicit reasoning process. Moreover, when you ask them to explain their moves, they often provide very sketchy rationales. They know how to perform, but they can't necessarily capture their knowledge verbally. This makes the development of expert systems especially difficult because the experts must somehow convey their knowledge to computer programmers for it to be expressed in an artificial intelligence language. If not all of our knowing can be captured verbally, however, any such attempt to translate expertise into words will fall short.

This, I believe, offers a compelling reason for utilizing the language of mathematics over normal verbal expression for capturing market understandings. If I have a set of market predictors, I can explore not only the relationships between these predictors and price change, but also the interrelationships among the predictors and their relationship to price change. Some simple interactions can be expressed in words, such as breakout trades working at one time of day but not at another. More complex interactions, however, interrelating a market's price change and volatility over multiple time frames, form a multidimensional conceptual space that eludes normal description. It is not surprising that statisticians rely on three-dimensional maps to describe the contours of predicted variables as a function of predictors. Pictures are worth a thousand words precisely because they convey information not readily expressed verbally.

It is unfortunate that many proponents of statistical modeling disavow any role for intuition in the markets and that many intuitive traders shun mathematics. I believe the two exist in a reciprocal relationship that is critical for successful trading. Traders' first market understandings manifest themselves intuitively, as felt tendencies, that traders can point to before they can fully describe them. These tendencies, however, can be investigated for their underlying similarities, their essential ingredients. These ingredients are promising candidate predictors in the development of empirical trading rules and systems.

In my own trading, I have found that many of my successful intuitive intraday trades reflect an awareness of an initial pullback in a nascent trend that permits a relatively low-risk entry. Although the newly developing trend can be tracked on traditional technical indicators, it is generally the case that I first experience this shift as a reluctance of the market to continue its prior direction, followed by a relative ease of movement in the new direction. By translating this experience into numerical form, translating reluctance and ease of movement in terms of the NYSE Composite TICK and short-term new highs and new lows in my basket of stocks, I can then attempt to create a more general trading model from my insight. I may find, for example, that when there is a breakout number of short-term new highs among the stocks that is accompanied by a two-standard-deviation upward move in the TICK, prices are significantly likely to continue upward for a particular period of time. In this way, I have furthered my learning by capturing in explicit form my basic intuitive understanding. No collection of expertise may be completely exhausted in verbal or even quantitative rules, but the shift from more tacit to more explicit knowing provides greater control over trading.

Indeed, this is Cleeremans's conclusion regarding the function of consciousness. *People have developed the capacity for explicit awareness to facilitate greater flexibility and control over their actions.* When clients in therapy become verbally aware of their tacit behavior patterns, they are in a better place to interrupt these patterns and to try something different. When traders can capture felt understandings as systematized trading rules, they retain the value of their subjective knowing, while attaining a measure of distance from distracting and distorting emotional responses. The most successful traders I have observed have been intuitive observers of the market who have been able to capture their intuitions as rules and who then trade in a rule-governed manner. Their rules—like their bodies—seem to know what to do in the market before they do.

CONCLUSION

The idea that traders know more than they know they know in the markets fits nicely with the solution-focused approach to trading emphasized earlier. Traders' best trading reflects their tacit knowing, and this is the foundation on which they build in cultivating trading expertise. Although it is instructive to review errors in entries, exits, and money management, a simple elimination of mistakes will not in itself build mastery. Rather, it is by discovering what one knows tacitly and translating this into explicit rules that one can establish personal templates for success.

These templates are best cemented by powerful emotional experiences. Sheer repetition is valuable in acquiring new action patterns, but the vivid *experience* of a new pattern registers more enduringly than mere verbal rehashing. In the therapy of Ken, Sue, and Mary, a crucial element in their learning was the experience of a powerful disconfirmation of their beliefs and expectations. If learning—that transition from tacit to more explicit knowing—can be accelerated through emotional means, then crisis should be a powerful learning tool, both in life and trading.

Chapter Seven

The Big Man beneath the Bed

It is not the presence of stress but the absence of well-being that afflicts the soul.

If there was a formula for lasting personal change, it might approximate the following: *Identify your greatest fears and face them as directly as possible, so that you find out they are not as powerful as they seemed.* If you were a child who was afraid of the dark, hiding under the covers would not be the answer to your fear. Rather, turning on a light to dispel the dark would show you that there were no monsters or bogeymen. Successful therapy shines a light on your personal fears and inhibitions, allowing you to move beyond them.

Crises are powerful catalysts for change because they force us to directly confront our worst fears. Just as what does not destroy us makes us stronger, as Nietzsche asserted, the crises we successfully face provide a sense of mastery that cannot be induced by mere conversation. Such crises, indelibly etched in our minds, hasten the process of emotional learning, moving us rapidly from tacit to explicit knowing. Brief therapy, in this sense, can be thought of as a tool for accelerated learning, truncating the normal, gradual movement from intuition to verbal understanding. In this chapter we will explore how

our tacit knowledge—the solutions that lie just beneath our verbal awareness—can point the way to resolving crises and can facilitate the development of traders, much as these solutions accelerate personal change.

BIG, SILENT WALT

Walt was an imposing medical student: at least six-foot-four and 250 pounds.
He was not gregarious. He had a quiet, intense demeanor and the sense of
always being on edge. Walt seemed removed from most people. He had few
friends and rarely smiled.

Among those feeling removed from Walt was his girlfriend, Janie. She
professed a deep love for Walt, but she finally reached the end of her rope
when Walt could not respond to a recent emotional dilemma that she faced.
In no uncertain terms, she told Walt to get help or the relationship was over.

I generally dislike meeting with people who are referred by others under
a threat of consequences. They rarely have the motivation to stick with the
intensive effort needed to make life changes. Walt, however, was an exception. He made it very clear that he loved Janie and would do anything to
rescue their relationship. He indicated that his emotional distance had caused
problems in prior relationships, including those with family members. "I feel
like there's a wall between me and other people," Walt confided, "and I don't
know why. I want to be there for Janie, but I shut down. She tries to reach
out to me, and before I know it, I can't even think straight." Filled with remorse, he admitted to wishes that Janie would just go away and leave him
alone. "I can't control myself," Walt said despairingly. "I totally shut her out.
She doesn't deserve that!"

"How many of your patients in your clinical rotations have you totally
distanced from?" I asked innocently, knowing full well that any such problems would have been referred to me.

Walt looked at me, horror in his eyes. "Oh, no. I've never backed away
from my patients," he assured me. Walt clearly prided himself on his concern for others.

"So in that situation, you *do* have control," I pointed out. "You can't tell
me that school has never alienated you and made you want to back away!"

Walt smiled.

"You *do* have the ability to relate to people in constructive ways. You're
doing it in your career every day. But for some reason that's not happening
in your closest relationships."

Walt listened intently. He was open to the idea that there were at least two Walts: (1) a professional self that could cooperate with others and handle frustrations in a constructive manner and (2) a relationship self that runs from intimacy. Making a problem "ego alien"—separating the person from the problem—is crucial to the change process. "The problem is not you," I often suggest. "The problem is your pattern."

In the next two sessions, Walt allowed me into his childhood memories. His father was moody and temperamental, capable of flying into a rage at a moment's notice. Arguments between Walt's parents were regular occurrences. Walt recalled going into his room as a little boy and hiding under his bed in order to avoid the sound of the disagreements. He loved his mother and sought her support, but he also resented her for not standing up for herself when his father was angry. He recalled that his mother lapsed in and out of depression and would leave the house untended for days at a time. Walt said that he also felt depressed on occasions. It appalled him that he might be like his mother, whom he saw as lovable, but weak. Like Mary, Walt was finding himself being someone he did not want to be.

Unlike Mary, however, Walt spent much of his time in the sessions out of touch with his emotional experience. When I first met him, with his large body and intense glare, I expected stormy sessions. Nothing could have been further from the case. Walt dutifully responded to my questions and seemed quite aware of the link between his father's anger and his own passivity. Indeed, he recognized that his father had felt belittled by his own father, leaving a generational legacy of insecurities. Walt was verbally attacked by his father on a regular basis, and he felt tremendous insecurity as a result. He refused, however, to get angry and fight back. He might feel depressed like his mother, but he would not *be* his father. He would not continue the generational pattern.

All of this Walt *knew*. Yet it didn't change a thing. The rational, professional self and the self caught under the bed, hiding from childhood turmoil, found little intersection.

I found myself becoming frustrated with our sessions. We were doing a good job talking about the problems, but we weren't touching the problems themselves. I knew that if therapy were going to be successful, we would have to effect an integration of Walt's "personalities." And that meant bringing the mother-father experiences into our sessions.

This is as close to an immutable law as one can have in psychotherapy. Change cannot occur unless problem patterns are happening in real time. Those provide the "gear shift" occasions when it becomes possible to introduce new understandings, new skills, new contexts, and new experiences. No amount of rational discourse can touch John Cutting's Mind #2.

Somehow, I needed a way to touch Walt's nonverbal mind.

CREATING POWERFUL NEW EXPERIENCES

Consider the idea that you can only change patterns once they have been activated. To overcome anxiety, you have to become anxious. To master depression, you must allow yourself to become depressed. No amount of avoiding anger, fear, self-doubt, or conflict will allow you to master these.

For traders, this means that *the greatest opportunities for change occur when trades are on and the emotional ebbs and flows are at their strongest.* It is on those occasions that traders can consciously make efforts to break their repetitive patterns and initiate new responses.

Mental rehearsals—playing out challenging situations in your mind and imagining using various coping methods—can be quite effective in breaking old patterns. But nothing substitutes for what behaviorists call *in vivo* exposure—when individuals create *actual* stressful situations and push themselves to institute coping measures. A patient with panic disorder who purposely accelerates his breathing, mimicking hyperventilation, can recreate many of the symptoms of anxiety. By conjuring up these symptoms and then practicing cognitive and behavioral self-control methods, the patient develops the capacity to face real-life anxieties.

My own most successful in vivo exposure came about in an entirely unplanned manner. For years, I had been uncomfortable with heights but never had to deal with the discomfort. The fear was only triggered when I had no barrier or support around me. In a plane or at a secure point on a mountaintop, I had no problem.

During a summer visit to a local recreation area, my son, Macrae, wanted to take a chairlift ride to see the scenery. I was a bit uneasy at the idea of sitting in a chair suspended from a cable; but because people were strapped into the chair and further protected by a bar that swung down in front of them, I decided that there was no danger of falling.

As we started up the lift, little Macrae sat on my lap, smiling and taking in the view. I quickly noticed that the restraining bar had become stuck and would not descend. We were traveling in an entirely unprotected chair. I realized that I could not afford to let Macrae see that I was concerned. If he became fearful and made a sudden move, he could fall from the ride. So, with a mammoth effort, I disregarded my fear and held Crae tight, pointing out features of the scenery and otherwise engaging his attention. He never realized that the ride was unsafe.

From that point forward, my fear of heights was never so great. I had faced the worst imaginable situation, and I saw that I could handle it. Having me experience heights, but in a way that I was responsible for someone else, was the best possible therapy. The immediacy of the situation forced me to cope in a novel fashion.

One of my favorite tools for trading development is a biofeedback unit that measures forehead skin temperature. As you shall see later in the book, forehead temperature offers a sensitive measurement of blood flow within the prefrontal cortex of the brain—that portion of the brain most responsible for focus, concentration, and attention. Temperature readings tend to rise when people are in states of relaxed focus ("the zone") and tend to fall during periods of frustration and distraction. By establishing a baseline for myself prior to the market open and hooking myself up to the feedback unit throughout the trading day, I can follow the rises and falls in my "zone" as a function of the movement in the markets—and in my positions

By establishing a very simple rule—never enter or exit a position when the biofeedback readings are below their baseline levels—I can force myself to break old patterns in real time. The biofeedback values become part of an entry/exit strategy in which frustration *cannot* drive my placement of orders. Either I find a way to relax and focus, or I don't trade. This real-time discipline has proven far more effective than any out-of-market exercises I could have undertaken. Like the chairlift ride, the biofeedback forces me to experience old threats in new ways.

And *that* is the essence of change.

REGRESSION: THE MIND'S TIME TRAVEL

I tried to explore Walt's experience and gain some of that real-life immediacy, but he would have none of it. When I asked for detailed accounts of his past, he gave me factual information only. When I probed for emotion, sights, sounds, and experiences, he gave me generalized descriptions. At no point during our sessions did he reveal any anger or hurt whatsoever. Frustrated, perhaps visibly so, I cajoled Walt, "I want to know how you *felt* in these situations. Close your eyes and get an image in your mind of Janie criticizing you. Tell me what that's like."

Walt did not comply. He scrunched up his body, folded his arms, and said—quite spontaneously in a pouting tone—"I don't want to!"

I stared at him, dumbfounded. A big, six-foot-four guy was appearing as a young child right before my eyes.

Walt realized what was happening. "I feel like a little kid," he said with stunned wonderment.

He was absolutely right. Before our very eyes, Walt had changed.

"Regression" was the term used by Freud. When old, unresolved issues are triggered in the present, people can regress to earlier modes of coping. That is how a person can be a mature professional and a raging child at the same time. There are two selves, linked by a portal in time. Under emotional duress, an earlier mode of behavior, thought, and feeling is activated, quite apart from the mature, reasoning mind. For a moment, Walt was suspended between two worlds—like the split-brain subject P.S. Walt's rational mind was attempting to make sense of behavior beyond his control.

I grew up in Canton, Ohio. Our family was close, taking frequent vacations together, watching television, and going to basketball games. My early recollections are positive, filled with memories of taking drives as a family, finding "secret places," and getting ice cream cones. My parents as children experienced less of this closeness. Both were estranged from their parents at a relatively early age; both were partly raised and supported by older siblings. They seemed determined to provide my brother, Marc, and me with the kind of warmth and cohesion that they had not enjoyed as children. And they succeeded.

Problems occurred as I became older and wanted to live within my own world. I vividly recall our first school dance at Mason Elementary School. While the music played and the awkward adolescents took their turns on the dance floor, I sat in the back of the room, completely absorbed in William Shirer's *Rise and Fall of the Third Reich*. By my eighth-grade year, a sympathetic teacher occasionally exempted me from classroom exercises so that I could go to the bookshelf and devour more texts. My regular after-school activity was my paper route, which afforded me the opportunity to spend time walking and daydreaming, free of the intrusions of others.

Understandably, this immersion did not work very well at home. My family members wanted close interaction, not individual reveries. It was difficult to find isolation at home, but my one haven from human interaction was the bathroom, where I could find solitude in showers and long bathroom rituals. From an early age, my best reading and thinking was done in the bathroom.

Years later, when my wife, Margie, and I became engaged, I moved into her home with her three wonderful children, Debi, Steve, and Laura. Within a matter of days, conflict erupted. The kids needed to get to school in time, and I was ruining their schedule. How? By spending inordinate amounts of time in the bathroom!

Completely outside my conscious awareness, my new family situation felt to me like the old one: close, loving, *too close*. I regressed to my earlier mode, taking lengthy showers and dawdling through my routine of shaving, hair combing, and so on. As a child, that mode of coping was reasonably constructive, allowing me to establish a measure of solitude without losing family cohesion. Later, however, in a very different life context, the lengthy bathroom routines were completely dysfunctional, creating conflicts. I had outgrown an earlier self.

Now, sitting in the café section of a Wegman's grocery store, writing furiously on the laptop while I sip my coffee, Philip Glass playing on the CD player in the background, I'm probably not much different from that boy who was reading Shirer during the dance. I do much of my writing in busy public places where I am unlikely to see people I know— an uneasy compromise between being in and out of the social world. It's not perfect, but it does keep me out of the bathroom.

ENTERING THE TIME PORTAL

Regression is painful for many people, so much so that they will go to considerable lengths to avoid situations that might take them through time's portal. Hanging out in a bathroom protects against the feeling of submerged identity; staying far from feelings guards against outbursts of rage. Walt, in our sessions, was reenacting what he had learned so well as a child: Go into hiding. There was no bed to hide under in my office, of course, but he could certainly hide in other ways. Symbolically, the therapy room had become his threatening childhood home, dredging up conflicts and anger. The more I pressed for feelings, the further Walt went into hiding.

It was the little boy sound of "I don't want to" that clued us both to the fact that this was an echo from Walt's past. Becoming the withdrawn partner in a relationship and regressing to the young child in our session were part and parcel of the same process. To change the withdrawal, we needed to find a way to break through to that childhood self. It was time to emerge from beneath the bed.

There are a variety of ways in which people can access thoughts and feelings lying just below conscious awareness, hypnosis being the best known. These methods access felt modes of knowledge by bypassing the critical, rational mind, much like Schiffer's glasses. Dr. Nathaniel Branden has written extensively on the use of sentence-completion techniques as tools for emotional self-awareness. The counselor will offer sentence stems to clients in rapid fire. Clients fill in those stems with the first phrase that pops into their minds, without planning or censoring. The words that emerge are often quite different from the individual's normal talk, establishing a direct link to suppressed thoughts and feelings. I've generally found that my best use of this method has occurred when my sentence stems are as spontaneous as the client's replies, creating a free-flowing interaction.

Still in awe over his childlike outburst, Walt was quite willing to participate in the exercise. We began slowly:

BRETT *(noticing that Walt has a remote, intellectualized look on his face, but is tightly crossing his arms in front of him):* Right now, I am feeling _____.

WALT: Stressed.

BRETT: If my arms could talk, they would say _____.

WALT *(hesitating):* I don't know.

BRETT *(escalating his voice):* My arms are tense, they're screaming out _____.

WALT *(frustrated, anxious, his voice a pitch higher):* I don't know, I don't know.

BRETT *(still escalating):* Tighter, tighter. I want to say _____.

WALT *(again, the childlike voice):* Back off!

BRETT *(now also sounding more like a kid):* If you don't back off, I'm gonna _____.

WALT *(clenching his fist):* Get you! *(He seems more absorbed in his body's anger.)*

BRETT: My fists are saying _____.

WALT: I'm mad.

BRETT: I'm mad about _____.

WALT: How people treat me.

BRETT: People treat me like _____.

WALT *(animated):* Shit!

BRETT: And that makes me want to _____.

WALT *(with great feeling):* Kill them!

Spontaneously, Walt broke from the exercise and uncrossed his arms. He clenched his fists and described in great, emotional detail how his father had once come home in a rage and yelled at his mother. Walt attempted to stop the fight, only to have his father attack him. Walt described the feeling of his father's body on top of his, his father's hands on his throat, squeezing the life from him. Only the impassioned begging of his mother kept Walt from being strangled into unconsciousness. From that point on, the family never discussed the episode. It, along with Walt, was swept under the bed.

The problem was not just withdrawal, not even just anger. The problem was murderous rage. Walt could not allow himself to be angry, to become like his father. At some level he was convinced that his anger would kill someone. Rather than act out the role of his father, he gravitated to that of his mother. Depression seemed a small price to pay. He would hurt himself but preserve others. Janie might resent his emotional unavailability, but at least he would not kill her.

During the workday, Walt was a warm, engaging student. He could reach out to patients, interact well with peers, and participate in a team with his residents and attending physicians. Once home, his hurt and anger unwittingly triggered by Janie, he shut down, regressing down the portal to the protection of passivity. He did indeed become a different person.

Notice how Walt's state changed over the course of relatively few sentence stems. The key was triggering a degree of frustration right there in the interaction. When I first asked Walt what his crossed arms are saying, he shut down with an "I don't know." By refusing to accept this answer and escalating the question, I raised the pressure. I took the role of Janie, badgering him to open up, provoking the very anger he most feared. When the anger finally emerged, it was as if a dam had broken, releasing pent-up waters. Walt's formerly passive self was suddenly filled with animation; his tight body, binding his aggression, now was alive and expressive. In this heightened state, he was immediately connected to a powerful emotional event, his fear of his father, and the fear of his own anger. As passive Walt, he was impervious to therapeutic talk; as angry, animated Walt, he was ready to face his history in a new way.

Behind the sentence-completion exercise is a therapist's trick that is quite relevant to traders. I was making Walt angry at me, prodding him until he gave expression to the emotions metacommunicated by his crossed arms. Walt felt that he could not afford to release his anger; his chief fear was that he would become his father. By allowing him to experience *controlled* anger in the session, therapy provided an emotional disconfirmation of his fears—an immediate, experiential affirmation that he could be angry *safely*. The choice, he realized, didn't have to be between angry, aggressive Dad and passive, depressed Mom. He could be someone different, angry yet lovingly connected to others at the same time.

He could only come to that realization, however, through a powerful emotional experience. If I had simply talked the words to him, he would have heard them in his passive way, and they would have had no effect.

Traders' understandings—whether of themselves or of the markets—are mediated by their states of mind. The trading implications are clear: *What you know about the market—and how you respond to what you know—hinges crucially on the mind frame you are in.*

To change your trading, it is necessary to first shift the gears of mind and body.

WHEN YOUR GEARS REMAIN LOCKED

"How could this happen to me?" The voice on the other end of the phone cracked, and all that I could hear for a moment were sobs. Her name was Mallory, and she was clearly in pain. "He promised me it would work out. I put everything I had into it, and now it's gone. What am I going to do? I can't just get out; I don't know what to do."

For the life of me, I could have sworn Mallory was talking about a failed marriage. But she wasn't. She was talking about her investment in a growth-oriented mutual fund recommended by her broker. It was down sharply, and Mallory felt trapped. She could not accept the loss, and she could not continue to expose herself to further punishment.

From talking with Mallory and others in similar situations, I've been struck by the ways in which people think of their investments in relationship terms. Perhaps this shouldn't be so surprising. People invest themselves in relationships with spouses, children, friends, and family members. The dynamics of risk and uncertainty are not so different, whether the relationship is romantic or financial.

My surprise came from the fact that people tend to use the same language when describing their portfolio concerns as their marital problems. Like Mallory, they begin their romance with their stocks with high expectations. Infatuated, they check quotes every day—or sometimes many times a day. When things are going well, they cannot help but share their joy with others and feel a loyalty and a bond with their chosen company. One older woman, holding a volatile stock that seemed clearly inappropriate for her stated financial needs, bristled when I raised the possibility of selling it. "It's been so good to me," she exclaimed. "How can I let it go?" Chastened, I dropped the topic. It was as if I had suggested that she contemplate putting her mother in a nursing home for the indigent.

When the romance with the stock doesn't work out, however, the feelings turn to denial, hurt, and anger. Mallory felt profoundly betrayed by her broker, by the Federal Reserve, and by the market. Worse still, her response to her fallen stock was similar to the response I have witnessed time and again among spouses who discover their partners have cheated on them. Lost is the sense of safety, security, and trust. Rarely is the hurt party ready to simply cut his or her losses and bring things to a prompt close. But neither can he or she blindly go forward in the status quo. Mallory's pain was not simply that of a financial loss, but also that of feeling trapped in an unsafe, hurtful situation.

Walt's case makes clear that people tend to act out the problems of past relationships in present ones, much as I misused the bathroom when I moved in with my new family. If you have unresolved feelings of anger toward a parent, damaged trust from a disloyal relationship, or fear and insecurity from past abuse, these experiences act as emotional lenses through which you inevitably view new relationships. These lenses, like the glasses used in Frederic Schiffer's experiments, affect how you respond to the world, creating seeming overreactions. *In point of fact, however, you never really overreact to a situation; rather, you react to both present and past.*

This, I have come to believe, happens in the markets far more often than is commonly recognized. Many of the dysfunctional patterns that people play out in their interpersonal relationships are duplicated in their financial investments. In the past two years, I can think of a host of examples from my trading contacts:

• Bill cannot make a firm commitment in a relationship, afraid that a woman will interfere with his career success. Bill is a day trader and cannot hold a stock overnight, despite massive statistical evidence that the lion's share of the market's advances during bull periods are attributable to rises at the market open, in response to overnight news and markets.

• Ellen does not diversify her portfolio, preferring to put all of her money in one or two stocks. When they do not reward her time, effort, and expectations, she feels depressed and dwells on her failure. She reacts with complete surprise when I point out that this was the pattern in her romantic relationships, as well.

• Ian has lost 40 percent of his trading capital in the past three months alone. Ian overtrades the market, trying to play multiple intraday swings each day, making highly leveraged bets on each trade. Intellectually, he understands the statistical concept of risk of ruin: the likelihood that, given enough trades, a string of losses will occur and devastate anyone who is overexposed with each trade. Emotionally, however, Ian needs the action. He also cannot settle down in his marriage and has had two affairs.

• Hector spends hours analyzing the markets and working on developing trading systems. Some of them are highly elaborate, and even ingenious. He finds himself second-guessing his systems, however, and overriding their signals. Invariably, this loses money for him, yet he feels compelled to tamper with his own research. As a child, Hector was badly hurt by the death of his younger brother. He spends considerable time with his own family and loves them greatly. Periodically, however, he entertains "irrational" worries that his wife or children might suddenly die.

Like Walt, all of these people are in pain. They are repeating destructive patterns blindly, and they seem unable to prevent them from recurring. Also like Walt, they are unable to simply talk themselves into doing things differently. Only powerful emotional experiences can help them reprogram the nonverbal minds that impel them toward self-defeat.

Every trade is made for a reason: a logical one or a psycho-logical one. When you become your own therapist, shifting gears and attending to your tacit communications, you learn to differentiate between the two reasons.

NOVELTY: THE KEY TO CHANGE

After Walt exploded in response to the sentence completion exercise, vividly describing his fear and rage at his father—as well as his fear of ever again provoking his father's anger—I posed a pointed question. I asked if, during the exercise, he had felt a desire to jump on top of me and strangle me. Aghast, Walt answered no. I then asked if he expected me to tackle and strangle him. Walt smiled and again said no. I approvingly suggested that perhaps he no longer needed to fear being angry, because he was *not* like his father and was no longer living with his father. Keeping himself bound up in passive muscle tension might have kept things in check as a child—much as my showers provided me with solitude—but this solution had lost its usefulness long ago. If Walt's anger really were the problem he feared it to be, surely I would have been the recipient of quite an attack in our meeting.

Once Walt unlocked his arms and fists, he could experience his past and face his fear and anger. He overcame his anxiety over his own rage by fully experiencing it—*and by seeing that nothing terrible happened.* Perhaps most interesting, however, is the fact that Walt *didn't know he was angry until we had performed the exercise.* What he knew about himself was a function of his state of consciousness: In one state, he was passive and completely lacking in self-awareness; in another state, he was vividly in touch with painful childhood memories and his reactions to these.

Sometimes counselors use such experiential exercises to heighten this emotional awareness. It is very surprising how shifts in the body's level of activity and arousal can spark overall changes in consciousness, which then fuel changes in moods and action patterns. One of my students, who suffered from long-term depression, recently took up a particularly active form of martial arts through classes with a master teacher. On her own, she constructed mental exercises where she visualized the people who had hurt her as she practiced her blows. With each strike and kick, she vividly imaged doing bodily harm to those people. The routines left her feeling empowered, channeling her frustration as anger and activity rather than as passivity and depression. Indeed, after a workout, she looked like a different person—alive, invigorated, not at all beaten down and victimized.

All of these techniques share one crucial element: They bypass people's usual mode of thinking and provide access to a new and different mode of experience. Without this shifting of the gears of consciousness, people would remain stuck in their usual frames of mind, endlessly repeating their same thoughts, feelings, and behaviors.

NOVELTY IN THERAPY: MAKING TRANSLATIONS

The idea that behavioral change is preceded by a shift in one's state of consciousness was the culmination of perhaps the most instructive exercise of my professional career. Hoping to better understand the dynamics of change in therapy, I conducted what I call a "clinical review of the literature." Most literature reviews are surveys of research, an attempt to capture the state of scientific understanding in a field. What I was trying to do was a bit different. I read every written work on therapy that I could find from the major authors of the past several decades. I especially focused on writings that contained transcripts of actual therapy sessions. These held the promise of describing what the therapists were actually doing, not what they *said* they were doing.

It was a far-reaching review, culminating in a lengthy journal article in 1992. I read works by analytically oriented writers such as Habib Davanloo, Lester Luborsky, Peter Sifneos, and Hans Strupp. I covered cognitive-behavioral works by David Barlow, Aaron Beck, Albert Ellis, and Joseph Wolpe. I threw myself into the strategic literature of Steve deShazer, Milton Erickson, and Jay Haley. All the while, I kept asking myself, "How does this work? How can theories and practices that seem so different produce similar and positive results?"

My sense was that if it were possible to isolate the elements that are responsible for emotional and behavioral change, traders—and other professionals—*could be empowered to become their own therapists.*

Two common elements leapt from the pages of these writings. First was what brief therapy writer Simon Budman called "novelty." All of the therapies were helping people see and experience things in new ways. They were introducing skills, promoting insights, providing original experiences. Many of the approaches had a distinctively creative element, opening the door to fresh ways of viewing oneself and one's world.

Second was what cognitive-behavioral therapist Donald Meichenbaum called the "translation" process in therapy. People typically enter counseling with a particular problem or issue on their minds. They are coming for help because the problem is interfering with their lives and they cannot address the concerns on their own. Therapists do not simply listen to the problem and then toss out answers. *Rather, they translate the initial complaint into some other conceptual scheme and offer a way out from that perspective.*

Consider a simple example: A trader comes to counseling indicating that he feels worthless. He lacks confidence in his trading and procrastinates putting on positions, waiting for every indicator to line up perfectly. Rarely does this occur, however, and he misses a number of moves as a result. This leaves him feeling frustrated and angry, which spills over to his personal life. Recently, his wife has had enough of his outbursts and has suggested couples counseling. The trader resists the idea of entering therapy with his wife. He already feels like a failure in one area of his life—trading; he doesn't want to feel like a loser in his marriage as well. Recently he has been feeling blue and can't muster the energy to keep up with his market research. Twice in the past week, he has missed golden opportunities to ride trending markets because of his lack of preparation. Now he feels like a complete loser.

What is troubling for this trader, adding to the immediate problems of poor trading and marital concerns, is his lack of understanding of why he is the way he is. He feels defective in some way. "I want to be more successful," he might say. "Why can't I be different?" The recognition that one is not in full control of one's thoughts, feelings, and actions can be acutely distressing.

Early in the counseling process, the therapist will offer an explanatory framework to the trader that makes sense of his troublesome experience. This translation, which takes the problem as described by the trader ("I'm such a loser") and puts it into a new perspective, occurs in every therapy. *Indeed, the various therapies actually seem to be different explanatory frameworks.*

So, for instance, a cognitive-behavioral therapist might say to the trader, "The problem is not that you are a loser. The problem is that you have learned patterns of thinking that *tell* you that you're no good." Or a psychoanalytic therapist might say, "Perhaps the problem is not that you're destined to lose, but that you have internalized a loser's mentality as a way of avoiding conflict with your hostile and competitive father."

These explanations may not be offered all at once and may not be offered in the first session. But every therapy seems to provide a novel framework for understanding human experience.

People fail to change—they stay in ruts—because they are locked into seeing themselves and their situations in a particular way. They are like Dr. Schiffer's patients, *only they have forgotten that they are wearing lenses.* People's emotional problems are the result of confusing their interpretations of the world—the lessons they have learned from the past—with the world itself. Once people become aware of the lenses they are wearing that distort their views of themselves, it becomes possible for them to change the prescription.

My translation with Walt was that *he* wasn't the problem in the relationship with Janie. Rather, the problem was his past mode of coping that was cropping up during their relationship. But notice that this translation didn't take hold until we could actually shift the emotional gears and experience the anger that he had so feared. Changing one's state of mind—experiencing oneself in new ways—greatly facilitates the process of changing those lenses.

The implications for trading are significant. After repetitive mistakes in the markets, traders become convinced that they are "bad traders," "unlucky," or just plain "losers." Instead of focusing on the trading, they now blame the trader. I have a near-foolproof way of determining when traders are ready to overcome their problems. The ones who are not yet poised for change view *themselves* as defective; they want me to fix *them*. The traders who are more likely to make rapid advances view their trading as the problem. They have made the separation between themselves and their problem patterns.

The translation that frequently opens the door to change is that problem patterns in trading are there for a reason. Like Walt—like myself lingering in the bathroom—people are reacting to the past as well as to the present. They are using old coping strategies to deal with new situations. And the strategies aren't working.

To repeat, if there is a recipe for success in changing yourself, it is this: *Find out what you most fear and then place yourself in a controlled situation where you can directly experience that fear.* Whether it is a fear of your own anger, a fear of heights, or a fear of pulling the trigger on a trade, the first-hand experience of seeing that you are stronger than your fear will begin a new surge of confidence. Nothing I could have said to Walt would have been as powerful as getting him angry and helping him see that nothing terrible happened as a result.

It sounds like a strange formula, but it works: Find what makes you most anxious as a trader; *then gradually and steadily pursue it.* You, like Walt, will emerge from underneath the bed once you realize, in your own experience, that anxiety points the way to your further development. You expand yourself by facing the unknown; sticking with the familiar and comfortable is stasis.

The fears experienced by traders come in many flavors:

• One young man had been successful in trading, but he was having difficulty increasing his size. He defined drawdowns in dollar terms rather than in percentage terms and became panicked if he was down by a certain figure.

• A day trader working at a trading firm had made money on an intraday time frame but was reluctant to hold overnight, even in the face of favorable odds. He told himself that the quick ins and outs were his bread and butter, but he chastised himself for not pursuing the larger opportunities when they were there.

• A woman who was trading for a living was uncomfortable diversifying beyond her one or two favorite trading vehicles, even though she could see profit opportunities elsewhere. The idea of trading commodities other than the Standard & Poor's (S&P) and the Nasdaq frightened her, although her trading system could easily adapt to those other markets.

• A man who had recently made the leap into full-time trading now found himself unable to execute trades that he had researched before the open. He always managed to convince himself that the market was somehow behaving abnormally. By the time he waited for his feelings of comfort to return, however, the move had already commenced, and he lapsed into guilt and frustration over the move that he missed.

In each of these cases, the traders were afraid of a healthy change. Their fear is of the unknown, the unfamiliar. By gradually facing their fears—making themselves ride the chairlift even in the midst of their anxiety—they can learn first hand that what does not kill them does, indeed, make them stronger.

THE ROLE OF CONSOLIDATION IN CHANGE

My literature review convinced me that although novelty is necessary for change, it is not sufficient. For change to take root, there must be *consolidation*. A new pattern must be repeated many times over before it is truly internalized. Without consolidation, people are apt to relapse into their old ways. Most people think of counseling as a mechanism for discussing and addressing problems. The truth is that when a person participates in successful therapy, a greater amount of time and energy is spent at home rehearsing and cementing solutions than within sessions working on problems.

Unfortunately, all too many people cease their change efforts as soon as they see gains, figuring that they have solved their problems and need no further self-work. That is a bit like saying that once a plant has begun growing in a healthy way, it no longer requires water and fertilizer. For new patterns of living and trading to take root, there must be continuous efforts at change.

There is a conundrum here that explains why so few people are able to change their lives. *It takes sustained efforts to cement changes, yet most people cannot sustain efforts without major changes.* People can begin diets, exercise routines, or counseling programs; but they have a harder time maintaining these.

Again, I go back to George Ivanovitch Gurdjieff for a full appreciation of the dilemma. Human beings are too fragmentary to sustain change on their own. No sooner does one self—one I—make a resolution than another self, triggered by an externally driven state shift, enters the picture and acts on a new set of priorities. Gurdjieff made self-observation a pillar of his work, so that individuals could realize that they possessed a multiplicity of personalities. Without a "magnetic center"—a new self organized around the process of change—it is unlikely that even the best of intentions can come to fruition.

The landmark National Institute of Mental Health collaborative study on depression described by Irene Elkin and colleagues studied a large number of patients receiving psychotherapy and medication for their problem. Participants received approximately 12 therapy visits. Despite efforts to utilize standard, effective treatments, researchers found relapse rates among the study participants approaching 75 percent. The 12-session treatments were enough to initiate change but not enough to cement it.

This phenomenon of relapse says something about succeeding in the markets. *Any techniques that you use in trading—whether for money management, self-control, or pattern recognition—require frequent repetition before they will become an ongoing part of your repertoire.* You internalize changes by repeating them, without variation, time after time after time. Your goal is to make the new behavior so habitual that you will feel strange to *not* act in that way.

My clinical review of the literature suggested to me that it didn't matter whether a particular therapy was behavioral, cognitive, or psychoanalytic. Change always occurred in a particular sequence. *And if we can follow this sequence intensively, changes can be made in far less time than is generally required by normal talk therapy.*

Examine this sequence and how it might apply to trading. Suppose you attend a Linda Raschke or Mark Cook seminar and learn a new trading technique. Or perhaps you read Jon Markman's *Online Investing* or Yale and Jeff Hirsch's *Stock Trader's Almanac* and discover seasonal patterns that might apply to your investments. Such sources assist you in adding new elements to your trading. But how can you make these elements yours, part of your normal, natural trading repertoire?

The first step in the change sequence is introducing the new trading methods while you are in a nonordinary state of mind: highly relaxed and focused, physically pumped up, emotionally aroused, and so on. As you saw with Walt, it is at those times of heightened experiencing that you will be best able to process information in novel ways. Anchoring your new pattern of trading to a distinctive state will also allow you to more readily enact the pattern any time you access its accompanying state.

Thus, if you want to use signals from a mechanical trading system to filter trading decisions you are currently making from price and volatility patterns, you might conduct a historical review, trade by trade, that illustrates how this filter would have affected your past trading. Keeping yourself in a highly focused and relaxed state, you would process how the trades would have gone without the filter and how they would have proceeded using the filter. Each time, you would play-act using the filter, as if you were actually putting on the trades.

The second step in changing your trading is rehearsing the new pattern repeatedly in a variety of actual trading situations. These could be paper-trading exercises or actual trading sessions. Three things are important: that you are (1) using the new method on fresh data in real time; (2) sustaining the same, distinctive state of mind that you first used in learning the method; and (3) employing the method with consistency, trade after trade. By enacting the patterns again and again—and especially by seeing, first hand, the results of the new change—you speed the process of internalization.

I am convinced that consolidation is greatly accelerated in trading through *exemplar-based education*. Later, I will explore that topic in detail, especially as it relates to implicit learning. Exemplar-based education is learning through examples rather than through direct, didactic instruction. Instead of reading about trading or listening to a lecture on trading, you look at examples of actual markets and the ways those might have been traded.

Seeing actual patterns time and again—and gaining a firsthand feel for their variations—appears to be essential in skill acquisition. Just as medical students need to see many patients and many variations of particular diseases before they become proficient at diagnosis, traders benefit from experiencing a variety of markets and trading setups.

When I first visited Victor Niederhoffer in his trading room, I was impressed by several large volumes on one of his desks. These were journals containing intraday entries for the markets going back a number of years. I was even more impressed by the number of statistical analyses he and his assistants ran during a trading session. They were constantly adjusting to the market, searching for tradable patterns.

Later, when I became involved as a guest instructor in Linda Raschke's trading chatroom, I noticed that she made a regular practice of posting charts after each day's session. These charts illustrated principles that had guided the previous day's trading. Carl Swenlin, the founder of the comprehensive Decision Point web site (www.decisionpoint.com), recently told me that this was also the idea behind his organization of "chartbooks" on the site. By organizing the stocks in the chartbooks according to relative strength and allowing people to click through many charts in a short time, he made it easier for traders to process large quantities of data. This, in turn, facilitated the detection of common themes and patterns in the market.

As you will see in the last chapter, these practices of repeated research, examinations of patterns, inspections of charts, and the like serve the psychological function of consolidation. They immerse the trader in market patterns in a way that simple instruction could never accomplish. Just as neural networks require many, many examples to develop their predictive connections, a trader's own neural networks seem to require a large library of examples to detect and to act on patterns. *It is the intensity and repetition of exposure that appears to be facilitative of learning*, whether it is learning new trading methods or new behavioral patterns.

Expecting that one could change simply by trying something a few times—or by attending a one-hour weekly session with a therapist—is as unrealistic as expecting to learn how to play good tennis with only an occasional lesson of instruction. Without repetition, the heart of consolidation, new patterns are unlikely to become self-sustaining.

In my own trading, I maintain a dedicated online brokerage account where the commissions are minimal. I use this account to practice trading new ideas and patterns with 200-share trades on the exchange-traded funds. The small trade size ensures that even if I make mistakes with my new ideas, I will not take a major financial hit. More important, however, the frequent small trades get me into the habit of observing new patterns, employing new methods, and acting upon them in real time. *No amount of retrospective chart review can substitute for real-time consolidation.* Only after trading the pattern many times, successfully, with the small trades will I consider devoting a larger share of my capital to the new method. By then, however, the method has become part of me.

When I first developed my composite "Power" indicator, combining several elements of my trading into a single statistic (price direction, velocity, acceleration, volatility, and so on), I was uncomfortable trading the new variable. Researching its past performance was helpful in convincing me that it had potential, but this did not give me the confidence to actually put my money on the line. That confidence came for me, as for Walt, when my expectations were disconfirmed in a real-life situation. On more than a few occasions, I expected the market to move in a particular direction based on my prior work. The models using the Power measure, however, made a completely opposite prediction. In each of these cases, my old trading methods turned out to be wrong, and the new work was supported.

This splash of cold water in the face, showing me how my earlier work was inferior to this new research, did more to build my confidence in trading the research than any historical testing. I really thought I had the market pegged, and then saw that I was wrong and that the new models nailed the move. Eventually I got to the point where I refused to put on a trade unless the Power models supported my position. It was the emotional experience of having my trading expectations dashed—and particularly the repeated violation of those expectations—that cemented my new trading style.

Yet another vivid example of consolidating an emotional trading pattern occurred when I took to heart the advice of Victor Niederhoffer and began holding more of my positions overnight. Up to that point, for purposes of risk management, I had closed my positions by the end of the day, not wanting to get hurt by overnight developments or unfavorable premarket news. Niederhoffer pointed out, however, that most of the long-term rise in the markets can be attributed to an upside overnight bias. Failing to hold a good position overnight is actually a highly risky strategy, in that it foregoes a significant opportunity for profit.

Fascinated, I replicated Victor's work by studying the S&P futures from April 1994 through April 2002. I looked at the total points gained attributable to the overnight action (yesterday's close to today's open) and the total points attributable to the daily session (today's open to today's close). Overall, during the period of my study, the S&P had gained a total of approximately 327 points. Of those, about 311 could be attributed to overnight gains! In other words, during the trading day, there was no overall directional bias.

Performing the research gave me the confidence to begin holding small positions overnight. In further research, I found that an unusually large number of the sizable overnight declines occurred during corrective market periods. That meant that if my trend readings from the Power measure were positive, the odds of a painful adverse overnight move were reduced. (Positive New York Stock Exchange [NYSE] TICK readings during the latter hours of the trading session were also useful in weeding out many nasty overnight declines.) Each time I decided to hold overnight, I reviewed the research after having placed myself in a focused, relaxed state. Again and again, I sought to create a conditioning: associating the calm focus with the overnight, "risky" trade. I knew I had become successful when I began feeling uncomfortable closing a position out early. By then, the overnight hold in the face of favorable momentum became automatic—a new part of the trading arsenal.

WALT'S CONSOLIDATION

In Walt's therapy, the consolidation occurred in a unique way. We created a dialogue between Walt and his body. I suggested to Walt that he really had two selves: (1) the person he thought of as Walt, complete with his usual thoughts and feelings; and (2) his body, which had no verbal ability but could speak the language of gesture and action ("body language"). It was the conversation from Walt's body that enabled me to make use of the sentence-completion work, and it was the shift in his bodily state that opened the door to his history and unacknowledged anger.

I suggested to Walt that he carry out a dialogue with his body at random intervals during the day. That meant attending to his state of tension, energy, and posture to decipher the meaning of his body's communications. We modeled this within our sessions each time that I saw Walt's body lapsing into either passivity or rigid tension. I reflected both these states back to him, referring to them as communications from his body that indicated he was feeling threatened by feelings of fear and anger. At those times, I reassured him that no harm would come as a result of experiencing these feelings, reminding him of his initial experience with the sentence completions. Once he became adept at reading his body's language during our sessions, we were ready to consolidate the efforts through homework.

The homework was straightforward. At random intervals during the day, he was to stop what he was doing and as soon as practical enter into a focused state where he could observe the feelings, actions, and tensions of his body. At those times, he was encouraged to make a key translation: When he felt passive or tense, he was to assume that some unmet need or perceived threat was present. *Passivity and tension were his body's ways of informing him about anger and fear.* Once he made this translation and identified the source of his feelings, he was to make an effort to give these feelings direct, verbal voice. In other words, Walt would use the information from his body to alter the way in which he dealt with situations.

Note the message: Your symptoms—passivity and rigidity—are not patho-logical. *Your symptoms are forms of information from an alternate self.*

Most of the problems that people bring to therapy and that traders bring to markets are metacommunications—useful, informative communications—from a hidden self, even when they seem to make no sense, as in the case of the Woolworth man.

Walt and I hit on an interesting technique to become aware of these metacommunications. As part of his work as a student, Walt carried an elec-tronic personal organizer. His unit kept the time and had a function for an alarm. Prior to the start of each day, Janie would set Walt's alarm for a ran-dom time between 8 A.M. and 6 P.M. When the alarm went off—at a time that Walt never knew in advance—he could carry out the exercise. If he was in class at that time or otherwise occupied, he would simply observe his body and wait until later to process the information.

Our approach was borrowed from Gurdjieff's "stop" technique. This was a method where the master would shout "Stop!" during the middle of inter-actions with students and require them to freeze in their positions. At those times, caught in awkward postures, participants could observe themselves in fresh ways. The alarm from Walt's organizer served such a "stop" function, but it also made Janie an active part of the consolidation. Gurdjieff realized that people are all asleep, bouncing from one "I" to another with no real aim, no authentic consciousness. The alarm was literally set to awaken Walt from his slumbers, to rouse him from falling back into old patterns.

After about a month of this daily work, Walt no longer required the alarm. The awareness of his body became part of his daily routine. He had devel-oped a "magnetic center."

Walt's stop exercise is very much related to the notion of "taking your emotional temperature" during trading. It is a means for interrupting nega-tive patterns and cueing the activation of new, positive ones. People's enemy is the sleep described by Gurdjieff: the tendency to lose awareness of them-selves and to fall into old patterns unthinkingly. It was only half in jest that a trader friend recently advised me to connect my biofeedback machine to my trading station so that I could not access data—or trading screens—un-less I were in the proper state of mind and body. Having to stay focused in trading to access the screen is very similar to having to stay calm for my son on the open chairlift. The new experience is invaluable in cementing a new pattern.

As it happens, simply having the numeric output of my biofeedback unit on a continuous basis serves much of the same function. I cannot lose sight of my mind's functioning and my body's state because it is always in front of me on a display. From this perspective, each trading session is also an exercise session for the mind, a part of the consolidation process that cements good habits. I am truly trading from the couch when the ups and downs of my couch indicator—the biofeedback—become a formal part of my trading system.

CONCLUSION

So often, clients ask me how they can become motivated to complete their work, lose weight, change their patterns, and so on. My answer is that motivated acts are fragile. If you have to motivate yourself to do something, it really isn't a part of you. Lasting changes become automatic, like brushing your teeth in the morning or driving your car while carrying on a conversation. *If you create a desired state and enter it with sufficient frequency, always in the same manner, it will crystallize and become part of you.* Once consolidation has occurred, the mindscape—and the trading arsenal—are changed forever.

Observe and interrupt old patterns, switch emotional gears, enact new patterns, and repeat these in as concentrated a way as possible: This, my literature review taught me, is what change is all about. The solutions in counseling and in trading begin as patterns people fear, then become patterns they enact with effort, and finally become automatic. The movement from tacit to explicit, transforming Walt's folded arms into directed exercises, is a hallmark of all personal change.

Chapter Eight

Buried Alive!

Nothing is more common, or more fleeting, than the great dreams of sleeping people.

Body language is one important form of communication from our nonverbal minds, but there are others as well. And these can provide important information about us and about our trading. Images, fantasies, artistic works, and dreams are but a few of the ways we communicate in a language of feeling. Therapists learn to become sensitive to these communications, for they often convey important clues as to people's repetitive patterns. Mary's dream, for example, crystallized her conflict between needs for attention and fears of exploitation. Even as her conscious mind attempted to reject the dream, her emotions and her bodily communications betrayed its importance.

In this chapter, we will explore more of these nonverbal communications and their relevance to the process of self-change. We will see that subtle markers, from our tone of voice to the rate of our eyeblinks, contain important information about our emotional states. We shall also see that fantasies are constructed realities that express some of our most basic human needs and motivations. By becoming attuned to the messages of our minds and bodies, we can ensure a firmer grounding in reality, much to the benefit of our happiness—and our trading.

THE ART OF TIMING IN THERAPY AND TRADING

Timing is central to both therapy and trading. The best trading idea can lead to ruin if implemented at the wrong time. Similarly, valuable insights in therapy are lost if they are introduced when a client is not ready to hear them. Successful therapists and traders are much like good comedians. They know how to time their interventions.

Beginning traders and therapists focus so much on *what* they are doing that they give little consideration to timing. As a result, a great deal of what they do seems ham-handed. This is particularly true of traders who rely on formulaic trading methods ("Sell when the 12-period RSI is overbought") and of neophyte therapists who import their lines from textbooks. There is a stilted quality to what they do, one that often ignores the context of the particular situation.

A recent trading correspondent described his bread-and-butter trades as "volatility breakouts." When the market consolidated after a rise or a decline, he would place an order just above or below the consolidation range, hoping to take advantage of a breakout. He was whipsawed frequently, but he managed to catch some nice trending moves. Overall, the relatively low batting average (due to the whipsaws) made his system a difficult one to follow. When he described his trades, I was struck by the degree to which he ignored the surrounding action in the market. Many times, the consolidation range he was trading for an upside breakout was evident on a Standard & Poor's (S&P) chart, while the charts of other indexes were clearly not in consolidation modes. This often led to failed breakouts. Because he mechanically took his trades without looking at the larger picture, he could not benefit from that information.

New therapists invariably give away their neophyte status by mimicking phrases they have read in textbooks or heard from others. I recall supervising one particularly mechanical therapist. The client indicated that he was so angry toward his wife that he could strike her. The therapist, taken a bit aback by the man's vehemence, stumbled and could only think to ask, "So how does that make you feel?" As you might expect, the man was quite in touch with his anger and let the therapist know about it in no uncertain terms.

Good timing requires a feel for one's work that can only come with re-peated exposure. Yet timing is not a mystical, intuitive gift. It can be acquired, usually by modeling someone who is accomplished.

Timing was an important element in the counseling with Mary and with Walt. Recall that when Mary was uncomfortable recounting her dream, I added to her discomfort by actually giving her the impression that I had a "personal" interest in her. Similarly, during the sentence-completion exercise with Walt, I raised the tone of my voice, quickened my pace, and called attention to his clenched fists. Many counseling interventions are of this sort, where the therapist times an intervention to alter the client's level of emotional experiencing. In both cases, with Mary and Walt, the heightened arousal allowed them to access memories that had been tucked away. Those memories were critical in understanding their present-day patterns.

Other counseling interventions do not seek to induce state-of-mind shifts but piggyback on changes that are naturally occurring. For example, a counselor may wait to point out a destructive pattern until the client is emotionally in touch with the consequences of that pattern. At such moments, the motivation to change is apt to be greatest, allowing the counselor to ride the emotional trend.

Some of the most promising opportunities for intervention in counseling occur during relatively subtle state shifts. These are manifested in the client's metacommunications: changes in their rate of speaking, emotional tone, body posture, and facial expression. Such metacommunications are known in the professional literature as *markers* because they signify a transition point from one cognitive and emotional state to another. Markers are important cues for traders as well.

Suppose a woman begins a counseling meeting by recounting several stressful things that happened during the past week. Her tone of voice and body posture are similar when describing each event, as she speaks quietly and nervously and sits on the edge of her chair. At the end of her recital, however, she mentions that she had a visit from a friend she hadn't heard from in years. With this new topic, her voice brightens, and she speaks louder and sits further back in her chair.

As a therapist, you might then ask the woman if she tried out the homework exercise suggested at the last visit. She immediately replies in the affirmative and says that the exercise was helpful. You notice, however, that when she talks about the exercise, she moves forward in her seat and lowers her voice, returning to the very same posture that she was in while she recounted the week's stresses. These markers are telling you two things: (1) that there is something stressful about the homework and the therapy; and (2) that whatever is stressful about these is probably the same thing that the client is wrestling with in other areas of her life. By attending to the markers and exploring the stressful aspects of the homework—perhaps even having the client perform the homework on the spot—the uncomfortable state can be heightened, opening the door for change.

Recently, I talked with a trader who was having severe and frequent arguments with his wife. I brought them together for a session and observed their interactions. Invariably, he would become impatient with her when she wanted his attention. He displayed this by adopting a curt, rejecting tone of voice, accompanied by an intense facial expression. His wife found this intolerable and would try even harder to win his attention. This came across in a demanding fashion and led to his efforts to push away even harder.

The situation was bewildering because the trader seemed to genuinely love his wife and certainly did not want to lose the marriage. It was clear to me, however, that their relationship was on the ropes.

At the end of the session, as we were readying to leave, I casually asked the young man how his trading was going. Immediately, to my surprise, his face returned to its intense expression, and he responded abruptly that things were fine. Fortunately, I had my wits about me and did not react negatively to his tone, as his wife had been doing. Instead, I attended to the marker—his physical and emotional change—and purposely adopted a softer, slower mode of speech. Looking him in the eye, speaking so that his wife could not hear, I said, "It's a pretty demanding market, isn't it? I've been trading for a while, and I still sometimes feel like I can't live up to the demands."

Almost immediately his face dropped, his eyes became teary, and he described a major loss that he had taken on a margined position. He explained, with his wife present, that he had hoped that he could make a lot of money in the market in a short time and, thereby, relieve her of the need to work while she had their first child. Instead, he lost the money and made it inevitable that she would have to work full time. He had not spoken to her of the loss and, indeed, subconsciously, dreaded her asking about his trading. To keep her at bay, he adopted his rejecting demeanor—the same attitude he enacted toward me at the end of our session.

In subsequent sessions, that behavior led us to a fruitful exploration of the demands of relationships and investments and the ways he met or avoided these. His state shift, assuming the same facial and vocal expression in both market and relationship situations, alerted me to the issue he was facing. My own shift, confessing my feelings of inadequacy in a lurching, volatile market, modeled for him a different style of interaction: one that *faced* problems, rather than pushed them away.

Successful traders and counselors use themselves as emotional barometers. Like poker players attentive to the tells of their opponents, they scan for the subtle cues that inform them when conditions are ripe for change. Whether you're trading from the couch or the couch is your trade, you become proficient when you learn to read the markers and use them to time your interventions.

MARKERS AND THE MARKETS

I find it helpful in my own trading to think of the market as one of my patients. Each day, sitting in front of the screen, I am in session. The market is telling me its story, written in upticks, downticks, trends, and consolidations. As in my counseling sessions, I attempt to catch the themes in the market's communications. I watch for the markers: the evidence of shifts in pace and tone, the overreaction and underreaction to news events, the depth of conviction of buyers and sellers on the market-maker screen, the relative activity of institutions on the buy and the sell sides. If I can stay focused, identify the themes, and time my interventions according to the markers, the odds are pretty good that I'll be successful. Conversely, if I'm caught up in my own reactions or especially if I am trying to impose the themes I want to hear, the chances are great that I will miss what is being said and pay the price.

Following the markets or holding a counseling session is much like attending a great symphony. The composer begins with the exposition of a theme and then develops this theme through rich variations and elaborations. In the ballet *Petrushka*, for example, Igor Stravinsky introduces distinctive themes for each character, including a melody for the title character, a puppet that wants to come to life. In the interplay of the themes, the interactions of the characters can be visualized: the soaring hopes of Petrushka, his love for the ballerina, his conflict with the Moor, and his eventual demise. Appreciating fine music, much like reading fine novels, requires an ability to abstract themes from the score and to follow their development.

In counseling sessions, as in great works of music, the dominant themes are generally expressed in the opening minutes and subsequently elaborated.

Skilled therapists are attentive to the communications and the metacommunications at the opening of a session. These generally establish the themes for the remainder of the visit, encapsulating the most important issues in the person's life at that time. Psychoanalysts sometimes refer to a triangle of conflict, in which themes are recapitulated in past relationships and present relationships and in the relationship with the counselor. Underlying the triangle notion is the awareness that themes are the glue that cements an emotional life.

Last week, a student began her meeting with me by spending an inordinate amount of time talking about trivia: the weather in Syracuse, her vacation plans, and so forth. Knowing that she had her board exams coming up in less than a week and chafing just a bit to get down to business, I jumped in and asked if she was having trouble with procrastination in her studies. She gave a surprised look, as if I were clairvoyant. There was no extrasensory perception (ESP) involved at all, however. I simply relied on the symphonic principle that there is a structure to communications, in which seemingly different topics express variations of underlying themes. Her avoidance of therapy work in the opening minutes of our session mirrored her larger avoidance of schoolwork.

There is a similar structure to market communications as well, allowing traders to place their stocks on a couch and read the themes. In the market, as in counseling sessions, the opening minutes of a trading day often establish durable themes. Sometimes the themes involve the outperformance of one sector over others, as in occasions when traders can see money being pulled out of old economy stocks and placed into technology, biotech, and other new economy shares. In the opening minutes of the session, I scan sector indexes for the performance of consumer ($CMR), cyclical ($CYC), financial ($NF), and technology ($MSH) issues, as well as for the performance of broader old economy stocks ($XMI). Even within a large group such as technology, it can be worth identifying themes that distinguish among, say, networking companies ($NWX), semiconductor manufacturers ($SOX), and computer manufacturers ($XCI). Occasionally all the groups will be up or down solidly, signifying a possible trend day for the sector or for the overall market. Much of the time, however, some groups will be outperforming others, sometimes significantly. These themes often persist through the session and can set up worthwhile trades.

Other themes that set up early in the market day may be somewhat subtler. I like to think of the markets in the stock index futures as segmented three ways: (1) the day session, from the market open (9:30 A.M. ET) to close (4 P.M. ET); (2) the overnight session, from market close to 8:30 A.M. Eastern Time (ET), at which point the next day's trading picks up, often in response to fresh economic news (the overnight session tells how the market is responding to overseas markets and overnight news); (3) the preopening market, from 8:30 A.M. to the open, reveals the market's response to economic data coming out that day. (Sometimes the data are released at 10 A.M., creating a larger window for viewing the response to economic news.) Does the overnight market significantly penetrate the previous day's highs or lows? Is the overnight range significantly extended following the release of economic data? Very often, the failure to take out prior highs/lows in the face of strong/weak economic data and overseas markets is a meaningful marker for a pending reversal.

As a market therapist, I keep my eyes open for early market strength or weakness—as revealed by futures premiums and the Dow, the New York Stock Exchange (NYSE), and the Nasdaq TICK—that fail to penetrate the price highs or lows from the previous night's Globex session. This suggests that fresh buying or selling is lacking, setting up a hypothesis that I may test the night session's opposite extreme. Conversely, a sharp breakout from the Globex range suggests that new buyers or sellers have entered the market, encouraging the hypothesis that a trending move may be afoot.

Volume and volatility patterns can form another valuable set of markers. There is a normal pattern of volume and volatility during a trading day, with the highest levels registering early in the morning, waning into the midafternoon, and then picking up in the later afternoon. Sometimes, however, volume levels become distorted, violating the usual smile curve of intraday volume. For example, afternoon volume may pick up on a breakout, nearing or exceeding opening levels. Such moves often serve as markers for fresh market buying/selling and, as such, tend to have legs.

The question for the trader is when a difference among sectors, price levels, or volumes represents normal, expectable variation and when it encapsulates a distinctive theme. Those who immerse themselves in the market and continuously follow the various groups in real time gain the ability to tape read meaningful deviations among the averages. I find it helpful, again following the Galtonian example of Victor Niederhoffer, to rely on counting exercises to determine if a theme is operative. For example, simple studies over a given lookback period can establish the average relationship between price changes in two averages and the normal variation from this mean. When

I see the price changes of averages moving away from their historical relationship by two or more standard deviations, I know it's a rare event, and one worth paying attention to.

As a short-term trader, I perform some of my counting in a simplified manner, simply scoring each minute in the market as up, down, or flat for each sector average I follow. When the averages are in sync, their cumulated up/down scores are quite similar. When they diverge greatly, however (and, again, I can ascertain this statistically by identifying the average divergence and the variation around this), I can hypothesize that money is moving out of one area and into another. This is generally a theme worth paying attention to, helping you make choices if you are contemplating buying, say, Dow versus Nasdaq futures or large cap (SPY) versus midcap (MDY) exchange-traded funds.

MARKERS WITH THE NYSE TICK

Other themes that pertain less to individual sectors also tend to show up in the market's opening minutes. A gap opening on an extreme TICK reading very early in a session will very often signify trending strength or weakness that persists through the day. Early dips that terminate at a zero TICK level—failing to get into negative territory—often suggest that selling will be modest through the day. Conversely, gains early in the day that cannot push into positive TICK territory generally occur in choppy-to-downward markets where rises will not be sustained.

At the start of each trading day, I make sure that I am aware of the recent *TICK range* for the most recent session. The TICK range is the difference between the highest NYSE TICK reading for the day and the lowest reading. I then utilize my nearest neighbor modeling to identify all previous days in my database with a similar TICK range. I specifically examine the average TICK range for the next day and the expected variation around this. My working hypothesis is that the coming day's TICK range will be within the range described by this average and variation.

This has important implications, creating a new set of markers. If a hypothesized market bottom early in the day occurs at a TICK level of −250 and the projected TICK range is 1050, I entertain the notion that the market will, at some point in the trading day, hit a TICK around 800. Right away that tells me two things: (1) that there is likely to be net buying for the day (positive TICK levels exceeding negative ones, which correlates with the day's advance-decline numbers); and (2) that a tradable bounce may be at hand, as the market moves from a TICK of –250 to +800.

Some of the most interesting junctures in the market occur when early themes are interrupted by *new* markers. This indicates that the themes are shifting, pointing the way to potential trend change. Those are the occasions when traders, like therapists, need to be their most nimble.

Suppose a market has been chopping around in the early going in a fairly narrow range, with the cumulative TICK neither exceeding +200 nor declining below –200. That is a market that a short-term trader might stay out of, given the low volatility and directionless trade. Suppose, however, the market breaks down to a new daily low on –750 TICK and rebounds only slightly on a rise back to a positive TICK level. What do you do?

Unless the market has been declining for a while, making this a last gasp decline, the winning move, on average, will be to place a short. The sharp downside move in the TICK and the violation of the trading range signify a change of theme. Up to the point of that decline, moves into positive TICK were taking the market to the upper end of its trading range. Now the moves to positive TICK are barely moving the market higher. This loss of efficiency is an important marker that generally heralds subsequent weakness.

An important marker—and one of the least well understood—is trading volume. Extremes of volume (which are correlated with volatility extremes) often occur toward the end of market moves, as the majority of traders attempt to hop aboard a train that has already left the station. If I am holding a profitable position and the market moves sharply in my favor on high volume, creating an unusually wide bar on the chart, I almost always will formulate a plan for taking profits. If the trend is *that* obvious, with traders clamoring to get on board, it is generally in its latter stages.

Volume markers can be difficult to discern, however, for short-term traders. As mentioned earlier, there is a natural tendency for volume to be highest toward the beginning and the end of each trading day and lowest in the midday hours. A given volume at 12:30 P.M. ET may be quite high for that time period but relatively low compared to the opening or closing volume. For this reason, I compute a statistic that I call *relative volume*. Simply stated, relative volume compares the volume at a particular period (from one minute to one hour) with the average volume for that period over the past X days. (In my own trading, I have a chart of average five-minute volumes for the exchange-traded futures [ETFs] and futures contracts I follow, with a 100-day lookback period.) This allows a trader to know, objectively, when volume at a particular period is high compared to its norm. When a trader sees a move out of a trading range at 10:30 A.M. ET on a five-minute volume that is three standard deviations above the normal 10:30 A.M. ET value, he or she will often see a continuation of that new trend. This is because the heightened relative volume designates an expansion of buying or selling interest. Conversely, when a trend has been in place and there is a sudden surge of relative volume, it often serves as a marker for prospective periods of consolidation or reversal.

(*Note*: As mentioned earlier, I prefer to measure volume in trades rather than in shares traded. This statistic is available from most real-time data feeds. Although the number of trades placed per unit time generally correlates well with the number of shares traded, there are times when the latter yields considerable distortion due to individual large-block trades, especially if you are following volume on a very short term basis. The number of trades is more sensitive to the buying and the selling activity of small traders, enhancing its contrarian potential.)

Many markers of change in the market closely resemble those in therapy sessions. Sometimes I open a window on my screen and observe the time-and-sales data flying by for a given stock. The screen captures every trade that is placed and the shifts in the bidding and the asking prices. At market turning points, you can often see a quickening of the screen's pace; you can also observe the uptick in pace when a dull consolidation range is broken and a new trend emerges. Floor traders are well acquainted with this marker, observing the noise levels in the pits for an indication of buying and selling interest. It is almost as if the market were acting like a therapist, shifting the pace and the tone of communications to emphasize certain points and to induce shifts in awareness.

Long periods of immersion in the markets are invaluable in helping traders become sensitive to these rhythm shifts. The trader's sensitivity, however, is like that of the therapist, in that the best move to make may be contrary to the rhythms. When a client's voice goes flat, that is often the best time to introduce emotion; when the pace of conversation slows, that cues a shift to a livelier topic. Similarly, a quickening of the trading pace late in a downside move may induce feelings of panic for traders long the market, as drawdowns mount. The proper couch-trading response, however, is the one that does not come naturally, viewing the panicky trader behavior as a marker for future reversal—and a possible long entry.

Themes and shifts in themes are seen in social conversation; in works of literature, art, and music; in psychotherapy; and in markets. Just as alterations of mind states precede psychological change, so do shifts in themes commonly accompany market changes. When the market is on your couch, you're listening to it talk and following its ever-changing, ever-fascinating permutations.

THE POWER OF DREAMS

Yet another parallel between traders and therapists is that both listen to their own emotional themes. For that purpose, few sources are more powerful than dreams.

Dream work holds a venerable place in the history of psychology. Ancients believed that dreams were portents from the gods. Freud theorized that dreams are a royal road to the unconscious mind, informing the dreamer of repressed conflicts. Carl Jung expanded on the Freudian notion, emphasizing that dreams are communications from the collective wisdom of unconscious minds, pointing the direction to solutions, not just problems.

What is definitely known is that dreaming is essential to mental health. Deprived of sleep, individuals first become tired and cranky, then disoriented. People with sleep apnea, a condition in which snoring interrupts their sleep, often experience reduced dreamtime, resulting in fatigue, poor concentration, and symptoms that mimic depression. It is interesting that medications for the treatment of depression often increase the frequency and vividness of dreams, perhaps helping to restore a vital function.

Freud emphasized that the manifest content of dreams—the story they tell—is generally less important than their latent content—what they symbolize. Although interpreting dreams is a perilous task, fraught with the risk of lapses into sheer mysticism, it is often the case that themes emerge across series of dreams. Indeed, these themes seem to capture important emotional realities.

Recall Mary's dream, in which I made a clear advance toward her. The dream was triggered when I displayed a personal interest in her artwork, which she subconsciously experienced as a personal, sexual interest. Her dream expressed her fear of replaying her childhood abuse, even as she consciously tried to dismiss the dream and its significance.

Many years ago, early in my graduate training, I found myself alienated from many of those around me. Worst of all, I did not feel adequately challenged in my work or sufficiently fulfilled in my relationships. I wasn't depressed; and to all outward appearances, I was doing fine. But something was missing from my life. Here is a dream from that period that I brought to my therapist:

> I am about to go off a large slide. The slide is hundreds of feet high. To get from the ladder portion to the slide portion, you must walk through a small room. I am a bit fearful, but I go down and, to my surprise, the ride is slow and not at all scary. I decide to go down again, but this time I am intercepted in the small room by Liz [my therapist]. She chides me for my first trip down the slide, pointing out that it was a gentle ride because I didn't even turn the slide on. She points out an on-off throttle switch in the room and a machine that allows me to choose a "coefficient of daily experience." My normal daily experience is a "1" coefficient. If I want more powerful daily experience, I choose a number greater than "1"; smaller than "1" will give a "grayer" experience. I settle for 1.15 and decide to go down the activated slide.
>
> —B.N.S. Dream Journal, entry for 8/21/77

Better than any therapist could, my dream honed in on my problem. If life is a slide, I was taking a gentle ride. In choosing a low "coefficient of daily experience," my ride was safe but unfulfilling. I needed to activate the slide, but not so much so that I would be filled with fear. A setting of 1.15—a modest, attainable challenge—was what I needed. A simple image of a slide captured beautifully the dominant life theme with which I had been struggling.

Two years ago, I had a horrible trading experience in which I held onto a losing position much longer than warranted, magnifying my losses. The hit to my portfolio was painful, but the emotional agony was even more so. Each day I acted out a tableau of hope, discouragement, despair, and helplessness. Experienced traders wisely counsel on the importance of cutting one's losses to avoid wiping out days and weeks of hard-earned profits. They recognize the sizable psychological toll taken when traders program their minds with negative experiences and messages during those periods where they hang onto their losers.

After one particular grueling day, in which my position started the day favorably only to reverse by the close, I had a most vivid dream. When I woke up, I immediately wanted to put the dream out of my mind—but I knew I could not. In the dream, I was in my boyhood town of Canton, Ohio. I was driving down Harvard Street along a strip that runs between 25th Street and

30th Street. I found myself dozing behind the wheel and awakened, surprised, to find that the car had remained on a straight path. As soon as I worried about it veering off the road, it began to drift and I realized that I was in the *backseat*. I vainly attempted to crawl to the frontseat in time to hit the brakes, but I realized it was too late. The car was headed toward other cars and a wire fence across from my old elementary school. As I cried out in my dream—*passionately cried out*—that I didn't want to die, I managed to awaken.

If a client brought me that dream, I would want to get him or her into that backseat, crying out for life. I *know* the meaning of that dream: the horror-filled recognition of living one's life aimlessly, out of control. If anything can shake one from sleeping behind life's wheel, it is the recognition of imminent death, the impending crash. As a trader, I was asleep at the wheel. I was about to crash. The vivid, emotional recognition that I wanted to live drove home the message of staying awake in my trading far better than any words of advice.

Once people recognize that they possess multiple minds, it isn't a great leap to view dreams as communications from one self to another. The emotional tone of a dream is more important than its outward content. Dreams that express fear usually capture something anxiety provoking in one's daily life. Dreams that are violent often speak to feelings of anger and frustration. If you're truly immersed in your trading, dreams will not tell you what to buy or to sell, but they may tell you something equally important: how comfortable Mind #2 is with the trading being done by Mind #1. My car crash dream suggested that I was aware of my self-destructiveness, even as I attempted to rationalize holding my losing trade.

DREAMS AS EMOTIONAL COMMUNICATIONS

Perhaps dreams are nature's way of providing people with alternate states that open them to creative reworkings of the mindscape. Dreams rarely occur in a normal state of mind; they are much more imagery and emotion filled than accustomed thoughts are. Access to that imagery and emotion can spark important trance-formations: shifts to new modes of thinking and feeling.

Incredibly, however, many people want to *analyze* dreams rather than re-experience them in a trance-formative way. They assume that the meaning of the dream is in the text, rather than in the experience, the *context*. To understand a dream, you have to *live* it. Talking about the car veering off the road is far less powerful than reliving the frantic struggle to get to the frontseat and watching the inevitable collision with the fence.

The experiential psychologist Alvin Mahrer utilizes a form of dreamwork in which clients are encouraged to actively enter their dreams in a vivid, fantasized way and to reexperience them. The dream, he believes, is less significant for its content than for the enhanced state of experiencing that it offers. He finds that when people allow themselves to fully immerse themselves in the thoughts, feelings, and actions of a dream, a transformation occurs in their experiencing. There is a breaking through the unpleasant feelings and images of the dream to a new, and often positive and integrative, experience.

Here is an illustration. Shelley, a swing trader, reported a dream of getting caught holding a long position in a plunging market. Watching her position deteriorate minute after minute in the dream, she literally felt as though she were bleeding to death. Subsequently, she reported great hesitance in taking a position in the market, fearful of taking a loss.

Shelley was asked to lie on her bed in a prone position and bang the mattress repeatedly, heightening her state of experiencing. After a series of bangs, she was instructed to continue hitting the mattress while visualizing her deteriorating position and screaming out, at the top of her lungs, "I'm going down! I'm going down!"

As Shelley poured herself into the exercise, her spontaneous cries on the mattress changed their form. From "I'm going down!" she began yelling, "I can't stop it! It won't stop!" This, in turn, gave way to "I can't get out! I'm trapped! It's going down and I can't get out!" Within a matter of a minute or two, Shelley's pounding the mattress became a frenzied pushing against invisible walls, as she acted out her desperation over exiting her helpless position.

Exhausted, she tumbled off the bed and began gasping exultantly, "I'm out! I'm free! I got out!" Her terror was replaced by an overwhelming feeling of freedom as she escaped her tormented position on the bed. Processing the exercise, she recalled a traumatic episode from her childhood in which her uncle was playing with her in the family swimming pool and held her head beneath the water for too long. Unable to emerge from the water and filled with fear, she nearly passed out before the "game" ended. She never returned to the pool again.

By reenacting the dream—and the episode from the pool—Shelley obtained a firsthand experience of facing and overcoming her worst fear. Mahrer finds that pushing oneself through the peak experiencing in a dream or uncomfortable event produces a qualitative shift in this experiencing, opening the individual to new modes of thinking, feeling, and acting. Instead of dampening negative states, the client is encouraged to blast through them and divest them of their power.

A trader once reported to me that he was troubled by a dream in which he was running from shadowy, menacing characters that were pursuing him. He was convinced that they were going to kill him and could not shake the feeling, even after awakening. It later came out that he had sustained a recent large loss in his trading. Consciously, he insisted that he had "come to terms" with the experience. Nonetheless, he admitted that his troubling dream had occurred immediately following a trading day when he had increased his size beyond his normal money management guidelines. His dream strongly suggested that he felt far more vulnerable than he was admitting. Armed with this information, he was able to closely monitor his position the next day and trim his exposure down to the sleeping level.

REPETITIVE DREAMS: THE THEMES OF LIFE

If dreams capture the momentary themes occurring in your life, repetitive dreams encode your *enduring* life themes. Like repetitive themes in a market—say, the relative outperformance of small and mid-cap stocks over their larger siblings for a period of months—these dominant life themes often form the basis for your most important and durable changes.

It is interesting that it was just such a repetitive dream that helped to shape this book. In past versions of the dream, I had the ability to fly and to move very quickly. This allowed me to remain beyond the reach of others, providing me with an indescribable feeling of freedom. During my writing of this book, early in the process, I found myself feeling stuck. To my dismay, I was facing a writer's block. When I reflected on the block, I realized that I was torn. Part of me wanted to write a book that was highly research based. I wanted a text that would be admired by my scholarly academic and trading colleagues. Another part of me wanted to write something more informal, much more personal, and geared toward the trading public. The result was paralysis: As soon as I would write in one style, a self-critic would jump in and interrupt the flow of words.

One day, I spent hours in front of the computer. At the end of it all, I had nothing of worth to show for my time. I was tremendously frustrated.

That night, I had a flying dream. It was one of my favorites, involving flying while playing basketball. Several players were attempting to block my shot, but I was able to soar over them en route to the basket. High in the air, I timed my descent to make a perfect slam dunk.

As I was at my apex and about to descend, however, I noticed the outer layer of the ball unraveling. Layers were stripped from the ball like sheets of paper. Indeed, as I struggled to keep the layers together and retain the round shape, the ball changed into a book. The sheets were pages from the book, and I was descending for my slam dunk. As I "dunked" the book atop a stack of other books (the books were thick library volumes; the top one had a plain white cover and was a book on tax and estate planning), a fragment from a song kept playing over and over: *"Hoppe, Hoppe, Reiter . . ."*

Please allow me a bit of explanation here. While writing the book, I was involved in establishing a family trust for estate planning purposes—a task I found necessary, but dull and time-consuming. The German phrase *"Hoppe, Hoppe, Reiter"* refers to a game, in which a child sits on the knee of a parent and bounces up and down as if riding a horse. The particular music in the dream was from the refrain of a song by a German group called Rammstein. The song, *Spieluhr* (Music Box), tells the story of a boy buried alive with his music box. When the winter wind blows through his grave, the music box is activated and the boy's heart is rekindled. Worshippers at Totensonntag, a festival for the dead, hear the music box and return the boy to the living.

From the moment I awakened, the significance of the dream was crystal clear. I was torn between writing a dull, scholarly volume and composing something that would be fun and personal. Slam-dunking the book on top of the dusty, dry volumes was a beautiful image for what I needed to do. The dream captured an important emotional reality. I, like the protagonist in the song, felt as though I had been buried alive. Indeed, I had buried the child— the sense of fun—in my writing. I would not overcome the block until I unearthed the soaring, slam-dunking, childhood sense of enjoyment that accompanies writing from the heart.

That dream was my personal Totensonntag. For the remainder of the writing, I never again experienced a debilitating block. *The verbal, rational me could not figure out how to write the book; but another part of my self knew very well, stating the message in image and song.*

HYPNOSIS: ACCESSING OTHER MINDS

Perhaps the most dramatic form in which life themes can be manifest is through hypnosis. It was hypnosis that convinced Freud of the existence of an unconscious mind. Indeed, it is impressive to see how people can access information in a hypnotic state that seems inaccessible in a normal mode. Changes made through hypnosis are true trance-formations.

Of well-known therapists, Milton Erickson is the acknowledged master of hypnotic trance. He used the trance state to interrupt client patterns and introduce new elements into those patterns. Many of his therapy sessions were very different from the normal talk therapy that is commonly associated with counseling. Erickson seemed acutely aware that normal talk in a normal mind state limits access to those facets of self that define one's normal identity. Only by accessing nonnormal spots on the continuum of consciousness, Erickson found, can people make extraordinary changes.

Jay Haley, in his book *Uncommon Therapy*, described some of the innovative techniques employed by Erickson. Erickson realized that it is not necessary to engage in elaborate inductions in order to promote a hypnotic state. Indeed, any situation that can firmly fix the attention of a client is sufficient to introduce an element of trance. Accordingly, many of Erickson's cases involved an element of shock and surprise in order to completely absorb a client's attention. Haley recounted the case in which Erickson met with parents who could not stop their adolescent daughter from sucking her thumb. Erickson agreed to meet with the girl on the condition that the parents would cease all efforts at getting their daughter to stop. They were not to discuss thumb sucking or in any way to comment on it.

Desperate, because nothing else had worked for them, the parents agreed. In an individual meeting with the daughter, Erickson took a different stance. He feigned indignation that the parents were ordering him to change their daughter, expressing the sentiment, "Who are they to be telling me what to do?" This, of course, gained the girl's attention. Furthermore, Erickson told the girl, he could not understand why the hell she just sucked her thumb daintily if she wanted to irk her parents. To really irk them, she should suck her thumb as noisily as possible.

The girl was completely absorbed in Erickson's advice, particularly when he used profanity. Once she was in the highly attentive state, he gave his instructions: She was to sit beside her father for 20 minutes each evening and "nurse your thumb good and loud, and irk the hell out of him for the longest 20 minutes he has ever experienced." Then, she was to join her mother for 20 minutes and do the same.

The girl faithfully executed the instructions, and the parents dutifully refrained from either commenting on the sucking or otherwise trying to make it stop. After several days of loud and effortful thumb sucking, the daughter began to lose interest in the task. She reduced the amount of time spent sucking her thumb and then skipped the exercise altogether. It had become a chore, with little reward. Within a few weeks, she had discontinued altogether.

Erickson recognized the power of highly focused, attentive states, realizing that these open people to processing information in a deep and lasting way. Thoroughly capturing a person's attention with unorthodox interventions, he could induce a degree of hypnotic trance without going through the usual process of induction. Changes that might have otherwise taken months or years were accelerated, given the deep level of processing associated with the attentive state.

Hypnotic procedures can be especially powerful in helping people induce emotional and behavioral changes, bypassing the usual conscious resistance to change. One of my favorite inductions is to have people sit in a chair in a very quiet, still manner and close their eyes. I ask them to hold their hands in front of them, spread apart by about two feet, with the palms facing each other. While they breathe deeply and slowly with eyes closed, I ask them to imagine that there are magnets slowly, slowly pulling their hands together. I suggest to them that as their hands are coming together, they are feeling more and more relaxed, more and more focused. When their hands finally touch, I suggest, they will feel completely calm and at ease. Moreover, I add, whenever they bring their hands together in this manner in the future, they will find themselves in the same calm, focused state.

This is a handy exercise, because it can be easily practiced at home, either with self-instructions (telling yourself that you will feel at peace when your hands touch) or with an audiotape. With sufficient rehearsal, the hand gesture becomes associated with the state of focused self-control, allowing you to enter the state simply by closing your eyes, taking a couple of deep breaths, and bringing your hands together.

One trader with whom I worked, Al, discovered how hypnotic work is internalized as part of a working repertoire. He had learned a new entry technique after attending a trading seminar. The entry worked well in backtesting, as long as it was accompanied by strict money management. The basic concept required the trader to identify short-term, low-volume pullbacks within markets trending upward on rising volatility. These became entry points to get on board a high-momentum market. (The risk, of course, was that of a reversal in a particularly high-volatility market; hence the need for careful stops.) Psychologically, Al found the pattern difficult to trade, as it required entering a market that had already moved nicely higher. He felt more comfortable trying to buy low and sell high, which required a bottom-picking clairvoyance that he, like most traders, lacked.

We adopted the magnet hands exercise to the trading pattern, having Al breathe deeply and slowly with his eyes closed. He moved his hands closer and closer together, as if pulled together by magnets, all the while imagining the pattern he was to be trading. When his hands came together and his fingers touched, I suggested, he would feel calm and confident in placing his trade per the system rules. After a few trials, using historical charts as his guide, Al became quite good at visualizing the pattern and entering a relaxed, focus state as he held his hands in front of him and moved them together.

His breakthrough came just several days later. Al was sitting in front of the monitor when a stock he had been watching paused after a morning spurt upward. The low-volume pause, coming early in the day after an opening gap upward, had the potential to trigger his system. Without even thinking, Al watched the stock carefully, *while holding his fingertips together, as if in a praying position*. This was the self-suggestion he had been rehearsing, now manifesting itself in real time. According to Al, he felt unusually clearheaded in placing his trade—almost emotionless. He had learned to create his own shift, anchoring the trading pattern to a new physical, emotional, and cognitive state.

Had observers been in the trading room with Al, they would have noticed the same kind of marker that therapists observe in their sessions: a change in breathing, in physical movement, and in emotional tone, signifying a transition to a focused and calm state. Moreover, the observers would probably notice that such shifts preceded Al's best trades, whereas those trades placed under greater physical and emotional agitation showed poorer results. Once Al could activate his own Internal Observer and control his state shifts during the trading day, he truly was trading from the couch.

Note, of course, that Al's use of the psychological technique would have been to no avail had he not adopted a valid, tested trading method. There is no merit in learning to be calm and collected while placing trades that lack an edge. Trading from the couch does not entitle you to lie down on the job. Emotional techniques allow you to consistently implement good ideas. They do not substitute for the ideas themselves.

Indeed, consider how damaging it would have been for Al to trade an invalid system. Suppose he implemented his trading ideas but did not incorporate any form of money management. The losses associated with occasional high-volatility reversals would have decimated his portfolio. Even worse, however, Al would have been at his most enhanced state of emotional experiencing at those times when his system is failing him. Sitting in front of the screen, emotionally charged, focused on every tick moving against him, Al would be rehearsing a host of fearful, negative thoughts—unwittingly programming his mind with the most damaging scenarios and messages. In a very real sense, he would be conducting effective therapy in reverse: altering his emotional state and then rehearsing the thoughts, feelings, and behaviors associated with poor performance!

This is a major psychological contributor to failure in the markets: Traders are most open to change—most receptive to internalizing their experiences—when they are wholly absorbed in the markets. And they tend to become most absorbed when they are losing. If a position is moving in their favor, traders can afford to step away and let the trade do its thing. But if the position is moving against them, it is human nature—the need for perceived control—to follow the market closely and to hang on every tick, looking for signs of reversal, hoping, hoping . . .

Al was successful because he used the exercise to become most focused and attentive when he was doing the *right* things in the market. This practice reinforced winning trading patterns. Had he not implemented proper money management, he most likely would have reinforced thoughts and behaviors associated with failure. Traders are accustomed to thinking of money management as a necessary (if somewhat prosaic) tool for preserving their accounts. Equally important, money management is a vital tool for psychological mastery. If you are going to internalize success, you need to *experience* success. Emotionally, you cannot afford to be at your most aroused and focused when you are experiencing failure.

For this reason, a disciplined, scratched trade where the market hits your stops is not a failure. It can, in fact, heighten your sense of control and mastery. One of the better pieces of advice I received as a neophyte trader was to move my stops to my entry price once a trade had moved decisively in my favor. The most damaging trades emotionally are the round trips: the ones in which you take an actual loss after losing a paper profit. Those are double failures: the failure to book a gain, and the failure to limit a loss. They are also some of the most emotional, frustrating trades. By moving stops to break even while you are ahead, you immediately gain the confidence during the trade of "I'm not going to lose on this one."

That is a feeling worthy of reinforcement: a sense of contentment that, over time, becomes a marker for successful trading.

THE WAKING TRANCE: DAYDREAMS

People tend to think of hypnotic states as unusual conditions that occur only in response to a professional hypnotist. In reality, however, people pass in and out of trance states frequently during an average day, as their degree of self-awareness waxes and wanes.

Daydreams are one of the most frequent daily trance states, as your image-based, nonverbal mind takes over for stretches of time and initiates communications with you. It is common to view daydreams as harmless fantasies or as idle wastes of time. However, when you regard daydreams as communications, you become more able to grasp their meaning and significance.

Daydreams reflect your unmet needs. If you cannot meet your needs at a given moment—and especially if these needs are pressing—you tend to find outlet for them in daydreams. A young man from an Asian family, Xiao, found it difficult to navigate between two cultures and sought my assistance. He had spent many of his growing-up years in the United States, but he still spoke his native tongue at home and followed the traditions of his homeland. Anger was rarely directly expressed in his home, especially toward elders. Xiao's reason for entering counseling was that he was troubled by intrusive thoughts. For long periods of time, he would fantasize various scenarios in which he confronted his professors, became angry toward them, and so on. This agitated him greatly, as he could not understand why he would keep thinking of such unacceptable and unprofessional behavior.

It turned out that Xiao had been treated shabbily by one of the residents during a medical rotation. The resident made a negative remark about "foreign doctors" and suggested that Xiao would have trouble passing the rotation because he could not relate to American patients. Xiao knew that this was not the case, but he did not know how to respond to the resident. It was unacceptable to express anger directly, so he did so through an indirect means: his daydreams! Once he could understand that the daydreams were serving a valuable discharge function, he could more readily accept them without agitation.

I often encourage traders to keep a journal of their daydreams as a way of learning about their unmet needs. Like Xiao, many traders find that their daydreams reflect unacknowledged feelings and impulses—ones that can easily distract attention and concentration.

Some of the most interesting daydreams that occur during trading follow winning trades. Recall Odean's research on the overconfidence of traders. When they go through a period of winning, they tend to trade more frequently and subsequently underperform the market. Behavioral finance research conducted by Mark Fenton-O'Creevy and colleagues in the United Kingdom suggests that many traders experience an *illusion of control*, in which they believe they are able to predict even random events. Such an illusion may very well underlie most trader overconfidence. Daydreams of glory, untold wealth, fame, and so on, speak volumes about traders' needs to have their perceptions of control validated. Some of these daydreams are simply imagined scenarios of what the market is likely to do—how it is going to break resistance, soar to new heights, or take out prior lows. Very often these fantasies are contemplated in a self-soothing way, to make traders feel better about their positions. They suggest a *need* for the trade to work out.

Unfortunately, such daydreams can become a straitjacket. Once you are locked into a fantasized scenario, it is difficult to be sufficiently flexible in your perception and thought that you can catch meaningful markers in the markets. This is especially damaging where the imagined scenario is for a long-term market move. The trader then utilizes the scenario as a rationale for holding onto losing positions and violating stops. With each disconfirming piece of market action, anxiety rises, as does the need to defend the fantasy.

I knew several traders who could not accept that the market was in a bull mode through the majority of the 1990s, preferring instead to focus on minute pieces of economic events that suggested an impending crash. To a person, they missed the market bottoms in the 1980s and 1990s and sought vindication for their errors. They spent a significant amount of time daydreaming about the coming economic collapse and the ways in which they would uniquely benefit from the event. Their trading was no longer dictated by reality; it was based entirely on their emotional needs to be proven right.

Later, in the early years of the new millennium, the shoes were on different feet and many traders with whom I corresponded could not believe that the Nasdaq stocks would not quickly return to their days of glory. People who had given up their jobs to pursue full-time trading were caught in a state of cognitive dissonance: They could not reconcile themselves to the fact that they had committed themselves to a market that had peaked. Their way of relieving the dissonance was to ignore the evidence and instead to indulge in fantasies of the markets coming back.

Once you begin to trade in a self-aware manner, the emergence of daydreams can become one of your trading markers, indicating that you are now more focused on unmet needs than on the markets. I recently found myself daydreaming about outsized profits on a short position in the S&P stocks.

The trade was solidly profitable, and, indeed, I had forecast the move to a number of my trading colleagues prior to the market open. I realized, however, that I had stopped watching the screen and stopped following my data with intensity. I was no longer in the zone; I was immersed in my own fantasy of success. That recognition led me to take money off the table before it could be lost and to reestablish my equilibrium. My fantasies became an important marker, enabling me to shift gears.

CONCLUSION

Your mind and your body are always communicating, even when you are silent. The flow of your thoughts, gestures, postures, activities, vocal tones, dreams, and daydreams all provide a stream of information, revealing your processing of events. The trader is thus doubly attuned, casting one eye and ear to the procession of market data and the other eye and ear to the flow of personal experience. Both sets of data encapsulate patterns that serve as markers for change events. These markers are the potential information in the noise: the signals that the trader can use to prompt his or her trading decisions.

A simple example illustrates the interplay of objective and subjective data in trading. A little while ago, the market experienced a bounce from a stiff decline in the S&P futures. During the bounce, I noticed myself feeling a high degree of certainty that the market was vulnerable to further decline. I could not put my finger on the precise source of the feeling, though I knew it had something to do with the lack of vigor of the rise compared to the prior decline. What was clear to me was that this intuition was not simply a case of hoping the market would decline. I had no position in the market and no particular desire either to trade that day or to trade from the long or short end.

I used the occasion to more carefully inspect the market action during the bounce. Right away I noticed that the lowest TICK value achieved by the market over the prior 10 hours was approximately −230. This struck me as unusual. I hypothesized that this might serve as a short-term overbought signal, thereby accounting for my sense that the market was vulnerable.

At that point, I inspected historical data and found that the most recent several short-term tops in the market also possessed this pattern: a minimum 10-hour TICK value greater than −300. I promptly e-mailed the observation to a few trading colleagues, a couple of whom validated my hypothesis with hard data. Armed with this information, our little group had a successful trading day with a double-digit decline in the S&P futures.

I believe this example challenges the usual dichotomies between "discretionary" trading and "system" trading, as well as the polarization of intuitive and quantitative methods. A debate has recently raged on the Spec List regarding the merits and demerits of technical analysis and "counting." Such debates, I fear, miss the essence of discovery in science.

As you can see from my trading example, subjective experience often provides the inspiration for hypotheses. My hypothesis of a weakening market began with a feeling, which was supplemented with a descriptive account of price change and TICK values. Once this qualitative hypothesis was framed, however, the counting work with historical data helped determine whether this hypothesis was valid—whether the observed pattern led to outcomes that were attributable to chance or that were truly nonrandom.

Technical analysis is a handy descriptive language for framing market hypotheses, just as the language of psychology can help convey subjective experience. If you are looking for markers in the markets, a picture *is* worth a thousand words and captures subtleties that ordinary language cannot. Like an X-ray, the charts and the indicator patterns of technical analysis can provide snapshots of market structure and a gross sense of whether that structure is normal or abnormal.

But technical analysis, like X-rays, is generally the beginning of diagnosis, not the endpoint. Radiology can identify a tumor, but only the counting of a blood test or a cytological analysis of a biopsy will determine definitively if the tumor is malignant. Similarly, the charts of technical analysis may reveal an unusual market pattern. Formal testing, however, is needed to determine whether this pattern contains information about the future.

Markers—those of the markets and those of traders—provide hypotheses. The successful trader is both open to these hypotheses and sufficiently skeptical to demand support for them. *The best trading is art elevated to science.*

Chapter Nine

Trance-Forming the Mindscape

Sustained attention makes for sustained intention.

Subjective experience, as we have seen, can both disrupt trading and serve as a fruitful source of market hypotheses. Extracting information from noise in our personal experience is not unlike the same process in following the markets.

In this chapter, we will explore subjective experience in greater depth, building on our core notion of multiple minds. If markets are relatively efficient, as the finance research literature suggests, the ability to process market events in fresh ways may be an important facet of pursuing a tradable edge. Such novel ways of processing can entail the use of ever more sophisticated mathematical tools; this is the way of data mining. Still another novel means for processing is to improve the information processing of the trader. In learning to process market information differently, we can make ourselves better generators of promising trading hypotheses.

THE RADIO DIAL OF CONSCIOUSNESS

Imagine that your mind is a receiver, like the radio in your automobile. This receiver has a dial, with a band of frequencies. At various frequencies, there are signals corresponding to radio stations. Some of these signals are strong, some weak. Some are formatted as news/talk stations; others feature rock music, country tunes, or religious broadcasts. Each frequency has different content and its own distinctive sound and feel. During an average day, you will spend most of your time at one or two points on the dial, tuned in to your accustomed stations. Indeed, you may spend so much time at those frequencies that you forget the remainder of the dial and miss out on what might be there. Instead, you listen endlessly to the same music, the same announcers, and the same commercials.

Most people utilize a relatively small bandwidth along the dial of consciousness. The shifts in effective therapy that I have mentioned represent those occasions when one moves from the comfort—and limitations—of one spot on the dial to a fresh frequency. *The goal of counseling is to enable people to control the knobs that move them from one frequency to another.* When you are stuck in a given frequency, it is all too easy to forget that the knob is even there.

The modern existential philosopher Colin Wilson vividly describes this dilemma in his book *New Pathways in Psychology*. Wilson pointed out that nature has endowed human beings with a most adaptive capacity: the ability to learn new behaviors so well that they can perform them automatically, without conscious effort. For example, when you first learned to drive a car, you needed to expend considerable mental energy on the task: recalling where each pedal was and what it did, watching for oncoming traffic, staying in the center of the lane. With practice, these actions became automated, allowing you to attend to other matters, such as conversations, while you drive.

This ability to automatize complex behaviors is evolutionarily adaptive. If each of your actions required effortful concentration, you would become quickly exhausted. Once behaviors become routine, you are freed to devote resources toward the acquisition of new action patterns, continually expanding your repertoire.

Yet, Wilson pointed out, your ability to act automatically comes at a dire cost. You live much of your life on autopilot, not fully conscious of what you are doing or why. It is that state of sleep described by George Ivanovitch Gurdjieff. You interact with friends and family automatically, drive to work automatically, perform chores automatically. In fact, during a great deal of the day, you are like a robot. You are stuck in a small bandwidth of consciousness, blind to what lies on either side of the dial.

Abraham Maslow was a pioneering psychologist who studied *peak experiences*: those moments in which people feel most alive and healthy. He found that unusually creative and productive individuals, whom he dubbed "self-actualizers," spent an unusual proportion of their time in the peak mode. Wilson observed that routine states of consciousness cannot sustain such peaks, which result from the shifts that occur when one moves effortfully from one spot on the dial to another.

This is the second-wind phenomenon that I discovered when using meditation-based techniques. Recall that if I sat completely still in a totally quiet room and focused all of my attention on a stimulus, I found that I rather quickly became bored and antsy. I invariably felt the impulse to allow my thoughts to wander, to shift my body, and to terminate the exercise. If, however, I did not yield to this impulse, a dramatic trance-formation occurred. I suddenly entered a new spot on the radio dial of consciousness. I no longer felt bored or antsy. Indeed, it took effort for me to rouse myself from this new, strangely pleasurable state.

Moreover, once I was in the new state, *I found myself thinking and feeling in very different ways.* Problems that had seemed insurmountable suddenly seemed minor. Patterns in the market that had eluded me stood out in bas-relief. It was as if I had changed lenses, as in Fredric Schiffer's experiment.

Gurdjieff once wrote that effort is the money one pays for self-development. Wilson's analysis and my personal experience support this conclusion. Focused acts of effort shift one along the mind's radio dial. Self-actualizing people have become so accustomed to absorbing themselves in their work—achieving what psychologist Mihalyi Csikszentmihalyi called the state of *flow*—that they routinely operate at high bandwidth, enjoying the peak experiences that come with an expanded mindscape.

Milton Erickson's surprising discovery, as captured by Jay Haley, was that even seemingly small interventions are able to move people meaningfully along the dial of consciousness, allowing them to experience themselves and their problems in very different ways. I recall one couple who entered counseling many years ago, on the verge of divorce. They engaged in frequent arguments, many times over trivial issues. Efforts to stop the arguments had been unsuccessful. Their problems were especially frustrating to them, given that their children were now out of the house and these should have been the start of their long-awaited golden years.

In the spirit of Erickson, I prescribed two tasks: (1) the couple was to plan an extended vacation together. They had long foregone travel plans due to childcare responsibilities, and I indicated to them that this was the time to dust off those plans. The stipulation was that they were to plan the trip collaboratively and in detail, itemizing each step in the itinerary, selecting the most interesting places to stay, getting the best hotel and travel fares, and so on. I pointed out that they were unique people with distinct priorities and naturally would have different preferences for destinations, lodging, and so forth. This could be expected to lead to *more* arguments, not fewer. And that situation led to the second task. (2) Whenever they argued, they were not to try to terminate the disagreement. To the contrary, they were to argue as heartily as they could. They had to agree, however, to conduct all of their arguments in their walk-in clothes closet while standing on one foot. This was to be their arguing space and mode. Under no circumstances were they to argue outside the closet or while standing on both feet.

They were a bit skeptical, but the couple complied. To their surprise, they enjoyed the process of buying travel books, fantasizing about trips, and making plans. Conversely, it only took two or three arguments in the closet for them to feel completely foolish. It is very difficult to muster resentment and to defend oneself while standing in a silly position in an absurd location. During their last argument, they broke down in complete laughter. They felt completely idiotic going into a closet, standing on one foot, and airing their differences.

Although the Ericksonian technique seems a bit strange, it makes sound psychological sense. The couple thought they should be free from arguing because the kids were out of the house and they now were able to do what they wanted. The reverse, however, was true. They had spent so much of their time invested in the children that there was little for them to communicate about. They could not rid themselves of arguments because even poor communications between them were better than none.

By substituting interactions aimed toward a common goal and creating an absurd context for the arguments, the couple gained a firsthand experience that they could enjoy each other's company without resorting to disputes. Moreover, the changed context for the arguments—standing in the closet on one foot—allowed each member to experience their disagreements in a very different spot on the emotional dial. The arguments, in no small measure, were part of the programming on the common frequency of their dials. By shifting to a different station, the couple was able to access new programming.

Context shifts are some of the simplest yet most powerful ways of moving to new spots on the mindscape. Most people occupy different states of mind, depending on the context they are in. With a spouse, a person might typically be in one frame of mind; at work, he or she can be in another. Where one stands on the dial is, in large part, an adaptation to the context one is in. By shifting contexts, people can gain control over their physical, emotional, and cognitive states.

A trader with whom I corresponded electronically, Eric, reported to me a strange phenomenon. He maintained two trading stations, one at his home and one at his office. Because he had a full-time job not associated with the markets, he had developed mechanical trading systems that allowed him to enter near the previous day's close and to hold for defined periods of time. This allowed him to benefit from trading without having to follow the market tick by tick.

To Eric's surprise, when he reviewed his account statements, he found that his trading performance at the office was much better than his performance from the home. This was completely unexpected because he was using the same systems and placing the same types of trades with the same stocks. When he carefully audited the trades, however, Eric found that he was most apt to deviate from his system at home, often anticipating signals rather than following them.

I suggested to Eric that, perhaps, he felt distracted at home and that this was interfering with his discipline and performance. He replied to the contrary. When he was at home, his wife and children were working and at school during the trading day, leaving him relatively distraction free. If anything, his home performance should have been superior.

Thoroughly befuddled, I asked Eric to phone me and walk me through his last two trades from the home station, recounting as much as he could: his entry strategies, the subsequent course of the stocks, how he felt while placing the trades, his thoughts and feelings as the trades progressed, and so on. Everything seemed perfectly normal until Eric mentioned that periodically he would get out of his chair and walk around the house while the trade was on.

I asked Eric if he typically roamed his office after a trade was executed. He responded no. When I asked why, he laughed and said, "Oh, it's that damned chair at home. Gives me a backache. I have to get up and stretch or I'll feel all knotted up at the end of the day." At the office, as it happened, Eric had an orthopedic chair that was particularly comfortable.

I inquired about other times in Eric's life when he had experienced back-aches or similar debilitating conditions. He promptly mentioned a difficult time in his grade school years when he was laid up for several months due to a severe bicycling accident. His bike was sideswiped by a car pulling out of a driveway, sending Eric tumbling to the ground at high speed. He was in chronic pain and required multiple casts to set the broken bones. He was prevented from playing with friends and attending school, and he felt acutely lonely during that time.

I asked Eric if he would be willing to perform a simple experiment. He was to switch chairs, bringing the home chair to the office and the office chair to his home trading station. Eric again laughed and refused, saying that he needed the orthopedic chair at work because of the amount of time he spent at his desk. He offered, however, to purchase a similar chair for his home, saying it was high time for the change.

Several weeks later Eric called me and reported that the experiment was successful. His home trading was going well. He was faithfully following his trading signals, he reported somewhat mystified; and he was making money. I explained to Eric that this made sense. When he was at home, feeling the twinge of his backaches, it activated highly emotional, painful, and de-structive memories from his childhood accident. He was no longer trading from the couch, observing himself and the market from a neutral stance. Rather, he was immersed in a spot on the mindscape that was anything but neutral. A simple change of context—where and how he sat—was suffi-cient to move him on the dial of consciousness, creating a difference in his trading outcomes.

CHANGING BEHAVIOR BY CHANGING CONTEXTS

Find the context that supports a problem pattern and then alter that con-text. This is a simple formula utilized by therapists in the Ericksonian tradi-tion. It is amazing that even lifelong, highly ingrained patterns can be al-tered with the right shifts of context.

A few months after I had begun my work at the medical center in Syra-cuse, New York, a director of a health professions program called me with a problem. There had been several complaints of racial tension within the entering class. Specifically, during exercises that required teamwork, white students avoided being paired with black students. The clear implication was that the black students were less qualified and capable than their white peers and would only drag the group down if included.

This exclusionary dynamic also played itself out socially within the class. White students and black students sat in their own groups and rarely interacted. Each felt that the other group was given unfair advantages; resentments were running high. In an effort to reduce the tensions, the director asked me to, please, give a talk to the class about racism. She wanted me to encourage the groups to work together.

As you have no doubt surmised to this point, I am profoundly skeptical of the ability of such talks to promote meaningful and lasting attitude and behavior change. A course lecture, with me talking and the students sitting and passively absorbing, would do nothing to help them experience each other in new ways. Indeed, they would be experiencing the world in their accustomed ways, for they would be operating in their normal, routine student contexts.

I agreed to do the talk, but with a key modification. The director had to agree to let me test the group on the content of the lecture and to make the test count as a significant portion of the semester course grade. She readily agreed.

Before I began the lecture to the class, I reviewed the two changed ground rules: (1) they would be tested on the lecture material at the end of the presentation, and (2) their test grade would count as a full examination grade toward their final semester average. Then I casually added, "Oh, yes. I forgot. We're changing the rules for the grading, too. The lowest grade achieved by any student will be the grade that everyone gets." When the class groaned, I quickly added, "But you're allowed to help each other and share answers. We'll make it a group test. It won't be considered cheating if you compare your answers."

The lecture proceeded routinely, and the students dutifully took their notes. At the end of the lecture, I announced that they had 20 minutes to review the information before taking the test.

For a few moments, no one moved. They didn't know how to study as a group. This was a wholly new context for testing.

Then, almost at once, the students shifted their seats and frantically began to check answers. The white students sat with the black students, and vice versa. No one was willing to be the one with the lowest score who dragged down the entire group. At the end of the exercise, everyone achieved a score of 100 percent. They had succeeded as a group, through cooperation. Everyone had served as a resource for everyone else; no one had dragged down the class.

As I left, I suggested that this could be a valuable way of studying in the future because everyone seemed to do quite well. Toward the end of the semester, the program director contacted me and happily reported that this, indeed, was what had happened. To consolidate the initial changes, she added several group exercises to the curriculum, in which everyone would receive the lowest grade achieved by any single student. Once the two groups of students began talking and collaborating, a few friendships formed, and new patterns of class interaction emerged. Even the students who had been most resentful were cooperating with those they had excluded, now that self-interest and group concern were aligned.

TRAUMA AND THE RADIO DIAL

Most of the techniques I have illustrated thus far take a person at one point on his or her radio dial and shift that person to another spot, while introducing a new pattern of behavior. Sometimes the dial shifts occur spontaneously; other times, they are induced through well-timed interventions.

Suppose, however, it is possible not only to shift within the dial of consciousness but to actually expand the dial. What if people could increase the sensitivities and the ranges of their receivers so that they could access different stations and even program new ones? This, I believe, is a most exciting horizon for applied psychology and for trading psychology particularly. *People can cultivate new patterns by programming them onto distinctive spots on their dials and then tuning into those frequencies whenever they choose.*

Such programming of new frequencies does, in fact, occur but often in a negative fashion. One of my favorite questions for psychiatry residents and psychology interns in my brief therapy course is: "What is the quickest, most efficient method for producing human change?" The beginning therapists are typically stumped, sometimes venturing guesses about various approaches to therapy about which they have read.

The answer, I reveal, is *trauma*. Trauma is the most effective, efficient, powerful mechanism for change. Through trauma, a single, powerful, emotional episode can produce lifelong changes in how people feel about themselves and the world. Trauma is the exception to the rule regarding consolidation. A single life event, if sufficiently powerful, is enough to reprogram the radio dial. The signal produced by such an event is so strong that it splatters onto the other frequencies, blotting out their signals. In a very real and frightening sense, the traumatized person is left with a radio dial stuck on a single frequency.

Joseph LeDoux, in his book *The Emotional Brain*, offered insights that can help in understanding the neurophysiology of trauma. Most of people's perceptions are mediated through their higher cognitive functions, associated with the outer, cerebral cortex. Indeed, many of the mind's thinking, reasoning functions can be traced to the cerebral cortex. Episodes that arouse strong anxiety, however, bypass the cortex and are processed in lower, more primitive structures, such as the amygdala. The amygdala is closely linked to motor functions and to the production of stress-related hormones. When traumatic events bypass the normal, rational awareness and elicit processing from the amygdala, a powerful imprinting occurs. Later events that are similar to the initial trauma can trigger the same amygdala responses, creating the flashbacks and extreme anxieties associated with post-traumatic stress disorder (PTSD).

Consider a simple example. I have always enjoyed driving and, in the past, have thought nothing of driving 15 hours at a stretch during vacations. Many years ago, however, I was a passenger in a car that was part of a carpool between Syracuse and my home at that time, Ithaca, New York. The driver took a righthand turn onto a state highway and pulled directly in front of an oncoming car. I was sitting in the front seat, where, unfortunately, the seatbelt was not working. When the other car hit ours, I was thrown through the back windshield head first, and our car was flipped upside down on its hood. My first memory after the impact was looking out the window and seeing blood dripping onto the ground from my scalp. A paramedic talked to me and explained that the "jaws of life" was being used to extract me from the vehicle. Carefully, they loaded me onto a stretcher and into an ambulance, concerned that I had sustained spinal injuries.

The doctors were amazed that the cut on my scalp and one on my wrist were my only injuries. I received a few stitches at the emergency room, and I was as good as new. For months afterward, however, I could not sit in the passenger seat of a car—even if the car was not moving. But I could drive my own car. As a passenger, however, I found myself continually scanning for oncoming traffic, especially looking to my left—the direction from which we were hit. Only after gradual, repeated efforts to sit in a car's passenger seat was I able to ride as a passenger without debilitating fear. Many years later, while riding in a friend's car, we took a turn onto a busy road and I immediately found myself frozen with fear, in the midst of a seeming panic attack. Only afterward did I realize that the turn was very similar to the one I had experienced in Ithaca, with an upward slope to the road and a store to the right. Although years had passed since the accident, the emotional impact was as fresh as if the trauma had occurred that very week.

Traumatic events can program such radically new spots on the dial of consciousness that people suffering from PTSD often feel that they are literally losing their minds. One woman I met with in counseling, Alice, was sexually assaulted and threatened with death. As the man leaned over her, knife in hand, she was convinced that she was going to die. She was powerless to stop the rape and could only close her eyes and blot out the pain in order to cope.

More than a year after the assault, Alice was seeking counseling because of problems in her relationship with her boyfriend, Jim. Often, when Jim attempted to initiate sexual contact, she found herself flashing back to the rape. On more than one occasion, she found herself pushing him away and screaming, even though she had welcomed the intimacy only a few moments before. Jim, of course, was bewildered by this behavior and felt that he had to walk on eggshells in any sexual encounter with Alice. Gradually, the distance between them widened, as the problems in their sexual life crept into other facets of their relationship, attenuating all physical expressions of affection.

Alice could not understand why she was reacting in such an extreme manner. The rape happened a long time ago, she told herself. She felt that she should "get over it." Yet, it continued to intrude in the most unexpected and disruptive ways. Just before their first session with me, Jim had made plans to stay home from work to be with Alice on her birthday. When he showed up at her house with surprise gifts, she became angry that he had sprung this on her without notice. Jim, taken aback at her reaction, became teary eyed, making Alice feel horrible for having hurt the man who so obviously cared for her. "Why am I doing this to him?" she asked in our first meeting.

Prior to the rape, Alice had been comfortable with sexual intimacy and was known to most people as a cheerful, carefree individual. By her account, and those who knew her well, the rape changed her personality. What was clear was that a variety of situations were sufficient to trigger Alice's reexperience of the rape. These included obvious triggers, such as physical touch, but also included seemingly innocuous situations, such as surprise. Any situation in which Alice felt out of control potentially served as a trigger, eliciting a complex set of responses, including anxiety, anger, and self-loathing.

One therapy for such a problem attempts to decondition the fear responses by gradually and progressively exposing the person to trigger situations while rehearsing coping skills that generate experiences of self-control. We placed a moratorium on all sexual contact between Alice and Jim and instead focused on nonsexual touch. Alice took the lead in guiding Jim, remaining in control throughout, as she reacquainted herself with safe physical contact. After much work on casual and sensual touch, Alice felt comfortable trying more sexual contact. With each successful experience, the traumatic conditioning was weakened, and Alice could reclaim the space on her dial of consciousness. It was a very special day when Jim and Alice came to my office, hand in hand, to tell me of their engagement.

The phenomenon of trauma raises a fascinating possibility. What if positive experiences as powerful as traumatic ones could be created and actually expand the bandwidth of consciousness? These "positive traumas" would be akin to the "corrective emotional experiences" described by Franz Alexander and Thomas French in their landmark work on psychoanalysis: experiences so affirming and impactful that they could reshape personality for the better, in ways as profound as Alice's assault.

Can the mind be directly programmed and expanded? Is it possible that people can alter their personalities without undergoing months and years of therapy?

I believe so.

DR. BRETT RECEIVES STRANGE COMMUNICATIONS

Half in awe, half in disbelief, I stared at my computer screen. The communication in front of me was unlike any I had ever received. As a director of student counseling, I was accustomed to receiving all sorts of electronic messages: e-mails requesting appointment changes, pleas for assistance, progress reports from clients. But this posting was a first in my years of practice. It read:

> destroy the rather shied way of the arctic cold. Build a ladder to all you know and whatever you can see in the new age. This is only the beginning. We have so much to do and it's all in front of you so make a pyre to visit every now and again and let flow the words and the sense of

> relief that is here. You know what you have to do it's clear and lies in front of you like a bear skin rug with soft fur in front of a fire. The warmth of your mind spreads out across you body with heat so intense that the fire burns deep inside you. Flaming embers wait with a strict impatience that will never be felt or heard. It's quiet but the flow continues and all is well. Rain the maker day with special flowers in sequence. Happy joy can see whatever is to be.

There was no signature, but I knew who had sent it. What didn't make sense was *why* it had been sent to me. Those who knew me recognized that I was the last person to be concerned with "whatever you can see in the new age." My greatest concerns from day to day were my family, short-term moves of the stock market, and whatever journal article or book chapter was in process. One of my favorite bumper stickers reads, "Forget world peace. Visualize using your turn signal." That's pretty much how I've always felt about the "new age."

But it was the line "Rain the maker day with special flowers in sequence" that alarmed me. That didn't sound right.

One nice thing about working in a department of psychiatry is that there is no lack of people willing to offer opinions about things that don't sound right. So I printed out the message and showed it to a few colleagues. The consensus was unanimous: My writer was probably bright, probably creative, and probably undergoing a psychotic break.

Over the next few days, further messages appeared on my screen. All had the same sound and feel. They were filled with vivid imagery and portentous meanings, interspersed with sentences that violated the bounds of reality. For instance:

> Hallowed are the great ones in the time of the western light. Burning out of control they light the sky with flashes of their brilliance from a depth that has rarely been seen. So many faces and places that they cover the sky in hopes of reconciling the way that we have to go. This is coming straight from the heart in feelings that whisper their power to you over broadcast bands with maximum intensity and power. Live the unit for the day has come. You have seen the way and it is here in all its glory with brightness in a wind of maize. How is the unit to be captured amidst

> the turmoil of the day and how are we to grasp the mean-
> ing of what is to be if we are constricted in a shell of stone?
> These are the questions that wrack your soul and that
> light the fusion of the western sky. Power denied has the
> way that lies deep inside. Vanquish memories in the ce-
> ment of day. Thrilling night has more glow than the cold-
> ness of day.

It is interesting that when I showed the printed messages to people who were not mental health professionals, the reaction was mixed. Some saw the writer as needing emotional help. Others simply viewed the writings as non-sense. "It's amazing how much someone can write without saying anything," was one comment.

Yet I was convinced that the writer was saying something. Common themes emerged across the messages: anticipation of a future path ("You have seen the way . . ."); the juxtaposition of warmth and cold; the need to leave memories behind and find a sense of power. Too, there was a recurrence of images: flashes of light, crystalline shapes, rolling seas, the sky. This was not a random collection of words or images. Like the Woolworth man, the writer was communicating something—and he was communicating it to me.

Most of my colleagues were quick to advise me to not return the communications. The consensus seemed to be that this was not a person to be encouraged. Though no one came right out and said it, the gist was: This person is crazy. Who knows what they might do? Don't give any encouragement.

MIND EXPERIMENTS

It was a holiday period, and the counseling business was slow. Two students had already canceled their appointments. That meant that I'd have time for my experiment.

In the past year, I had performed many such experiments. Most of these involved techniques for developing greater awareness and control over problem patterns. For example, I have always been prone to bouts of procrastination. From the time I was a boy, collecting money on my paper route, I recall avoiding the completion of tasks. Most of the time, these were not threatening or difficult tasks. They might be very simple things, like returning a phone call or running an errand. But I would avoid them until it was no longer possible to maintain the avoidance. Consequences—at least the fear of consequences—snapped me out of the procrastination.

Through my experiments, I found that my procrastination was highly state-dependent; that is, when I was in a certain physical and emotional state, I was much more likely to procrastinate than at other times. So, for instance, if I found myself procrastinating and then began a very rapid, strenuous, and abrupt set of physical movements (e.g., moving my arms and legs in mock-fighting motions), I would fairly quickly enter an energized state in which the procrastination seemed to melt away. Also, if I entered into a deeply meditative state and stilled the thoughts inside my head, I found it easier to pick up tasks and complete them.

This particular day, I had an interesting experiment to conduct. I had long noticed that, when I meditated, random images and sentences would often enter my mind. The same thing also occurred shortly after awakening from a deep sleep. Sometimes the intrusions took the form of emotionally neutral sentences, as in "That is the side that needs to turn." Other times, they appeared as images, such as a car that had plowed into a snow bank. Invariably the images or sentences were fleeting, and I would dismiss them from my mind and resume whatever I was doing. This day, however, I decided to investigate them more carefully. And I thought of an ingenious way to accomplish that.

I knew that the intrusions were most vivid when I entered into a deep state of focus and relaxation. This state could be accessed most successfully through highly repetitive music, such as the early works of Philip Glass. I found that, in that state, I had been able in the past to give myself hypnotic suggestions, using the technique of moving the hands together. Perhaps, I thought, I could use the state to implement other suggestions.

My idea was to enter into the focused, relaxed state while seated at my desk. When a random thought or image would enter my mind, I would type it on the computer. I'm a speedy typist, so I figured I could easily keep up with the stray thoughts that might drift by. In unspoken anticipation, I harbored the hope that I might unearth some interesting insight this way. Perhaps I would obtain an intuition about the future course of the market or a grand realization about Life.

I sat at the computer and began the induction, my headphones filled with Glass's *Music in Twelve Parts*. To enter the state, I close my eyes and gaze intently at the dark visual field. Eventually, in the darkness, I'll notice an area that is lighter than the rest. Very often, but not always, it is to one side of the visual field. I will then focus intently on the light and contract my eyes (as if looking at something very near) in such a way as to expand the light. Within a few minutes, the entire visual field is light, though my eyes are still closed. At that point, my gaze usually has drifted upward, and occasionally I will notice rapid pulsations of my eyeballs and eyelids. Although I am awake and fully conscious, it feels as though I am in a rapid eye movement (REM) sleep state. When I open my eyes, I typically feel very detached from the world, removed from the day's worries and concerns.

In the experiment, however, I planned to type when I entered the state, recording the flow of intruding thoughts. I wasn't sure what to expect. Would the act of typing destroy or alter the flow of thought?

As the experiment commenced, I found myself surprised that my fingers flew across the keyboard, typing the sudden flood of thought. I made a concerted effort to not censor or analyze anything I was typing, instead keeping my attention on the light. At one point in the exercise, I noticed a fleeting, intruding image: A child's drawing in primary colors. The sun was in the upper left-hand corner, and the top was a blue sky. A hand was coming from the right side of the picture, holding a watering can. Drops of water were falling on a row of daisies. The image lasted all of a second and was gone. Shortly thereafter, I stopped typing.

When I opened my eyes, I felt my usual detachment, but with greater intensity. I looked at the computer screen and read my typing. A chill went through me. The writing was unlike any other that I had produced. *Moreover, I could not recall having typed most of it.* The sentence that floored me, however, was: "Rain the maker day with special flowers in sequence." I knew, beyond a shadow of a doubt, that this referred to my image. But it was a sentence that could not have come from my well-ordered mind.

Half in awe, half in disbelief, I stared at my computer screen. I recall thinking that there was no way on earth that I could have written the New Age foolishness that appeared on my screen. I shuddered involuntarily. It was my first, and most powerful, realization that I was not a unitary self with a single mind and identity.

MAPPING THE MINDSCAPE

Subsequent personal experiments convinced me that people have much greater power in altering their mindscapes than they commonly recognize. As a writer, I discovered long ago that what I wrote in my more creative moments was often completely unrelated to what I had been planning to write. It was as if a hidden Muse had provided the thought and the inspiration for me. On those occasions, I have looked back on a piece of good writing with the sense of "How did I ever write that?"

It is fortunate that I am a relatively proficient typist and can get my thoughts onto the computer almost as quickly as they appear in my mind. When I'm immersed in my writing, I'm hardly thinking about what I'm going to say. The ideas come to me, and I type them out. It is not hard, at such times, to believe in the idea of multiple minds.

On one particular occasion, however, I decided to turn this idea into yet another experiment. I first placed myself in the deeply focused state by immersing myself in the Philip Glass music. As before, I placed my full attention on the light areas that appeared within my darkened visual field once I had closed my eyes. By this time, I had become rather good at entering the state of quietude. Now, however, I decided to extend it. To my surprise, I found that if I stuck with the exercise long enough, I hit not one but several points of second wind. Each time I felt tempted to end the exercise, I pushed myself yet further. Eventually, I extended the exercise for hours, remaining in a completely still, quiet position.

The results from the exercise were every bit as dramatic as those from any psychoactive drug. After several hours of total focus, my proprioceptive sense was greatly altered. The slightest movement in my swivel chair felt overwhelming and disorienting, like I was dipping and diving on a roller coaster. I lost all sense of which side of the room I was facing. When I did open my eyes, normal objects looked unusually vivid in color and shape. It was as if the hours of reduced sensory input had recalibrated my senses, making me sensitive to normal stimuli the way someone long deprived of food might gain a vivid sense of taste.

In the highly altered and attentive condition, I gained an appreciation for how artists and poets must see the world. The hours of complete darkness, almost totally free of thought and movement, made me exquisitely sensitive to the beauty of ordinary things in my room: the nuances of shapes and hues, the interplay of patterns on a tapestry, the richness of shadings created by the lights. I felt as though I could spend hours absorbing the beauty of it all. In the back of my mind, I also recognized that I was reacting quite uniquely to normal objects. My distinct realization was that my normal waking hours were so filled with stimuli—people talking, noises from roads, bombardments from television—that I spent much of my days in a state of overload without knowing it. I was like a glutton at a buffet, consuming so much each day that I no longer appreciated subtle and varied tastes.

My working hypothesis, which I am presently testing with biofeedback, is that there is a direct correlation between the amount of time spent in an experiential exercise, the intensity of experience, and the openness to change that is possible in the heightened state. In other words, deeper and longer trances produce a higher measure of cognitive and sensory recalibration, enabling one to more readily shift his or her mode of experiencing. After long sensory reduction, I felt that the simple scent of a garden flower would be sufficient to generate a state of heightened experiencing that would be as great as a dramatic intervention in a counseling session.

My recent efforts with forehead temperature biofeedback suggest that it takes a sustained period of quiet and focus to reach such dramatically altered experience. Indeed, the biofeedback readings do not begin to radically depart from baseline before 15 to 30 minutes of remaining still—and that is with some degree of practice. This suggests to me that people's normal states of mind are conservative: They are relatively resistant to short-term, sizable shifts. That would make sense because frequent large shifts would no doubt disrupt the continuity of daily thought and behavior. In order to function effectively in the world and to remain in control of their actions, people's states of mind must remain relatively stable.

By exerting significant effort through meditation, biofeedback, and the like, people can override the mind's natural settings and induce magnitudes of shifts that approximate those that occur during trauma. This requires both time and discipline and, hence, is not experienced in the normal flow of daily life. Csikszentmihalyi's work, however, strongly suggests that particularly creative individuals, immersed in their work, do achieve a measure of focus and concentration similar to that attained in my Philip Glass exercises. If so, they have developed natural means for expanding their mindscapes and cultivating new modes of perception and behavior. Indeed, they may have expanded their capacity for evolution by overcoming the usual conservative mechanisms of consciousness.

Can traders, I wondered, accomplish the same thing?

EXPERIMENTS WITH TRADING

Having improved my ability to enter this altered state, I moved to the next phase of my experimentation, which was to immerse myself in my usual homework before a day's trading, reviewing charts and indicator data to formulate hypotheses. I made a conscious effort to note everything but to avoid jumping to any conclusions about what I was seeing. (I must say that the latter was difficult—patterns seemed to jump out at me with unusual distinctness.) Once I had poured over the information and conducted a few tests, I then decided to spontaneously type out everything that came into my head about trading the day to come. I typed it rapidly, not censoring any of the ideas. I also wrote it as if I were writing a newsletter for public readership, complete with advice about what to do in various situations.

As with my earlier experiment, the writing came with ease. I found my fingers fairly flying across the keyboard. I was aware of what I was typing, but I was removed from it at the same time. It was a bit like watching my body do the typing.

Before reading my written synthesis of the market information, I extended the experiment still further. I closed my eyes again and reentered the focused state. This time I wore headphones connected to the computer. I had highlighted the text I had written; and once I was completely attentive, I clicked on a menu item in my Dragon Systems "Naturally Speaking" program that allowed the writing to be read to me in a synthesized voice. The voice had a clipped manner of speaking with a faint British accent. It read to me what I had written, and I absorbed it in my trance-formed state.

Listening to my own words spoken by another had an unusual effect, as if I were absorbing the thoughts of an expert consultant. The eerie and strangely irrational thought passed through my mind that I was hearing the voice of the Almighty. Nevertheless, I had the sense that I was hearing Truth:

> Extensive buying on Friday could not surmount the wall of resistance on Thursday, creating a line to trade against. Rallies that fail to break the line offer shorting opportunities, targeting Friday's lows as minimum objective. A break below Friday's lows has you shorting rallies. A sharp move above the wall on expanded TICK has you buying dips. Failure to rally in the morning will create weakness in the afternoon. Beware the disjunction of financial and industrial issues.

As I listened to the text of my writing, it was clear that the writing style was similar to the strange, descriptive prose from my earlier experiment. The phrase "Beware the disjunction" was not at all something I would normally say, and it was not something I would normally emphasize in my trading. Indeed, I wasn't consciously aware that there was any "disjunction" between financial stocks and the broader list of stocks that make up the Dow Jones

Industrial Average. When I checked the charts, however, it was clear that the financials—especially the brokerage stocks—were in a downtrend, even as the broader averages stayed in a narrow, flat range. My writing, it seemed, was alerting me to the theme being developed in the market, which cast financials as possible harbingers of the next move.

For better or for worse, I felt that I had a strategy going into the day's trading. I also had a sense of calm certainty that was unusual for me in trading. The observation of the breakdown in the financial stocks, which had escaped my normal attention to that point, convinced me that the altered mode of experiencing had opened me to new ways of processing market data.

Before the market open, I again invoked the quiet, relaxed state. My mind was still as trading began. The volume was fairly low for the opening minutes, and the market was relatively flat. I closed my eyes, taking it all in without forcing any conclusion.

That's when it happened.

A random thought popped into my head. But it was not simply a thought or even *my* thought. Distinctly, in my head, I heard the voice, in its clipped, British tones, say, "Master the disjunction." That was all. It was a simple phrase, but it came to me as if it had been read from the "Naturally Speaking" program.

I returned to my screen and noticed that the sector index for the brokerage stocks ($XBD) had broken down. The overall market was weakening, with waning TICK, but the Standard & Poor's (S&P) still appeared flat. Calmly, I placed my trade, going short. I was never so sure of a profit, never so certain of my target and of my stop points.

Minutes later, I covered for a profit.

At Friday's lows.

I had no feeling of success or elation whatsoever. There was no ego in the trade at all. In fact, I had the strangest feeling that I hadn't placed the trade in the first place. There was no doubt that the order was placed *by me*. But I swear: *I* didn't make that trade.

CONCLUSION

Earlier, I mentioned Ari Kiev's idea of "Trading in the Zone": achieving complete immersion in our processing of market data and acting on it. The case studies of neurologists Oliver Sacks and V. S. Ramachandran; the large body of split-brain research; the commonalities of experience among mystics in differing eras and cultures: These have convinced me that people, indeed, have *many* zones—more than people commonly recognize.

You might sometimes hear the (misguided) assertion that people use only a small portion of their brains for thought. The reality is a bit more complex. The average individual only accesses a fraction of his or her possible consciousness—as Gurdjieff pointed out, like someone who occupies a single room within a mansion, blind to its many splendid rooms. Creativity in any field of endeavor—whether it is trading, parenting, or counseling—comes from the ability to see the world afresh, from the vantage point of those different rooms. I know it sounds hopelessly mystical, and you know how I hate new-age speak. But I cannot deny the conclusion reached by Norretranders: *There is more to myself than my self.*

I believe that this is the greatest frontier of trading psychology. In learning to expand your radio dials of consciousness, you gain the potential to process market data in new and profitable ways. As the next chapter will make clear, you can perceive and know things in one state of mind that completely elude you in another. It is as if you contain multiple internal databases, but with restricted access to each. In cultivating the ability to trance-form the mindscape, you increase your access and become able to trade from a wider base of information.

In the spirit of the research of Andrew Lo and Dmitry Repin, I believe that biofeedback holds significant potential for the development of traders. Although traditional psychology—including much of this book—can formulate meaningful hypotheses about trading success, only hard research will validate or disconfirm these hypotheses. The great advantage of biofeedback is that it transforms subjective variables—emotionality, focus—into objective readings that can be submitted to statistical treatment. Biofeedback takes the Galtonian ideal of counting and applies it to personal experience.

Will trade stations of the future come with integrated consoles for measuring heart rate, skin conductance, muscle tension, and body temperature? Will traders practice their craft with wristband units for measuring pulse and blood pressure, much as professional athletes do? To the extent that trading is a peak performance sport, you can expect to see ever more sophisticated tools for the trader, just as you are witnessing more advanced software and hardware for trading. In ways that even Ayn Rand could not have envisioned, the pursuit of profit may accelerate your highest evolutionary strivings.

Chapter Ten

The Coat in the Closet

Demons risen make for fallen angels.

Although there is more to us than we normally assume, it would be a mistake to conclude that human nature is infinitely plastic. I sincerely doubt that any person could feel confident and successful if all they had experienced was failure. A lifetime of abuse and neglect will not suddenly give way to feelings of joy and fulfillment. New experience cannot be woven out of thin air. Ultimately, in self-development exercises, we are activating facets of our personalities that are latent and submerged, but present in some form nonetheless. To frame the issue in terms of our earlier metaphor, counseling takes signals on the radio dial of consciousness that are weak and systematically boosts the volume. Perhaps it is not so much that we create new frequencies as that we become ever better receivers for the faint signals that are out there for us to hear.

In this chapter, we will explore how traders can improve the reception of their mind's radio receivers by boosting weak but valuable signals. Instead of becoming lost in the programming at any given frequency, we can identify with the hand that controls the knob and changes the stations. Once on a new spot on the dial, it is remarkable to see how much more we can see and experience. What we know is truly a function of our states of mind and body.

STOPPING THE MORNING FRENZY

We were running late. Every morning, I see my wife off to work and get my children, Devon and Macrae, ready for school. And, sure enough, it seems as though every morning, something conspires to hold us up. Devon can't find her hair band; Crae is missing the favorite item he wants to take to school. All the while, I cajole, implore, and tear my hair out. Somehow, some way, we make it on time.

On this day, however, we were *really* late. I hustled the children along, reminding them at regular intervals that they needed to finish their breakfasts, comb their hair, put on their shoes, and make sure their homework was in their backpacks. After feeding the cats and preparing my lunch, I looked at my watch. We only had a few minutes to spare. Alarmed, I gave my customary bellow: "Let's go!" Devon and Crae tumbled down the stairs and dutifully began to put on their coats and boots, steeling themselves for yet another chilly, sleeting Syracuse morning. I did the same, reaching into the closet for my raincoat.

It wasn't there.

I looked across the row of coats on the left side of the closet. No raincoat. Very odd; I *always* put the coat there. I opened the right side of the closet. No coat. Time was truly getting away from us. I started to feel frantic. The children needed to be at school, and I had an important morning meeting. Worse still, my car keys were in the coat pocket. No coat, no car.

Now, more quickly, I returned to the left side of the closet and scanned the jackets and coats. One at a time, my eyes targeted the contents of the closet. No raincoat. Devon and Crae seemed to sense my mounting frenzy. They were unusually quiet, refraining from their normal morning bickering.

I glanced at my watch. We were late.

For a moment, I was enveloped in turmoil. I could sense the tightness in the muscles of my forehead, the racing thoughts, and the mounting panic. It was almost as if a voice were screaming inside my head: This *can't* be happening. The coat *has* to be here. I was dimly aware that my reaction was excessive. At some level, I knew that the world wouldn't collapse if we were a few minutes late. But it didn't matter: My body had decided that this was an emergency.

Then I *stopped*.

It had happened only a few times before: Suddenly, often in the midst of an emergency, I become eerily and unnaturally calm. I fix my vision, slow my breathing, and all at once the roiling waters become still. It's not at all gradual; more like flipping a switch. It happens automatically. And it's spooky. When I am *stopped*, I don't feel like myself.

I never recall having the *stopped* feeling as a child or a young adult. It has only occurred since my experimentation with the Philip Glass music and the altered states. It appears to be a relatively new spot on my radio dial.

STOPPING ON THE WAY TO NEW YORK

It was not the first time I had felt this way. Several months previous, Margie and I went for a short vacation to New York City. We had just crossed the Syracuse town line, heading south on Interstate 81, when we noticed the car in front of us drifting to the right. It was very early in the morning, and my immediate impression was that the driver had fallen asleep at the wheel.

That's exactly what had happened. As the car touched the rough edge of the road, the driver seemed to awaken and realize what was happening. He swerved the vehicle sharply to the left, impulsively trying to avoid veering off the road. It was the wrong move. The back end of the car fishtailed outward, as the car entered a skid. The driver tried to compensate by jerking the wheel back to the right, but it was too late. The car spun wildly in the middle of the highway. Not a single other vehicle was in sight.

It was strange watching the car careen out of control. It was like watching a movie; I was distanced from the unfolding events. The scene is implanted in my mind, an unusual occurrence because I rarely think in images. I didn't feel worry or concern. I simply touched the brake and stayed sufficiently far from the car that we would not become involved in the pending accident.

The car continued its leftward spin and careened off the highway, tumbling down a gently sloped embankment along the median. It tipped and landed softly on its side.

I turned to Margie as we pulled off the road. She seemed concerned, but didn't say anything. Faintly, I could hear voices from the rolled car. I placed my hands on the steering wheel and took a long breath. I had *stopped*.

In an unnaturally calm voice—a voice that didn't at all sound like my own—I explained to Margie that she should stay in the car and remain on the lookout for help. I would check out the accident.

I didn't feel a thing: not fear, not anticipation, not adrenaline pumping. Nothing.

I calmly walked to the car. There were two adults in the front seats and two children in the rear. The children were upset, but no one looked hurt. In an abnormally even voice, I explained to the mother what had happened. I calmly observed that their car had little damage, that the children looked okay, and that there was no sign of gasoline leakage or other danger. It was as if I were dictating a report into a transcription machine or perhaps were a machine myself. I felt no emotion: only the task demands of the moment.

As I turned toward our car, I observed that another vehicle had stopped. The driver had noticed Margie and offered assistance. He explained that he was a paramedic and indicated that he had summoned help on his cell phone. Within a few minutes, the help arrived. Everyone was safe.

When I returned to the car, I explained to Margie what I had seen. As I talked, I suddenly realized that the family could have been killed, that their car could have been filled with blood, and that the vehicle could have blown up. It was a *car accident!* As if a dam had broken, releasing pent up waters, I began to shake. I was a nervous wreck.

I had returned to being Brett.

KNOWING MORE THAN WE KNOW WE KNOW

As I surveyed the coat closet, I knew that this *stopped* feeling was exactly the one I had experienced on the highway. If I believed in spirits, I would say that I had become possessed. Occasionally, articles in the tabloids will describe people who say that they have been abducted by alien beings. Some people with a condition called Asperger's syndrome actually believe that they *are* aliens or can communicate with them. They realize that they are unlike everyone else and cannot explain the difference in any other fashion. That is how it feels to be *stopped:* as though a robot-alien has taken over. Perception is unusually clear at those times; there is no clouding of thought by doubt, desire, or fear. I feel like an efficient, accurate information-processing machine.

I turned to the children and very calmly explained, "I'm just going to be a minute. I need to find my coat." My voice seemed flat, a bit slower than usual, and as if it were coming from a great distance. Neither Devon nor Macrae seemed to notice anything amiss. They continued to wait alongside their backpacks, petting their multicolored, feline friends Ginger, Gina, and Mali. *They* didn't care if we were late to school.

More slowly than usual, I turned to the left side of the closet. Without hesitating—and with no prior thought or planning—I searched for the raincoat *between the other garments*. In a moment, the search was over. The coat had fallen from its hanger and had become trapped between two winter coats in the overfilled closet. I calmly put the raincoat on, retrieved the keys from the pocket, and gathered the children into the car.

As I drove to work, the clear, quiet mode persisted. It was a pleasant, calm, unruffled feeling, a bit distanced from the world. I pondered the question: *Was the coat really lost?*

At one level, it most obviously was. I searched high and low and couldn't find it. Yet at another level, I knew exactly where it was. Once I had *stopped,* I went to the coat with no hesitation whatsoever. The coat was lost to Brett, but not to the robot.

How much else might I know and not know that I know? How many market patterns go unnoticed by my conscious, frantic mind because they are caught between the usual indicators?

JOAN AND HER INNER VOICES

Joan was a bright, attractive woman in a challenging medical school program. She was the envy of her peers: successful, attractive, and popular. School was stressful for most of her classmates. They spent countless hours worrying about failure, cramming for the next exam. Not Joan. It seemed as though she could read the material once, absorb it, and pass with flying colors. In other people's eyes, she had it all together.

The reality was far different. Joan felt that she was a failure. She believed that she was "gross," "disgusting," and "fat." She had an eating disorder, a blending of anorexia (self-starvation) and bulimia (binge eating and purging).

In our first session, Joan made it very clear that she shouldn't feel this way.

She knew that she was popular, bright, and successful. At one level, she even knew that she wasn't overweight. "But I *feel* fat," she insisted, giving voice to her multiplicity. "People tell me how wonderful I am, but I don't believe it. I feel like an imposter. They don't really know what I'm like."

For the greater part of the academic day, Joan experienced few problems. Her focus was on her work, and she genuinely enjoyed learning about medicine and helping others. Indeed, that was one island of self-esteem amidst her negativity: Joan realized that she was a caring person and knew that she worked well with patients. She described the time when she spent an extra hour with an uneducated immigrant man who complained vociferously about his "family problems." He had been admitted to the hospital for complications related to heart disease and high blood pressure. The physicians on the service either dismissed his family-related complaints or indicated that he would be referred for family counseling after his medical problems had been addressed. Only after truly listening to the man did Joan figure out that these family problems were sexual ones. The man was experiencing erectile dysfunction in reaction to his blood pressure medication. Joan's face lit up with pride as she described the man's joy on learning that the problem was with the medication, not his manhood.

Once the working day was over, however, and Joan returned home, her focus turned inward and became unremittingly self-critical. She spent hours weighing herself, trying on her clothes, measuring her food portions, and standing in front of the mirror, all in the desperate hope that she could lose weight. At other times, she would lose all self-control, attempting to drown her disgust with her body in quarts of premium ice cream, cookies, and brownies. Her bingeing episodes left her even more despondent about her inability to lose weight and more disgusted with her body. Evenings thus became an endless cycle of self-loathing, attempts to lose weight, and efforts to soothe herself with food. She felt totally out of control. If positive reinforcement alone really did govern behavior, Joan should have been a paragon of self-esteem. She had experienced no lack of successes, no absence of acceptance and praise. She described her family upbringing as supportive and harmonious. Her parents were achievement oriented and clearly pushed their children to excel, but there were no abusive recriminations if grades, athletic performances, or piano recitals didn't work out well. Indeed, Joan mostly remembered receiving praise from her parents when she brought home good grades.

None of those positives seem to have been internalized, however. It seemed as though she clung to her negative self-image no matter what happened in her life and despite what others said or did. This, of course, was tremendously frustrating to those few people who knew about Joan's problems and wanted to help her. Sensing their frustration, Joan did her best to keep her eating problems a secret. In a desperate effort to keep her problems to herself, she avoided truly close friendships, only allowing people to see the competent, confident exterior. This further accentuated her feelings of isolation, failure, and worthlessness. By the time she came to counseling, she was seriously depressed.

When Joan first entered the office, she looked haggard. She acknowledged that she had not been sleeping well, and she said that she had been binge eating and forcing herself to throw up the food. It became a vicious cycle: She would feel depressed, eat to make herself feel better, feel guilty for eating, throw the food up, then feel depressed about her out-of-control behavior. Recently, she said, she had been losing valuable study time staring into the mirror, evaluating her body.

"So tell me what happens in front of the mirror," I suggested. "What are you thinking and feeling when you're standing there and looking at yourself?"

"I feel disgusting," Joan replied. "I don't like the way I look."

"Could you take me back to a specific time, recently, when you were standing in front of the mirror feeling disgusting?" I asked. "What were you thinking? What were you feeling? Try to put me in your shoes."

This is perhaps the most common question I ask in therapy: "Could you give me an example?" Talking about specifics helps to bring people closer to their experiences, toward a heightened emotional and physical state. Conversely, when people are overwhelmed by emotion and in serious crisis, I will stay as far from specifics as possible, trying instead to help them understand their feelings conceptually. Knowing when people come to counseling with too much structure—hiding their experiences—and when they are flooded with experience and need structure is a crucial element of helping. It's back to that idea of comforting the afflicted and afflicting the comfortable.

Joan looked away. "I don't know," she said. "I just don't like myself."

This is more of that Freudian "resistance." It is too painful for Joan to reexperience her moments of self-loathing, so she avoids my inquiry. By talking in generalizations, rather than entering into the emotional specifics of her times in front of the mirror, she is protecting herself from anxiety. Resistance to change, as I mentioned earlier, appears to be a fundamental feature of human consciousness, not just a response to anxiety, as in Joan's case.

It turns out that anxiety is an interesting phenomenon. Anxiety is generally thought of as a negative emotion, but it has its uses. The first therapist I ever had was Elizabeth Hoffmeister, a Jungian analyst in a small Kansas town. She was a sensitive, intuitive woman with a true gift for dream work. One day, after I had been rambling on in my ridiculously intellectualized way, Liz noted my avoidance and suggested that I *embrace* anxiety. We tend to be afraid of the unknown, she offered, but that is where our growth lies. We *can't* grow if we stay with the known, the routine, the familiar. It was from Liz that I developed the recognition that *the path to growth lies in following your anxiety, in venturing into the unknown.*

This is why it is not especially helpful to spend countless hours in sessions interpreting and analyzing resistances. Such work only helps to further distance people such as Joan from their emotional experience. Many times, through gentle pressure, the resistances can be challenged, opening the door to the person's rich emotional world. Indeed, the mere act of pushing past a resistance can, by itself, dramatically alter an individual's state and provide access to memories and perceptions that had long been hidden.

"Joan, please look at me," I requested. She immediately returned my gaze and I held it for a second. "Now, please close your eyes and use your imagination. You have come home from a long day at school. You haven't eaten all day, so you have had a large dinner. You feel a little full, and that reminds you of your weight. You get on the scale and look into the mirror. You've taken off your clothes. You're looking at your chest, your midsection, your hips, your thighs. What do you see?"

Joan was visibly uncomfortable with the evocative imagery. "I hate how I look," she cried out. "I look fat and disgusting. I *can't* go out. I don't want anyone to see me like this. I don't even like wearing my clothes. They feel tight after I eat. I just want to disappear. I feel gross." Joan's face was filled with anguish. There was no question that she saw herself differently from everyone else. Her body repulsed her, and she longed to lose weight. Nevertheless, she sabotaged every effort to successfully manage her food intake. What grabbed my attention most, however, was that she was tensing her muscles and digging her fingers into her skin as she talked, as if to hurt herself. Her words were saying "upset" and "pain." Her body, however, bespoke "anger."

Her pain truly tugged at me. I was tempted to try to reassure her, to tell her that she isn't disgusting; but I realized that this would be the wrong approach. It was what everyone else had been saying to her, and it certainly hadn't worked up to that point. She would have simply concluded that I could not possibly understand her and would have rejected any offer of support.

I was also convinced that talking about food, calories, and weight was the wrong way to go. Monitoring her eating and her weight would simply set me up in an unwanted, controlling role, poisoning our work. What was needed was a translation, a way out of this endless cycle of depression and self-hatred, restriction of food, frustration, overeating and purging, and further depression and self-hate.

Joan's problem, it seemed to me, wasn't so much an eating disorder as a self-image disruption manifesting itself through food and weight. Those tightened fingers, I suspected, held the key.

"So how are you doing in school?" I asked brightly.

Joan looked puzzled, slightly confused by the sudden change in topic and mood. "Okay, I guess," she said.

"What rotation are you doing now?" Like Walt, all third-year medical students participate in clinical rotations, where they work in various specialty fields, such as surgery, family medicine, and psychiatry.

"I'm doing OB," she said. "I really like it."

"Great," I enthused. "Tell me something. If you had a patient in OB-GYN who was going through exactly what you're going through—she looked like you do, felt like you do, had the same problems with food and weight and self-esteem—what would you say to her? How would you treat her?"

Joan answered immediately, smiling at the recognition of where I was heading. "I would try to help her not be so hard on herself. I'd hold her hand and tell her that she could be a wonderful person no matter how much she weighs." Joan's tone of voice had softened. She sounded compassionate.

"*Really?*" I did a mock double take. "That's what you'd say if she looked and felt like you? You wouldn't tell her that she is disgusting, that she is gross, and that she shouldn't go out in public?"

Joan laughed out loud. "No, I wouldn't say that."

"Why not?" I asked. "It would be true, wouldn't it? Why would you lie to your patient? Why would you say that she can be wonderful when in fact she's not?"

"It would be mean!" Joan exclaimed, as if stating the obvious. "You *can't* do that. It would make the problem worse. It wouldn't be right to judge her just because of her looks. It would be shallow."

"Are you shallow?" I asked.

"No, I don't think I am," Joan said firmly. "I think I'm good with my patients."

"I have a feeling you're right," I said. "You would try to see your patient for whom she is, not just for her looks or her weight. You would be kind to her, you'd take her hand, and you'd reassure her."

Joan nodded.

"So why is it mean and unprofessional to treat a patient harshly but okay to treat yourself that way? Why are you automatically less deserving than any patient walking in the door?"

For a moment, Joan's face went blank, her eyes filled with puzzlement. A tear started to form in her eye. "I don't know," she said very softly.

REPAIRING MULTIPLICITY

My goal was to call Joan's attention to her multiplicity—her wildly different frequencies on the radio dial. There is the sensitive, caring, Professional Joan, who is competent and supportive. Then there is Angry Joan with the clenched hands, gouging herself emotionally for every perceived shortcoming. When dealing with others, Joan can access her caring feelings: Professional Joan is much too concerned with being a successful student to say anything hurtful to a patient! But when dealing with herself, looking in the mirror, Professional Joan is submerged. In her place is Angry Joan, a vindictive, destructive person beset by her internal demons.

It was fascinating to see the transformation in my office. When speaking of herself, Joan was anguished, her voice and face tense, her posture rigid in the chair. Although her words spoke the language of depression, her face and body spewed rage and contempt whenever she spoke of her appearance, her weight, or her ambivalence toward food. When asked about her clinical work, however, her voice immediately became more matter-of-fact, direct, and smooth. Her posture eased, and she spoke with assurance. As with Mary and Walt, it truly was as if a different Joan had entered the room. But she seemed unaware of any of it. The transitions between Angry Joan and Professional Joan were seamless.

In the face of such duality, it became crystal clear that Joan's problem was not her eating or even her self-loathing. Her problem was her vertical split: the fragmentation of her being, her inability to access that part of her that was capable of reaching out and holding a hand. When she was immersed in her punitive self, she could not recruit her caring capacities. That prevented her from treating herself as she would treat a patient, a best friend, or a loved family member. If she could gain access to her professional, helping self when she dealt with eating and body image, she would have a powerful counterbalance to her angry, frustrated self. She wouldn't need to turn to food for gratification if she could cultivate the kind of relationship with herself that she enjoyed with her patients.

So it is with many traders. In other facets of their lives, they can process information rapidly and effectively, making constructive decisions and successfully navigating risk. In their trading, however, they find themselves repeating destructive patterns. Even when they are aware of these patterns, they cannot seem to control or to change them. They are locked on the radio dial, unable to find the knob.

TRIGGERS

Before exploring how Joan was able to bridge her divergent selves, take a look at the role of triggers in the shifts that occur among these selves. Triggers, it turns out, are the great saboteurs of trading.

Recall Chapter 8 and Alice's experience with the sexual assault. A number of triggers, some quite subtle, were sufficient to return her to the thoughts, feelings, and impulses associated with the traumatic event. When I experienced my automobile accident, many triggers set off my subsequent anxiety: sitting in the passenger's seat, making a righthand turn, seeing cars approaching from the left, and so on.

Although consciousness is generally conservative, keeping people locked into their normal frames of mind, powerful emotional events that are associated with particular cues can cause radical shifts. These cues become triggers for modes of processing that are quite different from the norms. Indeed, many clients in therapy—and many traders—recognize that their behaviors don't fit their usual personalities and are quite upset about that. They recognize that they have lost a measure of control over their lives.

One of Joan's triggers was simply the feeling of fullness following her dinner. She was quite busy during the day and did not have time for a complete lunch. As a result, she was hungry by the time she got home. She ate a good meal and at some point felt the sensations of fullness. This full feeling made her cognizant of her body and evoked the feelings she had experienced following bingeing episodes. Worse still, the fullness was associated with sensations she had experienced when she had gained weight. On the heels of these associations, Joan immediately became self-conscious and *felt* fat. The trigger of fullness became a switch that activated her negative sense of herself.

Problematic trading is often triggered in very similar ways. The trader who finds himself or herself placing orders impulsively is like the traumatized individual, reacting to stimuli in exaggerated ways. Some of the most common triggers for shifts in trading are those associated with distinctive emotional states. Consider the plights of the following traders:

- Trader A experienced a harrowing downturn in the crash of 1987, wiping out a significant portion of her equity. Now, when the market moves against her, she finds herself overcome with anxiety, unable to sustain even a normal drawdown. This leads her to bail out of positions at the least opportune time, generating feelings of failure and shame.
- Trader B was unpopular as a child because he was overweight and not athletic. Later in life, he was also unpopular with members of the opposite sex. He spent much of his adolescent and young adult life feeling bored and rejected. Now, as a trader, he finds it difficult to tolerate dull, flat markets where there is little volatility. He chronically overtrades these markets, undergoing one whipsaw after another, until he throws in the towel—and misses the eventual trending move.
- Trader C experienced the thrill of a major market coup early in his career, riding a high momentum stock to a massive gain, adding to his position along the way. Now, whenever he experiences a healthy gain on a position, he finds himself reliving his thrill and impulsively adding to his position. This makes him vulnerable to the inevitable reversals in his positions, which occur when he is maximally leveraged.
- Trader D finds that she responds to heightened market volatility with anxiety, even though the move may be in her forecasted direction. If she is not onboard the move when it begins, her anxiety is channeled toward self-recrimination over having "missed the move." This paralyzes her from making a high-percentage entry in the new trend and leaves her internalizing a potentially winning situation as a setback.

In these and so many other cases, the swings of the market act as triggers for mind shifts among traders. This fits nicely with the biofeedback research of Lo and Repin, who found that even experienced traders show heightened arousal in response to trend and volatility changes in the markets. Like Joan, these traders may go through much of the day functioning at a high level, feeling good about their work. Once the trigger is activated, however, another self takes over, leading them to process information about themselves—and about the markets—quite differently.

A great deal of seemingly irrational trading behavior is a subconscious attempt to avoid these destructive triggers. Restricting her eating was Joan's way of avoiding the trigger of feeling overly full. Tensing my muscles until they hurt while I am a passenger in a car was my way of steeling myself against an anticipated accident. Selling winners far too early is a defense against the anxiety of a drawdown; impulsively entering positions protects against those self-recriminations if an opportunity is lost. Tacitly, people know their triggers and fear them. Like Joan, traders will take extreme actions—even those that hurt their profit/loss statements—to avoid the triggers. For the bored trader sitting in the middle of a flat market, even the arousal of getting whipsawed feels preferable to the deadening sense of feeling powerless, like a loser.

How can traders overcome these triggers and their associated patterns? Perhaps they can replace them with alternate triggers: ones that elicit positive action patterns. What if they can create triggers for their solution patterns, so that they could cue these on demand?

JOAN'S LULLABY THERAPY

That was my strategy with Joan.

"I have an exercise I'd like for us to try," I explained to Joan. "It's going to sound crazy, and you'll probably feel weird doing it." Joan glanced at me nervously.

"I want you to begin your psychiatry clerkship early," I stated. "I want you to begin working with your own patient in psychiatry. Can you do that?"

Joan seemed completely befuddled. This made her all the more attentive.

"Listen very carefully. I want you to sit back and close your eyes. Breathe very deeply and slowly. Get yourself very relaxed. Now I want you to form an image in your mind of your new patient. Her name is Joan. She grew up in an achievement-oriented family, in which she received praise for doing well, in school and in sports. When she didn't do well and didn't receive the same praise, it hurt. So she got it into her head that she has to be perfect. She has to be a perfect student; she has to look perfect; she has to have a perfect body. But, of course, she's not perfect, so it's a trap. Whenever she falls short of perfection, she feels bad about herself. She's become very conditional in her feelings about herself. If she's not perfect, she's no good. Try to hone in on that image of your patient, Joan. She is hurting on the inside, wanting praise and acceptance. She is trying *so* hard to look just right, to act just right to get that praise. Can you see her in your mind?"

Joan was clearly uncomfortable. It seemed as though she were making an effort to not cry. "Yes," she said, her voice cracking just a bit.

"What does she look like?"

"She's little. She's a little girl. She's in her bed."

"What is she doing in bed?"

Joan smiled slightly. "She's doing what I used to do. She's holding a bear and listening to a song. A lullaby. It's the song my mom used to play when I got upset. She'd hold me and rock me, like I was a baby."

"Good. Now let's add to that picture. Try to get an image in your mind of grown-up Joan the medical student, the doctor-to-be. Imagine how she looks with her white coat on, the stethoscope hanging from her neck. She's walking from patient to patient on her rounds, stopping to talk with each one, helping them feel a little better. Can you play a little movie in your head, sort of like a tape you play on your VCR, and see her working with people in the hospital?"

"Yes, I can." Joan's tone was a little brighter.

"Now keep your eyes closed. We're going to hit the pause button on that VCR and blend the images. Joan the medical student, the doctor-to-be, is going to walk into the room of Joan the patient, Joan the little girl with the bear who tries so hard to be perfect. Can you see that in your mind? Can you see Joan the doctor coming over to the bed of hurting Joan? You're walking in the door, you see her on the bed in front of you, bear in hand . . . What do you see happening?"

Joan seemed immersed in the fantasy. "She's in bed with her teddy bear. She seems so small, so vulnerable. She doesn't know what's happening. Mom's not there."

"Where are you in the room?"

"I'm beside the bed, kneeling beside her. I'm reaching out to her on the bed and holding her hand."

"What are you saying to Little Joan?"

"That it's going to be okay. I'm there to help you. Everything will be all right. I'll take care of you."

"Is there anything else you're saying to her?"

Joan's voice broke, as tears ran down her eyes. "I love you. *I love you. I love you.*"

That evening, Joan had a homework assignment in therapy. Before dinner, she had to wear her white hospital coat at home and replay in her mind the images of Little Joan. I asked her to immerse herself in the lullaby and rock herself, as she focused on Little Joan. Then, as she prepared and ate her dinner, all to the tune of the lullaby, I wanted her to create an image of feeding Little Joan: sitting at the bedside, holding her hand, offering her food. If Little Joan worried about eating too much or becoming fat, she was to imagine herself offering love and reassurance, helping that little patient of hers.

Joan embraced the exercise. When she arrived home for dinner, she didn't just wash her hands. She wore her white coat and scrubbed, as if she were about to enter the operating room. She vividly visualized Little Joan as her patient and even made herself read up on her patient, as she would during a rotation. She learned about the connection between depression and eating disorders and the ways in which eating problems can serve a thwarted need for self-esteem. Most of all, she kept her compassionate mind-set as a physician-to-be. "Above all else, do no harm," she had been taught, so she refused to berate her little patient.

Perhaps most interesting of all was the way Joan became Little Joan when she immersed herself in the lullaby and the rocking. It was as if those sensations had become associated with a particular experience: a caring, nurturing experience. The result was an interesting exercise in multiplicity: simultaneously accessing the mature, care-giving self while activating the child-self capable of receiving nurturance. By rocking and humming the tune as she ate, Joan made eating an activity associated with a physician's caring, not unlike Mother's caring. No longer was it an exercise in self-loathing.

It would be an exaggeration to suggest that Joan overcame her eating disorder with just a few exercises. The reality is that it took quite a few meetings and many repetitions of the exercise before Joan joined her friends for a summer beach party wearing a new, revealing bathing suit. But one thing struck both of us after that dramatic session: She stopped binge eating and purging.

Joan couldn't feed herself properly, but she knew how to feed her patient. Cued by a white lab coat and a lullaby, she merged her compartmentalized selves and created a novel pattern—and, eventually, a new self-image.

WHEN EFFORTS AT CHANGE FAIL

To an outside observer, it might have looked as though Joan had undergone a personality change. A more accurate description would be that she had become more of the person she was already capable of being. The signal on her radio dial that corresponded to the loving, caring, physician was boosted, allowing her to access it even when she was not in her professional role. Had she not possessed this initial capacity for nurturance, it is highly unlikely that therapy could have worked for her.

Indeed, many of my greatest failures in counseling have occurred when I could not find a healthy, mature identity to anchor future changes. That piece of emotional health, no matter how seemingly small, is like a break in a sheer mountain face. If it is sufficiently deep and wide, it can provide a toehold for the upward trek.

Sometimes, however, there is no break in the rocks, or at least I fail to find one. It doesn't happen often, but it is striking when it occurs. Counselors in the addictions field are perhaps most familiar with the scenario: A person is referred for help by the family or by the justice system following multiple episodes of drinking. The person, however, is in denial. She doesn't feel that she needs help. There is no need to try various exercises or to examine particular patterns because there is no real problem!

A T-shirt once worn to a session by a client of mine read: "I don't have a drinking problem. I drink, I get drunk, I fall down. No problem!" The shirt was funny because it captured the thinking of the alcoholic. Some element of observation is missing. Without it, even the best and most sensitive interventions fall on deaf ears. It is very difficult and very frustrating to try to get a person to see what is plain to everyone else.

Perhaps that is why Alcoholics Anonymous (AA) approaches recovery very differently from traditional therapy. AA teaches that people must "hit bottom" before they can *own* their problems. They need to experience sufficient pain and consequences that they finally say, "No more!" AA regulars know that the worst thing you can do for a person in denial is to shield them from consequences. Addicts *need* to go through crisis and hit bottom in order to reach their turning point. Indeed, the grizzled veterans of recovery will employ tough love to accelerate the crisis. In so doing, they recognize that you can't simply talk people into their epiphany. "Bring the body and the mind will follow" is a popular AA slogan. Change occurs more through internalized experiences than through therapeutic insights. But even to bring the body to recovery, there has to be enough of a crack in the rock face for the person to acknowledge, "Maybe I do have a problem."

When people lack this duality—the ability to be an observer to their problems as well as an involved participant—therapy becomes every bit as hazardous as climbing a sheer mountain face.

One such incident occurred with an alcoholic man who was referred to me by the court system in Cortland, New York. I was a psychologist on the staff at the county mental health center, and, as is the case in rural communities, I was expected to handle just about any problem that walked in the door. Nothing, however, could have prepared me for this individual.

He was mandated for counseling because he had raped his five-year-old son.

I read the referral material from the court. The man had a history of alcohol-related offenses, including driving while intoxicated (DWIs), as well as several arrests for petty theft. The referral summary graphically depicted the physical damage done to the child; the emotional damage was left to the reader's imagination. The report indicated that the man at first denied that he had committed the act. Later, he said that he was drunk and didn't know what he was doing. Throughout, he minimized the damage that he had caused.

A cardinal rule in counseling is that one must develop a rapport with clients. As I have shown, the therapeutic alliance is a bond that forms between the therapist and the observing part of the client. Research consistently finds that the depth and the quality of that bond is the best predictor of the eventual success of counseling. It is obviously not helpful to the formation of an alliance to be harshly critical. After all, if people seeking help experience the therapist as blaming and punitive, they are unlikely to return for assistance. It is important, therapists are taught, to show a basic respect for clients—even when they act, feel, and believe very differently from you. Even when they rape their children.

I couldn't do it.

The man entered my small office, his demeanor nonchalant. He wore a flannel checked shirt and a worn pair of jeans and work boots. He sat down and looked for me to start the interview. I scanned his face and body for signs of discomfort. I could find none. Almost involuntarily, I blurted out, "I read through the materials from the court. *How could you rape your little son?*"

I immediately regretted my words. The question, however, didn't seem to upset him in any way. A hint of a half-smile crept over his face; and, with a slight shrug of his shoulders, he responded: *"Because my daughter wasn't home."* No pain, no remorse: I would have raped the girl, he seemed to be saying, but, hey, I had to take what was available.

This, I was certain, was the face of evil—not a cold, calculating, malicious intent, but the absence of any capacity to care.

Our interview lasted less than 15 minutes. The man wanted counseling visits to fulfill the judge's demands, but he could not specify any changes that he wanted or needed to make. Every fiber of my being wanted to help him out: out the door! I referred the case back to the judge, feeling a mixture of outrage and impotence.

Without the toehold, I had slipped down the mountain face. Moving the radio dial is of no avail if there are no signals to amplify.

CONCLUSION

It is time to return to that "fearless trading inventory" I had conducted a while ago. Recall that I discovered that many of my trades lacked consistency in execution. Recall also that I found that, when I performed my homework and remained focused on the market rather than on my profits and losses, I actually traded reasonably well.

If you have a valid, tested trading methodology (and this is a significant "if"), and if you are underperforming the method's historical performance, there is a real possibility that you, like Joan, are encountering triggers for state shifts that are getting in your way.

Just as Joan had at least two selves, one self-defeating and the other caring and affirming, many traders—myself included—have at least two trading selves. At times, these selves are in sync with the market, letting the hard work speak for itself. Other times, traders front run their trading signals, ignore their stops, double up on their losers, and pull the rug from underneath their winners. If you can examine occasions when you've traded in the zone and well out of it, you will find that, like Joan, you are carrying on very different internal dialogues at those times.

Activating your Internal Observer and noticing your self-talk as you are trading will tell you precisely who is doing the trading, which of the "I's" is in control. Many times, you do not identify the triggers as they occur, but you can recognize the negative self-talk that immediately follows. This self-talk has an automatic, scripted quality that is largely independent of the objective circumstances of the moment. It truly seems as though the trigger has pressed a "play" button in your head, activating a well-worn tape. Identifying the contents of those tapes is a very helpful step in being able to interrupt them. Many times, you can become sensitive to common phrases in your negative self-talk, such as "loser" or the catastrophizing "what if," using these to trigger a new, more constructive action pattern.

One way of accomplishing that is through what I call the "trading coach" exercise. This is a variation of the challenge that I posed to Joan. Recall that I asked her if she would say the same things to her patients that she had been saying to herself. She laughed at the very thought, knowing full well that she would never behave so destructively in a professional setting.

In your "trading coach" exercise, you are to go into trades as if you were a mentor to a developing trader. Your job is to teach this student how to become the most successful trader possible. Imagine that any position you contemplate, enter, or exit is your student's position. How will you talk with your student if the trade is going well? If the trade begins to falter? If the student is contemplating an exit or wants to hold on? Your job is to be the best coach you can be. Then compare that talk to the self talk you may have been engaging in before, during, and after you put on your positions.

Most people, like Joan, have a caring, constructive side that they access in their relationships, personal and professional. Too often, people cannot access this engaging self once they experience triggers associated with past losses, failures, and threats. By using their negative self-talk to trigger a coaching exercise, people—like Joan—can interrupt damaging patterns and replace them with their most positive ones.

This was the key to success for Ken, Mary, Walt, and Joan: They activated their Internal Observers as problem patterns were occurring and made conscious efforts to enact positive patterns *from their existing repertoire*. The vast majority of traders I have encountered do not need therapy. *Rather, they need to learn to become their own therapists*, by observing their triggers and shifting to new modes of thought, feeling, and behavior once their problematic tapes begin playing.

Generally, the successful trades come from immersion in the process of trading. The unsuccessful trades come from immersion in the potential outcomes of trading. The winning trader is immersed in the market, much as Joan was absorbed by her care for her patients. The losing trader is not really focused on the market. He is thinking about himself, his account statement, or his reputation.

A profitable exercise you can conduct is to replicate Joan's therapy on yourself, much as I conducted the inventory. Identify the contexts in which you already are enacting the role of the successful trader. Audit your trades and observe your patterns. Focus your attention on what you are doing right during those trades that work out well. And then, in the best solution-focused tradition, do more and more of what works—*and find the triggers that help get you into your positive modes.*

The goal is to create a model for yourself of "you, the successful trader." What you will find, if you observe carefully, is that this successful trader is a distinct self, complete with its own moods, internal dialogues, body postures, and thinking patterns. The idea is to find that spot on your mind's radio dial corresponding to that Successful Trader and then lock in a preset on that frequency. *You want to access that channel so many times that, eventually, you can summon it at will.*

All you need to reach your profitability goals is a replicable edge in the markets, a pattern to trade that tilts the odds in your favor. Once you've found that, the rest is consistency—doing over and over what works. Many traders with whom I have talked despair that they have not discovered more patterns to give them an edge. They buy books and attend seminars in the desperate hope of accumulating more sources of edge. That climb up the trading mountain face, however, must be tackled one step at a time, beginning with a single toehold. It is far better to internalize success from a single pattern than mixed results from many patterns.

As Linda Raschke has emphasized, if you can master even a single trading setup, you will have set into motion a model—an identity—that can be accessed and expanded many times over. Vince Lombardi once remarked that every game boils down to doing the things you do best and doing them repeatedly. The key is finding what you do best and making that a template for your future development. Joan changed when she brought her medical student self home for dinner. Traders change when they recruit those aspects of themselves that are focused, disciplined, and flexible and import those into their trading—even when there is but one source of edge. In the absence of consistency, any edge is valueless. Without the trading edge, however—the pattern as well as the consistency to follow it—the rock ledge of trading looks perilously steep and breathtakingly sheer.

Chapter Eleven

Pinball Wizardry

When people think they can change and when they think they cannot, they accurately forecast their outcomes.

Aristotle referred to humans as "rational animals." We humans constantly seek to explain the world around us and to extend our conceptual grasp. Toward that end, we build mental maps of people and events, much as the first explorers developed their maps of the world. Sometimes these maps are quite distorted; other times they are accurate guides for action. The field of behavioral finance has documented a number of cognitive and emotional biases that distort our mapmaking and mislead us in trading and investment decisions. To the degree that personal or all-too-human triggers interfere with our efforts to predict and to explain events, we as traders are unlikely to meet our Aristotelian potential.

In this chapter, we will explore the relevance of cognitive psychology for trading, with a special emphasis on modeling: the creation of mental maps. We will see that cultivating new maps that account for fresh experience is an important element in changing both our personalities and our trading. But to accomplish this, we must be willing to confront the errors and the omissions of our present maps. We must stop automatically following our maps and instead become mapmakers.

CREATING MODELS OF THE WORLD

A *model* is a representation of an object of interest. There are model homes, model cars, or models of the stock market. A good model captures the essence of an object, while discarding aspects that are not central to its identity. A model rocket, for example, is shaped like an actual rocket and possesses its own means of propulsion, but it lacks the size of the real thing and is constructed with different materials.

Scientists create models as ways to further their understanding of unknown aspects of nature. Reflected in the creation of a model is an underlying theory, an explanation of the patterns we observe in the world. If my theory describes human thought as a series of energy transformations within a closed system (as in Freud's early work), my model is drawn from physics and the laws of conservation. I am trying to explain cognition in recognizable, Newtonian terms.

As with the cognition/physics example, models in science typically draw on analogies, casting the unknown in terms that are familiar to us. On the one hand, behaviorism drew on models of animal behavior—principles of reinforcement and shaping—to explain how people acquire new action patterns. Cognitive approaches to therapy, on the other hand, owe their models to computers—they portray the mind as an information-processing unit that transforms cognitive inputs into emotional outputs.

As John Flavell observes, the developmental psychologist and researcher Jean Piaget emphasized that all people create models of the world to aid their intellectual grasp. He referred to these models as schemas and noted that they serve as personal maps. Such maps help people make sense of events and organize their responses to the world. When people encounter events that they cannot explain, they attempt to assimilate the events into their schemas, keeping their understandings intact. If, however, the fit is poor, people reach a point of disequilibrium. The maps no longer adequately represent the territory of their experience. People then accommodate, Piaget explained, and change their schemas to fit the new experience.

This accounts for what people have learned about change processes in therapy. People often come to therapy with maps that have been distorted by painful life experiences. They identify with these maps and try their best to assimilate new experiences into them. On many occasions, I have had clients respond to something positive I said by dismissing it, indicating that it is my job to be supportive of people. It is easier for them to disqualify feedback that does not mesh with their negative schemas than to acknowledge that their views of themselves and others are faulty.

One of the most powerful experiences people can create for another person is to extend themselves beyond the bounds of what is normally expected. For example, every student with whom I meet in counseling is given my home phone number and the opportunity to interact with me by phone, e-mail, or direct visit in between regularly scheduled meetings. At times, this has required meeting with someone late at night or on a weekend. I vividly recall one crisis call I received from a distraught student while I was on vacation with my family in Bermuda. I am not compensated for these extra contacts, and nowhere in my job description does it say that I should extend myself in such a manner. One student, amazed that I would meet with him at midnight before a major exam to head off a mounting anxiety problem, asked why I did this. My response was simple: *Because you're worth it.*

Many people have no schema—no mental filing cabinet—to hold such a concept. Without the ability to reconcile my actions with their schemas, they are prodded to accommodate to reality by altering those schemas. *Discrepancy—novel experience—creates change because it forces people to redraw their mental maps.*

This cognitive remapping can be observed among those developing their trading skills. At some point, after seeing their systems work on paper and then in actual trading, the schema of "I can't do this" is replaced by a growing sense of mastery and understanding. At one time, when you first slid behind the wheel of a car, you no doubt felt shaky about your driving skills. With repeated, successful experience, however, you reorganized your maps. Emotionally this manifests itself as a quiet confidence. You don't think about whether you'll drive successfully or not. You take it for granted; you *know* that you can do it.

For years, I had thought of myself as a nervous and not especially skilled public speaker. Then I found out that my graduate school scholarship required me to teach a large class three times a week. The first couple of weeks were agony; but after that, the teaching became routine. I gradually developed the ability to read my audience and acquired a sense for how to present the material in an engaging way. By the end of the course, I could walk in front of an auditorium of students and routinely deliver a fine lecture. Even more important, *I started to think of myself as a good public speaker!* Quite literally, the new experience shifted my internal model of myself, creating a new identity.

Recall the conclusion of Michael Gazzaniga and colleagues in their research with split-brain patients. When they asked patients to explain the actions of their left hands (which were processed by the relatively nonverbal right brain hemisphere), the patients readily invented rationales for their behavior. This led the researchers to conclude that a major function of the left hemisphere—John Cutting's Mind #1—is that of *interpreter*, making sense of experience. It is not a large leap to recognize that this interpreter is an important originator of mental maps, transforming raw experience into an internalized sense of self. People do so, Gazzaniga holds, through the creation of narratives. They create stories that explain their experience, much as scientists use theories to explain their observations.

The cognitive psychologist George Kelly made clever use of this narrative interpreter by encouraging his clients to construct ideal selves in their counseling. During sessions, clients would elaborate their idea of the person they would like to be, right down to the mode of dress, the manner of speech, and the body postures. The ideal selves were even named. They were very much like an author's creation, fleshed out in lifelike detail. Once clients constructed this ideal self, they were instructed to enter into unfamiliar social situations and to act the role of their ideal person. For example, a shy person might go to a mall and enact the role of the assertive, outgoing shopper. What Kelly found was that his clients invariably encountered positive feedback for their new role enactments, much as I received praise for my lecturing during my graduate years. Over time, the clients internalized this feedback, revising their self-concept in the direction of their ideal.

It is not too difficult to speculate what Kelly was accomplishing with his cognitive restructuring. In enacting a new role, clients needed to enter new states of consciousness. They had to adopt novel emotional patterns, physical states, and ways of thinking. They truly were, in Nietzsche's phrase, play-actors of their ideals. Through repetition and feedback, they literally programmed a new state on the mindscape, expanding their identity and behavioral repertoire.

This brings me back to an important point. *Your interpreter is always turned on while you are trading.* You will inevitably internalize your trading experience. And you will most deeply internalize those experiences that occur during times when you inhabit nonordinary spots on the radio dials of consciousness. If you feel unusually calm and confident, this will stand out to the interpreter. If you are particularly fearful and self-doubting, the interpreter will take note. Your identity as a trader is a distillation of those experiences that most stand out in your awareness. The interpreter does not need to make sense of routine facets of reality; *only nonroutine experiences will trigger your remapping efforts.*

This line of reasoning leads to an important psychological conclusion. *If you are to become successful in trading, you must learn to make losing routine.* No doubt this sounds more than a little odd and counterintuitive. But think about it. If you treat each trade as a hypothesis regarding market direction ("Under conditions X, Y, and Z, I predict the market will do A in B time frame"), then every trade should be stopped out when the hypothesis is disconfirmed. Moreover, to avoid the risk of ruin—the loss of trading capital that results from the string of disconfirmed hypotheses that can be expected over time with any trading system operating under less than perfect certainty—you will want to put to work only a portion of your capital on each trade. This combination of stops and money management makes losing an ordinary event. A limited loss on a high-percentage trade is not a failure or a bad trade. If your trades are 50 percent winners and you can keep the average losses half the size of the gains, you will make a fine living.

Again and again, I have noticed this mind-set among successful traders: *They treat losing trades as a cost of doing business.* Like a baseball player who realizes that making outs on 60 percent of his at-bats will get him to the Hall of Fame, successful traders realize they will strike out on a fair number of trades. Their skill is in recognizing the sour trades as early as possible and cutting them short. Psychologically, they never internalize losing experiences, even though they may have many of them. *Their interpreters simply don't act on routine events.* Conversely, imagine the trader who wins on 9 out of 10 trades but gives everything back in traumatic, uncontrolled losses on the other occasion. It is not difficult to imagine the sense of self that will be internalized from such a roller-coaster pattern.

Kelly's role therapy would make an ideal counseling method for traders. Rather than focusing on eradicating personal conflicts, the trader would define an ideal self: the trader she always wanted to be. This definition would be rich and detailed, right down to the data collected by the ideal trader, the ways in which the data would be utilized, the entries and exits to be implemented, the money management employed, the mind-set adopted, and so on. This fictitious ideal trader would have her own name and an ideally laid out trade station. Her pretrading routines would be defined, as well as her end-of-day activities.

Then, with as much conscious effort as possible, the trader would implement this ideal without exception. Every signal would be taken, every stop honored, and every routine followed. If the trader indeed utilizes valid, tested methods, this enactment over time would produce the same results as my lecturing in graduate school. The trader would internalize successful experience and revise her image in the direction of her ideal.

You have to enact success before you internalize success. No one talks himself into a revised mental map. Powerful, nonordinary experience, not well-intentioned "positive thinking," is the fountainhead of personal change.

MODELING YOURSELF AS A TRADER

The foregoing discussion clarifies why models of the ideal trader must come from one's own trading experience, and not from fantasy. When I audited my trading results, I found that my most successful trades were short term, where I had clear hypotheses to test, definite action points for entry and exit, and a limited time horizon so that I could devote full concentration to the trade. When I held positions longer, I inevitably suffered larger drawdowns when my hypotheses did not pan out, creating far more emotional circumstances for managing the trades. This, in turn, generated scenarios in which I held bad positions too long, doubled up on losing trades, and otherwise shot myself in both feet. Under such emotional conditions, I could not internalize a positive model of myself as a trader.

If someone were to ask me to fantasize the ideal trader, I might think of some big-time operative who moves millions of dollars with each trade, like a Warren Buffett or a Peter Lynch. I learned, however, that this was not the ideal that best fit with my cognitive and emotional makeup. I am much more effective focusing on one market at a time, with sharply defined parameters for my hypotheses and risk management. I am also far more effective approaching each day as a fresh event, trading larger positions on anticipated intraday moves and strategically managing overnight exposure. What this means is that I will rarely hit home runs. In baseball terms, I am less likely to be a Roger Maris, a Hank Aaron, a Mark McGuire, or a Barry Bonds than a Tony Gwinn, a Rickey Henderson, or a Lou Brock. My goal is to strike out rarely and to get on base (and maybe steal one) as frequently as possible. That is less glamorous than the long ball, and it poses a significant challenge. *In defining my ideals I need to first accept who I am and what I do best.* I perform reasonably well as a brief therapist and a short-term trader. Speed is part of my game. Put me in a long-term treatment facility or make me a manager in a value-oriented mutual fund, and I will fall well short of my potential.

　　The best models always come from within.

PLAYING MARKET PINBALL

A seminal experience in trading psychology came to me during my college days when I passed my time by playing pinball machines. Overall, I was a very average pinball player. I would keep some balls in play for a long time and lose others within seconds. My flipper control improved with experience, but it never became so precise that I could hit targets at will. And I never mastered the body control that true pinball wizards use to nudge the ball into the right spots.

　　I was persistent, however; and generally, after a time, I could identify an anomaly in the machine I was playing: a particular maneuver that could rack up points. I would then exploit this anomaly time and time again and attain respectable scores. For example, one machine that I played had ramps on either side of the machine and a number of targets in the center. The tempting strategy was to catch the ball on the flippers and then aim for the center targets when they were lit. Although this led to occasional high scores when my aim was good, it also led to an unfortunate number of lost balls that drained down the center, between the flippers.

　　It just so happened one day that I was playing the machine and the ball came down the right ramp to my left flipper. My hand had strayed from the button and instead of catching the ball on the flipper or hitting ball, I failed to engage the flipper at all. The ball then bounced from the left flipper to the right one. That seemed strange to me; I would have assumed that if you didn't use the flipper at all the ball would simply drain down the center. After numerous trials, however, I discovered, on this particular machine, that allowing the ball to hit the left flipper from its descent down the ramp invariably allowed the player to catch the ball on the right flipper. Once caught, the ball could be sent up the left ramp (scoring points) and would either then come down the left or right ramp. Either way, it could be caught again on the right flipper and sent back up the ramp. With a little practice, I could repeat this pattern dozens of times for each ball, accumulating points with each repetition. The amount of points gained was less than if I went for the center targets, but I very rarely lost the ball. As a result, I literally could play this machine all day on a single token.

To be sure, this did not make for particularly exciting pinball. It eliminated most of the sources of uncertainty by exploiting a high percentage pattern with great frequency. But the elimination of uncertainty and excitement was also a major reason for the success of the strategy. The game became almost entirely mechanical and routine, removing emotional interference from the play. Although I was never a great pinball player, I revised my mental map sufficiently to internalize the fact that I could be successful *on that particular machine*. Eventually, I discovered enough anomalies on various machines that I revised my maps one more time. Given enough time and experience, I became confident that I could locate anomalies in most machines.

It is interesting that those anomalies could only be discovered by pursuing odd and seemingly irrational strategies. Playing the pinball or video game the way the designers meant for the game to be played invariably created losses. For instance, years later, I was able to win in one video basketball game by taking only one kind of shot (a jumper from the corner). The game allotted this shot a sufficiently high percentage of made baskets that victory was assured. Varying one's shots or taking what looked like higher percentage shots was a sure way of losing the game.

To win in the markets, you only need to discover one such anomaly and play it consistently. Like a card counter in blackjack, you will still encounter uncertainty and losses. More important, however, you will have tilted the odds in your favor. With sufficient repetition, the results will show on the bottom line. And the interpreter will grab hold of those results and revise your identity as a trader accordingly. There are many different markets—commodities, equities—just as there are many pinball and video machines. The key is to crack the code, to find the anomalies.

And, as with pinball, these anomalies will be found when you investigate the counterintuitive strategies—buying when the market seems weakest, and vice versa. *It is at the emotional extremes that markets are imperfectly efficient; you cannot win by playing the markets the way designers meant for them to be played.*

I recently took pencil to paper and examined what happens in the

New York Stock Exchange Composite Index ($NYA) following those occasions when 5 percent or more of the traded issues made new 52-week lows on a particular day. My investigation spanned the period from 1978 to 2001 and identified returns 150 trading days (approximately 7 months) into the future.

There were 442 days in which 5 percent or more of the issues traded that day had made new annual lows. These tended to occur late in bear markets, when pessimism was running high and selling was most indiscriminate. It is interesting that the market was higher 150 days later approximately 88 percent of the time and by nearly 13 percent. For the sample overall (in keeping with the bullish tendencies of the 1978–2001 period), 150-day periods tended to rise on 73 percent of the occasions, but only by 6.5 percent. Those who bought at times when there was significant selling achieved returns twice as great as the norm. They had figured out the pinball machine.

CONTRARY TRADING: FADING THE MAPS OF TRADERS

Such counterintuitive trades work for cognitive reasons as well. Your interpreter is always attempting to make sense of the markets, even as it continually reshapes your sense of self. Much of the literature of technical analysis, valid and not so valid, is a set of heuristics, or rules, that help your interpreter cope with the ongoing stream of market data.

Because a picture is worth a thousand words and market charts encode a large amount of information in a single graphic, chart reading and the graphic display of indicators are a staple of most traders' arsenals. It is rare indeed to find a software package for trading that does not feature these elements.

Now there is nothing inherently wrong with reading chart patterns or interpreting oscillator displays. It's just that these reflect the way the pinball machine designers want you to play the game. It is unlikely that you will find the counterintuitive anomalies by trading moving average penetrations, RSI extremes, or other tactics built into every major charting program.

A more promising strategy may even be to trade against these shibboleths, taking the same seemingly irrational route that I followed when I chose to not engage my flipper. Trading against popular chart patterns is a particularly promising approach. Everyone is familiar with situations where people can perceive meaningful chart patterns in random number series. In any series of sufficient length, people are apt to see formations that look like double tops or bottoms, flags and pennants, and so forth.

If you think of chart patterns as market communications, you can see that an understanding of those communications needs to take context—those metacommunications—into account. Unfortunately, much chart reading does not do that.

The *text* of a communication is what is being said. The *context* of a communication is the set of circumstances surrounding the communication. You interpret most of what you hear situationally; that is, you draw on the context of communications to derive their meaning. A simple "How are you?" means something different when uttered by a doctor during an office visit than it does when spoken by the doctor at a cocktail party.

Students whom I see in therapy often remark to me that a first date went wonderfully because they spent hours discussing intimacies of their personal lives. Invariably, these dating situations do not work out. Why? Sharing details of one's life is inappropriate to the context of a first date. Normally, one would only reveal such information to a trusted confidant. If people speak of their lives indiscriminately, it is a sure sign of neediness: the impulse to get close quickly due to loneliness. It won't be long before both people find themselves over their heads, backing away from the vulnerable positions in which they have placed themselves.

Traders can be similarly heedless of context. Successful traders approach a new market position the way a rational person approaches a first date. They will wait for the market to prove itself before committing a large stake. By risking a limited amount of capital at the outset, they do not become emotionally entangled prematurely. If the anticipated move is for real, there will be plenty of time to get on board. If it is not for real, the losses will not be devastating. I refer to my small initial positions in the market as "pioneer positions." They are designed to scout the terrain and—more often than I like—are apt to get the arrows in the back. Plunging into a market, like becoming infatuated in a relationship, speaks more to the needs of actors than their objective circumstances.

Many technical market signals, such as chart patterns and oscillator readings, are interpreted mechanically. They are seen as possessing a fixed meaning regardless of the context in which they occur. I might pay attention to a double top or a head-and-shoulders formation if it occurred in the context of a market that had risen greatly, was now losing volatility, and was facing a rising-interest-rate environment. The same exact formation occurring after a lengthy, steep, volatile decline with interest rates falling might possess very different implications.

Its shortcomings notwithstanding, chart reading has been in use since the nineteenth century and is likely to retain its popularity well into the twenty-first. Once again, chart reading is fulfilling that human need to extract meaning from events, an element that distinguishes humans from most species. The human ability to perceive meaning in patterns of nature underlies every scientific achievement. Unfortunately, it also leaves people open to superstition and delusion.

Take the example of panic disorder, a debilitating anxiety condition. Many people who suffer from panic disorder also experience agoraphobia (a fear of public places). Panic disorder is a frightening condition in which a person can be stricken—without seeming cause—by sudden, intense feelings of dread and anxiety. Indeed, many people who first experience panic episodes truly believe that they are going to die.

What makes the panic all the more intolerable is that it often occurs out of the blue, not during periods of acute stress and threat. A person can be sitting peacefully in his or her car, stopped at a light, and suddenly experience overwhelming anxiety. That rubs violently against the human need to understand the world. A person has no ready filing cabinet in his or her mind for causeless dread.

As a result, panic sufferers arrive at ingenious—and wholly superstitious—explanations for their disorder. Without an obvious candidate for a causal explanation of the attack, the sufferer's interpreter kicks into overdrive, attempting to make sense of the senseless. If the attack first occurred in a car, the patient concludes that the car was the problem. If it happened in a shopping mall or in a crowd, the person will avoid malls and crowds. One client of mine had her first panic attack while driving on a thruway exit ramp. Thereafter, she avoided all roads with ramps, including unrelated ramps, such as those leading to parking garages. As the attacks multiply, the list of offending circumstances also expands, until the person is effectively agoraphobic—unable to leave his or her dwelling.

Market traders, especially in the throes of economic turmoil, are similarly apt to read meanings into even random events. Chart patterns, readily available to anyone with a computer, a newspaper, or an advisory service, are prime candidates for such rampant meaning making. Just as people are most likely to consult fortune-tellers when their lives are highly uncertain, traders are most likely to turn to charts and oscillators when their positions look most dicey. The need to know—to feel in control—is so strong that they will often prefer dubious answers to no answers at all.

From this perspective, chart patterns are as much a psychological tool as a true analytic device. They are a ready source of explanations for traders' confused interpreters. This, however, gives the patterns a certain value. If you know that anxious traders are apt to latch onto chart patterns to justify their positions, you can look to profit from those anomalous occasions when the chart patterns fail.

Most chart patterns involve consolidations—periods in which the market stays within a relatively narrow range relative to a previous trend. This is true of flags, pennants, double tops/bottoms, head-and-shoulders formations, cup-and-handle patterns, and the like. Any consolidation, by definition, entails a decrease of price volatility: Prices are moving less net distance per unit of time during the period of consolidation. When the market reverts to more normal, higher volatility, the result very often will be a trending move out of the consolidation range.

This is where the failed chart pattern comes in. Suppose a stock has fallen and now looks to be in a cup-and-handle formation, generally thought to presage a market bottom. Emotional investors, stung by the prior decline, are apt to latch onto this pattern as a rationale for initiating new long positions or for hanging on to existing longs. They are banking on the hope that the pattern will propel them to new highs, well above the top of the chart formation.

Should the pattern fail, however, there is a built-in set of emotional traders and investors ready to be disappointed. Their capitulation will add to the thrust of the move out of the consolidation area, creating a nice opportunity for the contrarian. Moreover, it is known from the availability heuristic research of Daniel Kahnemann and Amos Tversky that people will be relatively slow to revise their mental maps once they have latched onto a particular chart pattern. The promising "pinball" trade, therefore, is *identifying the earliest stages of a failure of a chart pattern as an entry point for a contrary move.* For example, suppose the market moves nicely higher, but the stock does not break out of its handle to resume its uptrend. At the first downside penetration of the handle base, you would want to be short, taking advantage of the stunned, paralyzed traders who will only bail out of their positions when they experience the pain of much lower prices. By playing the game opposite to the way in which it was designed, you can find unique niches of opportunity.

If you can identify contexts that do not support the validity of popular chart and indicator patterns, you may have the start of a successful contrarian trade. Thruway ramps have nothing to do with mental health, and charts do not move markets. In a world of panicky people, however, ramps and charts may be all there is to explain the inexplicable. The more visible the stock, the more popular the pattern, and the more the pattern is being bandied about by trading gurus, the more likely it is that you can make money by playing the game in an unorthodox way, fading the trading maps of the majority.

I have spent considerable research time analyzing one-minute data on the markets, including price, price change, put/call volumes, TICK statistics, E-Mini volumes, intraday advances/declines, intraday new highs/new lows, and the interplay of sector indexes in order to reverse engineer the trading strategies of the average trader. My goal has been to determine "how the designers want the game to be played" so that I can craft my own anomalous strategies. In short, I'm pursuing with the markets my college strategy with pinball machines.

After all this reverse engineering, what I can report with a reasonable degree of certainty is that the average trader is looking at price and price alone in two different (but overlapping) contexts:

1. The average trader seems to be sensitive to price breakouts to new highs and new lows and will piggyback on these breakouts.
2. The average trader seems to be sensitive to perceived support and resistance levels on charts and will activate trading strategies when these are hit—and especially when they are broken.

At the present time, these dynamics make trading false breakouts a promising strategy. Following an insightful column on the MSN Money site, Victor Niederhoffer and Laurel Kenner took some heat for questioning the shibboleth, "The trend is your friend." My research, however, suggests that they are correct. The markers that average traders employ to gauge trends are over-utilized and vulnerable to sharp reversals once these traders realize their errors. The winning strategy, at least for now, appears to be to identify the signs of failing breakouts and to use these as markers for contrarian trades.

INTERNAL MAPS AND INKBLOTS

One of the most revered instruments in psychological testing is the Rorschach Inkblot test. It is a series of 10 cards that depict complex inkblots. Some of the cards are colorful; others are black and white. The only instructions for the test are that the viewer should indicate what he or she sees in the cards. Perhaps part of the card looks like something; other times the entire card might call an object, a person, or an animal to mind. It is a bit like looking at the clouds and seeing what you can find in the shapes. There are no right and no wrong answers; the purpose is simply to allow people to use their imaginations.

The inkblots are known as a projective test because people tend to project themselves into their perceptions. What people see, especially in ambiguous situations, is a reflection of the content and the structure of their thoughts. The Rorschach inkblots are intentionally ambiguous, in an effort to force people to project more of themselves into their responses. The test is effective, because few people know what the psychologist is looking for. It is difficult to hide one's true feelings and personality on an inkblot test.

A sophisticated examiner can derive quite a bit of information from inkblot responses. First, the psychologist might look at the *content* of the responses: what the person sees. Are the perceptions mostly of people, or are people missing from the responses? That could say quite a bit about the social inclinations of the test taker. What are the emotional themes embedded in the responses? Are there many images of violence and conflict, or do the responses reflect greater harmony? And how many responses are there? Very anxious people will often provide a flood of responses, focusing on minute details within the cards. Depressed people, unable to respond to the external world, may see very little in the blots.

It is painful to observe the inkblot responses of an individual who has undergone emotional, sexual, or physical abuse as a child. The content themes of the responses almost always involve damage: broken objects, injured bodies, and so on. The responses also reflect tremendous anger, with such images as explosive volcanoes, bloody knives, and severed limbs. In such cases, what the person sees is a reflection of his or her traumatic life experience.

Second, the psychologist learns a great deal about people from the *ways* in which they see the cards. *What* is seen becomes less important than the way in which the perception is assembled. People with serious mental illness, who may lose contact with reality through hallucinations or delusions, will generally produce responses to the Rorschach test that are highly idiosyncratic and not well grounded in the blot itself. The term that psychologists use for this is *form level*. A poor form level indicates that the response is not justified by the contours of the blot itself. An example would be a long, thin, red area of a blot that the person says resembles a setting sun because it is red. In such an instance, the person is so responsive to the red color that he or she ignores the difference in shape between the blot area and the sun.

Color on the Rorschach test is indicative of emotion. A set of responses that makes extensive use of color suggests an active emotional life. The absence of color in a set of responses might indicate that the person is choking off his or her emotional experience. When an experienced clinician administers the Rorschach test, indicators such as color can be integrated with other test elements, such as form level, to obtain a rich view of the individual. For example, the person who saw the thin, red blot area as a setting sun might be highly responsive to color (emotionally reactive). This occurs, however, at the expense of form level (perceptual accuracy). Such a person is apt to misperceive situations in real life when he or she is in an emotional state—a condition not unknown to traders!

Indeed, I strongly suspect that many traders could learn a great deal about their internal maps and map making by taking the inkblot test. Consider the following patterns I've observed among individuals taking the Rorschach test:

• The person perceives one part of a blot accurately but then tries to make the whole blot fit that perception, introducing considerable inaccuracy. For example, part of a blot might look like an ear. The person will then say that the whole blot is a head, pointing to the one area as the ear. Although the ear detail shows good form level, the entire blot may look nothing like a head. This is seen among traders who focus on one or two pieces of data and concoct an entire market forecast on that basis.

• Some people respond to the blots very deliberately, carefully examining each detail before giving their response. Often they will reexamine the blot after giving the response, changing their answer each time. It may take quite a few minutes before they can arrive at a single response that they will stick with. Such people, often highly anxious, would have similar difficulty making trading decisions.

• Other people are highly impulsive in their response style. As soon as they are shown the card, they blurt out what they see, often focusing on the color of the blot area, and often with mediocre form level. Such impulsivity could be expected to lead to mediocre, emotion-filled trading decisions as well.

• People may give accurate responses with positive content themes when the blot area is seen as an object. When the blot is seen as a person, however, the accuracy decreases, and many more troublesome themes emerge. Similar situations can be observed among traders who are very successful in the markets and very poor in dealing with people. There are also Rorschach subjects—and traders—who display the reverse pattern.

• Action-oriented individuals will tend to see objects, animals, and people in motion; their responses describe a great deal of movement. More cerebral individuals will provide responses with less movement and more complex interplay of detail. There are similar differences among trading styles as well, with some traders relying on tape reading and floor experience, and others building and testing elaborate systems.

Of course, there is nothing magical about the Rorschach blots. The test could use clouds in the sky or pictures from magazines just as well. In fact, there is a test called the Thematic Apperception Test (TAT) that also acts as a projective instrument. It consists of a series of pictures of people in ambiguous situations. The test subject is asked to tell a story about the situation depicted on the card. One card shows a boy looking down, seriously, at a violin. My story, when I first took the TAT, involved a boy dreaming of becoming a world-famous concert violinist. Other people have produced different stories, such as a boy who is depressed because his violin is broken or who is upset because he cannot play the violin. Themes of achievement, loss, and failure are a few of the life stories that people tend to project into such pictures.

It is difficult to imagine any stimulus more ambiguous than the markets. Each market chart is a Rorschach test, encouraging viewers to project their hopes and fears and to read trends, patterns, and meanings into the up-and-down movements. The markets are especially interesting for a psychologist because they are a group administration of a projective test: You can see the ways in which different people are perceiving patterns in the same stimulus. As with the Rorschach or TAT, what people see and how they see it is as much a reflection of the viewer as of the market itself. Approaching the financial media from such a vantage point yields interesting insights. What commentators and traders focus on is a function of their mental maps, allowing rare insight into market consensus.

Of course, it helps to know which pundits to focus on when gauging the mental maps of the trading public. I generally look for market commentators that spend as much time hyping themselves as offering market information. In fact, whenever I see a newsletter or a column filled with the words "I" or "we," I know that the writer has a large ego investment in the forecasts being made.

On average, such forecasts are most likely to be biased by the writer's needs and emotional makeup. Indeed, Laurel Kenner and Victor Niederhoffer performed a study of firms that exhibited "hubris" in their corporate communications and found these to underperform the market. (The dramatic bankruptcy of Enron in 2002 is an especially vivid example.) In the terms of the Rorschach test, such writers and companies will be prone to misperceiving their markets, viewing reality in color-filled ways that lack good form level. Such hubris is a great contrary indicator, and a consensus among multiple such writers or firms (think back to the heady dot-com boom) is often meaningful.

Along this line, one of my favorite projective indicators for the market is the cadre of writers who feel the need to remind readers about the wonderful calls they have recently made. This is particularly significant if the writers have also been prone to bouts of silence following not-so-successful recommendations. It is when the writers are most full of themselves, most feeling the need to elevate themselves, that their judgment is apt to be clouded. They become like the manic patient—grandiose in their thinking, impulsively providing responses to the Rorschach cards that miss essential details.

I have generally found success fading the recommendations of such emotional gurus. Their market maps are distorted by their needs for recognition, and the emotionality of their communications is a measure of the degree of likely distortion. I recall one guru who remained steadfast in his support of Nasdaq growth stocks during the severe slide in the early years of the new millennium. Following market bounces, his opinions were voiced in a particularly strident manner, almost as if he were trying to talk the market higher or to convince others (or himself) that he was right. These strident communications invariably occurred within a few days of the ultimate market high, making considerable money for anyone trading from the couch.

For sheer projective test value, however, few market phenomena can beat the online bulletin boards in which people share their market perspectives. Here, the individuals posting their views are not constrained by the need to maintain an image of professionalism. What often emerge are raw responses to market ambiguity in which people project their most basic fear, elation, regret, and hope. I sometimes look for postings that are placed on the board at odd hours, such as very late night or very early morning. A person who is offering emotional perspectives at 3 A.M. is clearly desperate; the presence of many such people is a nice indicator of sentiment extremes in the market. A series of hopeful late-night postings about technology stocks early in 2001—in the midst of their historic decline—struck me as peculiarly lacking in form level. It was one piece of information that told me the decline had further to go.

Occasionally, I will post a market analysis to a popular bulletin board simply to gauge the response of readers. I generally lay out my reading of the market, the conditions under which I might go long or short, and my current leaning based on my observations. Occasionally, I will receive positive replies in which readers will share their own analyses; occasionally, I will receive no replies. Sometimes, however, my posting will strike a chord, and I will receive vitriolic, ad hominem responses. On one occasion, when I indicated a leaning to short the market on waning rallies, I was greeted with insulting remarks from several traders. One even accused me of undermining the economy by advocating the short side! If this were an isolated response from a single crackpot, I would pay no heed. The fact that several people, independently, felt sufficiently threatened by my analysis to attack me personally provided useful information. They *needed* the market to rise. Had they felt secure with their bullish stance, they would have had no need to attack.

Two days later, the market did in fact rise. It then sharply reversed and headed downward to new lows, culminating in a panicky selloff. At some level, I believe, those who posted attacks to the bulletin board knew that the market was vulnerable. This, however, conflicted with their existing positions, creating a psychological dissonance. Their attempts to quash my trading strategy were an effort at dissonance reduction. Their maps were no longer fitting market realities—and their emotional communications were the best evidence of the lack of fit.

At the time I am writing this, the most aggressive mental map I experience among longer-term market participants is the insistence that failed large-cap growth stocks—many of which are down significantly from their highs—will return to their prior glory and bail out their retirement plans. Any intimation that these stocks have seen their best days and that performance has swung to other market segments and themes is met with violent disagreement. I thought one middle-aged man was going to physically attack me when

I simply asked how younger investors would keep the market value of these stocks elevated above historic norms while the greater number of baby boomers cashed in their retirement holdings.

His response was no different from that seen in therapy sessions when I strike a nerve and point out something that is threatening to a patient. It is not disagreement, but *the need to reject evidence before evaluating it* that is significant. The best market forecasts are the ones people, at some level, know to be true but cannot reconcile with their interpreters. A trader whose portfolio is about to undergo death and dying will first experience denial and anger, and only later fear and capitulation. Great trades can emerge from the denial and anger phases, fading the positions of insecure holders.

MAPS AND THE LANGUAGE TRADERS USE

Imagine that two traders, John and Carol, come to my office for counseling. Both have the same presenting concern: They find themselves too quick to take profits and too slow to trim losses.

John presents his problem as follows: "Doctor, I don't know what's wrong with me. Maybe I have some need to lose money. Can you help me? When I put on a good position, I get too excited and take profits before the move is even halfway done. It's like I sabotage myself. But when the market goes against me, I hang in there while it goes down and down. I seem to be a glutton for punishment. I did that in my marriage as well. I stayed in that awful relationship for years. What's my problem?"

Carol has a different presentation: "Doctor, maybe you can help me. I work hard as a trader, but my results aren't what I'd like. I find myself rationalizing reasons for staying in bad trades and becoming fearful of seeing my profits evaporate. I need a way to stay steady and think clearly when the market is moving quickly. Can you help me?"

Here we have two people with the same basic concern, *but two very different problems.*

The key to understanding these traders lies in the language they use. *The words people employ are among the best windows on their mental maps.* John has defined the problem as himself. He views himself as a "glutton for punishment"; he sees himself as self-defeating. His mental map is skewed: He is not a person with a problem; he is a problematic person.

Carol, alternatively, does not personalize the problem. She sees a weakness in her trading execution, not a fundamental character flaw. Carol wants to solve a problem; John wants to change himself.

Psychologists are attentive to such linguistic subtleties, for they reveal a great deal about a person's self-perception. They also say quite a bit about how people view markets.

One of the pleasures of writing columns for financial web sites is the opportunity to hear from readers. Their e-mails provide valuable insight into the minds of traders during turbulent market times.

After a column I wrote in February 2001 for the MSN Money site, several readers responded with their concerns about the falling market in technology stocks. Sometimes these letters ask me to perform a crystal ball act: Where do you think this market is headed? Should I hold or sell?

These questions, however—asked in the face of an historic one-year decline from over 5000 in the Nasdaq to under 2000—were different. "What is this market doing?" was the gist. People were not even focusing on tomorrow's market. They were simply trying to make sense of the present.

Fear and greed generally get top billing in market psychology writings, but there is much to be said regarding trauma and disorientation. The manner in which readers responded to my column said to me that they were neither bullish nor bearish. *They were paralyzed.* In fact, the results to a subsequent informal poll I took of reader-respondents showed that not one had decreased their positions during the fateful market drop, despite media reports of "capitulation." That was an important factor in my analysis that the bear market had not yet ended at that juncture.

Cognitive therapy is based on the understanding that people's responses to the world are mediated in part by their ways of thinking. The language people use is a window that reveals how they think. Their meanings of the world are reflected in the words they choose and the ways in which they organize those words.

Consider a job applicant for the position of company CEO (chief executive officer). The firm is looking for a person who can be a strong and effective leader. The applicant has a positive track record at a smaller company and qualifies for an interview. He is asked a question about his experience at the smaller company and responds: "I've seen some ups and downs at the XYZ Company, but fortunately the ups have outweighed the downs. Several manufacturers were attracted to us as a supplier during my tenure as president, and those accounts significantly boosted our production and market share. The resulting jump in our share price helped me retain our key managers due to a generous stock option plan. I'm seeing some challenges on the horizon, including a slowdown in the general economy and rises in labor costs, especially health care. This past quarter, those factors ate into our margins somewhat. We've remained profitable throughout, however, and I believe the economic downturn will leave us stronger than ever."

On the basis of this reply, what might you hypothesize about the candidate's suitability for the position? The average person might look at the content of the words and conclude that this is a successful, positive-thinking leader. A psychologist, however, would entertain reservations about this candidate.

Although the words are positive, the ways in which they are structured are revealing. Notice that the candidate never speaks of himself in the active tense. Things have happened to him; he has not truly described any leadership. This is reflected in the fact that his language does not place him in an active role. How he constructs his sentences says more than the sentences themselves.

There are few words in the English language more powerful than "I." Whenever you utter an "I" sentence, you are using the language to reflect important psychological realities. How you experience and construct your world is often manifest in your "I" sentences. Do your "I" sentences contain more positively tinged words or negatively tinged ones? More active verbs and adverbs or more adjectives and passive verbs? I strongly suspect that the ratio of "I" to "me" in a person's speech is a nice "technical indicator" of the degree to which a person views himself or herself as an active agent in his or her life. "I" can do things, but things can only happen to "me."

Your understanding of the market is similarly revealed in your language, as in the example of my column readers. This is also revealed in online bulletin boards and chatrooms devoted to the market. The content of these message boards and rooms is not particularly important. One person might tout a group of stocks; another might pan them. The language used in the postings, however, often speaks volumes.

One simple gauge is a measure of the frequency of emotional words in the posts. Some postings are relatively factual and focus on news, earnings, product developments, chart patterns, and so on. Others are highly emotional and either attack or praise companies, industries, economic policies, and so forth. As a psychologist, I don't care whether writers are pro or con; what is relevant is that they are emotional. In general, increased emotional processing of information is seen at important market turning points, when bullishness or bearishness is at extremes. This is a valuable marker for the couch trader.

During the aforementioned tech-stock decline, postings vilifying Federal Reserve (Fed) chairman Alan Greenspan reached a frenzied pitch. It was difficult to find a message board without numerous postings blaming personal losses on Fed policy. This suggested that a significant number of traders were processing market information in an emotional mode, contributing to rising market volatility. That set up a number of profitable short-term trades based on (temporary) pullbacks in volatility.

The language of the market can also provide useful clues as to emotionality. I monitor put option and call option volumes every five minutes of the trading day to look for significant expansions. Instead of computing the traditional put/call ratio, I simply examine the degree to which total option volume for each five-minute period compares to its relative norms (the average option volume for that same five-minute period over the past 100 days) and to the most recent set of five-minute periods. The total option activity is a gross measure of emotionality. High levels of emotion often occur at those points when traders are playing the game in the ways it was intended to be played. This can serve as a marker for a promising contrary trade, for it reveals the models under which traders are currently operating.

CONCLUSION

Once you become sensitive to the structure of language, reading financial web site columns, watching financial news programs, and participating in online chats take on a new dimension. Your language reflects your worldview; every time you speak, you reveal. People will rarely disclose their true feelings in what they say, but they cannot hide their feelings in how they say it. Good poker players, psychologists, and traders know the value of "tells." Your words, feelings, and actions reflect the models you employ to make sense of the world.

More than once I have heard successful traders indicate that they figure out the right thing to do in the markets by determining what could happen to frustrate and to hurt the majority of traders. At first this may sound paranoid—and, believe me, I have often thought the market had a personal vendetta against me—but it may in fact reflect a profound understanding of one's model making.

Time and again, I have seen situations where bulls and bears were dueling it out in the chatrooms, only to find the market mired in an ongoing consolidation range. Similarly, it has been at the gloomiest market periods, such as the days following the September 11, 2001, World Trade Center attack, that the market has been able to mount meaningful rallies.

The function of markets is to efficiently allocate capital within an economy. To accomplish this function, they must, over time, reward risk assumption. If the assumption of risk systematically produced inferior returns—if stocks consistently returned less than savings accounts—business formation and expansion would essentially come to a halt. The mental models of the markets formed by the majority of traders define what they perceive to be the safe, certain path. Although such models may produce acceptable returns on particular occasions, overall, they *must* be punished if risk is to be rewarded by the markets. When I saw the dramatic capital inflows into bond funds and money markets in the wake of the September 11 disaster, I knew it was time to shorten the maturities in bond portfolios and to take profits at the long end of the curve. The panic response of the market—whether to the upside or the downside—is rarely rewarded. Rather, the market rewards those who create anomalous maps, finding the nonobvious ways in which the trading game has been designed.

Chapter Twelve

A Session at Gunpoint

In tensions, we find intentions.

The role of extraordinary mind states in accelerating change helps to explain why crises are times of both great turmoil and great opportunity. It is when our mental maps are most challenged that we are apt to feel disoriented and threatened. Yet this is also when we are likely to stop assimilating events to our maps and instead accommodate the maps to our discrepant reality. Change requires that we provoke the crises that challenge our constructions of self and markets, shaking up what we have taken for granted so that we can approach life and trading anew.

In this chapter, we will explore the role of crises in change and the ways in which we can afflict our comfort through the strategic pursuit of unsettling events. If we learn to embrace crisis, we have taken a large step toward becoming our own change agents—across all facets of life.

JACK, MAN IN CRISIS

There is an unwritten law in counseling: The probability of the occurrence of a crisis is directly proportional to the therapist's proximity to Friday afternoon. All week can be slow; it doesn't matter. At 5 P.M. on Friday, someone is going to call and will be hurting. And every fiber of your being wants to ask, "Can it wait until Monday?" But you don't ask. You cheerfully set the appointment for 6 P.M. and practice a new apology for a late arrival home.

There are times, like right now, when I'm sitting in my supermarket café perch, my laptop looking slightly out of place amidst the early-morning weekend shoppers, that I love what I'm doing. I've just broken through a major obstacle with a student who has been through hell, and I think we'll work everything out just fine. I've also reviewed three years of data on the Dow TICK ($TIKI) and Standard & Poor's (S&P) futures premium, and I believe that I've refined a tradable short-term pattern that I can test out. So many ideas . . . so little time.

Then there are times like Friday afternoon, when I wish I had banker's hours—or no hours at all. After back-to-back meetings with people in varying states of distress, the finish line looks very far away at 6 P.M.

That's how I was feeling when Jack entered my office. During the hour previous to Jack's arrival, I tried to convey a message to a client by challenging his persona, his comfortable view of himself. In the aftermath of the subsequent misunderstanding, I wasn't sure that he would return to counseling. Holding my head and lamenting the lightning stroke with which I had delivered my message, I was, in Borges' words, a case study in contrition and weariness.

Jack was a big man, in every sense of the word: tall, broad shouldered, and stocky. He looked haggard and emotionless. He wore a sweatshirt and jeans, both of which needed a good laundering. Everything about him screamed *depression.*

Within 30 seconds, my energy returned. Jack stated his intention to kill himself. Not with fear, not with anguish, just very straightforwardly. He would plant his car into a tree at 60 miles per hour. It was plausible enough to qualify as an accident, he explained, and to allow his children to inherit the insurance money. A brief empty feeling in the pit of my stomach told me that this was not the usual "cry for help." This was the real thing.

"I'm here because people keep telling me to talk with someone," Jack explained. "But I've made up my mind. I don't want to live. I won't live this way." With that, he covered his face and collapsed into silent tears.

It takes a certain kind of person to enjoy crisis intervention. Everything that happens in long-term therapy is condensed into a single session in crisis intervention: getting acquainted, learning about the person, shifting gears, developing and implementing a plan for change. Such speed is not for everyone; after all, more people drive the Toyota Camry than the BMW M3. Crisis intervention is the NASCAR of counseling. No comfortable analytic couch and careful interpretations, à la Freud; just a stripped-down carbon fiber cockpit and a heady blur of passing events and rapid reflexes.

It's strange, but good crisis counselors don't think about the speed once the session has started. They don't think about the finish line, or the fact that people might die. As with trading, it is a complete absorption.

Only the absence of anxiety permits such absorption. For me, the calm that comes during a life-or-death counseling session arises from the understanding that the cards are stacked in favor of life. If people wholeheartedly want to kill themselves, they certainly don't need to consult a therapist. Counseling is of no value to them. The fact that they seek my help says that an important part of them wants to live, wants a way out. Few people *really* want to die. They simply want an exit from an unbearable situation. The part of them that seeks counseling is looking for an alternate escape route. That confers an important edge.

The collapse of time in crisis situations means that the participants are racing, not strolling, through the labyrinth of fate. A single session may very well determine an alternative future where the stakes are life and death. Everything seems heightened in such circumstances; each intervention assumes particular significance. A small turn of the steering wheel at 150 miles per hour affects the vehicle far more than at 15 miles per hour.

I didn't need an advanced degree in a mental health profession to see that Jack was in an unbearable situation. Even through his haggard features and silent tears, I could see that he was a proud man, not one who would normally seek help from a professional. His overt distress meant that he had not fully bought into his suicide plan. He wasn't totally resigned to a highway death. His tears, I thought, are my greatest assets.

"I've lost my wife," Jack explained. "I've lost my children. Look at me!" he exclaimed, pointing to his ragged clothes. "I used to be a happy person. I owned my own business; I had a family. Now I got fucking nothing. I'm just like every other asshole out there." As he talked, Jack became increasingly angry and agitated. I half expected him to leap from his seat and start smashing my furniture.

Actually, however, his anger gave me tremendous relief. Depression and anger are opposite sides of a single coin that depicts causes of problematic events. At one side of the coin, depression attributes those events to the self, looking inward for sources of blame. At the other side, anger casts a gaze outward, finding blame in the actions of external agents. Sometimes people oscillate wildly between anger and depression in a mad dance to make sense of a painful reality. Experienced therapists don't merely see the one side of the coin and then the reverse. Rather, they develop that spherical, Janus-like vision that allows them to see both simultaneously. Anger bespeaks hurt and loss; depression attests to resentment and frustration.

Clients, of course, enter counseling without such perspective. When they are angry, they simply see others as bad, themselves as innocent bystanders. When they are depressed, it is the reverse. This, fortunately, has its uses. Overtly angry people, on average, are less apt to harm themselves than depressed ones are.

I discovered that Jack had always been on the edge of crisis. As a child, he was an outgoing troublemaker, the black sheep of a large Greek family. After several scrapes with the law, his parents banished him from the home. He learned to fend for himself during those late teen years, drawing on a combination of hard work and shrewdness. Longing to prove to his parents that he was not a failure, he fixed his sights on becoming rich. In his early twenties, with the help of a friend, he started trading. His initial foray was wildly successful, as he caught the sweet spot in a roaring bull market. On a roll, he expanded his trading stake by agreeing to invest other people's money. Too late, he discovered that the bull market was the better part of his success. With his first major market correction, he sustained unbearable losses. He was forced to liquidate his holdings and to return pennies on the dollar to those who had trusted him.

The loss devastated him, yielding his bout of depression. The shattering of his dreams seemed to confirm his worst fears—that he really was a good-for-nothing. His world completely disintegrated when his wife, tired of the turmoil and long hours, took the children and moved into an apartment building owned by a family friend. In a mix of shock, amazement, and anger, Jack related how this friend billed him an inflated rent for the apartment, figuring that Jack would have to pay the sum as part of "child support." Suspecting that his wife was part of this scheme, Jack decided to pay the man a visit. At this point, he gestured to a bulge in his waistband and, with an enigmatic smile, explained that he had taken his two good friends with him: Smith and Wesson. The "friend" adjusted the rent downward, but not before Jack's standing with his wife was irredeemably tarnished.

Jack gave me a hard look after relating the story. He was scanning for my reaction. I could tell this was my first test. How would I respond to this tale of violence? *How would I counsel someone who was sitting in front of me with a gun in his waistband, inches from his hand?*

Somehow I managed a smile and a lighthearted tone. "Well, thanks for telling me about the landlord," I ventured. "I guess this means you don't want to hear about my new fee schedule."

Suddenly the Jack-the-depressed-man became Jack-the-big-shot-trader. The hearty man exploded with laughter, flashing a winning smile that made you feel like you were the center of his world. If I didn't mind his two friends, he said, he didn't mind talking with me.

Such tests are not unusual. Indeed, two psychoanalytic researchers, Joseph Weiss and Harold Sampson, maintained that tests lie at the very heart of therapy. Transference, they suggested, is actually one grand test: an effort by patients to rework their pasts by replaying them with their therapists. The therapeutic alliance is the patients' way of trying to help the helper become the parent they never had. Freud had cast transference as a pathological phenomenon, the mechanical repetition of early conflicts in later relationships. For Weiss and Sampson, however, transference is a highly constructive phenomenon. People pose tests for their therapists for the same reason that traders pose tests for their trading: *They are in search of needed developmental experiences.*

Jack was making it clear to me that he was a bad boy. He did not conceal the bulge under his waistband that no doubt belonged to his friends Smith and Wesson. The content of his messages bespoke pain, loss, and depression. The process, however, was quite different. Jack was challenging me to reject him, as his parents had rejected him. Or, more in keeping with Weiss and Sampson, he was challenging me to accept him, as his parents never had.

Because we barely knew each other, it was too early to shift the focus from content to process in an explicit fashion and to point out to Jack what he was doing. That would have only made him feel uncomfortable at a time when he was reaching out. With humor, I tried to respond to his process with my own. The metamessage of my joke is: I'm not afraid of you, and I'm not ashamed of you. I can accept you as a bad boy.

The rest of Jack's story came quickly. He kept long hours managing the trading, but he began partaking of the booze and the readily available women that accompanied success. Intoxicated by an excellent start and a sense of invulnerability, he stopped treating his trading as a business and left an increasing share of the details to others. He suspected, but could never prove, that a partner skimmed funds from the operation. For a while after the initial market drop, Jack scraped by financially, aided by money that poured in from two investors. When his performance lagged, however, the flow of new money ceased, and his friends became increasingly restive. Jack was forced out of the market, only to now face his neglected wife and children.

There was a long pause, the laughter now a distant echo in the room. "I'm not doing this any longer," he said quietly. "I'd rather be dead."

FACING LIFE'S CHALLENGE

So what do you say to someone who packs a handgun and has a plan to kill himself? This is where the traditional skills taught in professional school break down. Jack doesn't need a psychological analysis or any of those prefabricated techniques: open-ended questions, reflections, summarizing statements. *He needs a reason to live.* Unfortunately, that's not on the syllabus for most graduate courses in psychology.

What the crisis counselor can never, ever do in such situations is show doubt, confusion, or fear. That other person is looking for an answer and needs you to have one. If you hit the panic button and show a lack of confidence, your credibility is shot. No mood, no message, no resolution. It's okay to feel uncertainty. It is *not* okay to show it—even when a gun sits in a waistband, not three feet from your temple.

Is it confidence that allows the therapist to sit there calmly in the midst of a storm? Or is it the fear of not being confident? And does confidence help people weather crises, or do they first live through the storms and then develop confidence?

I sat calmly with Jack for the same reason I sit calmly with a large position that is hovering at breakeven. I know I will internalize however I respond, however I act. *First, behave according to your ideals; the feelings come afterward.* Acting out of control only reinforces the loss of control.

So I hang in there with Jack, as with a big position on the line. And I watch for the markers, even as butterflies dance in my stomach.

WHEN THE GAME IS ON THE LINE

It was the 1992 National Collegiate Athletic Association (NCAA) basketball tournament. Coach Mike Krzyzewski's Duke University team was in the midst of an epic tournament battle with the University of Kentucky in a national semifinal game. The game went to overtime, with five lead changes in the final 30 seconds alone. Each time one team made a clutch basket, the other responded in kind. It seemed as though the team who held the ball last would win the game. Each execution was flawless.

It was Kentucky that took the last crack at victory. Shawn Woods penetrated into the lane and threw up a runner. It banked in, leaving 1.4 seconds remaining on the clock.

Coach K later would explain his approach to the subsequent huddle during a time out. "The first thing I think you have to tell them is 'We're going to win,' whether you completely believe that or not." The players at that moment are at a fragile point. Their season is on the line, and the odds seem stacked against them. The coach's only ally is the desire of the players to believe and the capacity of those players to absorb the faith of their mentor.

The mood, then the message. Fear and crisis, words of confidence.

Grant Hill threw the ball the length of the court. Christian Laettner caught it at the top of the key, turned to the basket, and released his shot, seemingly in a single motion.

It hit nothing but net.

The players jumped in jubilation. Thomas Hill clutched his head and cried out, in a timeless moment of relief and disbelief. In the span of less than two seconds, his team had gone from defeat to victory.

The best athletes create their own moods and messages. That is a big part of what makes them special. Few people gave Muhammad Ali a chance to win against the undefeated George Foreman in Zaire, Africa. By 1974, Foreman had devastated every foe in the heavyweight division, including multiple knockdowns and a quick dispatch of that consummate warrior, Joe Frazier. Ali, even after his imprisonment for failing to participate in the Vietnam draft, still had speed, but Foreman had unquestioned power. The only hope for the aging "Greatest" one was to keep away from Foreman's vicious hooks, much as he had stayed away from the similarly intimidating Sonny Liston.

Interviewed before the fight, Ali explained the source of his strength. If he only thought of himself and big George Foreman, he was scared. But if he believed that God was with him, Foreman didn't seem big at all. He was little, conquerable. For weeks before the fight, Ali taunted Foreman as a "mummy," emphasizing his foe's slowness and inability to keep up with someone who could "float like a butterfly, sting like a bee." Clearly, Ali was talking himself—and the public—into believing that this was a real fight, a match that he could win. It was, indeed, a page out of the Liston book, where Ali had ridiculed the "ugly bear" and, in a burst of genius, feigned insanity in order to rattle his intimidating opponent.

George Foreman, however, was not intimidated.

Bolstered by faith, Ali came out for the first round and did what no one expected. He did not stay away from his foe. He entered the ring swinging, hitting Foreman with one righthand lead after another. The enraged Foreman came at Ali like a bull, pounding the body and swinging for the head at every opportunity. By the end of the first round, it was clear that Ali could not keep Foreman away. He could not keep dancing for an entire fight in the 80-plus degree heat and humidity of Zaire. Some commented that, in the break between the first and the second round, it was the first time they had seen real fear in the eyes of Ali.

There he sat between rounds, staring into space. It was his moment for self-counseling: crisis counseling. Suddenly, pulling himself up before the start of the second round, he led the crowd in a cheer: *"Ali bomaye!"* (Ali, kill him!) The crowd responded, and Ali fed off their energy. He proceeded over the next six rounds to do what no man had ever done, what no one predicted he would—or could—do. He allowed Foreman to hit him. And hit him. And hit him. It was the rope-a-dope; Ali invented it on the spot to demoralize his opponent. With each body blow, Ali taunted the larger Foreman: "Is that the best you can do? You hit like a sissy!"

Even more enraged than before, Foreman swung wildly at his tormentor, missing numerous shots to the head that would have felled any opponent. By the seventh round, it was clear that Foreman was spent. Starting the eighth round, Ali knew his foe was unable to sustain his power. "Now it's my turn," Ali announced at the bell. And it was. An overhand right put the big man on the canvas and made Ali, once again, world heavyweight champion. Ali had transformed his fear into invincible braggadocio, the enthusiasm of the fans feeding his self-made image. (Years later, the bitter Foreman would make his own personal transformation and regain his boxing stature, this time as an engaging media figure.)

Perhaps it wasn't his overhand right or even his ability to take the punches that were Ali's greatest accomplishments that night in Kinshasa. Ali had become his own therapist, shifting gears, turning crisis and adversity into inspiration and opportunity. Through his fear, he stayed sufficiently mentally flexible that he could craft a new strategy on the spot.

Ali, I believe, would have been a phenomenal trader.

THE EDGE IN CRISIS COUNSELING

One of the advantages of doing therapy for a long time is that you get to the point where you have pretty much seen everything. When things get hairy, I reassure myself by recalling the close calls of my younger days as a professional. The worst such incident involved going to a client's home after receiving a nighttime crisis call. It was a foolhardy move; the right thing to do was to contact the police and the hospital. But, ever the eager helping professional, I entered the home, only to find the client holding a knife to her neck. For two nerve-wracking hours I talked with her until she agreed to put the knife down and to set up therapy meetings. At one point, she threatened to turn the knife on me.

Once you've been to Hell and back, one arm thrust away from a plunging knife, the idea of suicide becomes a lot less threatening. That is what I try to communicate to the person in crisis. I've worked with people who have lost their careers, their loved ones, and their possessions. I've worked with alcoholics who have hit bottom, with not so much as a driver's license to their name, haunted by memories of the abuse they have inflicted on others. They were able to turn themselves around. It *is* doable. Even when everything else seems hopeless. Even when there is 1.4 seconds left on the clock . . .

My optimism stems from yet another edge that counselors have in crisis situations. Clients who contemplate suicide already enter therapy in an altered mood. They are all emotional nerve endings, overwhelmed with anxiety, depression, and anger. The message they need to hear is one of hope: There *is* a way out, even if it isn't clear at the moment. And I will be there to help you find that way out, just as I've helped others.

As a counselor, you might be shaking inside, doubting if there will ever be a happy ending. It doesn't matter: You look that person in the eye, get off the stool, and get the crowd into the action: *Bomaye!* There *is* a way out.

What you see in situations like that is nothing short of remarkable. Almost like osmosis, your confidence becomes their confidence. In the heightened state of crisis, the message flows freely from counselor to client. The person who had been bent over with inner torment suddenly sits up straight, looks you in the eye, and musters the energy to express some optimism. A less scientifically oriented observer might conclude that some form of possession has occurred, as if the spirit of the helper somehow entered into the body of the person being helped. You may not have said anything different from what others had been saying to the client for weeks, but you had the credibility and those other people didn't. The mood was ripe for change for you, not for them.

On this occasion, with Jack and that suspicious bulge in his waistband, a strong dose of hope and optimism was just what was needed. But this time, I didn't quite come through.

Because I was busy having my own flashback.

DR. BRETT'S TRADING CRISIS

It was 1982. The stock market had been weak through much of the past year. Each bounce off the low points seemed feeble, suggesting to me that further declines were in the offing. In fact, the advance-decline line, a measure of market strength, was dipping to multiyear lows. I went short in the summer, anticipating one last plunge that would take the Dow toward its 1974 lows.

My timing couldn't have been worse. Soon thereafter, my short position encountered the most powerful rise in years. With considerable anxiety, I rode out the August spike, waiting for the market to pull back and bail me out. It did pull back modestly, only to give rise to an equally powerful upward thrust in the fall. Stunned, I covered the position. My profits from the past five years were lost. I had totally misread the market.

Totally.

It's impossible to describe the feeling of true depression. It is more than discouragement and defeat. It feels as though your soul has been torn from you. Amazingly, I functioned at work, but inside I was empty. I felt like a zombie, shuffling aimlessly from activity to activity. There was no joy, nothing to look forward to. Every single day, I lived with the idea of killing myself. But even that seemed pointless. For what seemed an eternity, I went through the ritual of getting up, going to work, and helping other people. But there was no one home, no one inside. Later, a friend told me that I looked frightening during that time: scuffed shoes, hair ragged and uncombed, eyes lifeless.

Just like Jack. When I saw him, it was as if I were facing myself years ago. It was a self I had swept under my mind's carpet but recognized too, too well. Nietzsche was right: When you stare long into an abyss, the abyss also looks into you.

Slowly, wearily, I told Jack my story. I'm not sure what that big, boisterous guy expected when he came to a therapist, but I'm confident he didn't expect to hear his counselor's tale of suicidal depression.

I told Jack how the market was to be my way of making it big and proving myself. I needed to prove myself to my parents, who were successful themselves, to the people who hadn't believed in me, to myself. Making a killing was going to redeem me from the humdrum of daily life. I was going to *make it*. As I made money over the first years of trading, the profits were nice, but modest. They brought no redemption. So I increased my bet size, using margin to place more money on the line than I actually had in my account. The plunge of 1982 was going to set me free, cementing my career as a trader. Instead, it plunged me into depression.

I explained to Jack that my depression was followed by a wild period of drinking and dating, a frantic effort to escape the black hole. Bottom came in a bar in Homer, New York, after several rounds of Scotch and a particularly potent (and probably adulterated) smoke. There was a band playing that evening, but I couldn't make out the words or the tunes. The sounds seemed to emanate from within, feeling almost like liquid swirling inside my head. I was immobilized, recognizing that I was very, very impaired. I dared not leave my seat; I knew I would never stay vertical. After an indeterminate time (and the same tune swirling through my skull), I pulled myself together and made it to my car. By that time, I was sober enough to drive with extreme caution and the roads were empty enough to reduce the risks of accident. After a night of throwing up, I awoke to the guilty sense that I could have killed someone on those roads. My thoughts were clear, though my head was throbbing, and my words echoed Jack's: *I can't keep living this way.*

There was something powerful in that realization. Only a couple of weeks later, I got drunk for the last time in my life—at a New Year's party where I met Margie, the woman who would become my wife and the one great love of my life. Seven months after that, we were engaged; the following year I took a major pay cut to do the work I really wanted to do: student counseling. From the pits of head-throbbing despair, my life had turned 180 degrees.

Jack listened with rapt attention. Once slumped over, he now held my gaze. He chimed in with his tales of partying and infidelity. He talked of his own depression, born of the unavoidable sense that he was responsible for his own downfall, that he would never amount to anything. For a few minutes, the boundaries blurred, the conversation as liquid as the music years ago. There was no counselor, no client. Just two people who had undergone similar agonies, reveling in battle stories and war wounds.

I broke the spell.

"Hell, Jack," I said. "You don't care about the money or the trading. That's not why you're depressed. If that's what it was, you could take your gun, hold up some people, and grab as much as you need. But that wouldn't prove anything. You wanted to prove your parents wrong, you wanted to make something of yourself. That's what you lost, not just the trading stake."

Jack seemed deep in thought. My voice lowered just a bit as I suggested, "I bet you can hear people's voices in your head, telling you you're never going to amount to anything." Jack nodded. "And that depresses you," I said gently, "the thought that they might have been right."

Jack's eyes widened with surprise as he wondered, "How do you know that?"

I offered my best, thin smile. "It depressed me, too."

CREATING CHANGE BY CREATING NEW ROLES

Telling clients of your own travails is not exactly textbook therapy. Nor is it something I would think of doing in most professional situations. Taking a one-down position, however, introduces a most unexpected element into the process. People often rise beautifully to the challenge.

For several years, I participated as a group therapy leader on an adult in-patient psychiatric unit. Such hospital units serve one purpose primarily: to keep people safe. In this era of cost-consciousness, people are hospitalized when they are a danger to themselves or others or when they are so out of touch with reality that they cannot properly care for themselves.

The clients on the unit were beaten down. Many had experienced long-term physical, sexual, and emotional abuse. Others had long-standing problems of depression, schizophrenia, and bipolar disorder. Occasionally, it was difficult to separate out what was "mental illness" and what were the long-term effects of myriad tranquilizing medications. Vacant eyes, a shuffling gait, and low tones of despair were the typical signs of lifelong emotional difficulties and chemical treatments.

In the group sessions, sustaining a conversation was a major undertaking. Fearful of ridicule, certain that their problems could be of no interest to others, the participants sat with eyes cast downward, barely responding to direct inquiries. Just an hour later, however, sitting in the dayroom, these same patients would engage each other in animated conversation, often sharing difficult and significant personal stories. It was especially eye-opening to see how they dealt with crises. When one person hit a low point, contemplating suicide, even the most noncommunicative individuals would rally to their support, offering friendship and guidance. At such points, it was often difficult to discern that these were chronic psychiatric patients.

It struck me, after one tooth-pulling session of group therapy, that the problem was that *I* was the therapist. If I am the helper, what role is left for the others? They can only be helpees. When the clients were in the dayroom, however, there were no patients and therapists. Everyone helped everyone. And everyone was needed. The patient role meant not being needed, not being of use to anyone—except, of course, when dealing with other patients.

The next session, I tried an experiment. Speaking in a low, somber voice, I explained to the group that I would not be able to talk very much for that meeting. I indicated that there was a significant health problem in my family and that I was afraid for our daughter's well-being.

The therapy room was perfectly quiet. Nothing like this had happened before.

"What's wrong with your daughter?" one member asked tenderly. She was a young woman who had been abused as a child, one of the members who rarely spoke.

"She was diagnosed with a tumor near her brain," I explained. "It's going to take major surgery. I'm just a little freaked out, that's all. They say that the success rate for the surgery is high."

"I never knew you ever freaked out," a young man with long hair remarked with astonishment. I could tell that "you" referred to the plural, to all therapists.

"It would be nice if that were true," I smiled. "I wish I never had anxious feelings or suicidal feelings or depressed feelings."

A slight gasp was audible. "*You've* been suicidal?" one member asked in amazement. It was if she had said, "*You've* been to Mars?"

"Of course," I replied, a slight hint of annoyance in my tone. "What do you think I am, a robot?"

"It's just that none of you ever talks about it," the first woman explained. "You get to know us and we don't know anything about you . . . "

"Yeah," an angry young man chimed in, "It's like you just sit back there watching and judging us."

"Okay, fair enough," I offered. "What do you want to know about me?"

"Have you ever lost anyone you were close to?" the young man challenged.

I paused for a second. "Twice," I said. "My grandfather died, and I was the first to discover his body in the apartment. I knew he was sick, and I went to visit him in the afternoon, but he had died. For a long time I felt guilty, wishing I had stopped by to see him in the morning. At least he wouldn't have died alone."

I paused again and plunged in with both feet. "My wife and I also lost a child during a pregnancy. It was very difficult. I'm very afraid of losing another child."

An older woman, who had been depressed and silent throughout our sessions, suddenly stirred. "I'm sorry," she said. She started to speak further, then hesitated, started, and paused again. "My husband died just before I came here to the hospital," she explained. "He killed himself." She broke into tears. "We had been fighting. We were always fighting. But I never thought he'd kill himself. I feel like I killed him."

The abused young lady left her seat and hugged the sobbing woman. The angry man was visibly touched. "My dad left us when I was five," he ventured.

The silence was gone from the room, never to return for the remainder of my tenure as group leader. If an observer had entered the room at that moment, it would have been difficult if not impossible to discern who was the doctor and who were patients. In the space of a few minutes, we had created new identities.

LEAPS AND TEMPOS

So what is happening in the therapy with Jack and the group in the hospital? The answer can be found in music.

In his *The Listening Book*, W. A. Mathieu refers to *leaps*, in which the musician makes a sudden movement from one scale tone to another. He explains that leaps tend to be filled in by the subsequent melody, as in the development following the first two notes in *Somewhere Over the Rainbow*. Technical analysts rely on the very same phenomenon when price action creates a gap—a sudden, discontinuous move from one price level to another. People's equilibrium-seeking tendencies lead them to find a middle ground between the extremes of a leap or a gap.

The leap in therapy is from one structuring of the relationship to another. When the sessions begin, I am cast in the role of therapist. Jack and the people on the hospital unit are the patients. I initiate the questions, they respond. They tell me how bad they feel, I try to find a solution. The very structure of the situation keeps the participants locked in narrow roles.

It doesn't take much of a change in the structure of a musical piece to alter its emotional tone. Philip Glass's music derives much of its power from exploring the nuances of change: the ability of the listener to adapt to repetition and to become highly attuned to small shifts in structure. When a Glass piece on the CD is over and moves to the next track, the absorbed listener experiences a leap—a sudden, discontinuous transition. The effect is jarring.

It is precisely such a leap that occurs in therapy when a counselor steps out of role. By withholding the expected response, the therapist makes it impossible for clients to respond with their normal patterns. This creates fluidity, opening the door to filling in the gap with new action patterns. The "music" of therapy is radically altered if I disclose my own problems or appear to be more vulnerable than the people I am helping. Not infrequently, ones-who-need-help fill in the leap and respond with a trance-formation, exiting the loop of their own problems and reaching out as ones-who-can-help.

The participants in therapy, like those in any significant relationship, create a musical score with their interactions. That score has themes and tempo, a distinctive timbre and texture that reflect the states of the "players." When one party alters a parameter of the score, by restructuring the relationship or simply by shifting his or her tone of voice or volume level, the musical creation is changed, opening the door to new variations, new themes, and new tempos.

This has profound implications for altering the behavior patterns of traders. If traders want to accelerate their changes, they need to act not just differently, but *radically differently* from their norms in order to create a leap.

While incremental change might be necessary for the person who has been traumatized, and hence needs a sense of safety, taking baby steps may not be the best solution for most people.

Consider a practical trading example. I recently reached the point where my research and trading had been going sufficiently well that it was time to increase my size. Nevertheless, I found myself balking at the move. No doubt I was being extracautious, lest my hard-won confidence turn out to be over-confidence.

No one ever overcame a fear by avoiding it, however. Instead of increasing my size incrementally, which would have been a concession to my fear, I decided to immediately double my positions for my normal trades. Making this leap was my way of using my actions to reinforce confidence, much as I had done as Jack's therapist. I may not have felt totally confident, but I was going to act on the premise of confidence, and thereby reinforce confidence.

Moreover, I realized that I was creating a new role for myself. I had always thought of myself as a "small trader." I knew that I would never change this identity by nudging my size higher and becoming a "less small trader." If my goal was to trade size, I needed to gain familiarity with myself as a "large trader."

I won't pretend that this was an easy period in my trading. Doubling size doubles dollar drawdowns and more than doubles one's susceptibility to emotional whipsaws. Sitting in front of the screen, continually reassuring myself that these were the same trades that I had been making successfully, and allowing the markets to buffet me with random movement were not unlike Ali's ordeal in Kinshasa. All I could do was absorb the blows, keep myself psyched, and wait for the moment when I could say, "Now it's my turn!"

My turn came when I decided to create one of my nearest-neighbor models of the New York Stock Exchange (NYSE) TICK indicator. The model identified all days in the past three years that were similar to the most recent day with respect to the behavior of the TICK. This allowed me to see how the market performed subsequent to each of these past occasions.

The TICK had been extremely strong for a while, so I queried the database to give me all historical periods in which TICK was strong but price had not gone to a new high. The results hit me in the face. Whenever the TICK had been strong and price had not followed, the market weakness did not end until the TICK—and price—came tumbling down.

Armed with what seemed to be solid research, I doubled my normal size and shorted the market, despite the fact that it had already been down for a while. I made the leap—and kept nervously glued to the screen—but stayed grounded in the research. I would not close the position unless the market hit a new high or unless the TICK sold off.

As the trade turned profitable, I found my normal calm confidence returning. I could appreciate that this really was no different from my other trades, size notwithstanding. I took my profits, but I didn't feel elated. To the contrary, it seemed routine. I was adjusting to the leap and it was feeling more normal. *It was becoming part of me.*

If traders have the courage to stick with their leaps, they have the potential to internalize a new set of experiences and to draw a radically different map of the self. One trader I knew, Dwayne, indicated to me that he had a problem with impulsive trading. He became caught up in market action, especially around times of volatility, and ended up in trades that were not well thought through.

I encouraged Dwayne to make a major leap. For a while, he was not to trade more than once a day and he was not to trade unless both of his trading systems solidly pointed in the same direction. At first, he balked. "I might not trade for the whole day!" he complained.

"That's the point," I explained. "If you want to be in control, you can't do it by being *less impulsive.* Let's take a few trades where you are totally in control, and see what that feels like."

Dwayne carried out the exercise faithfully and placed a good number of winning trades over the ensuing weeks. Unable to gain excitement by overtrading, he poured his energy into research and planning, discovering new directions for his trading. By the time he finished our little experiment, he seemed less interested in returning to frequent trading. But he realized that he could now fill in the gap and trade more often while remaining in control. Having experienced control for a while, he felt like it was becoming part of him and would not leave—even if he increased the frequency of his trading.

If you want to achieve an ideal, shift your actions radically in the direction of your ideal, and spend enough time in that mode to internalize the results. If you have defined your desired end reasonably and stick with the initial awkwardness, you will have created a new role for yourself, much like those patients on the hospital unit.

I strongly suspect that the duration and the extent of the leap is directly correlated with its results. This may account for much of the success of experiential and brief dynamic therapies, which immerse clients in experiences that they have been warding off, creating massive shifts from accustomed modes. The therapy of Habib Davanloo is quite unusual, in that it features a vigorous confrontation of each and every client resistance. Over the course of an extended session, clients become increasingly agitated and frustrated by Davanloo's maneuvers. Eventually this spills out as a direct expression of anger and resentment—the very feelings that they often have been withholding. The leap to a new, angry state, but now with none of the feared consequences, is a powerful corrective emotional experience. Like Walt, Davanloo's clients discover that they can be angry without being destructive.

The majority of trading problems appear to involve a faulty regulation of personal control. Some traders are overly inhibited in the markets, unable to pull the trigger and act on their plans. Others are impulsive, unable to follow routines and discipline, and continually trading outside their plan. The most helpful emotional leaps for the *inhibited* trader are those that involve shifts to highly energized, action-oriented states: the pounding on the mattress advocated by Alexander Lowen, the immersion in experiencing described by Alvin Mahrer. The most productive leaps for the *impulsive* trader accomplish the reverse: dampening reactivity through increased focus, relaxation, and physical stillness. With sufficient practice, these leaps open new frequencies on the radio dial, reinforcing traders' abilities to program themselves.

This, I believe, accounts for the distinctly powerful effects I have experienced from long periods of immersion in physical and cognitive stillness, immersed in the Philip Glass music. Much like the sensory isolation tanks of John Lilly, the biofeedback and music exercises create a leap so radical that it is virtually impossible to access old behavior patterns. Moreover, I have found that, enacted with sufficient frequency, these highly altered states become more familiar and more easily accessed. Where long hours once were needed to achieve the leap to a highly focused state, only minutes are now required. Moreover, I find periods of intense absorption appearing spontaneously during the day with increasing frequency. Radical departures from norms, whether socially induced or cultivated through directed techniques, appear to accelerate change, breaking old patterns and cementing new ones.

CONCLUSION

"I want to really make it, like you," Jack explained to me. "Do you think I can do that?"

Jack was not referring to my income, which was embarrassingly modest by his former trading standards. He wanted to know if he could make a living by being a good person: a successful trader, husband, and father. It is interesting that Jack felt worse about his shortcomings as a family man than he did about his trading losses.

"Then I'd really have something," Jack explained. "I want something that's really mine."

"Your success didn't feel real?" I asked.

"No," he admitted. "I always felt like I was screwing up, giving my family the short end. And I couldn't face the people who gave me money to invest. One of them was a bad guy. I thought he was going to come after me."

I now realized why Jack packed his gun. And, from the depths of my flashback, I understood why his businesses imploded.

"What I found out, Jack, was that as long as those negative voices were in my head, no amount of profits in the market were enough. I would always have to go for more, take on more risk, until everything collapsed. Once I got the voices out of my head, I could take some money off the table. It hasn't made me rich, but I can do well and feel good about it."

There it is, the translation: *The problem isn't your business loss; it's the internal script that keeps you in the role of a loser.*

"You mean if I can forget my past, I can be a success?" His tone brightened slightly.

"No!" I stressed. "I mean that if you can overcome your past, you *will* be a success no matter how much money you're making at the time."

I could see the wheels turning in Jack's mind. His gaze was intense. His shoulders, once sagged, were now straight. It was another of those trance-formations that makes this work so special.

A smile crossed Jack's face, and I thought I detected a slight narrowing of his eyes and a shady, sideways glance. "So what do you think about this market?" he asked.

Okay, so it wasn't a *complete* transformation.

Within a few months, however, he was in a good job, making a fresh start with his children, and pursuing a new relationship. He was another survivor from the brink. Crisis—that painful, all-consuming sense of hitting bottom—provided the mood, opening him to a new set of emotional messages: You're okay as you are. Those messages could not penetrate when he was his old self, pursuing life in his usual way. Under conditions of crisis, however, the very same ideas could turn his life around.

In one state, Jack, like myself, was locked into a pattern. In a different state, emotionally attuned to the destructiveness of his ways, he could reorganize his life. Crisis was the catalyst, the very soil from which novel life directions sprouted. Jack, like me, like Muhammad Ali, had found a way to downshift in the midst of crisis and to change his direction: *He no longer needed success in the markets to be a success in life.*

Chapter Thirteen

A Dose of Profanity

We take our truth as coffee, with or without sugar.

What allows traders to so utterly reject their old ways that they can leap to new alternatives? The answer, interestingly enough, is anger. Of all the emotions, anger perhaps receives the least attention among psychologists—far less than anxiety and depression. It is precisely because many people cannot tolerate their own anger, however, that they find themselves anxious or depressed in the face of aggressive impulses.

Channeled properly, anger can be one of our most constructive emotions, generating energy that can catalyze a host of changes. In this chapter we will take a look at how we might harness the feelings of frustration and anger that stand in the way of trading and use them to propel us into leaps of change.

UNDERSTANDING YOUR RELATIONSHIP WITH YOURSELF

To begin the exploration of anger, take a look at the relationship you have with yourself. Once you appreciate how restructuring a counseling relationship opens possibilities for change, allowing an individual to assume and internalize new roles, it is but a small step to recognize how you can guide your own change by *shifting your relationship with yourself.* Many of the changes I have helped people make have entailed learning ways of talking more constructively to themselves. This was particularly evident with Joan, who transformed angry self-talk into a nurturing dialogue.

One of the most helpful exercises traders can undertake is keeping a journal of their internal dialogues. Internal talk is a conversation between the "I" and the "me": It is a direct measure of your relationship to yourself. And, truly, what is self-esteem but the *quality of the relationship you have with yourself?*

When people keep a journal of their ongoing stream of thoughts, their conversations with themselves become visible. It becomes possible to return to the conversation, to examine it, and to evaluate it. They gain the observing capacity to ask themselves: How am I talking to myself? Is this how I talk to other people? Is this how I want others talking to me?

It is eye opening to examine a written journal and to see how much of your time is spent in damaging self-communications. Worst of all, these conversations tend to be most poisonous when you are emotionally aroused and, therefore, most likely to internalize their negativity. How you talk to yourself after a difficult loss in the market will play a disproportionately large role in defining your subsequent emotional reactions: your confidence going into future trades, your sense of mastery and control, your motivation. Sadly, many people carry on relationships with themselves that would be identified as emotionally abusive if conducted between two other people. Like Jack, people harbor deep insecurities that become more deeply engrained with each act of guilt, doubt, and self-blame.

One of the ways this manifests itself in trading is the inability to reverse scratched trades. Suppose that you identify a high-probability trade based on a forecast that a particular stock will rise over the next two weeks. Instead, the stock stays in a narrow range for the next 10 trading sessions, even as the market is rising. You realize that the trade hasn't worked out and take a small loss. The question now becomes: What is your internal dialogue at the time you take the loss? Too often, the conversation consists of frustrated statements, discouragement, and negative feelings. You tell yourself that the trade was a *failure*, and—even worse—you might process the trade as if *you* are a failure.

This negative processing takes a toll on your ability to learn from the market action. Caught in self-flagellation, you lose the focus and the motivation to take the reverse trade when conditions warrant. Many times, a failed high-probability trade is giving you valuable market information. If a stock that is expected to rise fails to move higher on a market rally, it may be particularly vulnerable during the next correction. It is difficult to reverse your thinking about the trade, however, if you are self-absorbed. A trading audit may reveal an ability to honor stops and take modest losses, but also a failure to capitalize in a positive way on this information. The inflexible trader can cut losses on the long position but not reverse and go short when conditions dictate. The internal dialogue is a likely culprit.

This dialogue can be shifted, as you have observed in the counseling with Sue, Mary, Walt, and Jack. To accomplish such a shift, you want to adopt new roles in your relationship with yourself, rehearsing the constructive self-talk that you would want to hear from others. Unfortunately, mere positive thinking is unlikely to dislodge the negative dialogues. What it takes is emotional experiences, like those created in therapy. How can you create such experiences for yourself? This is where anger becomes a valuable ally.

DAVE, THE NARCISSIST

Dave irritated me from the moment he entered my office. A short, thin, nervous-looking medical student, he arrived several days before Step One of the medical board exams. Much of the irritation was due to the last-minute nature of his request. Dave was encountering studying problems, and he wanted help immediately. Not soon—*immediately.*

How people request assistance is often suggestive of larger personality patterns. Some ask for your time almost as if they are an imposition, interrupting their request with apologies for distracting you with such minor problems. Others are matter-of-fact, as if scheduling an appointment with their accountant. Still others couch their request in elaborate emotional outpourings, gushing about their problems before a meeting can even be established.

My least favorite people are those who call directly into my office, bypassing the secretary. They immediately launch into a presentation of their problems, heedless of the possibility that a counseling session might be in progress. Or they request an appointment for a seemingly routine concern within the next few minutes or hours—something they would never do with their primary care physician or attorney. "I want it, and I want it now" seems to be the operative mind-set.

Psychologists refer to this as regression. Under stress, people revert to modes of coping that were utilized during formative periods of their development, much as I entrenched myself in the bathroom when I moved into the home with my wife and children. The term for this particular type of regression is *narcissism*. Under the strain of current conflicts, the person returns to the egocentrism of childhood. Just as children might press their demands, ignoring the constraints of reality and the needs of others, clients can make demands of therapists that are breathtaking in their self-absorption.

So it was with Dave. He knocked on my door during a meeting with a client and asked to be seen *right now*. "What's going on?" I asked, doing my best to place my body between him and the individual in my office, even as I contained my annoyance over an interrupted session.

"I'm trying to study for the boards," Dave responded. "I'm totally losing it. I haven't slept in two days, I'm behind with all the material, and there's no way I'll be able to get through it all. I want to go into neurosurgery. If I don't do well on the boards, it will ruin everything."

"I'm in a meeting right now," I said. "Could you wait for a few minutes in the waiting room right around the corner? I'd be happy to talk with you once I'm done."

I realized that I had a committee meeting next on my agenda. This would have to take a backseat, however, given the anxiety on Dave's face. "But I *can't* wait. I have to study," Dave complained, practically pouting.

I stared at him incredulously, now feeling pressured by the time taken away from my other student's session. "What would you like me to do?" I asked. I was about to add, "Kick the student out of my office so that you can talk?" but I thought better of it, partially because it might alienate him, partially because he just might take me up on the offer.

"I'll go to the waiting room," Dave responded glumly.

I went back to the meeting in progress, already steeling myself for a session I knew I would not like.

REGRESSION AND MULTIPLICITY

What does it mean for a person to regress to a different level of functioning? As you saw earlier, the idea of regression presupposes a backward travel in time, a reversion to modes of perception and response more appropriate to an earlier point in development than to one's present-day context. But it also presupposes that the person is capable of occupying multiple mind spaces.

Sometimes these mind spaces collide at a particular moment of insight, as when Walt recognized, "I'm acting like a little kid, not like the adult I truly am." The self-as-child, the self-as-adult, and the self-as-observer suddenly merge in a seamless testament to the complexity of personality.

Developmental levels are often reflected in this multiplicity: This was a seminal recognition of Jean Piaget. I vividly recall the first time my daughter, Devon, saw herself in a videotape. The camcorder footage had been taken just a few minutes before and now was displayed on our television. Her eyes grew wide as she saw herself on the screen; and, in her most excited three-year-old voice, she exclaimed, "TWO DEVONS!" It was a classic Piagetian moment. Unable to reconcile the realization that she was both the watcher and the person being watched, she concluded that there must be two of her.

If Devon had come to that conclusion as a grownup woman, her belief in two Devons might have reflected a psychotic process. Psychosis itself is a regression, a return to more literal understandings and identifications. Had the Woolworth man said that he *felt* like an empty department store, he would not have been viewed as mentally ill. It was his insistence that he *was* a store that triggered his diagnosis.

What, then, are we to make of Rorschach inkblot test results in which a single person generates multiple developmental levels of response? Here is a classic example: A respondent will see the first card as a bat or a butterfly, outlining the markings—wings, head, and so on. This is a popular response and in no way violates the bounds of reality. The next card, however, with its red markings, may elicit a response very different in its structure and content. The client may see the top red details as seahorses and the bottom gray area as a landscape. The entire response is offered as "bloody seahorses going for a walk through the mountains."

This is not so far from little Devon. Unable to reconcile different perceptions—red as blood, seahorse shape, and gray area as mountains—the client fuses them into a whole that violates reality. Offering a response of bloody, walking seahorses and showing no signs of the incongruity of the response—even after pointed inquiry—is an important clue that regression has occurred.

The inkblot test is a showcase of multiplicity. It chronicles the shift in and out of mind states in response to ambiguous stimuli. Indeed, the experiments with automatic writing and the Branden sentence completion exercises are similar, projective tests: Give a person a stimulus, and then ask them to respond automatically, censoring nothing. The spontaneous flow of speech, writing, and perception reveals shifts in information processing that only make sense if it is assumed that minds are capable of moving forward and backward in time.

If the mere color of a Rorschach card is enough to trigger a regressive response, how much more likely is it that traders will find themselves traveling backward in time in reaction to a breakout on a chart? I have seen situations in which a trader has displayed extreme behavioral and emotional patterns in response to a single wide-range bar on a real-time chart: anger, depression, self-recrimination, and anxiety. What is most striking is that these reactions were not present in any shape, manner, or form for hours preceding the market event. One trader told me of beginning the trading day calm and confident and then regressing to anxiety when market reactions to a news event threw his trading plan askew. He had an opportunity to get on board the developing market trend, but he watched the entire move from the sidelines, unable to place a trade. Later, he described the feeling as the same helplessness he had felt as a boy when larger peers picked on him.

That trader wanted help for his anxiety problems. He didn't realize that anxiety was only the tip of the problem. The more fundamental problem was that he did not have his hand on the radio dial of his consciousness. The market was controlling his state of mind, rather than his state of mind placing him in control of his trading. It is one's lack of control over one's mind— not the specific problems associated with any particular mind-set—that poses the greatest challenge for trading.

NARCISSISM AND REGRESSION

A fundamental feature of that form of regression known as narcissism is that a person becomes so wrapped up in his or her own experience that the person cannot properly respond to social contexts, especially the needs of others. When Dave seemingly expected me to truncate my session in progress in order to address his current crisis, he strongly resembled the client distorting a Rorschach card. Under emotional duress, he was unable to accurately assess and to respond to the social situation at hand.

The narcissism continued well into the start of our session. Once Dave sat down, he launched into a nonstop account of his chronic anxiety, his many unsuccessful efforts to resolve the anxiety, and his fears over failing the exam because of his level of stress. He seemed vaguely aware that he was caught in a nasty feedback loop, with anxiety fueling fear of failure fueling further anxiety; but he seemed completely unable to slow himself down. He never inquired about me, about counseling, or about how much time we had available to us. He was thoroughly absorbed in his own fears and needs. I could have been anyone to him.

For a time, I let Dave ramble, hoping that he would exhaust himself and allow me to squeeze in a few words.

No such luck.

He continued in a rapid, nervous monologue, jumping wildly from one topic ("I've always been anxious, I always freak out on tests") to another ("There's nothing else I want to do; if I don't get into neurosurgery, I don't know what I'll do"). Once in a while, he would tell me, "You've gotta help me"; but as soon as I began to offer a question or a comment, he interrupted and continued his monologue about his nervousness.

Suddenly the phone rang. Dave's nonstop flow of anxious talk stopped. At least, I thought darkly, he didn't try to talk while I was on the phone. Regression notwithstanding, that set him slightly ahead of my children on the developmental ladder!

Not quite.

As soon as I returned the phone to its cradle—not a minute after it rang—he launched into a tirade. "Don't people have any respect for your privacy? Do you always get interrupted like this?" It was clear that he did not want anything intruding on his session, *even as he had intruded on a previous client.*

Narcissism. In that emotional state, people can see flaws in others that they are utterly incapable of seeing in themselves. Just like the hidden coat in the closet: In one state, people are blind; in another, they can see clearly. How can they be capable of such extremes of ignorance and insight, maturity and immaturity? *Who are these people, anyway?*

THE STATES OF DAILY EXPERIENCE

The crucial insight of Colin Wilson is that people spend their lives in relatively few distinctive states of consciousness. The Austrian psychologist Hermann Brandstätter and the American Ed Diener have asked ordinary people to maintain diaries in which they periodically describe their conscious states. This time sampling of experience is far more reliable than retrospective accounts based on self-ratings. Indeed, it is not at all unusual for therapists to make such diaries an active part of counseling. Having clients or traders keep a journal of significant weekly events is a useful way for the therapist to enter into their worlds.

An interesting picture emerges from such diary work. Eight basic emotional states define the bulk of human experience: (1) joy, (2) relaxation, (3) activation, (4) fatigue, (5) sadness, (6) fear, (7) contentment, and (8) anger. If you imagine a grid in which the *X* axis is anchored by *excitation* on the left and *inhibition* on the right and the *Y* axis is anchored by *positive* at the top and *negative* at the bottom, you can obtain a simple view of these common states. People's states are experienced as either pleasurable or aversive, as either activating or sedating. The fear experienced by Dave is negative and activating; its opposite is a state that is positive and restraining, such as relaxation or contentment.

Brandstätter reported an interesting finding. Low arousal states are most likely to occur in highly familiar physical and social environments. Higher arousal is found in the presence of unfamiliar people and places. The degree of emotion is intimately connected to contexts: If you want to feel sedate and relaxed, you should immerse yourself in common, routine situations. Conversely, if you are looking for emotional stimulation, you might seek high degrees of novelty.

This makes sense when you think about the choices confronting people in everyday life. Someone who is feeling overtaxed by their work might want a peaceful, relaxing, stay-at-home vacation. A different person, less stimulated on the job, might opt for trips abroad to novel destinations. The researchers Robert McCrae and Paul Costa have found the desire for novelty to be a trait-like dimension. Some people are highly open to new experience and tend to be stimulus seeking. Others are more attracted to security and stability and avoid change. You can conduct an interesting personality test by simply asking people which restaurants they typically visit. The stimulus seeker rarely visits the same restaurant twice; the stability seeker frequents a few, favorite haunts.

An important conclusion follows from this. *In exercising control over your physical and social contexts, you are titrating your conscious experience and thereby regulating your openness to change.* During most of your life, you follow rather set routines: You wake up at a certain time; you follow morning rituals of washing, brushing teeth, and eating; you travel to work via a particular route; you keep set working hours and return home for dinner; and you spend time in an accustomed way with family, television, and household chores. These routines limit the emotional, cognitive, and physical states you are likely to experience during any given day. Indeed, the work of Brandstätter suggested that routines dampen everyday experience, keeping people from states of high emotional arousal. This has the potential to both deaden daily experience and to keep the social machinery well lubricated. After all, it is taxing to deal with such highly aroused people as Dave!

As the music of Philip Glass revealed, repetitive stimuli, such as loops of music, can be sufficient to induce a state of trance. Indeed, an entire genre of electronic dance music is based on this. Given Brandstätter's research, your daily routines might be viewed as long-duration loops, and *much of your daily experience can be conceptualized as a form of trance*. This is very close to the analyses of George Ivanovitch Gurdjieff, who viewed ordinary states of consciousness as forms of sleep. It is indeed amazing to think of all the information that you discard when you are in your usual frame of mind. When you are driving your car, you rarely note the uniqueness of the scenery; when you walk from one place to another, you fail to observe your surroundings. Most of your actions are performed automatically, without self-awareness. Such autopilot is efficient, but also not so far from the limitations of awareness you experience during hypnotic induction.

This contradicts the common understanding of mind states. Hypnosis is normally viewed as a transition from one state to another—from usual, wakeful consciousness to trance. Perhaps, however, hypnosis is simply a tightening of the loop of everyday routine, reducing the duration of the loop and intensifying the accompanying focus. The transition from a normal state to a hypnotic one may be an intensification of trance, not a true induction.

Charles Tart, one of the pioneers of consciousness studies in psychology, described consciousness as a "world simulator." The function of conscious experience, he proposed in his text *Waking Up*, is to simulate the world and to enable one to navigate within it. The simulations of action people experience in video games are more or less realistic, depending on the memory allotted to the programs. All things being equal, a 128-bit game machine will render more detailed, realistic graphics than a 16-bit one. People's states of consciousness, in a sense, determine the bits to be allocated to their world simulations. During much of routine experience, people function as 16-bit machines, generating highly partial renderings of the world. Tapping into wider values and vistas, it is as if one's simulator gains an expansion card, leaping by megabits to more vivid, realistic experience.

Colin Wilson observed that when the mind's energy level wanes, its ability to extract meaning from events drops precipitously. In one state of mind, people, like Proust, can perceive vistas of meaning in a single event. The majority of time, however, people move aimlessly through life's rituals, as if they were blindfolded. As the analyst Thomas French once wrote of psychosomatic illness, the problem is not so much the presence of emotional conflicts as the depletion of psychological resources—like the inability to access the expansion card. William James was correct when he asserted that the human condition is as if one has developed the habit of moving only one little finger, heedless of the whole of one's bodily organism.

EFFORT AND PARTIAL CONSCIOUSNESS

If you are to master the emotional challenges of the markets, the following insight is crucial: Dave's problem—and the problem of most traders—is not anxiety or self-doubt. Locked in a single mind state, operating in a 16-bit mode of consciousness, Dave cannot process the information required by his board exam. In a similar way, traders trapped in states of boredom, fear, and elation are closed to wider vistas of meaning, unable to process the significance of market patterns in front of them. Acquiring new data, or new ways of slicing old data, will not help them if they cannot draw on their resources for data processing. Most traders do not need a shrink; they need help in *expanding* their conscious control.

A number of approaches to self-development take James's observation quite literally. These emphasize increased awareness of physical posture and movement as a means of cultivating expanded states of consciousness. Reviewing modalities such as the Alexander Technique, autogenic training, biofeedback, progressive relaxation, the Feldenkreis Method, and Reichian therapy, Michael Murphy explains in *The Future of the Body* that altering motor patterns helps to broaden behavioral repertoires. Just as people are limited to a narrow repertoire of thought and emotional patterns, they tend to become frozen into a rigidly circumscribed set of postures and movements. Indeed, people's cognitive, emotional, and physical limitations are of one cloth, reflecting the poverty of their habitual states of consciousness. Therapies enrich people's states through differing means, some by changing thinking patterns, some by promoting novel emotional experiences, some by introducing unaccustomed postures and movements. The gateways to change are manifold.

If you pursue an activity for a sufficient period of time, focusing all your effort in that activity, your mind will adapt to the situation with a new spot on the radio dial. And it is very likely that the problems that seemed so insurmountable in your initial mind state will be experienced very differently in this new one. Consider the following examples:

- Thoroughly absorbed in writing, the writer loses all self-awareness and is amazed to see how quickly time has passed. In this state of flow, previous concerns simply did not enter consciousness.
- The runner begins to fatigue, feeling discouraged about her workout. She presses on, however, and catches her second wind. Shortly thereafter, she experiences a state of runner's high, feeling completely energized and refreshed. Her prior discouragement vanishes.
- The stressed executive enters a sensory isolation tank, which allows people to float on salt water in a completely dark and soundproof environment. Consistent with the observations of John Lilly, the executive begins to feel bored and understimulated and then adapts to his surroundings. He emerges in a peaceful state, his stress completely vanquished.
- A trader is battling a tendency toward impulsive trading, especially at the market open, as he fears missing a major trend. He begins a trial on a biofeedback machine connected to a VCR. In this trial he has to maintain an elevated forehead temperature in order to watch a movie. As soon as his temperature falls below a threshold, the movie pauses. After 40 minutes, he learns that he can keep the movie running by keeping his body totally still and placing all internal dialogue and frustration out of his mind. At the end of the session, he feels oddly removed from the emotions of the market and places his morning orders without pressure.
- A trader who has been overly cautious in exploiting opportunities uses her morning weightlifting routine to get herself in the proper mind-set for the market open. Using the high-intensity routine developed by the late Mike Mentzer, she concentrates her effort in a relatively short period of lifting, generating tremendous effort during her final repetitions. She emerges from the workout with her muscles feeling engorged from the enhanced blood flow, which becomes her marker for a pumped-up mind-set. Her prior hesitation is forgotten, and she aggressively pursues her edge.

Effort is the key to the acceleration of change. You can eliminate problem patterns that have existed for years simply by placing yourself in a mind/body space that is radically different from your norm—and then programming that new space with your desired patterns. Your reluctance to make such efforts—your comfort with your existing mind/body state—is your greatest obstacle toward change. It is not coincidental that the military places recruits through rigorous exercise and training when they want to instill soldiers with the desired mental and behavioral patterns. *Change cannot be achieved in comfort—ever.*

Traders of the future may pursue self-development through means that look far different from weekly talk sessions. Virtual reality domes and sensory isolation tanks may become as common as home theaters, placing technologies of consciousness in the hands of average consumers. These will be the home gyms of the mind, dedicated to expanding consciousness and identity rather than to eradicating problems. It is wholly unnecessary for basically healthy individuals to explore conflicts and problems in months and years of psychotherapy if they can acquire the capacity to navigate the mindscape. The awful music one hears on the radio of the mind is only a problem if one cannot change the station.

ACHIEVING A NOVEL MIND FRAME

The relationship between novelty and states of consciousness sheds important light on the approaches most psychologists would take to the situation with Dave. Although he is an experienced student, Dave approaches each test as a novel situation. He becomes immersed in the threat of failure, sending his level of bodily arousal through the roof in a classic fight-or-flight response to emergency. For Dave and for traders, the key to overcoming performance anxiety is to eliminate the sense of emergency. By introducing elements of familiarity and repetition into the equation, Dave can shift toward less-aroused states, and he can experience less interference with his studying.

A common way this is done is through a method known as "systematic desensitization." Anxious individuals are shown how to focus and calm themselves, using such techniques as deep breathing and progressive muscle relaxation. Once they become relatively proficient at these methods, the state of relaxation is paired with stressful situations in a gradual manner. Typically, this is accomplished through the use of a hierarchy. People are asked to create a scale of stressful events that extends, say, from 0 to 100. At the 0 end of the continuum are situations that are minimally stressful; toward the middle are somewhat stressful circumstances; and at the 100 end of the hierarchy are severe stressors. They are then encouraged to imagine various scenarios, starting at the bottom of the hierarchy and working their way up—all the while performing the relaxation technique.

The idea is that through repetition people learn to associate calm and relaxation with formerly anxiety-producing situations. Dave, for instance, might begin by pairing relaxation with looking at his textbook, then reading in his book, then taking sample tests, then taking the actual test. He would not move to the higher spot on the hierarchy until he had fully achieved relaxation at the current level. This work can be greatly facilitated by the use of imagery. A trader, for instance, could pair the relaxation with imagined scenarios of facing drawdowns before tackling live trading situations. The use of imagery creates practice situations that would be difficult or impossible to construct in everyday life.

With only days left until the board exam, I naturally gravitated to such techniques for Dave. Cognitive-behavioral methods are well suited to between-session homework assignments, thereby taking maximum advantage of time. Seeing our time passing quickly, I interrupted Dave's flow of anxious talk and slowly, calmly explained to him that there were techniques available to help people reduce their level of arousal. "These are techniques that draw upon our body's ability to calm down by changing our rate of respiration," I explained.

Dave looked a bit uncertain, so I stressed, "We have enough time to put this into practice." I looked him squarely in the eye. "If necessary, I'll meet with you every day between now and the exam to make these techniques work." *Bomaye!*

Dave blinked and, as if emerging from a daydream, sat up straight and began to sputter, "No, I've tried that, and it doesn't work. You can't understand what I'm going through. I try to open the book, and I just start freaking out. I keep thinking there's too much material, I'm too far behind, I'll never pass. I'm going to have to decide on my specialty next year, and what if I can't get into neurosurgery? That's all I want to do. How am I going to explain to my parents that I can't get a residency? I need to be studying, but I can't."

My gaze was quite fixed on Dave as he spoke. My awareness felt unusually sharp and clear. It was absolutely apparent that he hadn't heard a word I had said. He had dismissed the desensitization idea without even hearing what it was all about. Then, like an activated tape loop, he launched into his previous litany of worries. During this worry mode, his speech was nonstop; he never once looked to me for a response. I had the distinct feeling that he was talking *at* me, not to me. Seeing him, hearing his litany of worries, I knew that he was not in control in a very fundamental sense. *Something had taken him over.*

Realizing that my attempt to speak slowly and calmly had not made a dent in Dave's aroused state, I took a different approach. Of all the self-change schools, the method known as NLP—neurolinguistic programming—is perhaps most attuned to the importance of states of consciousness in change. Inspired by the hypnosis work of Milton Erickson, NLP relies on shifts in the pacing and the framing of communications with clients to induce states of "trance." John Grinder and Richard Bandler, in their text *Trance-Formations*, emphasized the need to establish rapport with clients before attempting shifts. This rapport can be cultivated by carefully tracking the tone, speed, and content of the client's communications and pacing one's own communications to match those of the client.

So, instead of slowly and calmly invoking hope, I mirrored Dave's state. I sat up straight and talked to him in the same tone that he used with me. Almost in a single breath, I stressed, "You're telling yourself that there's too much work, you'll never get through it all, you'll fail the exam, your life will be a failure, and that is getting you worked up, and the more worked up you get the more these thoughts flood into your mind, and the less able you are to study, so you get more worried and fall further behind and feel like there's even more work and you won't ever get through it all . . . "

Dave did not smile at my anxious rendition of his problems. But he did slow down a notch. "You have to help me," he pleaded. "The test is only a few days away."

"Then we're going to have to break that vicious cycle," I said, also slowing down slightly.

"I *can't*," Dave exclaimed, his tone sounding far more like, "I *won't*." "You don't understand. My anxiety isn't like what other people go through. I pick up the book and just start freaking out. I keep thinking, 'This is too much. I'll never get through it all . . . '"

Dave, again, was off to the races. It was the strangest feeling. He was looking not just at me, but right through me. This time, however, I interrupted Dave right away. "Dave," I said gently, "you already told me that. You're saying the same things over and over again. I can see this is what happens when you study: The same thoughts and feelings keep coming up. We need to figure out what we're going to do to break that pattern."

"I've already tried that," Dave cried out. "I *can't* break the pattern. I need something different."

I could feel my anger rising. Dave and I were in a loop. Each time I suggested a strategy, he responded with a "Yes, but . . . " The more I conveyed the sense that he could overcome his anxiety, the more he seemed to immerse himself in that very state. Dimly, I was aware that Dave *needed* to be anxious. Emotionally, he seemed convinced that being under stress would keep him "sharp," would help him get through the material—even as he recognized that it was destroying his work. Shifting to a nonaroused state was too threatening. He equated nonarousal with nonmotivation: an absence of focus. *He would never allow himself to slow down.*

I couldn't shake my anger, though. It had been there from the very start. The narcissism; the looking right through me; the strange, almost tape-recorded quality of his anxious thoughts; the yes-but response mode: All of it angered me. I could feel the tug of my anger, wanting to lash out, to "interpret" his resistance, and to end this silly dance. I knew, though, that this would be ineffective. Gradually, I found myself becoming as aroused as Dave. My heart was pounding. I shifted in my seat; I felt ready to pounce. But pounce how? Pounce on what?

I didn't know what to do. Every fiber of my body felt primed for attack. Again, I shifted my position, trying to get comfortable in the large recliner chair in my office. I dared not attack Dave, frustrated though I was. But I couldn't just sit there, growing more agitated by the minute. The thought struck me: *This is what Dave is going through*—all pumped up and nowhere to go. I had absorbed Dave's state. *I had become Dave.*

Without second thought, I left my seat and sat cross-legged on the floor beneath Dave, arms loosely at my side. "Let me think for a moment," I said to Dave, quietly. I closed my eyes and immediately felt calmed, but highly alert. It was as if sitting on the floor had shifted me out of agitation. Strangely, Dave remained quiet as well. The sight of his therapist sitting in an unusual position no doubt raised his curiosity, perhaps taking his attention from his internal worries.

"I would really like to help you," I said to Dave, looking up from my seat on the floor. "But I can't. You're absolutely right. Your anxiety is different. Other students are worried about failure, and they get stressed out; but what you are going through is much greater than that. That's why nothing works for you. It's not an anxiety problem. It's an anger problem. You're angry; you really hate yourself. Look at what you tell yourself every single day: You'll never get through the material, you're going to fail, you'll never have a career in surgery. Such hateful messages! If this were a simple anxiety problem, I could help you in just a few days. But changing someone's basic feelings about himself is a much more involved job for counseling. There just isn't the time."

Dave looked stunned, his eyes beginning to mist. He didn't say a word.

"I wish I could help you," I said softly.

Tears streamed down Dave's face. He no longer looked anxious. His face contorted with the effort of restraining a sob, he looked down at me. "Why do I hate myself?" he asked, obviously tormented by the thought.

I didn't respond. The seemingly absurd thought crossed my mind that I was sitting in the "fighting form" posture described by Carlos Castaneda in his adventures with the sorcerer Don Juan. For the life of me, however, I could not recall the specifics of that posture.

"You *have* to help me," Dave implored.

My heart went out to him. This last request was not narcissism, and it wasn't even about the test. It was genuine despair. He was not asking for academic help. He wanted help in caring for himself.

"Maybe we can try something," I began hesitantly. "It's a long shot, and it's pretty different. But if you're willing to give it a shot, I am, too."

Dave's eyes widened just a bit as he nodded vigorously. His body was telling me "Yes!" Not "Yes, but." Just, "Yes."

It was a start.

CHANGING THE POSTURE OF MIND

It was not the first time I had noticed a change in posture affecting my state of mind. One of my favorite personal exercises, when I feel myself getting discouraged or depressed with trading, is to play highly uplifting music at a greater than normal volume. It helps if I am wearing headphones, immersing myself in the sound, and if I am standing and moving around. Any normal sitting or reclining position will sustain the stream of internal thoughts and maintain the negative state. So I keep moving to the music, sometimes jogging while wearing the headset. It is difficult to sustain a discouraged state while simultaneously invoking emotional and physical arousal. It is the physical posture and movement, combined with the musical elements, that evoke the new perspective.

A similar principle appears to be at work when one enters a meditative posture or a position associated with prayer. Having meditated for a while, I often find that my altered state begins shortly after I enter the cross-legged posture, sitting quietly, hands on my knees. Most unwanted emotional states—anger, depression—are associated with typical postures. You can observe them much as you can infer a cat's state from its physical cues: arched back, raised fur, and so on. Your body communicates even when you do not, capturing in gesture and posture a set of private experiences. It is not coincidence, as Lowen noted, that depressed people experience themselves to be no-bodies, whereas individuals of authentic self-esteem project themselves as some-bodies. Depression is a deflation of the body and its vitality.

My repositioning myself on the floor is a message to Dave, albeit a nonverbal, nonconscious one. Dave's anxiety—his physical tension and accelerated, nonstop speech—is also a conveyed set of meanings. People's problem patterns are communications—often preverbal ones—to self and world. From the Woolworth man's insistence that he is a discount department store ("I am empty") and Mary's efforts to push others away ("I'm afraid of getting too close") to Jack's bad-boy antics ("I'm going to make you deal with me") and Sue's decision to leave school ("I won't be like my mother"), *symptoms have meaning*. Symptoms are communications to one part of the mind from an Other.

Dave is caught in a loop of anxiety. Internal pressure to succeed generates fear, which triggers helplessness, which accelerates fear and further pressure. Transiently, he is capable of experiencing other states, but the loop keeps drawing him in. He is stuck on the radio dial of consciousness. In an important sense, he is *not* conscious. He is lost in his fear, unable to stand above it and select an alternative state. Indeed, he believes it to be *necessary*, equating a reduction in arousal with a loss of motivation. What is significant about Dave's presentation is not his anxiety, but his immersion in anxiety and the degree to which he clings to his distress. The communication, which I failed to read until well into the session, was unambiguous: "I *need* to stay vigilant!"

How many traders act out Dave's very pattern, convinced that the very anger and stress they face will give them the edge in the markets? Is it any wonder that they resist change if they think that decreasing their emotional intensity will also diminish their drive for success? Only when confronted with the real possibility of *never* changing might they, like Dave, consider trying something different.

I must say that I felt strangely energized by my posture, sitting on the floor at Dave's feet. The perspective was different, and the sensation of the floor beneath me was unique, heightening my alert state. Castaneda's "fighting form" posture was one of vigilance, sitting in a circle, protecting him from attackers. My own sense of wanting to pounce was transformed into just such a sense of vigilance and heightened awareness once I left the chair and sat on the floor. I no longer wanted to lash out at Dave. The energy was transformed, manifesting itself as a state of profound readiness for action, not unlike the coiled tension of a runner poised at the starting line.

I had felt this potential-energy-on-the-verge-of-becoming-kinetic before. Often, before major tests, public performances, or important events, I will experience a state of intense physical tension that I can only discharge through pacing. That was how I felt with Dave—not angry, but ready for action.

"Okay, Dave," I said while standing up. "I'll need you to stand in front of me."

Dave readily complied. He stood in the center of my office, facing me.

"What we're going to do is very simple," I said. "Instead of *you* telling yourself certain things about the test, *I* will say them to you."

Dave looked a bit puzzled.

"I'm just going to say to you the things you've been saying to yourself, okay? And I'd like you to tell me how you feel."

Dave seemed ready to try anything.

Slowly, I circled Dave, keeping my eyes directly on his all the time. At times I moved close, too close to him, violating his physical space. My pacing never stopped as I moved around him, repeating his own phrases in a gradual crescendo: "Look at how much material there is for the boards. You're never going to cover it all. You're so far behind, you'll never catch up. You're gonna fail this test big time, and then what are you going to do? There's no way you'll ever make it into a surgery program, and there's nothing else you want to do. Can you imagine what you're going to tell your parents? And are you doing anything about it? No! You just keep freaking out and falling further behind . . . "

My tone had risen to a near shout. The pacing, the eye contact, and the loud, accusatory tone brought to mind a drill sergeant, breaking down his recruits so that he could build them up. As my litany continued, I could see Dave growing red in the face. He seemed none too pleased at finding himself in the role of military recruit. He didn't say a word, but his muscles were tensing. His face grew taut.

I picked up the pace and hammered away. "No one else is going through this," I exclaimed. "They're busy studying, and you're just freaking out. You can't even postpone the test because then you'll just have longer to think about it and get totally anxious. Even if you did start studying, it wouldn't matter. You're so far behind you'll never catch up. There's too much material. You'll never get through it all . . . "

Dave looked ready to explode. He was glaring at me, his face red, his fingers clenched in a half-fist. It seemed to me that he would be able to contain himself no more.

"AND WHAT DO YOU HAVE TO SAY ABOUT THAT?" I yelled.

"*FUCK YOU!*" Dave screamed, his hands held above his head, his body shaking. He seemed ready to strike at any moment, thoroughly immersed in anger toward his tormentor.

So much for developing rapport in the first session!

I grabbed Dave by the shoulders. The room seemed alive with energy, both of us vitalized by the physical discharge. "Good for you," I said, looking him deeply into the eyes. "Good for you. You *do* like yourself after all. You were able to get angry. You were able to say, 'Fuck you!' to those negative thoughts."

Dave caught on immediately. He nodded in recognition of this unexpected development.

"Do you think that you can say 'Fuck you!' to your negative thoughts at home, the way you just did here? All you have to do," I suggested, "is imagine that I'm standing over you, saying those angry things to you. Close your eyes, and get an image of me hovering over you, telling you how far behind you are. Then really let it out. I don't care if you wake up the whole neighborhood. Tell that voice in your head, "Fuck you! I'm not going to let you make me hate myself!"

Thus was born an innovation in counseling: *Fuck You Therapy*. Not as dignified, perhaps, as psychoanalysis or structural family therapy, but it worked. Dave couldn't get relaxed, but he *could* get angry. And when he was angry, he was standing up for himself instead of attacking himself. He felt empowered, not paralyzed. Anger kept him aroused and motivated, but it did not leave him vulnerable. For him, the physical postures and expressions of anger were much more potent than meditation. Anger allowed him to stay vigilant, and he needed to be vigilant for this test.

After several days of venting his anger, Dave was able to successfully sit for the exam. He is currently working in the field of his choice, as a neurosurgeon.

That, however, was not the truly dramatic trance-formation. After all, Dave had been passing tests throughout his education. I was confident he could pass this one. At the end of our session, once we had processed the profane outburst, Dave spontaneously turned to me and called our session to a halt. "Well, I'm taking too much of your time," he stated apologetically, noticing that the clock had gone well beyond the traditional therapeutic hour.

I wheeled around to face him. He seemed genuinely contrite at having run over his allotted time. "Besides," he smiled, "I've gotta start studying."

Not a shred of narcissism. The trance-formation was complete: from "See me *now*" to "I'm sorry for taking your time." Dave seemed at that moment as sensitive and understanding as any medical student. He even smiled when he mentioned studying! Multiple states. Multiple personalities. Multiple information-processing streams. Multiple minds. Through a little profanity and a shift in posture, Dave had found a new spot on the dial.

CONCLUSION

Ask the average trader about the psychology of trading, and you are apt to hear some variation on the theme of "You need to eliminate emotion from your trading." As the case of Dave reveals, and as I have shown repeatedly in these pages, this is a very limited formulation. Eliminating Dave's loops of anxiety and negative thinking was critical, but it could not be accomplished by simply ridding him of emotion. Rather, invoking different, more powerful emotional patterns allowed him to shift engrained ones. And physical posture and movement were important components of that shift.

Traders operate under a distinct psychological handicap: Their work naturally provides them with limited physical activity. Sitting in front of a screen, monitoring quotes while staying relatively still, invokes a very limited range of physical and cognitive states. This is conducive to the maintenance of routines, including self-defeating ones. Odd as it may sound, one of the first pieces of advice I would give to a trader on a cold streak is to process market information in a radically different way. Instead of thinking about the market, talk the trades out loud. Instead of sitting by the screen, pace the office. Instead of continuously following the market, break away from the screen and perform some vigorous exercise. Each shift may be sufficient to help the trader process market action in a new fashion and to act on it differently. If at first you can't succeed, therapist Jay Haley once remarked, try again—then do something different.

I have encountered many Daves on financial bulletin boards and in chatrooms. They are so absorbed in their anxieties that they cannot properly assess their investments. Every step they contemplate seems fraught with risk: If they buy or hold, they might lose money; if they don't buy or hold, they could lose an opportunity. They beg for advice, but they cannot follow any that is given because any action promises failure. Their response to the world is "Yes, but . . . " and their resulting paralysis yields a harvest of guilt and self-blame.

Dave was able to successfully sit for his exam because of two important shifts, First, he was able to understand that what he had been experiencing as anxiety was actually self-directed anger. The thoughts "There is too much material; I can't get through it all" and "I'll never be able to go to a good residency if I don't do well on the test" amounted to self-accusations. He would appreciate that these were hostile, damaging communications once I framed them as statements in an interpersonal conversation. When I talked his thoughts to him, making their angry component more obvious, his natural response was to defend himself. The "Fuck you" outburst, combined with his change in posture and facial expression, told me that he had mobilized his self-esteem and moved beyond anxiety.

Second, Dave was able to shift his anger from me toward his problem pattern. Initially, his outburst was directed toward me; I was his tormentor. I quickly praised his profanity, however, and—while he was in his aroused state, with his esteem mobilized—I proposed that he could become angry at his negative thoughts. *The "Fuck you" outbursts were now a therapeutic tool he could use to confront his anxiety.* If he could stay angry at the negative thoughts, he would sustain a mode incompatible with self-anger. He had been telling himself that he needed to be aroused and vigilant in order to pass the test. This kept him from accepting any relaxation technique. By giving him a way to stay vigilant while defending himself, I was able to help him stay in a constructive mode during his studying and test taking.

Many traders feel a similar need for vigilance. Day traders and short-term traders of leveraged instruments, such as futures and options, in particular, sometimes harbor an unspoken belief that they need to be *on* the edge in order to *have* an edge. Many will even turn to drugs in the mistaken belief that this will sharpen their edge. Unfortunately, the increase in their arousal makes trading an emotional roller coaster in which their dominant experience is a loss of control. I recently spoke to a day trader who recounted the number of smashed computer monitors at his firm. Underlying the tension of trading among his peers was the same anger experienced by Dave. Venting it toward themselves or acting it out against their computers simply reinforced their frustration level.

Dave's counseling suggests an alternative with powerful implications for traders: *Instead of directing anger at oneself or one's environment, it is possible to become angry at one's own problem patterns.* Indeed, becoming angry at these patterns is a powerful step toward separating oneself from them and maintaining the stance of the Observer.

Many times, it is possible to identify and to angrily challenge the internal dialogues that accompany trading problems. Earlier I mentioned the example of a trader who becomes upset when he misses the price high on a short sale or the price low on a purchase. He waits and waits for his stocks to return to these levels so that he can stop berating himself for the missed opportunity. Instead, he finds himself missing entire trending moves—and beating himself up even worse!

By focusing his attention on his perfectionism and venting his frustration toward his perfectionistic "tapes," he can distance himself from this destructive pattern and enter positions once trending moves are under way. Each time he feels tempted to engage in picking tops or bottoms, he has to vividly imagine the consequences from his worst trades and direct his anger at his perfectionism. At times, this might mean shouting his angry reaction aloud, confronting the perfectionistic thoughts as an enemy. Associating his old pattern with pain instead of safety, he will be able to accept taking pieces of market moves, perhaps viewing the "missed" portion as an insurance policy that helped guarantee that the odds are tilted in his favor.

Like Dave, this trader learned that it is very difficult to identify with a pattern he hates. Anger is sometimes construed as a negative emotion. It is, in fact, a potent tool in the arsenal of those who would trade from the couch. If you can identify a repetitive pattern that interferes with the attainment of your goals and if you can make this pattern your enemy, expressing all your frustration and rage at it, you will have changed your relationship to yourself. Instead of identifying with the problem, you now become a fighter combating the problem, reinforcing your will—and your control. Note, however, it wasn't just anger that shifted Dave, but the experience of total rage. Once again, the extent of the leap created the rapidity of the change.

Chapter Fourteen

Trading from the Couch

The greatest changes you can make are already occurring.

In these pages, I've attempted to open the door on the therapy room. We have entered the heads of people like Ken, Sue, Phil, Mary, Jack, Dave, Walt, and Joan. We have also looked inside the counselor's head, exploring how human change processes require far more than simple talk. Perhaps we can now pull together some of the lessons from these case examples and summarize how they can enable you to become a more effective trader.

PROPOSITIONS FOR TRADING PSYCHOLOGY

Time and again, you have seen that the ways in which people are wired to process information clash dramatically with the ways in which they need to be wired to effectively trade the markets. It is for this reason that becoming a successful trader very often entails becoming a different sort of person. Success in the markets is less a matter of learning one or another psychological technique than it is systematically developing one's capacities for sustaining effort and purpose. The parallels to weightlifting strike me as particularly apt: Progressive, sustained, targeted efforts result in extraordinary development.

How can traders begin to develop gymnasiums for the mind and the spirit? Following are 11 of the major themes explored in this book. Together, they form a framework for understanding the psychology of trading and the steps to be taken in self-development.

1. *Behavior is patterned.*　You observe patterns in the markets. You appreciate themes in music and literature. Human behavior is similarly organized. Rarely do you have 12 different problems. More likely, you experience a single, general problem pattern that is manifested in a dozen ways. You cannot change by focusing on each concrete manifestation. The key is changing the underlying pattern.

2. *Your trading patterns reflect your emotional patterns.*　The patterns that interfere with trading are usually extensions of patterns that are present in other areas of your life. The field of behavioral finance has identified information-processing biases that systematically skew decision making, especially under conditions of risk and uncertainty. These biases include overconfidence, endowment effects, and frame-driven biases. Other biasing influences that affect trading are extensions of maladaptive patterns from your personal history. If you become overly enmeshed in your personal relationships, you are apt to enact a similar pattern in your trading. Conversely, if you have difficulty in maintaining commitments in relationships, you might also have difficulty maintaining commitments in trading. Much of problem trading is a generalization of the cognitive biases and emotional influences that are present in daily life.

3. *Change begins with self-observation.*　It is impossible to break a pattern unless you can see it happening in real time. Most patterns are automatic; you don't recognize when they are occurring. Before figuring out what you should do in a positive way, it is important to stop doing what isn't working. Typically, that means interrupting problem patterns when they first appear and distancing yourself from these patterns. Because such patterns generally appear across numerous facets of life—not just in trading—much of your daily experience can fuel your self-development as a trader. Intercepting and redirecting anger and frustration toward a spouse, for example, will provide powerful fuel for mastering the same emotions during trading. You begin the process of change when you sever your identification with your problem patterns, and you continue that change when you initiate identifications with positive patterns.

4. *Problem patterns tend to be anchored to particular states.* If there has been a dominant theme in this book, it is that people possess multiple streams of information processing, owing to the brain's division of labor. Some of these streams are verbal and explicit; others are nonverbal and tacit. The ways in which you blend these modes creates distinctive states, each with its own unique experience of self and world. When you enter a particular state through emotional, physical, or cognitive activity, you tend to activate the behavioral patterns associated with that state. As a result, you move in and out of problem and solution patterns many times a day, as your state of mind shifts in response to external, daily events. This vulnerability to state shifts undermines your ability to sustain purpose, making it difficult to adhere to such disciplines as diets and exercise programs. To the degree that you cannot sustain your intentions, you are unlikely to consistently profit from even the best-researched trading plans.

5. *Our normal states of mind, which define most of our daily experience, lie within a restricted range of our possibilities.* Your immersion in daily routine keeps you locked in routine mind states. This traps you in problem patterns that have been anchored to these states. The heart of counseling is the introduction of new, constructive patterns during times when a person is operating outside of their emotional, physical, and cognitive norms. Attempting different change techniques—such as positive imagery or self-talk—is unlikely to succeed if those techniques are administered during periods of normal, routine functioning. The psychological techniques that are most powerful in accelerating change create positive traumas, providing new experiences during extraordinary states of cognitive and emotional processing. Ordinary human consciousness—not necessarily any abnormalities associated with mental disorders—is the enemy of profitable trading.

6. *Most trading occurs in a limited range of states, trapping traders in problem patterns.* Traders tend to place greater emphasis on the data they process than on the ways in which they process those data. What you are capable of seeing is determined, in part, by the mind state you occupy. When you are processing the self-relevance of information, you tend to suppress your processing of patterns within that information. This creates distortions in the ways in which you trade, as you make decisions more for psychological reasons than for logical ones. You have seen that traders often occupy different states while they trade compared to while they research and plan their trading. Markets possess the uncanny ability to activate patterns associated with emotional arousal and cognitive bias. As a result, traders find it especially difficult to stick with trading strategies, even when these have been well formulated.

7. *People in general, and traders specifically, enact solutions as well as problem patterns.* If a person were wholly dysfunctional, he or she would not survive. Most people have dysfunctional patterns, anchored to specific states, and exceptions to those patterns, which are anchored to different states. The challenge is, thus, one of making the shift from one set of states to another. Identifying constructive patterns that already exist and learning to access them in an intentional manner is one of the quickest means of psychological change. This requires self-observation with a different focus. The purpose is to identify occasions of success in formulating and following trading plans. The goal is to become highly aware of those situations—within and outside trading—in which you do function as a highly intentional human being. Once you distill the essence of what you are doing when you are at your most intentional, you will be better equipped to recruit those capacities in trading.

8. *Although emotional mind states are associated with distortions in the processing of market information and in trading, eliminating emotion is not necessarily the secret to improving trading.* Removing a negative will not, in itself, create a positive. Traders can utilize positive emotional experiences to identify constructive solution patterns and to create an anchoring of new, positive patterns. Successful traders appear to cultivate new trading methods, based on careful observation and research, and to anchor those methods to distinctive cognitive, physical, and emotional modes. In so doing, they become highly attuned to market patterns. These traders also become sensitive to markers of change in those patterns, much as therapists are attuned to their clients. Effective traders thus experience significant emotion, but they do not become lost in their feelings. They have so finely calibrated themselves that they can utilize their emotions as market data, informing their research strategies.

9. *Success in the markets often comes from doing what doesn't come naturally.* An important research study conducted by Charles Lee and Bhaskaran Swaminathan at Cornell University found that high-volume rising stocks tend to continue to outperform the market over a period of months, but they subsequently underperform over a period of years. (The Nasdaq tech stocks from the late 1990s through the early years of the twenty-first century are a prominent example.) Lee and Swaminathan refer to this phenomenon as a *momentum life cycle.* My own research suggests that these life cycles occur on even shorter time frames, especially within the noisy equity futures markets. The market that rises on high volume and high TICK tends to continue upward in the short run and then correct. Conversely, when large pluralities of issues are making new lows, some of the finest prospective re-

turns on the long side are seen. It is human nature to extrapolate trends into the future and to climb aboard high-momentum markets and seeming breakouts. It is also human nature to become committed to these positions, even in the face of evidence that they are not working out. Traders' emotional reactions to the markets serve as hypotheses for how other traders may be responding—which, ironically, may be the worst way to play the inevitable reversals of market life cycles. Emotional tugs to enter a roaring market or to abandon a plunging one very often point the way to successful contrary trades.

10. *The intensity and the repetition of change efforts are directly responsible for their ultimate success.* The new, constructive patterns that are likely to stick are the ones that have become associated with highly distinctive states of mind and that have been overlearned. Conditioning new patterns to a distinctive state of mind makes it easier to summon those patterns any time you reenter that state. This connection becomes internalized most readily when it has been rehearsed intensively. It is rare that insight alone will create change; more often, *doing* things differently allows you to make the change part of your ongoing repertoire. The greatest challenge to changing yourself as a trader is also the greatest challenge to change in therapy. It is relatively easy to initiate change, but it is far more difficult to sustain it. Without consolidation, people are likely to relapse into their habit patterns. An essential ingredient in change is to repeat a desired pattern again and again in the same way, at the same time, in the same situations on every occasion that presents itself. At first, enacting new behaviors will require conscious effort. With repetition, however, the behavior becomes automatic, an internalized part of the self.

11. *Trading success is a function of possessing a statistical edge in the markets and being able to exploit this edge with regularity.* Trading failure is most likely to occur when you trade subjective, untested methods that possess no valid edge or when you are incapable of consistently applying edges that are available. Improving your psychology as a trader by itself will not confer an objective edge. Developing or purchasing a valid trading system will not in and of itself make you a great trader. The development of trading systems and the development of yourself as a trader thus must proceed in concert. *You are only as good as the methods you implement and as your ability to implement the methods.* My very strong sense is that the process of discovering patterns in the market and of formulating plans for trading these helps to cultivate those very capacities for sustained effort and purpose that subsequently empower

trading. Immersion in the markets as an analytical, neutral observer enables traders to remain neutral and analytic during periods of market turmoil and uncertainty.

Changing yourself as a trader requires the recognition that you are every bit as patterned as the markets you're trading. Change begins with repeated and intensive self-observation. Keep a journal of all trades, the reasons you made the trades, the states you were in while placing the trades, and the outcomes of those trades. Over time, isolate the trades that went awry and the patterns common to those. Then isolate the successful trades and their shared ingredients. Imagine that, trapped within you, is a self-destructive trader about to go bankrupt and a master trader poised on the brink of success. How does that self-destructive trader make decisions? How does that master trader operate? Once you can answer those questions, you are better positioned to do less of what doesn't work and more of what will bring you to your goals.

I strongly suspect that even the most successful traders have a constructive side and a destructive side—a self that is capable of mastering the markets and a self that is capable of implosion. The traders who are ultimately successful have found ways of continuously accessing the mastery they possess. The ones who fail may be every bit as knowledgeable and experienced, but they remain locked in states that undermine their goals. Overcoming problem patterns is only half the game. The equal challenge is to cultivate successful patterns that can be invoked at will. This is only possible to those who have developed a high degree of intentionality—the capacity to sustain significant effort and purpose.

CHANGING YOUR MIND: APPLYING THE PRINCIPLES

It is not uncommon in counseling to hear people lament, "I know what my problems are, but what can I do about them?" Intuitively they recognize that insight is necessary but not sufficient to generate and to sustain change. Once you *know*, it becomes time to *do*. What can you do to effect change *now* in your trading patterns?

Change, like problems, follows particular patterns, many of which are illustrated by the counseling cases from the previous chapters. If you distill these change patterns, however, you can see that there are three broad change strategies that are of greatest relevance to traders:

1. *Dampening intrusive emotional patterns.* It is not unusual to find particular emotional reactions interfering with the processing of real-time market information. This is why so many traders believe that the holy grail of trading psychology is to eliminate emotional influences altogether. When you notice a pattern of anxiety, euphoria, discouragement, or self-blame interfering with your trading, the first step is to identify specific situations that elicit the emotional reaction. For instance, one trader might overreact to missed opportunities; another might face his or her strongest reactions when handling larger positions.

Knowing what "pushes your buttons" is half the battle. This requires cultivating the Internal Observer, your ability to stand back from your immediate situation and perceive the pattern that you are enacting. Keeping a journal is a helpful method for developing the habit of self-observation, as is meditation. I have generally found that slowing the mind and body and removing myself temporarily from situations goes a long way toward activating my Observer.

Once you have identified the triggers for these disruptive emotional reactions, it is possible to dampen the reactions by repeatedly exposing yourself to the triggers under controlled conditions. For instance, if you find yourself reacting to declining markets with anxiety and self-doubt—even when you don't have a position on—repeated exposure to declining markets, in paper trading and in real time, can be very helpful. *The key to controlling anxiety is performing a highly non-emotional activity during the exposure.* Relaxation exercises under conditions of intense cognitive focus, for example, can be performed during the exposure to declining markets, as you literally train yourself to respond less emotionally to the downdrafts. It is not necessary to wait for actual market drops to perform this exercise; invoking meditative calm while vividly imaging declining markets can also prove useful. As mentioned earlier, performing such exercises with intensity and frequency will cement the new pattern, allowing you to respond to actual declining markets with greater calm and focus.

One variation of this exercise, derived from eye-movement desensitization and reprocessing (EMDR) therapy, involves engaging in a boring, routine pattern while exposing yourself to a highly emotional market situation. One pattern I use involves repetitively tapping fingers on my knees, alternating one and two taps on the left and the right knees. The boredom of the routine pattern is paired with the emotional situation (such as a stop being hit), extinguishing emotional reactions and allowing for a more neutral processing of market action.

John Cutting's work showed that there is a division of labor within the brain between centers that process self-relevant, emotional information and those that process patterns in the world around you. When one hemisphere is activated, the other tends to be suppressed. This can catch you in highly emotional states where it is difficult to identify and act on market patterns. By immersing yourself in nonemotional processing, such as meditation, self-hypnosis, or repetitive tapping, you suppress and dampen your emotional processing. This builds a sense of control and reinforces your Observer. With sufficient repetition, it is possible to enter highly focused, nonaroused states in a matter of seconds, dampening feelings of anxiety, self-doubt, and overenthusiasm.

2. *Shifting out of old patterns by making radical leaps.*   A second set of methods for altering unwanted patterns of arousal involves making radical shifts in your behavior patterns. These "leaps" or "gearshifts," as I have referred to them, push you beyond your normal comfort zones to alternate mental, emotional, and physical states. Once in these states, it is possible to process information about yourself—and about the market—in new and potentially more constructive ways. If I am feeling discouraged and burned out, for example, I may undertake particularly strenuous and extended physical exercise to pump up my mind and body. Conversely, in a state of anxiety, I will pull away from the screen and engage in a prolonged biofeedback session in which I must remain completely still and bring my physical arousal to unusually low levels.

Such shifts enable people to access previously hidden modes of thinking, feeling, and acting. I have repeatedly observed peak-performing athletes provoke fights on the field, pumping themselves up in the process. Coaches, similarly, will incite their players with confrontations and tongue-lashings. I showed you how Dave was able to become enraged at his patterns of negative thinking, fueling his efforts at passing the exam. When you leap to a new mind state, you not only abandon the patterns associated with the old state, but also activate new potentials.

The act of radically shifting to another mode may be more significant than the specific mode to which you shift. The extraordinary act of effort required to achieve a breakaway from the gravity of your habitual states confers its own momentum. The ascetic acts associated with many of the world religions make sense in this context. When people renounce worldly pleasures, they make a supreme effort that allows them new access to states of mind and spirit. It is not by coincidence that monks seek the Almighty amidst a vow of silence, that nuns achieve a commitment to Christ by renouncing conjugal relationships, that Jews fast to achieve a state of atonement, or that Buddha found enlightenment after days of solitude beneath the tree. Extraordinary efforts are required to sustain extraordinary departures from normal functioning.

Although some radical leaps involve shifting to polar extremes of experience, such as jumping into a tub of freezing water when one is feeling bored and lethargic, other leaps are achieved by blasting through emotional reactions already present. In a sense, this variation of the gearshift strategy is the opposite of the first, dampening approach. For a person who is feeling anxious and uncertain, for example, the goal is to accentuate this experience by entering more deeply into it. This can be accomplished through the use of imagery, enacted role-plays, the reexperiencing of dreams, and so on. Therapists such as Alexander Lowen and Alvin Mahrer have found that, once immersed in this heightened experience, people undergo a transformation to a new state and understanding. The anxiety over a volatile market, for example, may give way to expressions of anger, as prior losses are recollected and reexperienced. In expressing and making sense of this anger, the trader diminishes much of the prior fear.

From this perspective, blocking your emotional responses, rather than the responses themselves, may be the greatest obstacle to effective trading. Many times these blockages are maintained physically, as chronic muscle tensions and physical inhibitions. This is why some of the most effective strategies for deepening your experience involve the achievement of new physical behaviors and states. In freeing your body and allowing yourself to fully experience fear, frustration, greed, and overconfidence, you can break through to the opposite side, where these feelings no longer control you. Not infrequently, people are afraid of making the effort needed to fully experience themselves because they tacitly believe that they will become overwhelmed in the experience. Actually blasting through a negative emotional state provides a powerful affirmation of one's trance-formative capacities.

Such bursts of effort, to new states or through existing ones, may not resolve the particular issues creating one's state of mind—if, say, my poor juggling of home and trading responsibilities are burning me out. The shifts, however, can break self-destructive loops in time to salvage a trade. Moreover, you may be pleasantly surprised to find that it is easier to address those outstanding personal issues once you have switched mental and emotional gears. In general, the unwanted behavior patterns that affect traders are either inhibitory (problems in pulling the trigger) or excitatory (problems with impulsive trading). By making strong physical and emotional efforts during periods of inhibition and strong efforts at self-control in times of excitation, it is possible to quickly exit these modes before they intrude on trading.

3. *Cultivating new behavior patterns.*   This group of strategies seeks to develop positive action patterns, rather than to dampen or exit old, maladaptive ones. It is grounded in the recognition that, usually, there are exceptions to problem patterns in which you act in highly constructive ways. These solution patterns can form the foundation for change efforts, as you enact more of what is already working for you.

The first step in enacting this solution-based strategy is a different kind of self-observation. It is necessary to observe what you are doing right: what is working. This is where an audit of your trading can once again prove useful, focusing on trades that have been well executed. (Note again that well-executed trades are not necessarily the most profitable ones. It can be very useful to audit trades in which you have successfully cut losses short, for example.) Such an audit is best taken from a trading journal in which you have carefully noted the reasons for making each trade, your thoughts and feelings at the time of placing the trade, and the outcome of the trade. Very often, such a journal will reveal patterns among the positive trades that otherwise would escape your attention.

You may find, for instance, that trades based on particular market configurations are especially profitable. Such was the case when I reviewed the minute-to-minute action of multiple sector indexes at the time I placed short-sale trades. A pattern that became evident was that short trades placed at times of multiple divergences among the indexes (some making daily highs; others falling x percent short of their daily highs) tended to be more successful than trades placed when a greater proportion of indexes were at or near their highs. This trading pattern thus became one that I wanted to internalize as part of my strategic repertoire.

Anchoring such a solution pattern to a distinctive state—a unique cognitive, physical, and emotional mode—can greatly assist its internalization. People achieve most distinctive states by either greatly reducing or increasing their normal level of arousal. Meditation is an arousal-reduction strategy; physical exercise can be used to heighten arousal. I have found pacing continuously around my house while verbally rehearsing my new trading strategies and scenarios to be especially helpful in building positive action patterns. Others with whom I have worked have benefited by mentally rehearsing strategies in states of self-hypnosis or in the highly aroused states achieved during physical workouts.

Discovering the anchors that work best for any particular trader is, to a large degree, a matter of trial-and-error. It is especially important that your subsequent trading be performed in the same state you have been rehearsing while invoking the solution patterns. I do not want to be trading while sitting silently at my station for hours if I have been rehearsing solutions while pacing and talking. I am much more likely to successfully identify and to act on the solutions if I am processing the market while pacing and talking out what I am seeing. Indeed, I have found that often I can see what the market is doing only after I have spoken it aloud during my stream of consciousness processing while pacing. Looking at charts and data provides the raw material for processing, but integrating the information into meaningful patterns sometimes only occurs once I have shifted to another mode.

The solution pattern you rehearse may be a pattern in the market data, as in my example in the previous paragraph, or it may be one of your own behavioral patterns, as in the case of rehearsing the ability to stop a losing trade or let a winning trade run. Anchoring works by simple classical conditioning. By repeatedly pairing a desired pattern with a distinctive state of mind or physical state, you become better equipped to identify and to act on that pattern whenever you invoke that state. What you see and how you construe information is dependent on the state you are in. By practicing constructive behavior patterns in a unique state, you gain control over the subsequent enactment of those patterns.

Sometimes traders are unable to identify their own solution patterns. In such cases, all is not lost. A powerful strategy that relies on the same logic is to extract those solution patterns from a mentor and then systematically anchor them to a distinctive state and become the play-actor of those ideals. If I learn a trading pattern from a teacher, for example, I might rehearse this pattern repeatedly by placing myself in a state of intense focus and concentration and then reviewing the manifestations of the pattern in my historical data. I will activate this same focused state and paper trade the pattern in real time, before actually undertaking small trades with the strategy. Through this repetition and anchoring, the role-played trading method begins to feel more natural and eventually is internalized as part of my repertoire. The simple act of focusing oneself can then aid in recruiting the trading method.

Most of the change efforts you will undertake in the markets will boil down to one of these three strategies. You will either be attempting to dampen unwanted reactions, leap to discrepant states and patterns, or cultivate novel, positive ones. There are many, many variations on these strategies and an infinite number of creative ways of putting them into practice. Ultimately, however, their success is contingent on the quality of your self-observation at the outset—pinpointing the changes to be made—and the extent of rehearsals once the change efforts have begun. Very often people are successful in initiating change but not in sustaining it. Performing exercises many times on a daily basis and performing them in the same way each time greatly facilitates consolidation.

And that leads to the most powerful trading psychology strategy of all: having friends and family that are supportive of your efforts at self-development. In pursuing aims with extraordinary effort, you are not leading a normal life. This calls for remarkable understanding from those around you. Normal people do not stay up for hours at a time at night, typing automatic thoughts on a keyboard. They do not stay connected to biofeedback and sound-and-light machines while trading or processing market data. For others to not only tolerate but also value this departure from normality is rare and special. Whatever insight and experience I have captured in this book could never have been achieved in the absence of supportive family, mentors, and colleagues.

MATCHING YOUR TRADING TO YOUR PERSONALITY

One of the most profound pieces of market wisdom I have ever encountered appeared in an article by Linda Bradford Raschke. She advised beginning traders to focus on one or two tested market patterns and simply trade these. If you have done your homework, these patterns by themselves should provide you with a decent living. The patterns you will trade will depend on your approach to the markets, which, in part, will be shaped by your personality and your financial goals.

After having surveyed a number of frequent traders with Linda, I came away with two impressions regarding trading and personality:

1. *Many traders who report emotional problems in the market are experiencing difficulties because their trading is understructured.* By this I mean that

they have not carefully defined the patterns that trigger their entries and exits and often lack explicit mechanisms for money management. I do not at all believe that all traders need to trade mechanical systems, but I would say that the majority of distressed traders I have encountered would benefit from becoming more *rule-governed*. The best educational services I have seen for traders, including Linda's, limit themselves to a core group of tradable patterns that have been tested. These services then remain faithful to their methods. When traders lack this structure and discipline, it is very difficult for them to internalize confidence. Their trades are particularly vulnerable to emotional intrusions and occasional debilitating losses. Rules go a long way toward keeping traders reality grounded.

2. *Many traders who report emotional problems in the market are experiencing their difficulties because they have not found a good fit between their trading styles and their personalities.* Tolerance for risk is, in part, a traitlike personality variable. When traders with low tolerances for risk expand their holding periods, they are going to be particularly vulnerable to the enhanced drawdowns that come with the territory. Similarly, a trader with a visual, intuitive learning style may find it difficult to stick with a mechanical trading system. Many traders I have surveyed or interviewed have methods or systems that they want to work, but they have not asked the hard questions as to whether these methods or systems are ideal for them. As a therapist, I am accustomed to processing subtle markers in my interactions with people. It is not surprising that my best trading makes use of this skill. When I have attempted to trade in other styles—especially mechanically—the results have been poor. I simply cannot trade something I do not feel and perceive firsthand. Conversely, my good friend and successful trader Henry Carstens is a marvel at developing trading systems and, I strongly suspect, would find it very difficult to trade in a discretionary manner. The issue isn't so much one of which approach to trading is best. Rather, it is important to *find the proper fit between the trader and the trading.*

I strongly suspect that some people have personalities that simply are not well suited to trading. Not everyone possesses the necessary blend of flexibility and analytical decision-making skills. Similarly, not everyone possesses the requisite emotional maturity and self-discipline to become a successful trader, just as not everyone possesses the skills to be a world-class basketball player or surgeon. From the limited data Linda and I collected, I would say that trading will be an uphill battle if you are generally prone to high degrees of emotional distress (anxiety, depression, anger) and if you tend to be impulsive, poorly disciplined, and not particularly conscientious in everyday life.

True, there may well be emotionally volatile, undisciplined traders making a fortune in the markets. I must say, however, that the ones I have observed have not kept their fortunes. To a person, the successful traders I have observed have been methodical and highly rule governed. I believe a careful reading of Jack Schwager's *Market Wizards* books supports this conclusion. The methods and the rules differ for various traders—some are scalpers, some are swing traders; some are more discretionary: Some are more mechanical. All of them, however, appear to have plans and techniques that they have observed and researched exhaustively, honed carefully, and implement faithfully. These plans and techniques are extensions of their personalities, capturing the distinctive ways in which they process information and handle risk and uncertainty.

THE GREAT FRONTIER: DEVELOPING TRADING EXPERTISE

A review of research convinces me that the greatest strides in the psychology of trading will come not from psychotherapy, but from the field of learning. Recent developments in cognitive neuroscience suggest that learning—like emotional change—can be accelerated under the proper conditions. This has profound implications for the training and development of traders.

The implicit learning research of Arthur Reber and Axel Cleeremans indicates that people acquire complex skills such as spoken language long before they are capable of verbalizing the rules of spoken language. Their knowledge is tacit or implicit, held at a level beneath explicit verbalization. A series of clever experiments utilizing artificial grammars—strings of letters that are combined by sets of rules—indicates that such implicit learning is not at all uncommon.

Pretend that I have invented an artificial grammar that follows this pattern: UFMAG. I will flash those five letters, one by one, to the participants in the experiment. Every time I flash the letter "U," it will be followed by an "F." Each time I display the letter "A," the next letter will be a "G," and so on. It is relatively simple to create grammars of varying complexity by altering the number of letters in the grammar and the rules that govern the letters' appearance.

The key to the experiment is that the subjects are not told the underlying rules of the grammar. They are first shown strings of letters that are grammatically and ungrammatically formed (i.e., that follow or don't follow the rules) in an acquisition phase. Then, in a testing phase, they are asked to determine whether presented strings of letters are grammatically formed. Subjects are corrected when they get an item wrong, but they are not informed why they were wrong. They then move quickly on to the next item. This occurs over a large number of trials.

Over time the participants become quite adept at determining whether the strings of letters are grammatical. They seem to pick up the pattern that underlies the grammar. If, however, you ask the participants to state their reasons for determining the grammaticality of the strings, they cannot verbalize the rules. Indeed, they often insist that the patterns were random and that they were merely guessing well. Their learning appears to be implicit in that they know something but don't necessarily know that they know it.

In his book *Implicit Learning and Tacit Knowledge*, Arthur Reber pointed out that subjects are capable of learning even highly complex grammars under noisy conditions. For instance, in one set of studies, participants were asked to predict the appearance of an event, a flashing light. The appearance of the event on any trial N, however, was dependent on what had occurred at trial N–j, where j was varied between one and seven across trials. Surprisingly, participants were able, over time, to predict the appearance of an event based on what had happened many trials ago—again without being able to verbalize the basis for their predictions. Moreover, when a noise element is added to the acquisition phase, in which a varying percentage of the elements presented to participants are randomly derived, implicit learning still occurs.

What seems clear is that participants in the implicit learning studies are learning complex patterns: patterns too complex, Reber noted, to be learned in a single afternoon. In one study, participants learned to predict the production level of a sugar plant, given the underlying rule Production = $2w - (p + n)$, where w was the number of workers in the plant, p was the previous trial's output, and n was a noise factor. Reber asserted that knowledge acquired implicitly underlies performance that could be accounted for by conscious knowledge.

What is the nature of this tacit knowledge? Evidence suggests that participants in implicit learning studies are acquiring knowledge of statistical regularities among the data. Reber noted that, if events E1 and E2 occur with probabilities .80 and .20, respectively, the guesses of participants over time will approximate .80 and .20 for the events. It is not necessarily the case that participants ever acquire the true rules of the grammar or sugar production task. Rather, they seem to build implicit representations of the probability of events determined by those rules.

The key to implicit learning appears to be the large number of trials (generally one thousand or more), prompt and accurate feedback, and a high degree of focus and concentration on the part of the participants. If, for instance, the participants are distracted with other tasks during the implicit learning trials, the quality and the amount of learning will diminish significantly.

Cleeremans proposed that human beings are processing the information during these studies much as a neural network processes data. They establish connections among events based on statistical regularities. When these connections are sufficiently strong, they reach the threshold of awareness and become explicit. What people know, therefore, exists on a continuum from *tacit* to *fully explicit*, with many gradations between. This sets up potential clashes between what people know—their verbal, explicit understanding— and what they sense. Indeed, this is what Reber found in his review of research. When participants are told the rules underlying the learning trials, or when they are prompted to search for rules and the rules are relatively simple, explicit thought appears to aid performance in the implicit learning experiments. But when the rules are so complex that participants cannot figure them out for themselves, efforts at explicit rule finding actually hinder performance. It appears that the tacit encoding of information in these studies is relatively independent of the accustomed, explicit learning processes.

Summing up these studies in *Implicit Learning and Tacit Knowledge*, Reber concluded that participants can learn to utilize complex structural relationships in presented data in a completely nonreflective manner. I propose that traders acquire expertise in the markets in a very similar manner. They immerse themselves in complex, noisy stimuli (market data) and gradually acquire information about the regularities among these stimuli. Once they have achieved an extended degree of immersion—far before they can verbalize what they know about the markets—traders gain a sense for when markets are likely to rise and to fall. It is only after the patterns have been overlearned that they can be verbalized and captured in explicit rules and trading systems.

If this is the case, then a key to developing trading expertise may be the degree of immersion with which one approaches the markets. By following markets day in and day out for a number of years and carefully following trades that are placed, traders may internalize rules of the markets much as children internalize the rules of spoken language. To the degree that traders approach their work on a part-time basis and/or lack immersion in the real-time patterns of the markets, their learning is apt to be impaired.

This lack of immersion may also help to explain why so many people undertake trading and why so few actually succeed at making it their living. Quite simply, they cannot survive their learning curves. If the implicit learning of market patterns requires thousands of trials—as for the participants in Reber's and Cleeremans's studies—it would have to be a dedicated student—and perhaps also one with deep pockets—to undergo the inevitable frustration of the learning period. Then too, traders may not trade with sufficient frequency to obtain the exposure necessary to internalize market patterns. If a trader places only two orders per day, it would take over two years of trading to achieve the number of trials found in an implicit learning study. Even this, however, might not be sufficient to trigger tacit learning. The trials in a typical implicit learning study are very closely spaced, preventing any interference from intruding explicit thought and emotion. For the trader who is trading only twice daily, there is plenty of opportunity for such interference. It would be surprising if such distantly spaced learning trials could generate the learning necessary for internalized market expertise. Most traders may fail to learn market patterns not because of their emotional difficulties or self-defeating tendencies, but simply because of their lack of sufficient exposure to the markets.

IMPLICATIONS OF THE IMPLICIT LEARNING RESEARCH

This line of reasoning can be followed through to its possible conclusions. If implicit learning accounts for trading expertise, one would expect to see the best evidence of tacit knowledge among traders who have been immersed in trading, with frequent learning "trials." These would be floor traders, scalpers, and other very high frequency traders. In following the markets minute by minute, day after day, and in placing and following dozens, if not hundreds, of trades each day, the floor trader is a natural field study in implicit learning.

It is interesting that among the traders Linda Raschke and I surveyed, several had floor experience or were very high frequency off-floor traders. It was clear to us that these traders were utilizing methods different from those used by the others. They were less likely to rely on elaborate research for their decision-making and much more likely to cite "instinct" in entering and exiting trades. The successful traders in this group did operate in a rule-governed way, but the rules were relatively simple heuristics that helped limit losses and that governed overall activity. For example, one of the traders automatically exited a position after it had moved against him by only several ticks. This strategy led him to enter and exit markets quite frequently, increasing the number of "learning trials" available to him.

Such a rule helped reduce this trader's losses when he was wrong about the market, but, from his account, similar rules were not governing his entries. He had developed a feel for market momentum, the action of the strong and the weak players, and the patterning of the bids and asks. His knowledge was implicit, in that he knew enough to be successful on the floors but could not verbally duplicate his knowledge so that his listeners could replicate his performance.

Moving from such scalpers to frequent but less frenetic traders, such as Linda, one finds that an increasing proportion of market knowledge—and market decision making—is explicit. Linda can indeed verbalize many of her rules for trading and illustrates these with examples each day for members of her trading chatroom. It is far from clear, however, that all of what Linda knows is subsumed in her rules. She does not take a trade every time a verbalized pattern occurs; rather, she seems to have an implicit sense for when these patterns might pay off and when they might not. Her trading is highly rule governed, but not mechanical. Implicit knowledge plays an important role in helping her apply her trading rules. Someone who simply read Linda's rules and mechanically applied them would be unlikely to obtain her trading results. No doubt this is because Linda has spent many years, day after day, immersed in the markets and in frequent trading.

Moving further out the time line to swing traders and intermediate-term traders, who might be trading only one or twice a week or month, it becomes increasingly clear that learning trials occur too infrequently and with too much spacing to permit implicit learning. Unless the trader found some other means to generate the implicit learning trials—by faithfully and intensively reviewing charts, historical market data, and so on—little tacit knowledge could be expected. Successful longer-term traders could thus be expected to rely far more on explicit rules and systems as a basis for their entries and exits. Good examples of such rule-based, longer-term trading are contained in Yale Hirsch's *Stock Trader's Almanac* and Jon Markman's *Online Investing*. Yale focuses on seasonal patterns for the broad market, such as the tendency of markets to perform much better during the latest and earliest months of the year, as compared to the middle months. Jon identifies model portfolios based on such screening criteria as momentum and growth. Other Markman portfolios draw on seasonality patterns among individual stocks and stock sectors. By utilizing the rules from such research as decision-making aids, longer-term traders who have not internalized an implicit feel for the markets can still give themselves an edge. After all, if a trader's hunches do not contain (tacit) information, eliminating those hunches from decision-making processes makes a lot of sense.

If I am correct in surmising that the time frame of the trader plays a significant role in determining the relative importance of implicit, intuitive knowing versus explicit knowledge in trading, the psychological techniques reviewed in the previous chapters take on a different cast. Techniques for maximizing focus, for dampening intrusive emotional and cognitive reactions, and for becoming highly sensitive to personal and market markers would be especially helpful to the scalper. This is because all the scalper needs to know to make a successful trade is already present in his or her experience. The most successful psychological interventions will be those that remove interference from this tacit knowing.

Longer-term traders have much more time than scalpers do to think about their positions and to act out personal patterns from other facets of their lives. They are most likely to benefit from techniques that undermine problem patterns by leaping to new states and by anchoring solution patterns in distinctive modes of experiencing. The longer-term trader, relying more on explicit rules than on tacit knowledge, will also benefit most from an immersion in formal research and from an increasing formulation and anchoring of trading rules.

Trading failure could be expected among longer-term traders who attempt to trade intuitively and from scalpers who attempt to overanalyze their trading. The longer-term trader lacks the tacit knowledge to trade intuitively, due to insufficient learning trials. As a result, he or she is apt to fail in extracting the signal from the noise. The scalper, conversely, needs immediate access to his or her implicit knowledge and cannot afford to second-guess what is already known. Overanalyzing trading for the scalper would be analogous to a pitcher's becoming overly aware of his delivery, aiming the ball instead of delivering the pitch fluidly. The interference of explicit processing is apt to undermine the natural, tacit performance.

Are some people more talented as implicit learners than as explicit ones? Do highly complex, noisy markets better lend themselves to implicit learning than to efforts at explicit formulation? There are many unanswered questions triggered by this research literature. It is quite conceivable that different people possess distinct information-processing strengths and weaknesses and that markets possess varying degrees of signal and noise. *Finding the right fit between cognitive style, trading style, and trading vehicles may play a crucial role in determining the success or failure of trading.*

GREATNESS AND THE ACQUISITION OF EXPERTISE

Studies of accomplished individuals in creative and scientific fields suggest that many years of practice, study, and apprenticeship typically precede the internalization of world-class skills. Reviewing research on genius, R. S. Albert pointed out that the key to extraordinary achievement is *productivity*, the ability to generate large volumes of varied contributions. Dean Keith Simonton, in his text *Greatness: Who Makes History and Why*, similarly noted that renowned individuals are driven by unusually strong motivational forces. Indeed, one of Simonton's more provocative findings was that eminent contributors to their fields produce the same proportion of unsuccessful works to successful ones as do lesser contributors. Their eminence is due to the fact that they produce so many more works than their peers that the odds of making a lasting contribution are greatly enhanced. But to sustain such productivity over a long span requires unusual dedication.

This dedication is first manifested in the willingness to undergo a prolonged period of learning and practice. K. Anders Ericsson, in his edited volume *The Road to Excellence*, noted the "10-year rule," in which 10 years of intensive preparation are necessary for the cultivation of expertise in chess and in other domains. Ericsson and colleagues studied the acquisition of expertise by collecting diaries from skilled and amateur musicians. They found a direct correlation between the number of hours spent in deliberative practice and the degree of expertise of the musician. By the age of 20, the top group of violinists, for example, had spent over 10,000 hours on deliberative practice. Ericsson's review of studies further suggested that concentration is an essential ingredient of deliberate practice. The best-performing musicians practice with the greatest intensity, but they also take frequent naps to combat fatigue. They not only practice for more hours but also obtain more from each practice session due to the intensity of their focus.

Francis Galton was correct when he indicated that great individuals seem to be urged by inherent stimuli to achieve their eminence. This can only happen among individuals who derive pleasure and fulfillment from the effortful pursuit of goals. This goes back to Mihalyi Csikszentmihalyi's notion of *flow*: the intrinsically rewarding state that creative individuals experience when they are immersed in their work. Work itself generates a state-shift for the creator and is anchored to a positive place on the creator's radio dial of consciousness. It is difficult imagining sustaining high-quality practice and skill development over 10 or more years in the absence of such inherent stimuli.

And yet, there is something beyond the intrinsic pleasure of effort that appears to impel the high achiever. Without confidence, a deep belief in his or her success, no one could sustain years of effortful pursuit of life's goals. In his insightful autobiography, *The Education of a Speculator*, Victor Niederhoffer told the story of first meeting the tennis and squash coach at Harvard, Jack Barnaby. Before Niederhoffer had even started playing the game, he announced to Jack that he would be the best player ever. Sure enough, after 14 months of hard work, Niederhoffer was the National Junior Champion. The abiding belief in the self, yoked to a love of work and effort and aided by a depth of concentration, appears to be a potent combination in generating success in life—and in the markets.

Niederhoffer's checkers coach, Tom Wiswell, left behind a legacy of proverbs about winning that his student shared in his book. "Success does not come all at once," Wiswell noted. "Even for masters it comes in stages, separated by years" (p. 168). But, Wiswell explained, "Only those with passion can become masters" (p. 168). The capacity to sustain passion over years makes for success in markets as well as in marriages.

Could it be that greatness in trading follows the same patterns observed among artists, scientists, and squash players? If so, one would expect the expert trader to have spent a sustained period of time immersed in the markets, following market action, practicing trading, and maintaining a high level of focus and concentration. *These are the very same conditions that generate optimal implicit learning.* Expertise appears to be gained by maximizing the number of learning trials and by maximizing one's focus during these trials so as to extract the most learning possible. When this can be sustained over a lengthy period, the result is an internalized set of skills that, like the competence of the violinist, cannot be readily captured in verbal form.

ETCHING THE BRAIN

An important implication of the implicit learning research is that any technologies that could accelerate market exposure would be of immense benefit to the development of traders. These technologies would include, first, ones that simulate and/or play back market action for traders so that they can immerse themselves in market patterns even outside normal trading hours. It is in this context that my practice of creating flash cards from past market data makes particular sense. By printing out the best trades for each day and what the markets were doing prior to those trades, I create a set of learning trials that can be rehearsed on demand. This is similar to Linda Raschke's exercise of posting charts for seminar attendees and asking them to predict the upcoming market action. In flashing one chart after another and providing ready feedback, she is, in essence, accelerating learning by stepping up the implicit learning trials.

I believe there is much to be gained by such exemplar-based education. When traders experience a large number of examples of trading patterns in a compressed fashion, they may gain the ability to implicitly abstract essential features of markets that are ready to move. The key to this experience is generating enough examples and presenting them in a closely spaced manner. As I mentioned earlier, when I recently talked with Carl Swenlin, developer of the Decision Point web site (www.decisionpoint.com), he seemed to be sensitive to the learning needs of traders. He said that by organizing the charts both by indicator (looking at a given indicator across multiple markets) and by market (looking at a variety of indicators for a single market), the site provides "an easy way to quickly review different perspectives." One of my favorite exercises with the site is to rapidly click chart after chart of different sector indexes and market indicators, keeping my mind as loose and open as possible. Very often, a sense for a big picture will emerge that can provide the basis for more hard-nosed testing.

Recently I have begun experimenting with a computer program (HiJaack Pro) that captures graphic images of my trading screens for ready use as flash cards. An additional feature assembles these images into "movies" that can be viewed on demand. Such a technology has the potential to greatly expand the number of implicit learning trials, as each trading day can be captured as a number of minimovies. The advantage to capturing the data in moving form is that it potentially sensitizes the learner to the unfolding of the patterns and the sequences that precede tradable market behavior. Conducting the trials with the same data and the same displays that one would experience in trading could be expected to enhance the transfer of implicit learning to real-time trading.

A second set of technologies with the potential to accelerate the development of trading expertise is biofeedback. If, indeed, the learner gains more from the implicit learning trials by maintaining a high level of focus and concentration, then any techniques that expand one's focus could meaningfully increase the efficiency of learning. At present, I am experimenting with forehead temperature feedback as an indirect measure of blood flow to the brain's prefrontal cortex. As cognitive scientist Elkhonon Goldberg emphasized in his text *The Executive Brain*, this region is largely responsible for our concentration, decision making, and other executive functions. To the degree that the activation of the frontal lobes can be increased, executive control over behavior and the ability to process new information is potentially expanded.

Goldberg cited a range of evidence suggesting that the exercise of brain regions contributes to their development, including cognitive exercises that enhance the functioning of the frontal lobes and that forestall the deterioration associated with aging. He envisions gymnasiums for the mind, which promote cognitive fitness. Rather than attempt to cultivate specific mental processes, Goldberg asserted, people might try to actually reshape the brain. The intensive use of biofeedback to exercise the brain regions responsible for concentration may be among the most promising ways in which traders can maximize their learning and develop expertise. Perhaps it is possible to accelerate this development to the point that the normal 10 years needed to achieve expertise could be reduced significantly.

Is it possible that trading techniques, executed faithfully, could actually reshape the brain? I believe so. In a remarkably encyclopedic text, *Zen and the Brain*, neurologist James Austin traced the biochemical and structural changes in the brain as a function of Zen meditation. His comprehensive review points to glutamate (an excitatory amino acid neurotransmitter) and GABA (an inhibitory transmitter) as key players in the reshaping process. It is interesting that GABA is created from glutamate with the aid of an enzyme, GAD (glutamic acid decarboxylase). Research suggests that about 40 percent of all nerve cells are GABA producers and another 30 percent produce glutamate. Austin referred to these transmitters as the yin and yang of neurology, in that they largely control the inhibition and the excitation of response patterns. Injected GABA, for example, will inhibit aggressive and hyperactive responses in animals; reducing GABA will create hyperexcitability. Among humans, benzodiazepine medications (minor tranquilizers, such as Xanax and Valium) enhance the transmission of GABA, reducing agitation.

Austin noted that if excess glutamate from nerve cells overactivates the receptors from the next (postsynaptic) cell, it causes this cell to die. Among the sites most affected by such glutamate production are those responsible for the creation of stress-activated peptides that serve as messengers to the hypothalamus and amygdala. Austin hypothesized that "repeated, deep extraordinary states of consciousness" may "etch" the brain by selectively destroying nerve cells, including those involved in "dysfunctional, overemotionalized behavior" (p. 656). Moreover, glutamate receptors in nerve cells appears to modify the excitability of the next cells, improving memory and task performance among animals.

Goldberg cited research in Russia that found that L-Glutamic acid, of which glutamate is the sodium salt, improves functions associated with the brain's frontal lobes, including insight and time sequencing. The Zen practitioner may thus create traitlike changes in personality both by etching away negative emotional response patterns and by selectively enhancing cognitive abilities.

A variety of techniques in addition to meditation, such as hypnosis, may also expand focus and concentration and thus aid the implicit learning of market patterns. I am convinced, based on my personal experiments with the Philip Glass music, with the sound-and-light machine, and with the biofeedback that some of the best mental gymnasium exercises consist of cultivating and sustaining highly extraordinary mind states. The acceleration of learning may very well depend as much on the learner's state as on the organization of the material being presented. At present, I am experimenting with biofeedback not only to stay in the zone, but also to explore zones of various depth and intensity. My goal is to determine whether staying in these zones during trading can ultimately enhance learning and performance.

My working hypothesis is that the repeated, intensive performance of mental gymnastics alters the balance of information processing between brain hemispheres. Cutting links a variety of psychopathologies to the relative overactivation of one hemisphere and the suppression of the other. Anxiety and depression are most clearly linked to right-hemispheric activation; schizophrenia and other thought disorders appear lateralized to the left hemisphere. Each hemisphere plays a unique and crucial role in cognition. As V. S. Ramachandran and Sandra Blakeslee noted, the job of the left hemisphere is to create belief systems or models and to fold new experiences into this system. That is the "interpreter" discovered by Michael Gazzaniga and Joseph LeDoux. The right hemisphere is responsive to abnormalities in experience that conflict with existing models. For that reason, Ramachandran and Blakeslee refer to the right hemisphere as a devil's advocate.

Traders clearly need the ability to form mental models of the market (left hemisphere) and to quickly revise these when anomalies occur (right hemisphere). This requires a distinctive set of cognitive gifts: the ability to be highly attuned to experience, to assemble robust mental maps (trading plans), and to flexibly modify these maps on the basis of experience. These are among the same gifts that distinguish practitioners in other fields, from chess players to psychotherapists to fighter pilots. It would not surprise me if careful study of expertise in these fields yields further insights into the characteristics and the development of superior traders.

Conversely, a great deal may be learned about problems in trading by studying people who lack these capacities. Allow me to propose a "Trader's Syndrome A" that typifies traders who appear to have difficulty in creating and modifying plans. This syndrome is characterized by:

- *Inattention*—The trader has difficulty sustaining attention and demonstrates distractibility and low task vigilance.
- *Behavioral disinhibition*—The trader tends to be impulsive, responding rapidly and inaccurately to tasks.
- *Deficient rule-governed behavior*—The trader exhibits difficulties in adhering to task rules and demands.

Now consider the converse of this trader's syndrome, Trader's Syndrome B. It is characterized by:

- *Hypervigilance*—The trader rigidly locks onto a limited set of stimuli, losing forest for trees.

- *Behavioral inhibition*—The trader tends to be overanalytical, experiencing paralysis when it is time to act.
- *Inflexibility*—The trader becomes overly focused on task rules and demands, losing flexibility in responding.

Trader's Syndrome A is taken from Russell Barkley's diagnostic criteria for attention deficit hyperactivity disorder. Syndrome B is an apt description of an anxiety disorder. The extremes of these "syndromes" capture the majority of problems faced by traders. In performing mental gymnastic exercises that strengthen the functioning of the executive centers, the frontal lobes, people may cultivate a path between these extremes. This path may best be described as *flexible focus*. It is a state familiar to those who have undertaken meditation or biofeedback disciplines.

Goldberg cited a variety of evidence to challenge the notion that the adult brain loses its plasticity. He noted that adult rats, placed in an enriched environment with wheels and toys, develop 15 percent more neural cells than unstimulated mice. What, however, if traders can create their own stimulations, accelerating developmental changes that might otherwise occur over 10 years of training? This truly is one of the most exciting frontiers in the psychology of trading.

THE QUEST FOR MARKET MASTERY

When Jack Schwager asked Market Wizard Ed Seykota what advice he would give the average trader, Seykota's response was instructive. Give your money to a superior trader, Seykota advised, and find something that you are truly good at. When Schwager asked how the average trader could transform himself, Seykota responded that average traders do not transform themselves—only superior traders do that.

In years of reading literature on trading and the markets, I have come across few better pearls of wisdom. Find your passion: the work that stimulates, fascinates, and endlessly challenges you. Identify what you find meaningful and rewarding, and pour yourself into it. If your passion happens to be the markets, you will find the fortitude to outlast your learning curve and to develop the mastery needed to become a professional. If your passion is not the markets, then invest your funds with someone who possesses an objective track record and whose investment aims match your own. Then go forth and pour yourself into those facets of life that will keep you springing out of bed each morning, eager to face the day.

It is far better to struggle in the service of one's dreams than to find instant success at meaningless work. The greatest joy in life, George Bernard Shaw once wrote, is being used for a purpose you recognize to be mighty. The greatest fields—those that are a calling and not a mere job—give one room to expand and develop oneself. There is only one valid reason for trading the markets, just as there is only one valid reason for being a psychologist, a dancer, or an architect: *because it is your calling*, the arena that best draws on one's talents and passion for self-development.

It is in this context that trading and investing can be truly heroic activities. The anthropologist Joseph Campbell has studied heroic myths across various cultures and has discovered a common underlying theme. The hero is one who faces a worthy, but daunting challenge. Unable to easily vanquish his foe, the hero must descend into the underworld to gain a boon that allows him to achieve his ends. This descent is frightening and fraught with peril, but it hardens heroes for their eventual conquest.

If traders are to be successful, they must fight sobering odds and surpass the efforts of many competitors. They are not automatically equipped for the challenge. Their descent into the underworld requires that they face their personal demons, fighting those cognitive and emotional tendencies that would distort their efforts at identifying, understanding, and trading market patterns. If they are to succeed, they must become more than they are; they must exercise a control and a mastery well beyond that demanded by ordinary life. Like the mythical Greek hero Hercules, successful traders will find their clubs insufficient to kill off the many-headed monster Hydra; like Theseus, the mythical King of Athens, they will be tempted by the Sirens as they avoid the perils of the marine monsters Scylla and Charybdis. As with Hercules, too, their success will come from their ability to accept assistance and to employ new weapons. Like Theseus, they will avoid the Sirens' song and navigate the narrow path only through steely self-discipline.

This mythic challenge also provides the joy of competitive games and sport: With each match, the combatants enact a new heroic struggle, facing new foes, digging deeper into themselves as they descend into their own underworlds of risk, reward, pain, and ecstasy. As spectators to the sport, people vicariously share in the athletes' adventures, thereby absorbing a measure of their heroism. In cheering for the exploits of an Olympic hockey or soccer team, fans place themselves in the spiritual shoes of their heroes, ennobling themselves in the process.

There are few arenas left in life where the independent individual can enact the heroic struggle. The Gold Rush of the late 1800s captured the imagination of the public because it so thoroughly embraced Campbell's heroic myth. An individual could cross the desert and face myriad dangers in order to strike it rich. Over a century later, the emergence of the Internet promised a similar boon, where individual entrepreneurs could pioneer a worldwide medium and reap magnificent rewards.

These thrilling pursuits, however, are exceptions to the rule. More often, people live and work in large social units, fulfilling highly circumscribed roles, where their unique contributions are difficult to assess. People enjoy a security of job and home unknown to Hercules or Theseus but also have few direct outlets for their heroic impulses. In small ways, people can face and overcome challenges on the golf course or in pursuing the next round of sales targets, but the grand dimensions of heroism are missing. There can be no greatness without danger, no uplifting conquest without a facing of the underworld.

This, I believe, is the eternal allure of the markets. With a reasonable stake and an online account, each person can undertake his or her own gold rush and enact the highest entrepreneurial quest. Like salmon that swim upstream to spawn, sperm that pursue the egg, and prospectors who dig for precious metal, many will be called and few chosen. It matters not. What matters is the dignity and the dimension of soul conferred by one's noblest impulses. It is not desirable to rule in hell *or* to serve in heaven; far preferable, to paraphrase Ayn Rand, is to fight for tomorrow's Valhalla in order to walk its halls today.

If this book has offered a few signposts for your journey, it has achieved its goal. Many great-souled individuals have walked this path before you and me. Learn from their example and, especially, from the greatness within you. There are times right now when you, even in small ways, achieve the glory of the gods. Absorb the lessons from these. And when all your cunning, understanding, and tools fail you, find the benefactor who will hand you the torch that will sear the Hydra and the mirrored shield that will allow you to view and kill the hideous Medusa.

If you can remain pure and steadfast in your pursuits, you will face more than your share of risk and uncertainty, loss and lost opportunity. At the end of it all, however, I am confident that you and I will sit around a great table and bask in the eternity of the slain heroes who gather in Valhalla.

Bibliography

Albert, R. S. (1992). A developmental theory of eminence. In R. S. Albert (Ed.), *Genius and eminence* (2nd ed., pp. 3–18). Oxford: Pergamon.

Alexander, F., & French, T. M. (1946). *Psychoanalytic therapy: Principles and applications.* Lincoln: University of Nebraska Press.

Austin, J. H. (1999). *Zen and the brain: Toward an understanding of meditation and consciousness.* Cambridge, MA: MIT Press.

Barkley, R. A. (1990). *Attention deficit hyperactivity disorder: A handbook for diagnosis and treatment.* New York: Guilford.

Borges, J. L. (1964). *Labyrinths: Selected stories and other writings.* New York: New Directions.

Branden, N. (1997). *The art of living consciously: The power of awareness to transform everyday life.* New York: Simon & Schuster.

Brandstätter, H. (1991). Emotions in everyday life situations: Time sampling of subjective experience. In F. Strack, M. Argyle, and N. Schwartz (Eds.), *Subjective well-being: An interdisciplinary perspective* (pp. 173–192). Oxford: Pergamon Press.

Campbell, J. (1973). *Hero with a thousand faces.* Princeton, NJ: Princeton University Press.

Castaneda, C. (1975). *Journey to Ixtlan: The lessons of Don Juan.* New York: Pocket Books.

Cleeremans, A. (1993). *Mechanisms of implicit learning: Connecticut models of sequence processing.* Cambridge, MA: MIT Press.

Cleeremans, A., Destrebecqz A., & Boyer, M. (1998). Implicit learning: News from the front. *Trends in Cognitive Science,* 2(10), 406–416.

Cook, M. D. (2001). *Staying alive: Trading defensively for maximum profit.* www.traderslibrary.com: Trade Secrets Video Series.

Csikszentmihalyi, M. (1996). *Creativity: Flow and the psychology of discovery and invention.* New York: HarperPerennial.

Cutting, J. (1997). *Principles of psychopathology: Two worlds, two minds, two hemispheres.* Oxford: Oxford Medical Publications.

Davanloo, H. (1990). *Unlocking the unconscious.* Chichester, England: Wiley.

Diener, E., Sandvik, E., & Pavot, W. (1991). Happiness is the frequency, not the intensity, of positive versus negative affect. In F. Strack, M. Argyle, and N. Schwartz (Eds.), *Subjective well-being: An interdisciplinary perspective* (pp. 119–139). Oxford: Pergamon.

Elder, A. (1993). *Trading for a living.* New York: Wiley.

Elkin, I., Shea, M. T., Watkins, J. T., Imber, S. D., Sotsky, S. M., Collins, J. F., Glass, D. R., Pikonis, P. A., Leber, W. R., Docherty, J. P., Fiester, S. J., and Parloff, M. B. (1989). National Institute of Mental Health Treatment of Depression Collaborative Program: General effectiveness of treatments. *Archives of General Psychiatry,* 46, 971–982.

Ericsson, K. A. (1996). The acquisition of expert performance: An introduction to some of the issues. In K. A. Ericsson (Ed.), *The road to excellence: The acquisition of expert performance in the arts and sciences, sports and games* (pp. 1–50). Mahwah, NJ: Erlbaum.

Fenton-O'Creevy, M., Soane, E., & Willman, P. (1999, August). *Trading on illusions: Unrealistic perceptions of control and trading performance.* Academy of Management Conference, Chicago, IL.

Flavell, J. H. (1963). *The developmental psychology of Jean Piaget.* New York: Van Nostrand.

Galton, F. (1869). *Hereditary genius: An inquiry into its laws and consequences.* London: Macmillan.

Gazzaniga, M. S. (1998). *The mind's past.* Berkeley: University of California Press.

Goldberg, A. (1999). *Being of two minds: The vertical split in psychoanalysis and psychotherapy.* Hillsdale, NJ: Analytic Press.

Goldberg, E. (2001). *The executive brain: Frontal lobes and the civilized mind.* New York: Oxford University Press.

Grinder, G., & Bandler, R. (1981). *Trance-formations: Neuro-linguistic programming and the structure of hypnosis.* Moab, UT: Real People Press.

Gurdjieff, G. I. (1984). *Views from the real world: Early talks of G. I. Gurdjieff.* London: Arkana.

Haley, J. (1986). *Uncommon therapy: The psychiatric techniques of Milton H. Erickson, M.D.* New York: Norton.

Hastie, R., & Park, B. (1997). The relationship between memory and judgment depends on whether the judgment task is memory-based or on-line. In W. Goldstein and R. M. Hogarth (Eds.), *Research on judgment and decision making: Currents, connections, and controversies* (pp. 431–453). Cambridge: Cambridge University Press.

Hirsch, Y., & Hirsch, J. A. (2002). *Stock trader's almanac 2002.* Old Tappan, NJ: Hirsch Organization.

Isen, A. M. (1997). Positive affect and decision making. In W. M. Goldstein and R. M. Hogarth (Eds.), *Research on judgment and decision making: Currents, connections, and controversies* (pp. 509–536). Cambridge: Cambridge University Press.

Kelly, G. (1963). *Theory of personality: The psychology of personal constructs.* New York: Norton.

Kiev, A. (2001). *Trading in the zone.* New York: Wiley.

Lazarus, R. S., & Folkman, S. (1984). *Stress, appraisal, and coping.* New York: Springer.

LeDoux, J. (1996). *The emotional brain: The mysterious underpinnings of emotional life.* New York: Touchstone.

Lee, C. M., & Swaminathan, B. (2000). Price momentum and trading volume. *Journal of Finance, 55,* 2017–2069.

Libet, B. (1985). Unconscious cerebral initiative and the role of unconscious will in voluntary action. *The Brain and Behavioral Sciences, 8,* 529–566.

Lo, A. W., & Repin, D. V. (2001). The psychophysiology of real-time financial risk processing. Working paper: Massachusetts Institute of Technology Sloan School of Management.

Lombardi, V., Jr. (2001). *What it takes to be #1: Vince Lombardi on leadership.* New York: McGraw-Hill.

Lowen, A. (1995). *Joy: The surrender to the body and to life.* New York: Arkana.

Mahrer, A. R. (1989). *Dreamwork in psychotherapy and self-change.* New York: Norton.

Markman, J. (2001). *Online investing: How to find the right stocks at the right time.* Redmond, WA: Microsoft Press.

Maslow, A. (1998). *Toward a psychology of being (3rd ed).* New York: Wiley.

Mathieu, W. A. (1991). *The listening book: Discovering your own music.* Boston: Shambhala.

McCrae, R. R., & Costa, P. T. (1996). Toward a new generation of personality theories: Theoretical contexts for the Five-Factor Model. In J. S. Wiggins (Ed.), *The Five-Factor Model of personality: Theoretical perspectives* (pp. 51–87). New York: Guilford.

Meichenbaum, D. (1977). *Cognitive-behavior modification.* New York: Plenum.

Mentzer, M. (1997). *Mike Mentzer's high intensity training program.* New York: Advanced Research Press.

Murphy, M. (1992). *The future of the body: Explorations into the further evolution of human nature.* Los Angeles: Tarcher.

Niederhoffer, V. (1997). *The education of a speculator.* New York: Wiley.

Norretranders, T. (1998). *The user illusion: Cutting consciousness down to size.* New York: Penguin.

Odean, T. (1999). Do investors trade too much? *American Economic Review,* 89, 1279–1298.

Ornstein, R. (1997). *The right mind.* San Diego: Harcourt Brace.

Ouspensky, P. D. (1971). *The fourth way.* New York: Vintage.

Pennebaker, J. W. (1993). Social mechanisms of constraint. In D. M. Wegner and J. W. Pennebaker (Eds.), *Handbook of mental control* (pp. 200–219). Englewood Cliffs, NJ: Prentice-Hall.

Pirsig, R. M. (1974). *Zen and the art of motorcycle maintenance.* New York: Morrow.

Plous, S. (1993). *The psychology of judgment and decision making.* New York: McGraw-Hill.

Polanyi, M. (1967). *The tacit dimension.* Garden City, NY: Anchor.

Ramachandran, V. S., & Blakeslee, S. (1998). *Phantoms in the brain: Probing the mysteries of the human mind.* New York: Morrow.

Raschke, L. (2001). *Trading my way: Professional trading techniques.* Wellington, FL: LBRGroup.

Reber, A. S. (1993). *Implicit learning and tacit knowledge: An essay on the cognitive unconscious.* New York: Oxford University Press.

Sacks, O. (1996). *An anthropologist on Mars.* New York: Vintage Books.

Schiffer, F. (1998). *Of two minds: The revolutionary science of dual-brain psychology.* New York: Free Press.

Schwager, J. D. (1989). *Market wizards: Interviews with top traders.* New York: Harper & Row.

Schwager, J. D. (1992). *The new market wizards: Conversations with America's top traders.* New York: HarperBusiness.

Shapiro, F., & Forrest, M. S. (1997). *EMDR: Eye movement desensitization and reprocessing.* New York: Basic.

Shefrin, H. (2000). *Beyond fear and greed: Understanding behavioral finance and the psychology of investing.* Boston: Harvard Business School Press.

Sherry, C. J. (1992). *The mathematics of technical analysis: Applying statistics to trading stocks, options and futures.* Chicago: Probus.

Simonton, D. K. (1994). *Greatness: Who makes history and why.* New York: Guilford.

Sperry, R. W. (1969). A modified concept of consciousness. *Psychological Review, 76,* 532–536.

Steenbarger, B. N. (1992). Toward science-practice integration in brief counseling and therapy. *Counseling Psychologist, 20,* 403–450.

Steenbarger, B. N. (1994). Duration and outcome in psychotherapy: An integrative review. *Professional Psychology: Research and Practice, 25,* 111–119.

Steenbarger, B. N. (2002). Brief therapy. In M. Hersen and W. H. Sledge (Eds.), *The encyclopedia of psychotherapy.* San Diego, CA: Academic.

Steenbarger, B. N. (2002). Single session therapy. In M. Hersen and W. H. Sledge (Eds.), *The encyclopedia of psychotherapy* (pp. 669–672). San Diego, CA: Academic.

Steenbarger, B. N., & Budman, S. H. (1998). Principles of brief and time-effective therapies. In G. P. Koocher, J. C. Norcross, and S. S. Hill (Eds.), *Psychologists' desk reference* (pp. 283–287). New York: Oxford University Press.

Talmon, M. (1990). *Single-session therapy: Maximizing the effect of the first (and often only) therapeutic encounter.* New York: Jossey-Bass.

Tart, C. T. (1987). *Waking up: Overcoming the obstacles to human potential.* Boston: Shambhala.

Tversky, A., & Kahneman, D. (1982). Causal schemas in judgments under uncertainty. In D. Kahneman, P. Slovic, and A. Tversky (Eds.), *Judgment under uncertainty: Heuristics and biases* (pp. 117–128). New York: Cambridge University Press.

Weiss, J., & Sampson, H. (1993). *How psychotherapy works.* New York: Guilford.

Wilson, C. (1972). *New pathways in psychology: Maslow and the post-Freudian revolution.* New York: Taplinger.

Index